THE
COMMONS

Roger A. Lohmann

Foreword by Jon Van Til

THE COMMONS

New Perspectives on Nonprofit Organizations and Voluntary Action

Jossey-Bass Publishers · San Francisco

For sales outside the United States, contact Maxwell Macmillan International Publishing Group, 866 Third Avenue, New York, New York 10022.

Manufactured in the United States of America

 10% POST CONSUMER WASTE

The paper used in this book is acid-free and meets the State of California requirements for recycled paper (50 percent recycled waste, including 10 percent postconsumer waste), which are the strictest guidelines for recycled paper currently in use in the United States.

Library of Congress Cataloging-in-Publication Data

Lohmann, Roger A., date.
   The commons : new perspectives on nonprofit organization and voluntary action / Roger A. Lohmann. — 1st ed.
      p.   cm.—(The Jossey-Bass nonprofit sector series)
   Includes bibliographical references and index.
   ISBN 1-55542-476-7 (alk. paper)
   1. Voluntarism—United States. 2. Associations, Institutions, etc.—United States. 3. Corporations, Nonprofit—United States. I. Title. II. Series.
HN90.V64L64   1992
361.7′63′0973—dc20   92-13058
                                        CIP

FIRST EDITION
HB Printing   10 9 8 7 6 5 4 3 2 1   *Code 9275*

The Jossey-Bass
Nonprofit Sector Series

Contents

Foreword   xi
   by Jon Van Til

Preface   xv

The Author   xxi

Introduction: Rethinking the Nonprofit Issue   1

1. Current Approaches to Nonprofit Organizations
   and Voluntary Association   23

2. A New Approach: The Theory of the Commons   46

3. The Evolution of the Commons
   in Western Civilization   83

4. The Varieties of Common Action   127

5.   The Economics of Common Goods   158

6.   The Politics of the Commons   177

7.   The Role of Gifts and Other Exchanges   196

8.   Charity, Self-Help, and Mutual Aid   215

9.   Volunteer Labor and Prosocial Behavior:
     The Psychology of the Commons   235

10. The Values of the Commons   253

11. Summing Up   272

     References   277

     Name Index   327

     Subject Index   337

Foreword

Books that shape emerging fields of scholarly endeavor are like this one by Roger A. Lohmann. Their analysis is as acute as that of a policy analyst, which Lohmann was trained to be. Their purview is as broad as the interdisciplinary field of social work, the field Lohmann teaches. Their vision is that of the poet, which Lohmann proves to be with his original images of the subject of voluntary action. And their writing is as crisp and expressive as that of the social critic, which Lohmann also succeeds at being in this persuasive and original work.

I first started reading the papers of Roger Lohmann some years ago and was startled by the power of the metaphors he applied to the world of voluntary action and nonprofit organization. The concept of "the commons," to take the primary example, embodied brilliantly the core value of voluntarism in society: to create a protected space for the collective expression of what people find most important in their lives.

I made space for Lohmann's vision in the preface to my own book *Mapping the Third Sector* when I wrote: "It is within these commons—in neighborhood associations and interest groups, in houses of worship and secular places of contemplation, in nonprofit organizations and social clubs—that people communicate across the chasms between different life experiences and create meaning and value for their lives. It is in these modern commons that people learn the arduous joys of sharing what is good within the complex web of contemporary society."

Roger Lohmann has written a book that is in many respects the first definitive large-scale theory of the voluntary and nonprofit sector. Up until now, theory has largely been descriptive (an example is that of Michael O'Neill) or middle-range (the largely economic theories of Henry Hansmann, Estelle James, Dennis Young; the largely sociological work of Albert Meister, David Horton Smith, David Knoke; and the largely political work of me and Jennifer Wolch).

Readers, accustomed to earlier theory, should approach this book as though they were embarking on a voyage to a new land. Think of it this way: we divide our institutions into four major sectors to accomplish our societal tasks. Corporations and businesses (the first sector) make most of our products and hire most of our labor: they provide jobs that amount to 80 percent of the country's payrolls. Government (the second sector) provides a military capacity and a number of ancillary regulatory and welfare services: it meets about 13 percent of the national payroll. Voluntary and nonprofit organizations (the third sector) address a number of educational, charitable, and membership purposes: their payroll amounts to more than 7 percent of the national total and is supplemented by much valuable voluntary effort as well. Finally, households and informal organizations (such as neighbors, kin, and so on—the fourth sector) perform the lion's share of home management and child raising, though without the benefit of the transfer of cash.

What Lohmann does is to help us look at the work of the third sector so that it becomes as familiar to us as that of business, government, and the family. He reminds us that voluntary choice is at the core of this sector, rather than the more febrile legal or economic concepts of "nondistribution constraints" and "sector failure" cited by earlier theorists.

Lohmann's broad-scale theory transcends disciplines; it is original, robust, and powerful. Moreover, the theory forces those who believe they know something about this field to think about it anew. The theory of the commons forces those who have swallowed the nonprofit metaphor whole to contemplate the wisdom of their diet. It fortifies those who have seen in voluntarism the core value of the sector with the power of that vision, both in empirical reality and normative preference. And it invites those who have yet to approach the work of the third sector to do so in a clear and caring fashion.

The Commons is a significant work. It has the potential of defining a field at the point of its full scholarly emergence. The author has done his work: it is now for the rest of us to read, learn, and apply.

Camden, New Jersey Jon Van Til
August 1992

To my wife, Nancy

Preface

Sometimes the most familiar objects can be extremely difficult to speak and think about clearly. Such is the case with the patterns of human association we ordinarily denote as "nonprofit organization" and "voluntary association." Empirical findings and middle-range generalizations about such entities are expanding very rapidly; in the process, however, some of our cherished assumptions about the exceptional role of volunteerism in American culture and the charitable nature (or lack thereof) of nonprofit purposes are eroding or being transformed. Conventional categories, such as the distinction between "profit" and "nonprofit" motives or orientations, and broad distinctions between competition, cooperation, and conflict are no longer sufficient in a global village of pluralistic cultures, insecure families, bureaucratic states, and mixed economies.

Nonprofit and voluntary action studies have a major problem of theory. For many readers, *theory* is an ugly, intimidating term that suggests irrelevance and impracticality. For others, *theory* has very exacting connotations of assumptions, precisely defined terms, and clearly stated propositions. *The Commons* seeks to be theoretical in neither of these senses: it seeks to talk generally (and interestingly) about the social, economic, and political structures and processes of nonprofit and voluntary action and at the same time to redraw some of the major internal and external boundaries of the field. In undertaking this task, I made an effort to recondition some traditional, and even archaic, terms and to draw attention away from preoccupation with nonprofit corporations as sole representatives of the field as a whole. Nonprofit organizations, voluntary associations, and several other distinct types of related organizations are, in the theory which is offered here, subsumed within a larger category called *the commons*.

Audience

The Commons is written for all those who care deeply about the practice of social democracy and who continue to marvel at the multitude of ways in which people with similar interests seek out one another and commit themselves to shared purposes and joint actions of all types. In particular, the theory of the commons is addressed to investigators, students, and practitioners of the several subfields of the science of association, which de Tocqueville called "the mother science": social workers, sociologists, political scientists, economists, anthropologists, psychologists, lawyers, fund raisers, accountants, foundation staff members, volunteer coordinators, grant writers, and anyone else with a serious intellectual interest in this fascinating topic.

Organization of the Book

The introduction sets out the nature of the task undertaken in this book; it is built around and addressed to the expanding group of nonprofit organization and voluntary action researchers whose current quest is defining a commons devoted to the study and understanding of common action.

Chapter One reviews the current state of nonprofit and voluntary theory. Nonprofit corporations and nonprofit organizations are considered, along with nonprofit, voluntary, third, nongovernmental, independent, and various other sector conceptions.

Chapter Two sets out a basic theoretical framework called the theory of the commons. It begins with a consideration of eight alternative assumptions, and thus systematically attempts to adjust the theoretical footings of nonprofit and voluntary action theory. The chapter highlights the marginal status of nonprofit "firms" and shifts the focus to the much broader category of associations, clubs, groups, and gatherings that make up the commons. The term *commons* and its adjective form, *common,* are elaborated in terms of participation, shared objects and resources, mutuality, and fairness. Endowment is said to encompass cultural, as well as material, resources. Civilization is said to be the endowment of societies and cultures. The positive implications of patronage in terms of support and protection are emphasized. I coin a special term, *benefactory,* to summarize social organizations whose purposes involve giving and gift exchange in some fundamental way.

Endowments of voluntary action in Western civilization are the theme of Chapter Three. Although the American nonprofit corporation may be a unique phenomenon, there is abundant historical and anthropological evidence of the prior existence of associations, endowments, and commons of many types throughout the history of the West.

Chapter Four is devoted to broadening the range of recognized benefactories; it examines, in addition to the association and social agency, other types of benefactory such as the solo trusteeship; public bureaucracies in the arts, sciences, and charities; common places or spaces devoted exclusively or primarily to commons; campaigns and committees; scientific, religious, and professional conferences; and cooperatives and disciplines. Other types of commons examined include fiestas, foundations, holidays, journals, political parties, pilgrimages, institutes, secret societies, sciences, and trusts.

Chapter Five suggests ways for extending conventional nonprofit economics beyond its present concerns with revenue-oriented nonprofit service producers to the analysis of commons and comments on the production model.

Chapter Six addresses the question of the relation between the state and the commons. The relation is reciprocal because democratic states arise out of the political activity of parties and political interests to function as dominant protective associations in societies. Because of its singular position, the state must be constitutionally restrained from exerting control over common activities. We do this in the United States through the provisions of the First Amendment, with its related guarantees of freedom of speech, religion, assembly, and redress of grievances.

Chapter Seven expands the range of the theory of the commons by examining four types of nonmarket exchange involving voluntary labor and the exchange of common goods. These are termed tributes, gifts, potlatches, and offerings.

Chapter Eight explores the social structure and process of the nonprofessional charity world. Current explorations of mutual aid, self-help groups, volunteerism, and related topics suggest that the professional, publicly funded world of social service contracts between state agencies and professionally staffed nonprofit corporations has grown up alongside another world of helping volunteers, friends, and neighbors. Charitable activity that involves mutual aid, self-help, and volunteers offers preeminent examples of commons in operation.

In Chapter Nine a large and somewhat unwieldy body of psychological research is introduced, reviewed, and shown to bear upon traditional issues and concerns of nonprofit and voluntary studies. Although its theoretical implications do not appear to have been closely examined, "prosocial" behavior appears to be emerging as a broad rubric for linking such important topics as altruism, charitable behavior, responses to fund raising, bystander behavior, free-riding, and other topics. Prosocial behavior involves both selfish (egoistic) and unselfish (altruistic) motives on the part of the actor (Dozier and Miceli, 1985).

Chapter Ten links the descriptive and explanatory discussions of the commons with the normative and value issues that practitioners, in particular, must struggle with. Rather than the misplaced reliance upon productivity, maximization, and efficiency, the standards of satisfaction, proportion, hermeneutics, conservation, and prudence are suggested. Chapter Eleven is a brief recap of central aspects of the theory.

The epigraphs to the chapters are slightly edited extracts from Alexis de Tocqueville's famous Book Two, Chapter 5, "Of the

Use Which Americans Make of Public Associations in Civil Life."
Gender references to "men" have been modernized and specific
references to Americans have been removed. This was done simply
for reasons of historical currency, human dignity, and optimism.

Acknowledgments

Writing a book of this sort is a long-term process, combining periods of working alone preceded and followed by rare opportunities
for dialogue and common exchange of ideas and thoughts. Jon Van
Til understands far better than most journal editors what it takes
to transform half-formed "bright ideas" into something more. He
has done for this project what he has done for dozens of others,
encouraging and questioning and teasing out more implications.
His editorship made the *Journal of Voluntary Action Research* a
true intellectual commons.

The Association for Research on Nonprofit Organizations
and Voluntary Action (ARNOVA) has been for me a genuine scholarly commons. I owe a particular debt of gratitude to several colleagues and fellow ARNOVA members: Ellen Netting, Steve
McMurtry, Bob Herman, Felice Perlmutter, Steve Wernet, Nancy
McDuff, Thomasina Borkman, George Floro, and Jeff Brudney.
Numerous anonymous reviewers of conference papers and manuscripts also offered helpful comments and advice at various stages.

My colleagues and students at West Virginia University, particularly Ernie Barbeau and Barry Locke, also helped to shape my
thinking on these issues over a number of years. Mary Sue Bracken,
Seinam Hahm, Debbie Williams, and my secretary, Penny Dailey,
also contributed to this effort in many important ways.

Most important to me are the love and the sacrifices of my
family growing out of this project: my children, Melissa and Andy,
and daughter-in-law, Lisa, have always been generous and tolerant
to a fault in sharing me with this and other projects. And I appreciate more than I can ever say the willingness of my wife, Nancy,
to handle more than her share of the routine tasks of daily life while
being brilliant at her own career.

To everyone who in any way contributed to this work, I say
thanks. A great many authors might have been cited from the volu-

minous and rapidly growing literature. I tried, for the most part, to cite key works within and less well known works outside the field that seem most likely to contribute to enriched common understandings. The achievement is ours in common, but, of course, responsibility for all errors in fact and in judgment is mine alone.

Morgantown, West Virginia   Roger A. Lohmann
August 1992

The Author

Roger A. Lohmann is professor of social work at West Virginia University. He received his B.A. degree (1964) in English and journalism from St. Cloud State College in Minnesota; his M.P.A. degree (1970) with an emphasis in social gerontology from the School of Public Affairs, University of Minnesota; and his Ph.D. degree (1975) in social policy from the Florence Heller Graduate School for Advanced Studies in Social Welfare, Brandeis University.

Lohmann is director of the Nonprofit Management Academy and a faculty associate of the Regional Research Institute at West Virginia University. He is also an associate of the Korean Social Policy Institute, Seoul, Korea, and was associate editor of the *Journal of Applied Gerontology.*

He is the author of *Breaking Even: Financial Management in Human Services* (1980), which has been translated into Korean. He is a board member of the Association for Research on Nonprofit Organizations and Voluntary Action (ARNOVA) and moderator of an electronic list server on BITNET/INTERNET for researchers and others interested in nonprofit and voluntary action. His other memberships include the Council on Social Work Education, Social Welfare History Group, Network for Social Work Managers, Association for Community Organization and Social Administration, Society for the Study of Symbolic Interaction, and Southern Gerontological Society.

Lohmann's current research interests include comparative and historical organizational studies. A recent book chapter addresses the evolution of social planning in the field of aging. He is currently working on a volume of historical studies of the management of Hull House, the Russell Sage Foundation, and other nonprofit and public social service and social action organizations.

He teaches graduate courses in aging and long-term care and in the administration of nonprofit human services, a course on the history of social policy, and an interdisciplinary undergraduate honors seminar on American philanthropy.

THE
COMMONS

Introduction:
Rethinking the Nonprofit Issue

Nothing is more deserving of our attention than the intellectual and moral associations.
—Alexis de Tocqueville

People, it has been said, form associations at the drop of a hat. In fact, almost any such occasion may well inspire the formation of more than a single new association: perhaps one society will be devoted to promoting hat dropping as recreation, and another will be dedicated to keeping records on the longest and highest recorded drops. A third group may form to raise funds for victims injured while bending over to retrieve their dropped hats, and a variety of ethnic, religious, nationality, gender, and other self-help organizations may be formed so that those who have dropped their hats may share this and other common experiences. Furthermore, the network of organizations connected in some manner with the issue of hat dropping may give birth, at some point, to a kind of hat droppers' subculture or even a broad social movement devoted to transforming society.

While the tendency to organize for any civil purpose was once thought to be a uniquely American characteristic, recent events have raised important doubts about the accuracy of this view. In the 1970s, news stories about small groups of Russian dissidents meet-

1

ing in apartments and passing *samizat* literature hand to hand in the face of rigorous attempts at repression by a totalitarian state were among the many widely available clues that civil associations are a broad phenomenon. Throughout the world, "American-style" associations and nonprofit organizations have been adopted with an ease and for a diversity of purposes that contradict the supposed culture boundedness of these social forms. Yet few are exact copies of the American way of associating; they are more like Andrew Lloyd Webber musicals—seemingly infinite variations on a central theme.

The amazing revolutionary social, political, and economic events in Eastern Europe and the Soviet Union that began in 1989, accompanied as they were by reports of the formation of hundreds and perhaps thousands of new clubs, groups, and associations, provided proof for those who needed it that what we Americans tend to call nonprofit organization and voluntary action is part of a worldwide phenomenon. Either the world was adopting American-style voluntary association practices or (and this seems more likely) our perceptions were catching up with tendencies deeply embedded in a great many different cultures. Many people are still not exactly sure which is the more plausible view.

This book is devoted to formulating a new multidisciplinary view of nonprofit organization and voluntary action to address this and other issues. Scholars have made great strides in recent years in analyzing in detail many separate aspects of nonprofit organization and voluntary action. A recent bibliography, for example, contains more than 5,000 scholarly and literary listings on philanthropy and the nonprofit sector (Foundation Center, 1989). However, specific research agendas have been based on an increasingly threadbare conventional wisdom about the nature of nonprofit and voluntary action built up largely from American experience over this century. As in any field heavily influenced by practical concerns, many topics and issues of nonprofit organization and voluntary action and more than a few questions of major importance have gone largely unaddressed simply because no research agendas have crystallized around them.

In first looking at nonprofit and voluntary action, we might easily grant the rather obvious and frequently repeated (yet simplistic and misleading) assessment that nonprofit endeavors are characterized by the negative condition of lacking a profit. In doing so, we may still be at a loss for any real explanations of why and how these endeavors occur as they do. And we may be hard-pressed to identify those positive traits or characteristics most closely associated with such nonprofit endeavors. Do churches, volunteer fire companies, nonprofit charities, and symphony orchestras, for example, really have anything in common with professional associations, scientific journals, or service clubs? Moreover, do any of these or other "tax-exempt entities" really share any common characteristics with the political parties or cemetery associations that they are classified near in the Internal Revenue Service Code (Biemiller, 1991; Sloane, 1991)? Or is the nonprofit sector actually only a residual category of disparate and dissimilar groups—a kind of Victorian attic of the unrelated and irrelevant castoffs of a profit-oriented civilization?

For most of the recent history of social science, such questions have been of interest to only a handful of researchers and scholars at any given time. However, in virtually all of the social sciences, interest in nonprofit and voluntary action has grown very rapidly within the past decade. The number of active research projects under way in this area has gone from a mere handful to dozens and perhaps hundreds in only a few short years. This growing interest was inspired in part, of course, by politics. As early as the mid 1970s and definitely after 1980, a newly vigorous conservative movement professed an agenda of limiting government by transferring many of its current activities and functions to the voluntary sector—the "thousand points of light." Another motivation for the increase in research was empirical; data such as reviewed in the next chapter suggest dramatic increases in the number of nonprofit organizations in recent years as well as substantial growth in public support and donations for voluntary action. Upon closer examination, however, the data also point toward several entirely new and related recent developments—the growth of support groups and self-help groups being one of the most dramatic examples.

Rethinking Nonprofit, Voluntary, and Philanthropic Studies

Present interest in the nonprofit sector involves more than interest in simple growth and novelty, however. For a number of scholars, a rethinking and reordering of some of the larger questions of the place of nonprofit and voluntary action in the social world is overdue (Billis, 1991; Langton, 1987; Ostrander, Langton, and Van Til, 1988; Salamon, 1987b). Yet, despite tremendous progress made by research in this area, important questions about the fundamental nature of charitable and philanthropic action remain unanswered.

Such rethinking is, inexorably, a theoretical enterprise (see, for example, Langton, 1987; Ostrander, 1988). Yet empirically oriented and practice-oriented social researchers and practitioners interested in voluntary action are often highly suspicious of any exercise that smacks of theory per se. A colleague at a recent meeting of the Association for Research on Nonprofit Organizations and Voluntary Action (ARNOVA) put the matter rather directly when she asked me, "Why do you think we need a new theory of the nonprofit sector?" To a considerable extent, this book is an attempt to answer that question.

More formal considerations notwithstanding, any social theory is first and foremost an expressive vocabulary; that is, a communication matrix, or an expressive medium for articulating ideas and asserting premises. In the terms presented in this book, theory, to the extent that it is accepted and utilized, constitutes a common good. It can offer a broad framework of shared terms, understandings, nominal and operational definitions, assumptions, and conventional approaches within which discrete but related issues can be formulated and research questions can be addressed by many investigators.

Undoubtedly, some new terminology (or revitalized old terminology) is needed in the study of the nonprofit sector. Virtually everyone who attempts to say anything meaningful about this area eventually stumbles over the expression of certain key ideas. Researchers and scholars frequently find it necessary to add qualifiers to their work such as, "Of course, we are not looking at many other activities that are voluntary in the sense that they are noncoerced."

Devising a suitable vocabulary with which to share experiences and interact with others about common, shared issues and concerns is preeminently a theoretical task. The kinds of hesitations, qualifications, and stumbling over words characteristic of the dialogue about nonprofit and voluntary action are clear signs of theoretical exhaustion, and they point directly toward the need for some enhanced theoretical language with which to discuss nonprofit and voluntary action. It would be convenient, of course, if such new theories were to spring forth full blown, as if from the mind of God. The social sciences, unfortunately, have been noticeably short on divine inspiration and must settle for a faltering human dialogue, full of fits and starts, misstatements, and false leads. This book is conceived as a part of that dialogue.

Four-Part Dialogue

Four interrelated aspects of the ongoing dialogue over rethinking the nonprofit area are uppermost in importance. First, research on matters of importance to nonprofit and voluntary studies in the work of scholars in the broader scholarly community should be given more attention. It may be desirable, in other words, to expand the paradigm of nonprofit and voluntary action in a number of directions more or less simultaneously.

Second, in talking about important nonprofit and voluntary action issues, less attention should be focused upon the arcane jargon and particular perspectives of early isolated work in discrete academic disciplines. In many instances, independent scholars who were working in relative isolation, rather than within the multidisciplinary academic community that has now emerged in this area, may have found it necessary to adopt unwarranted assumptions, misleading terminology, and unsuitable premises simply to fit their work within hostile or unsympathetic academic traditions (Milofsky and Hall, 1989). Instead of swearing continued allegiance to arcane terminology, we should pay more careful attention to the tremendous language resources available to the common community of speakers of English.

Third, less effort overall should be expended on the convention that research on nonprofit and voluntary studies is a value-free exercise in objective science and greater attention should be paid to explicit consideration of the underlying values operating in the arenas of nonprofit, voluntary, and philanthropic action. Fourth, additional attention should be paid to questions of parsimony and the economic and thoughtful use of language in describing and discussing these matters. Each of these four issues will be addressed more fully in the following pages.

In this book, I shall be engaged in a task of theory building and will be primarily concerned with three considerations: (1) developing descriptive terms and language that allow for adequate identification of the phenomena of nonprofit and voluntary action as we observe them; (2) developing explanations for the phenomena labeled by these terms; and (3) framing the descriptions and explanations within the context of values that we can observe people in the nonprofit sector using. My inspiration for this effort came, at least in part, from Bernstein's challenging work (1976) on restructuring social and political theory.

Expanding the Scholarly Community

Today, nonprofit and voluntary action research is a viable multidisciplinary concern of interest to researchers, scholars, and practitioners in many different disciplines and professions. Aspects of the broad issue of the role of nonprofit and voluntary studies in society are of importance to people in a dozen or more disciplines in the social sciences and humanities, and other aspects are of potential interest and significance to people in a great many other fields in the humanities and the natural and life sciences. Furthermore, the sciences, humanities, and other academic disciplines and professions are themselves examples of nonprofit, voluntary, and philanthropic action. Indeed, understanding the social organization of any scientific interest or discipline, from the study of nonprofit and voluntary activities to the study of the anatomy of wombats, is critical to understanding the central concept of this book.

In some cases, interest in nonprofit and voluntary action is a matter of day-to-day attention to practical questions and immediate concerns. For example, issues of accountability in social services can have a direct impact upon the ability of workers to continue delivering service to clients or of solicitors to raise funds (Milofsky and Blades, 1991). In other cases, major issues of importance to interdisciplinary theory and research are buried deep behind layers of arcane and specialized jargon within a particular field. For example, the distinctive organizational theories of religious bodies are sometimes grounded in sacred beliefs and buried deep within theologies.

Much of the contemporary knowledge in nonprofit and voluntary studies has emerged in interdisciplinary settings explicitly devoted to the topic. For more than two decades, the Association for Research on Nonprofit Organizations and Voluntary Action, formerly the Association of Voluntary Action Scholars, has provided a national and international forum for multidisciplinary discussion and consideration of important issues in nonprofit and voluntary action studies. Through its annual conferences, proceedings, and journal, recently renamed the *Nonprofit and Voluntary Sector Quarterly*, ARNOVA has embodied many of the principles of nonprofit and voluntary action that interest its members.

Recently, the discussion has been expanded with the creation of two new national periodicals, the *Chronicle of Philanthropy* and *NonProfit Times*, and two new academic journals, *Nonprofit Management and Leadership* and the international *Voluntas*. More than a decade ago, Yale University broke new ground with the formation of the Program on Nonprofit Organizations. INDEPENDENT SECTOR, a coalition of national voluntary associations, sponsors an annual research conference. More than forty academic centers and programs devoted to nonprofit and voluntary action research and teaching have also been developed. Even so, the bulk of the scholarly work on nonprofit, voluntary, and philanthropic action, as befits the topic, is still being done by independent scholars at institutions of all sizes and descriptions, from the largest and most prestigious universities to small, independent, one-person consulting firms and think tanks.

Taken together, these developments indicate the existence of a scholarly community. Such a scholarly community is in itself evidence of what I will be identifying as a "commons" in the pages that follow. Membership in a scholarly community is not always simply a matter of affiliation or even of regular attendance at conferences and meetings. Such activities merely define the formal core of contemporary scholarly communities. These communities also typically include peripheries as well; in this case, the periphery includes those people whose teaching, research, or practice is influenced by the body of nonprofit and voluntary action studies but who do not participate directly or formally in these studies. The renaissance of nonprofit and voluntary action studies has been sudden and dramatic enough so that its periphery extends throughout most of the social sciences.

We must be careful to avoid thinking of the periphery only in terms of a passive audience. Despite a certain level of coherence and integration of efforts in the core of this particular commons, we cannot overlook the simultaneous existence of a host of independent scholars in a variety of disciplines and settings who have made important contributions to our collective understanding of nonprofit and voluntary phenomena. Much of the material produced by such past and present "independent operators" may be well known to members of the interdisciplinary community of nonprofit and voluntary action scholars. For example, the central metaphor of this study—the commons—was first derived from an essay by a biologist. Hardin (1968) succinctly posed what has become known as the "free-rider problem" in "The Tragedy of the Commons."

Reconnaissance on the Periphery

My review of material for this book suggested that some of the independent research efforts and work in nontraditional disciplines may have major implications for the rethinking of nonprofit studies. A great deal of interesting and seemingly relevant material is to be found in anthropological studies of other cultures and in medieval and ancient history (Anheier, 1987; Kerri, 1976; Ross, 1976). For example, a ruler in ancient northern India whom writers in English call Asoka deserves to be ranked as one of the world's notable philanthropists. Asoka patronized the institutional base of Buddhism just as Constantine did with Christianity. He endowed hundreds—perhaps thousands—of monasteries, monuments, and temples and legitimated a distinctive set of Buddhist ethics about giving and fund-raising practices.

Although attention has been lavished on various practical aspects of the contemporary relations between government and the nonprofit sector, systematic political insights are rare in nonprofit and voluntary action theory. Perhaps as a result, politics as nonprofit and voluntary action and important political activities in political conventions and campaigns, party finance and organization, and interest group behavior have been largely ignored or only touched upon lightly in the existing nonprofit and voluntary studies literature.

Furthermore, any enterprise that seeks to deliberately expand the paradigm of a field by bringing in new evidence and additional questions must also raise the issue of parsimony as an objective of sound social theory or risk simply adding to the cacophony. The qualities of appropriate brevity, succinct presentation, and avoidance of redundancy are normally considered to be desirable characteristics of any sound theory. However, parsimony is far easier to talk about than to achieve in a multidisciplinary context characterized by differing sets of assumptions that are taken for granted, variations in definition, and variable emphasis of even basic terms and concepts. In a scientific world characterized by multiple exploding universes of knowledge and discourse, it is difficult even to gain access to all of the relevant materials, much less organize and collate them. In such a context, it is tempting to view any attempt at theoretical synthesis and parsimony as hopelessly naive and utopian.

Nevertheless, one of the principal justifications of the effort reflected in this book is a desire for greater parsimony in nonprofit and voluntary action theory. If the example of other sciences is a guide, classification and taxonomy are beginning steps toward more parsimonious theory. To begin this process, I suggest that particular concerns found in six different social science disciplines form the emerging skeletal structure of a multidisciplinary theory of the commons. In the following brief sections, each of which is expanded later in the book, I introduce and label aspects of this theoretical anatomy.

Altruism

In some instances, independent examinations of issues in nonprofit and voluntary action studies speak directly to matters of central importance to a particular academic discipline. For example, a number of psychologists have been interested in the motivation associated with charitable and philanthropic behavior. Several studies of bystander behavior, for example, shed important light on the central issues of what motivates people to give aid and donations and to engage in other forms of giving and helping behavior.

I will deal with these and other psychological concerns under the label of *altruism theory* and will suggest that they are part of a pattern of concerns and theoretical issues involving motivation and individual aspects of behavior included in what I am calling the theory of the commons. In the context of contemporary nonprofit and voluntary studies, altruism theory can be seen as addressing behavior that occurs outside the family and that is not motivated by profit or gain.

Philanthropy

Researchers in sociology have been interested in a set of concerns related to altruism theory for many years. They have shown considerable interest in the organized social relations of the associations, formal voluntary organizations, and social institutions of the nonprofit world. *Philanthropy theory,* in this sense, is concerned broadly with the social organization of attempts to make the world a better place. Fisher (1986) defines philanthropy as voluntary giving, voluntary service, and voluntary association for the benefit of others. Nonprofit organizations and voluntary action are thus the principal medium of philanthropic efforts.

Some researchers have examined primarily the internal and extramural relations of formal organizations, including interorganizational coordination and community relations. More recently, applied social scientists in gerontology and other fields have done extensive research on informal support groups.

These concerns might be called charity organization theory, as they once were, or community organization, as they were more recently. Early in the present century, Amos Warner ([1908] 1988) went so far as to suggest calling them "philanthropology." In this book, I shall designate them simply as philanthropy theory and attempt to encompass the broadest possible range of concerns involving the social organization of all efforts at social improvement.

Patronage

As noted earlier, one of the less-often examined areas of nonprofit and voluntary studies is the political aspect of charitable and philanthropic behavior. This topic is actually part of a broader pattern of concern with the theoretical implications of patronage relations. Aspects of *patronage theory* have been of interest to an interdisciplinary community including historians and political scientists. Some of the most fascinating contributions to patronage theory come from the work of classicists, art historians, literary critics, and musicologists.

Patronage is the giving of either protection or support (Gifis, 1991). Patronage theory is concerned with an extremely broad range of hierarchical relations between patrons (or donors) and their clients. Such phenomena include status, power, authority, and the state and all of its relations to the nonprofit sector, not just nonprofit service vendors but also political parties and party caucuses and conventions, interest groups, political campaigns, and related political phenomena. Patronage theory explicitly includes not only the patronage of the nonprofit sector by the state but also the unique forms of political patronage by which the democratic state is constituted and expressions of power and authority within nonprofit organizations and voluntary associations.

Gifts

The broad horizons of patronage theory open up to multidisciplinary scholars of nonprofit and voluntary action a significantly expanded view of the area. The same may be said of a little-known area of specialized study in anthropology and archeology. Following the lead of the French anthropologist Marcel Mauss, a small but diverse group of researchers has made significant advances in understanding variations on the gift exchange in a cross-cultural context. The *potlatch* for example, is an important kind of serial gift exchange found in a number of different cultures.

Gift theory is a fitting label for cross-cultural and comparative studies that form an increasingly important aspect of our collective understanding of nonprofit and voluntary action. Because it deals with what is often behavior of central significance in cultures very different from our own, gift theory must be approached very cautiously. In its broadest sense, gift theory is concerned with the consequences—including social integration and social equilibrium—arising from various forms of nonmarket and noncoercive exchange.

Charity

Many American social sciences, social work and parts of sociology in particular, originally arose in the wake of the reform Darwinism of Lester Ward (1967) and remain heavily committed to the pragmatic use of social science for social improvement. *Charity theory* is concerned with conscious, deliberate understanding and use of altruism, philanthropy, patronage, and gift theories for the purpose of organizing and carrying out social-improvement projects directed at aiding those in need.

Norms and ethics endorsing and advocating individual acts of charity can be traced to the brink of Western history and beyond. Organized eleemosynary efforts to aid the poor and disadvantaged were well established by the early Middle Ages. Beginning late in the nineteenth century, the scientific charity movement established the base of the contemporary model of social service with emphasis upon efficient and effective organization and the adoption of established routines and "methods" of charitable practice (Walter, 1987). Creation of the legal category of nonprofit corporations and the granting to such corporations tax-exempt status can be seen as byproducts of those same efforts.

Endowments

Another major question of general importance that has been receiving increased attention in recent years involves the economics of nonprofit and voluntary action. In its most general form, nonprofit economics is concerned with the economical use of a society's endowment—the social surplus of a productive society diverted from future production, public goods, and private consumption and dedicated to various charitable and philanthropic purposes. Like other economic theories, *endowment theory* is a theory of means. In this case, however, the concern is with the use of a society's endowment—its culture and its wealth—to define much of what we conventionally think of as civilization. Ultimately, then, endowment theory is concerned with how a civilization uses what it currently possesses and what its people know to strive for common goods.

Business

Some researchers and scholars working in the area of nonprofit organizations and voluntary action are very enthusiastic about what might be called the *nonprofit business perspective*. In general, this approach is based on a categorical assumption, a critique, and a viewpoint. The categorical assumption is that not-for-profit organizations, especially those that employ paid staff and receive fees or other compensations for their services, are more akin to commercial business organizations than they are to voluntary membership organizations. The critique based on this assumption is that these same organizations are often managed poorly and operated inefficiently and are, all in all, rather poor specimens of private enterprise. The resultant viewpoint is one placing heavy emphasis on management problems and perspectives.

Native Language Resources

One of the most basic common goods of any society or group is the spoken and written language that its members share and through which they are able to express their thoughts, ideas, and aspirations. Therefore, I am fundamentally concerned with the endowment of terms and concepts inherent in nonprofit and voluntary action studies. The objective of this book is modest in this regard: to state in words as plain and ordinary as possible what appear to be some of the most important aspects of how and why certain nonprofit and voluntary actions occur.

The theory of the commons as presented here does not answer all questions and resolve all issues about the language used in this area of study, for in truth it is not yet fully clear what all of the issues and questions raised by an adequate interdisciplinary theory of nonprofit and voluntary action may be. Moreover, at least as many relevant disciplines are left out of this book, for practical considerations, as are included. For example, important contributions by geography and regional science, archeology, accounting, and several additional major subfields of history are not discussed. Another field of major importance only touched upon here is legal studies, in which a virtually unbroken chain concerned with inheritance, trusts, foundations, and other relevant matters leads back to Roman law. We might expect that insights from each of these fields would broaden and enrich nonprofit and voluntary studies considerably. I leave to others more familiar with the fields, however, the task of elucidating materials in those areas. It is sufficient to note that nothing currently suggests that evidence from any of the areas that are neglected would overturn the basic insights offered in this book.

As befits its subject matter, this book is in part a lighthearted language experiment; that is, an effort to create word-pictures that describe the ways in which people in the nonprofit world think about themselves and their social worlds when things are functioning about as expected. It is also partly an experiment in setting aside the materialistic and utilitarian nonprofit paradigms that have so often guided public discourse and research on this topic.

I make no inflated claims about the overarching significance or public gravity of the language of the commons as used in this book. The theory as presented here will not immediately cure human greed, ignorance, or stupidity. Yet some of its implications, if consistently followed through, do appear to promise significant impact on policy at some point in the future.

To those people suspicious of such cautious claims, take note: if physicists can indulge themselves with the fascinating wordplay of using words like *up, down,* and *charm* to give added meaning to their data, why can social scientists not do likewise? Initially, it will be sufficient if the model presented here stands on its own as a description and explanation of an important slice of social, economic, and political life. If it does, its practical significance may be more appropriately assessed on a later occasion.

I do not suggest that what follows is presented as an objective or value-free exercise. Theories of nonprofit and voluntary action, like theories of the family, suffer from our limited abilities to describe and explain without simultaneously evaluating in every sense of the word. In the case of nonprofit and voluntary action, utilitarian theory—certainly through economics but also through psychology, political science, and the sociology of organizations—has proven to be particularly susceptible to this shortcoming.

For some people, the calculus of costs and benefits has become a universal index to what is rational. Yet it would be the most repulsive kind of reductionism to suggest that the fantastically diverse pursuits of nonprofit action should be directed or governed for all time by the narrow insights of twentieth-century cost-benefit thinking. Enlightenment, virtue, beauty, rapture, truth, salvation, perfection, community, art for its own sake, and untold other nonprofit objectives sought by the philanthropists, philosophers, artists, scientists, athletes, religious people, and charitable people of human history stand on their own merits as human endeavors. They do not need to be thought of in terms of utility maximization or goal attainment to be seen as reasonable pursuits.

In developing the language of the model presented here, I sought to use what might best be called poetic license. My intent is to create a semantic model of various key elements of nonprofit and voluntary action. I devoted considerable time and energy to simplifying the basic terms. In particular, I tried to avoid four- and five-syllable nouns ending in *tion* wherever and whenever possible. (*Information* and *rendition,* it must be acknowledged, slipped through.) In addition, I avoided meaningless metatheoretical formalisms like *outcome* and *input* whenever possible.

Substantial effort went into exploring the connotations of ordinary English words that might be used in the model, particularly those with a history of practical use in this area. The English language is remarkably rich in ways of describing and discussing aspects of nonprofit organization, voluntary action, and philanthropy. Ordinary speakers of English have been dealing with nonprofit, voluntary, and philanthropic issues in their daily lives for many centuries.

Some terms, like *dower* and *benefice,* were retrieved from linguistic oblivion. Others, like *endowment, commons,* and *repertory,* had to be given slight tweaks to bring out latent or hidden implications of theoretical value. A few terms, most importantly *benefactory,* were deliberately constructed (in this case, by analogy with the terms *manufactory* and *factory,* and *factors* of production) with an occasional dash of pun intended.

Terms such as *endowment, foundation, benefit,* and *trustee* stretch back hundreds of years and are anchored deep in Western culture. Chalmers (1827), for example, used the term in roughly the sense intended here nearly two hundred years ago. Other terms (including borrowings from Latin, like *benefice* or *fideocommisia,* or from Greek, like *koininia*) express important contemporary ideas but either have never been adopted or have fallen into complete disuse and may be beyond recall.

In calling upon these rich linguistic reserves, any theory of nonprofit and voluntary action necessarily becomes a kind of reflexive exercise by demonstrating (or failing to demonstrate!) some of the very principles it asserts. All speakers of a common language are members of an association of sorts. They are also mutual beneficiaries of common meanings and the resulting outlooks and worldviews that condition their actions in infinite subtle ways. At another level, the communities of researchers and scholars interested in nonprofit and voluntary studies declaim and sustain their joint interests through modes of communication and interaction and in so doing dramatize and demonstrate their subject matter.

Using poetical language as a basis for social and political theory is not as whimsical as it may at first appear. Much existing work on nonprofit and voluntary action relies upon literary devices, sometimes unintentionally. Nonprofit economics in its current state has been built up from market economic theory with a whimsical series of analogies, ironies, metaphors, similes, and wordplay; nonprofit organizations are treated as if they were profit-oriented firms (Crew, 1975). Such similes are a common poetic device, often used for irony or other dramatic effect. Nonprofit leadership is characterized ironically as "entrepreneurship" (Young, 1987). In the same vein, some terms used in the field are suggestive of nothing quite so much as Lewis Carroll. The pretzel logic evident in compound negatives such as "the unrelated business income of the nonprofit, nongovernmental sector" is truly worthy of the Red Queen in *Alice in Wonderland.* What can one possibly be asserting in such a phrase? Such phrases often seem to operate at a strictly poetical level. Regrettably, at times they appear to convey largely negative images of disheveled, disorganized, unfocused and unmanageable establishments peopled by the confused, impractical, and erratic.

Overview of the Theory

The first task of any theory is to establish a suitable nomenclature. I call the interdisciplinary theory set forth in this book the *theory of the commons*. The theoretical rationale for using this name will become increasingly clear as the theory unfolds. The term *commons* plays upon many relevant meanings and connotations. For example, the conventional wisdom of a group is sometimes called common knowledge. The Anglo-American experience of common law arose out of custom and conventional practice and the much broader experience of common lands held in joint tenancy or ownership.

Several U.S. states, including Pennsylvania and Massachusetts, are self-identified as commonwealths, and the economic transformation of Europe was undertaken under the heading of a common market. Clubs and membership organizations, including the Smithsonian Institution, frequently have common rooms for the mutual use of members. Public elementary education often occurs in common schools and is thought by many to emphasize common sense, which was also the title of a political polemic at the time of the American Revolution. That revolution was undertaken as a common action of the people of the United States against Great Britain, which already included its famous House of Commons (Ryle and Richards, 1988). Then as now, it was common knowledge that many of us engage in commonplace tasks, some of which may be undertaken for the common good. Each of these connotations of the term *commons* is related to the others and, as we shall see, to the fundamental ideas of nonprofit, voluntary, and philanthropic action as well.

A number of contemporary academic uses of the term *commons* support the usage in this book: Edney and Bell (1984) call their decision-making game, in which teams of participants harvest resources from a shared pool, *a commons game*. And, there is a rich tradition in social philosophy concerned with the *common good*, a term used roughly as I use the term in this book.

The term *commons* as it is used in this book may refer to a club or membership organization; social movement; political party; religious, artistic, scientific, or athletic society; support group; network; conference of volunteers; or to several other forms of what we think of as nonprofit or voluntary social organization. As developed here, the term is an ideal type; it distills an essential set of related characteristics that are seldom if ever empirically observable in pure form. As an ideal type, we should expect to find in any empirical commons evidence of altruistic motives and behavior; philanthropy; charity; patronage; various forms of donations and gift giving; and programs that involve search, investigation, learning, and other ways of expanding common endowments.

I hope that readers of this book, including members of the Association for Research on Nonprofit Organizations and Voluntary Action and all those interested in nonprofit and voluntary studies, may see themselves as collaborators in a commons of which I am also a participant. The goal of the book and of the theory of the commons is partially to clarify the nature and purposes of the tasks facing this particular commons by pointing toward future directions for research and study of the many other commons in contemporary society.

Attention to common purposes and objectives by the participants of any commons can be expected to result in *common goods,* which are distinguishable not only from the private goods on sale in the marketplace and the public goods of the state but also from *the* common good. Common goods differ from public goods in that no assumptions need to be made about the universal desirability of common goods. In most instances, it is sufficient that common goods are shared or held jointly by members of a particular commons, even in the face of indifference or hostility from others. Common goods may be transformed into true public goods only under very special circumstances.

Any set of common goods suitable for further use are said by the theory in this book to constitute an *endowment,* and the full set of all endowments in a society or group of societies is seen as constituting a civilization. The endowment of any commons ordinarily consists of its treasuries of money, property, and marketable goods; its collections of precious, priceless objects; and its repertories of routines, cults, skills, techniques, and other meaningful behavior learned by participants in the commons or passed on to others for the common good.

Any endowment is a dynamic entity. Treasuries, collections, and repertories carried forward into the present constitute a common heritage, and those endowments made available as resources for future use make up a common legacy. Oft-quoted commentaries by de Tocqueville ([1862] 1945) and others on the unique American penchant for voluntary action, for example, point to such action as an important part of the heritage of American civilization and presumably its ongoing legacy as well. Children who learn basic repertories of voluntary association in scouting groups, churches, or synagogues grow up to be adults who organize parent-teacher associations, little leagues, new political parties, interest groups, and professional associations.

Practicality alone does not define an endowment. Among primitive tribes, past or present, many of the same skills that go into tool making also go into decorative and ritual art forms (Van Gennep, 1960; Smith, 1972a). It is usually a moot question whether practicality preceded or flowed from decoration and ritual. Endowment theory, therefore, is concerned in part with the special circumstances of the rational choice between carving an ax and decorating a ceremonial pipe. In the life of any people, such choices may be equally as momentous as the better known "guns and butter" choice between food and defense.

The social organization of any commons may encompass one or more benefactories, consisting of the organized social relations between patrons, clients, and various intermediaries or agents and devoted to various forms of gifts, grants, or benefits. Two major contemporary types of benefactories are those engaged in various problem-solving efforts and those engaged in presentations of various types.

Other complex acts in the commons may link various benefactories together in a variety of ways. Thus, the conduct of voluntary action research (like any other research) may be a particular form of problem solving, and the discussion of that research at a scientific meeting such as the annual ARNOVA conference or publication of the findings in a scholarly journal constitute presentations. Yet conduct of the research and presentation of the findings are clearly part of the same larger act (which we call "the research").

These and other acts derive their meanings in part from one another and from the commons that encompasses them.

Commons are not physical entities or places, although a variety of common places may be set aside for shared uses. Indeed, the architecture of such common places and the unique architectural forms that express and facilitate common values is itself an important area of inquiry completely outside the repertory of the modern nonprofit and voluntary action scholar. (A few scattered examples of such research can be found. Taylor [1979] considers prisons and "moral architecture," for example.)

Commons consist principally of acts incorporating dialogue or interaction and building up successive understandings and the aggregation of separate meanings between participants. Such aggregations may include events, situations, organizations, and other complex acts that link together many separate events and typical situations.

The theory of the commons explicitly departs from the sociological practice of treating society as an aggregation of many separate institutions. Instead, the theory conceives of society as composed of four fundamental institutional sectors: households, markets, the state, and, of course, the commons. The sociologist Arnold Rose, an early student of nonprofit and voluntary action, set forth a similar conception more than three decades ago: "Voluntary associations consist of all classes of functioning groupings except families, the formal government (including its specialized organs such as schools and armed forces) and economic enterprise" (Rose, 1960, p. 667). The popular characterization of the commons as the third sector is usually derived by ignoring another sector—the household sector. No harm is done (and the phrase *third sector* remains intact) if we merely acknowledge households as the fourth sector. See Ross (1977) for an appraisal of Rose's work on voluntary associations.

A fundamental goal of the theory of the commons is to set forth a base for greater common ground among disciplines in a model of nonprofit and voluntary action as rational behavior. Although the issue of the rationality of common behavior has often been treated as a matter of little importance to social researchers, it is of critical importance in the politics and economics of nonprofit and voluntary action and, as we shall see, is also important in establishing the practical basis for action in the commons. To accomplish this, I shall attempt to set the concepts of the theory and its values within a limited *rational choice theory*.

A fundamental goal of the theory of the commons is to set a base for greater common ground among disciplines in their understandings of nonprofit organization, voluntary action, and philanthropy as value-laden social action. This task has taken on additional importance since the collapse of the Soviet empire and the crisis of public legitimacy in the United States. The familiar world of the welfare state representing a moderate alternative between socialism and laissez-faire capitalism may, in the long run, be more completely transformed by the revolutionary events of 1989 to 1991 than by decades of fulminations against the "mixed economy" and "reluctant welfare state" by ideologues on either the left or right.

Conclusion

Van Til's metaphor (1988) of conceptual maps concisely sums up the status of third sector studies today. Both nonprofit organization and voluntary action studies have been historically distinct intellectual maps that appear to be converging at the very point where the compass of philanthropy studies—long thought extinguished—shows signs of pointing toward a number of new and interesting landmarks as well.

A great many different disciplinary maps of parts of the emerging territory are waiting to be discovered—in law, social work, history, anthropology, public administration, sociology, political science, economics, and many other fields of study. Some of the more important areas of study that overlap disciplinary boundaries have been labeled in this chapter as altruism, philanthropy, patronage, gifts, charities, endowments, and business maps.

By present consensus, the vast terrain of society has been divided into three sectors: state, marketplace, and the awkwardly unnamed "third sector." This introduction offered a brief synopsis of some of the main terms of a theory of the commons, which seeks to name and further map this third sector. A number of additional terms and concepts as well as further explication of these basic terms will be introduced in the chapters that follow.

In Chapter One, I shall examine a number of existing perspectives on the nature of nonprofit organization and voluntary action. Taken together, these perspectives delineate many of the major areas of interest to nonprofit, voluntary, and philanthropic studies as the field is currently emerging and also raise a number of unresolved issues and questions.

Current Approaches to Nonprofit Organizations and Voluntary Association

Political and industrial associations strike us force-
ably; but the others elude our observation, or if we
discover them we understand them imperfectly because we have hardly ever seen anything of the
kind.

—Alexis de Tocqueville

Generally, there are thought to be two centrally defining concepts
of nonprofit, voluntary, and philanthropic studies. First, the most
pervasive and characteristic forms of nonprofit and voluntary behavior are nonprofit formal organizations. Second, the network of
nonprofit organizations defines a socioeconomic sector known variously as the nonprofit, voluntary, independent, or third sector in
contrast with the profit-making sector of business and the public
sector of government.

For many people, this nonprofit sector (or "the sector") is the
province of simpletons, knaves, and fools: those who lack a clear
understanding of their goals and purposes and must therefore be
aided in clarification; those whose declared purposes mask and conceal their real interests in personal gain and profit; and those whose

goals and purposes are irrational, foolish, impractical, and unattainable. For others, particularly true believers of all stripes, the sector may equally be viewed as the province of the wise, brave, good, and foresighted. In this chapter, I shall examine further some of the contemporary expressions of these formative ideas by looking at a good deal that is worthwhile in the ideas as well as certain nagging theoretical problems.

The Nonprofit Organization

The conventional way of approaching the sector is through the legal and economic category of the nonprofit organization—a residual category arrived at by negation or exclusion (Lohmann, 1989). According to Anthony and Young, "A non-profit organization is an organization whose goal is *something other than* earning a profit for its owners. Usually its goals are to provide services" (1984, p. 35, italics added). Precisely what these other purposes may be is not evident in such a definition. (But see Elkin and Molitor, 1984.)

Nonprofit and voluntary action scholars agree that the simple presence or absence of profit is, by itself, an insufficient indicator of a nonprofit organization. For example, today people are concerned about the enormous profits of professional sports and their distribution to players in the form of large salaries and bonuses. Yet when the Cincinnati Red Stockings went on the first professional baseball tour in 1869, the total profit from the tour was reported to be $1.69. Therefore, in its early years, was professional baseball almost a nonprofit activity? The general consensus among nonprofit and voluntary action scholars would be that it was not.

It is largely to distinguish intent from result that some authors prefer the term *not for profit* instead of *nonprofit*. However, this usage is distinctly marginal. *Black's Law Dictionary*, Kohler's *Dictionary for Accountants*, *Webster's Third New International Dictionary*, *Funk and Wagnalls*, and the *American Heritage Dictionary*, among others, make no mention of the term *not for profit*. The principal object of using this term appears to be to distinguish bone fide nonprofit organizations from failing businesses (which are nonprofit in an entirely different sense) without excluding successful nonprofits that may incorrectly call their undistributed surpluses profits.

The issue has been further complicated by statutes in a number of states (New York, California, Pennsylvania) that now allow types of not-for-profit business corporations whose purposes fall largely outside those under consideration here (Oleck, 1980). Those people who prefer the term *not for profit* may safely pencil in the letter *t*, two hyphens, and the word *for* wherever the term *nonprofit* occurs in this book. Note, however, that this work is grounded in the view that those two hyphens and four letters fail to resolve any of the underlying theoretical problems presented by the nonprofit concept.

As mentioned earlier, Anthony and Young (1984) have pointed to two defining characteristics of the nonprofit organization: preoccupation with something other than profit and a tendency toward providing service. The first point is hardly an exclusive criterion, unless one adopts the peculiar view of contemporary exchange theorists that any and all attainments of goals, realization of objectives, or fulfillments of purpose is profit (see, for example, Becker, 1976; Alhadeff, 1982; Blau, 1967; Homans, 1961). On the basis of such an approach, the nonprofit world would indeed appear to be limited to the confused, deceptive, and uninformed. Anthony and Young, however, clearly regard these two criteria alone as insufficient to define nonprofit activities. They go on to expand their initial criteria to nine.

1. The absence of a profit measure
2. The tendency to be service organizations
3. Constraints on goals and strategies
4. Less dependence on clients for financial support
5. The dominance of professionals
6. Differences in governance
7. Differences in top management
8. Importance of political influences
9. A tradition of inadequate management controls

A key assumption of much of the current management literature on nonprofit organizations that is widely shared by accountants, economists, public and business administrators, and others is that "the absence of a single, satisfactory, overall measure of performance that is comparable to the profit measure is the most serious problem inhibiting the development of effective management control systems in nonprofit organizations" (Anthony and Young, 1984, p. 39). In the same vein, Gifis (1991) says that a nonprofit corporation is one chartered for other than profit-making activities. Thus, this particular construction of the theory of nonprofit organizations begins with the critical assumption that nonprofits are a flawed or incomplete form of for-profit organization. Advocates of this position tend to assume, based on the absence of a consistent performance measure, that nonprofit organizations as a class are inherently more inefficient in the conduct of their affairs than comparable for-profit organizations.

It is important to note that this is an assumption, rather than an empirical finding, although it is seldom presented as such. Furthermore, it is an unjustified assumption in that systematic empirical evidence of generalized inefficiency as a defining characteristic of nonprofit organizations is simply nonexistent. In charity theory, for example, it has been assumed for decades that greater efficiency was needed in the delivery of social services (Lee, 1937). As early as 1906, the Cleveland Chamber of Commerce was calling for improvements in the efficiency of charitable activity (Lubove, 1965). Yet, incredible as it may seem, there has never been an empirical or comparative study that establishes that charities are less efficient than profit-oriented organizations. The matter rests entirely upon theoretical deduction. (And upon a theoretical lacuna, as we shall see below.)

A somewhat different approach to defining the nonprofit organization has been taken by scholars who are less interested in nonprofit management and more interested in policy issues. Hall (1987, p. 3) defines a nonprofit organization as "a body of individuals who associate for any of three purposes: 1) to perform public tasks that have been delegated to them by the state; 2) to perform public tasks for which there is a demand that neither the state nor for-profit organizations are willing to fulfill; or 3) to influence the direction of policy in the state, the for-profit sector, or other nonprofit organizations." This approach expands the other-than-profit approach to recognize what some sources call the nongovernmental organization (NGO) as well as the possibility of autonomous action.

This approach is particularly evident in the distinction between museums (nonprofit) and galleries (for profit). According to the National Academy of Art, as cited by DiMaggio (1987, p. 195), "All American museums are nonprofit . . . because the definition of *museum* the American Association of Museums (AAM) adopted excludes proprietary enterprises that mount exhibitions for public view." From this vantage point, the first-order distinction between profit-oriented and other activities necessitates a second-order distinction like nongovernmental organization because the nonprofit heading encompasses both public (or governmental) and private (or nongovernmental) endeavors.

Legal Types of Organization

Current legal terminology makes a number of organizational distinctions worth noting here; for example, an *association* is "a collection of persons who have joined together for a certain object" (Gifis, 1991, p. 32). This meaning is very close to the original meaning of the term *company,* which is "any group of people voluntarily united for performing jointly any activity, business or commercial enterprise" (Gifis, 1991, p. 83). A *corporation* is an association of shareholders created under law and regarded as an artificial person, with a legal entity entirely separate from the persons who compose it and the capacity of succession, or continuous existence. A corporation is able to hold property, sue and be sued, and exercise other powers conferred upon it by law (Gifis, 1991).

The issue of succession has attracted little interest among nonprofit and voluntary action scholars. It will be treated later under the twin headings of heritage and legacy. The heritage of Anglo-American nonprofit law, for example, is clearly traceable to the 1601 Statute of Charitable Uses that was adopted by Parliament in the same year as the Elizabethan Poor Law (Gray, [1905] 1967).

Legal terminology offers several clear alternative models of nonprofit organization with interesting implications. First, legally, a nonprofit corporation is not an organization but a legal personality. A *cooperative association* is "a union of individuals, commonly laborers, farmers or small capitalists, formed for the prosecution in common of some productive enterprise, the profits being shared in accordance with capital or labor contributed by each" (Gifis, 1991, p. 101). Perhaps nonprofit organizations are distinctive forms of cooperatives. A *syndicate* is a group of individuals or companies who have formed a joint venture to undertake a project that the individuals would be unable or unwilling to pursue alone (Gifis, 1991). Nonprofit organizations may be constrained forms of syndicates. Many of the nonprofit systems, networks, collaboratives, and federations have something of the character of syndicates.

The Nondistribution Constraint

Hansmann (1981b, 1987) points out that the legal concept of nonprofit does not rest on the theoretical basis of profit or profit-seeking motivation. In law and tax policy, the concern is not with profit or how it is earned (by service or otherwise) or with any of the other criteria given by Anthony and Young (1984). The key issues in state and federal public policy have been two. First, the critical question for attaining the legal designation of a nonprofit corporation is, in most cases, charitable purpose, broadly defined. Second, the critical issue in attaining exemption from taxation is not the absence of profit but rather "the nondistribution constraint" (Hansmann, 1987). Legal and ethical restriction on the distribution of any resulting surpluses to owners or shareholders is the defining characteristic of nonprofit organization (Simon, 1987).

The Nonprofit Sector

The second formative idea of contemporary nonprofit and voluntary theory is the concept of the nonprofit sector. Together, nonprofit organizations are said to make up a distinct sector consisting of a number of discrete but related nonprofit organizations, possibly classifiable into nonprofit "industries." According to O'Neill (1989), this sector owns roughly 10 percent of the property in the United States, has as many employees as the federal and state governments combined, and has a bigger budget than all but seven nations.

Even though there seems to be widespread agreement about the existence of this sector, there is little agreement over its definition or organization. Anthony and Young (1984) offer one conception of this sector, discussed below. The chapter outline of O'Neill's *The Third America* (1989) offers another, somewhat different, classification. The National Taxonomy of Exempt Entities (NTEE) offers yet a third conception, and the Internal Revenue Service (IRS) Code, with its labyrinth of classifications, offers a fourth (INDEPENDENT SECTOR, 1987).

In general, these various efforts at distinctions point to at least two of the greatest and most controversial ambiguities in the contemporary field of nonprofit and voluntary studies. First, should clubs, associations, and other types of membership organizations be considered as part of the nonprofit sector or as a separate sector? (See, for example, Smith, 1991.) Second, is the nonprofit sector defined exclusively by formal organizations or are the activities of membership organizations, individual volunteers, informal groups, and private acts of charity and philanthropy to be included as well?

Equally controversial, especially among public administration theorists, is the issue of whether federal, state, and local governments are nonprofit organizations. Federal and state nonprofit laws do frequently mention private nonprofit organizations, and there is a long tradition in public administration, in particular, of treating private and public nonprofit organizations as members of a single class. Public agencies do, typically, lack a profit orientation. On the other hand, including them as part of the nonprofit sector initially appears to make a complete muddle out of attempts to deal with the interaction between the nonprofit sector and the public sector. As we shall see in Chapters Seven and Eight, it is indeed possible to make a satisfactory distinction between state and commons without forfeiting the equally useful distinction between commercial and nonprofit ventures.

The issue is further complicated by introducing the question of tax exemption. As already noted, the IRS standard of nondistribution of profits to stakeholders offers a distinct alternative to the profit-motive criterion. Indeed, as we shall see in Chapter Three, the concept of profit motive (and the underlying distinction between self-interested and altruistic behavior) is an unnecessary oversimplification of the range of observable behavior. Although some contemporary nonprofit managers will undoubtedly be unhappy with the results, it may indeed be possible to make a stronger theoretically grounded distinction between tax-exempt and tax-eligible nonprofit organizations.

Nonprofit Typologies

Analysts of the nonprofit sector have long been concerned with deriving an appropriate classification scheme for nonprofit organizations. The following classification of nonprofit industries, for example, was offered by Anthony and Young (1984): (1) health care organizations, (2) educational organizations, (3) membership organizations, (4) human service and arts organizations, (5) the federal government, and (6) state and local governments. Note that items five and six explicitly incorporate governmental organizations into the nonprofit sector, rather than segregating them into a separate public sector. The IRS Code (see Exhibit 1.1) offers a somewhat different way to categorize nonprofit organizations.

The IRS approach, however, is only one of several classification schemes used by federal agencies. The Bureau of the Census, in its Censuses of Services, classifies nonprofit organizations into nine major categories by program: (1) hotels, camps, lodges; (2) research, testing, and consulting; (3) amusement and recreation; (4) health services; (5) legal aid; (6) education; (7) social services; (8) membership associations; and (9) educational, scientific, and research organizations.

Probably the most complex classification scheme emerged from a project spearheaded by INDEPENDENT SECTOR (1987) that devised the twenty-six–item classifications shown in Exhibit 1.2. This National Taxonomy of Exempt Entities (NTEE) was subtitled "A System for Classifying Nongovernmental, Nonbusiness Tax-Exempt Organizations in the U.S. with a Focus on IRS Section 501(c)(3) Philanthropic Organizations." This ambitious schema attempts to embrace the full range of nonprofit, voluntary, and philanthropic activity. Each category is assigned a letter of the En-

**Exhibit 1.1. IRS Classification System
Under Section 501 of the IRS Code of 1934.**

501(c)(2)	Title holding corporations (5,758)*
501(c)(3)	Charitable corporations (366,071)
501(c)(4)	Civic leagues, social welfare organizations, and local associations (131,250)
501(c)(5)	Labor, agricultural, or horticultural organizations (75,632)
501(c)(6)	Business and trade associations (54,217)
501(c)(7)	Social/recreational clubs (57,343)
501(c)(8)	Fraternal beneficiary societies and associations (94,435)
501(c)(9)	Voluntary employees' beneficiary associations (10,668)
501(c)(10)	Domestic fraternal societies, orders, or associations (15,924)
501(c)(11)	Teachers' retirement funds (11)
501(c)(12)	Benevolent life insurance associations of a purely local character (5,244)
501(c)(13)	Cemetery companies owned and operated by members (7,239)
501(c)(14)	Credit unions (6,032)
501(c)(15)	Mutual insurance companies (967)
501(c)(16)	Corporations for financing crops (18)
501(c)(17)	Supplemental unemployment benefit plans (726)
501(c)(18)	Employee funded pension trusts (3)
501(c)(19)	Veterans' organizations (23,062)
501(c)(20)	Legal service organizations (167)
501(c)(21)	Black lung trusts (15)

*Numbers in parentheses are the number of active organizations on the IRS master file in 1985.

Source: U.S. Internal Revenue Service, 1985, p. 70. As cited in Weisbrod, 1988, pp. 176-177.

glish alphabet as part of a complex four-part coding scheme that also distinguishes group, program, and beneficiary characteristics.

The NTEE is, in part, a refinement and expansion of concepts incorporated into a social services classification project completed a decade earlier (Sumariwalla, 1976). By itself, however, the NTEE is not a sufficient typology for theoretical purposes. It merely supplies labels for major categories of presently tax-exempt organizations. It provides us with nothing in the way of a rationale for the inclusion or exclusion of particular categories or any of the relationships between them.

Exhibit 1.2. NTEE Major Group Code Items.

A	Arts, culture, humanities
B	Education/instruction and related—formal and informal
C	Environmental quality, protection, and beautification
D	Animal related
E	Health—general and rehabilitation
F	Health—mental health, crisis intervention
G	Health—mental retardation/developmentally disabled
H	Consumer protection/legal aid
I	Crime and delinquency prevention—public protection
J	Employment/jobs
K	Food, nutrition, agriculture
L	Housing/shelter
M	Public safety, emergency preparedness, and relief
N	Recreation, leisure, sports, athletics
O	Youth development
P	Human service, other
Q	International/foreign
R	Civil rights, social action, advocacy
S	Community improvement, community capacity building
T	Grantmaking/foundations
U	Research, planning, science, technology, technical assistance
V	Voluntarism, philanthropy, charity
W	Religion related/spiritual development
X	Reserved for new major group (future)
Y	Reserved for special information for regulatory bodies
Z	Nonclassifiable (temporary code)

Source: INDEPENDENT SECTOR, 1987.

Size of the Sector

One of the issues that has been of particular interest to advocates of the nonprofit concept is the size of the nonprofit sector. Until quite recently, there was little demonstrated interest in information of this type. Even today, major questions about measurement remain. Nevertheless, we can get an approximate idea of the size of the sector from a variety of existing sources. The following discussion is based on two sources: information on organizations is based on a series of tables published in the appendix of Weisbrod's *The Nonprofit Economy* (1988) and information on nonprofit employment is taken from *Statistical Abstracts* (U.S. Bureau of the Census, 1987).

Working from IRS data, Weisbrod (1988) estimates that there

were 887,000 nonprofit organizations in the United States in 1985. Of this number, 366,000 are estimated to be tax exempt; that is, meeting the requirements of Section 501(c)(3) of the tax code. The 1985 figures for the other IRS categories are listed in Exhibit 1.1. My primary focus in this work is the tax-exempt charitable organizations, which are often thought of as the core of the nonprofit sector, although many of the perspectives offered apply to other categories as well.

Salamon (1987b) reported significant regional variations among the number of nonprofit organizations in the United States. The South fell below the national average of 47.1 organizations per 100,000 people, and the Northeast, northern Midwest, and West were above this average. Of course, this finding could simply mean that nonprofit organizations in the South are larger than those in the other regions. Data on expenditures suggest exactly the opposite, however. Nonprofit expenditures in 1977 were below the national average of $323 per capita in both the South and West and roughly half the per capita expenditures of $522 for the Northeast.

Hodgkinson and Weitzman (1986) estimate private contributions to nonprofit organizations in the three decades after 1955 to range between a high of 2.7 percent of national income in 1963 and a low of 2.21 percent in 1979. Over that same period, there was an uninterrupted decrease in contributed funds as a proportion of aggregate expenditures by nonprofit organizations. Figures varied from a high of 70.7 percent in 1957 to a low of 31.2 percent in 1984. In 1980, private giving was most important among religious organizations (93 percent of total receipts) and least important in health services (9 percent of total receipts). The proportion of governmental support was highest in civic and social action organizations (44 percent of total receipts) and health and human services groups (43 percent of receipts). Service fees made up the greatest portion of total support for educational and research nonprofit organizations (79 percent of receipts), with all other categories falling at least 25 percent lower.

Two Subclasses of Nonprofits

Existing data and conceptualizations suggest the existence of two quite distinct subcategories of nonprofit organization, as well as a third type that represents a mixture of the two. According to a random sample of 274 IRS-990 tax reports, existing nonprofit organizations are clearly bimodal on the question of resource inflows (Weisbrod, 1988). For the largest single group of nonprofits (47 percent of the total), contributions, gifts, and grants constitute less than 20 percent of total financial inflows. Fees, service charges, and other revenues that "meter" activity levels account for the largest portion of the resources of such organizations. For the second largest group of nonprofit organizations (27 percent of the total), the reverse was true: contribution, gift, and grant support comprised 80 percent of total financial inflows. (The remaining 26 percent of organizations fell between these two clear modes; they received from 21 percent to 79 percent of their resources from revenues or public support.)

This bimodal distribution provides empirical support for a dichotomy introduced by Robert Anthony (1978) between "Type A" nonprofits, which generate revenues that meter their levels of service activity and thus could reasonably be expected to be "firmlike" in their behavior, and "Type B" nonprofits, which rely on public support in the form of gifts, donations, contributions, or grants and for which there is no particular reason to assume any revenue-metering or other "firmlike" characteristics. In between are the mixed (A-B) type organizations seeking to successfully blend firmlike and nonfirm tendencies.

It is important to note that these data are from a relatively small sample of the measured or counted portion of total nonprofit, voluntary, and philanthropic organizations in the United States. The legal protections of incorporation and the expectations of tax exemption are probably applied disproportionately to type A organizations, while type B organizations may be somewhat more inclined to rely upon factors such as trust and mutuality between donor and recipient. Thus, type B nonprofits may be disproportionately represented among the unreported organizations and underrepresented in the data above. At any rate, the primary focus of this book is on the quarter of organizations that are clearly dependent primarily on support for revenue. We must, for the time being, leave open the question of the degree to which the perspective offered here applies to type A groups.

Counting the number of organizations may not give a true picture of the role of the total nonprofit sector. Some researchers have instead looked at paid employment in the sector and located nonprofit employment within a broader service sector (Ginsberg and Vojta, 1981). According to Rudney (1987), employment in philanthropic organizations tends to be primarily in labor intensive services and totalled roughly 6.5 million in 1982. This was roughly 13 percent of total private (nongovernmental) employment, and it was an increase of 43 percent since 1972. While philanthropic organizations employed only 5.7 percent of all workers (including governmental) in 1980, they employed 14.1 percent of all employed professionals and 15.3 percent of all service workers. In 1980, 40 percent of all employees of nonprofit organizations were professionals and 36 percent were service workers. Data on employment, however, also present a distorted picture of nonprofit organizations, voluntary action, and philanthropy, because they concentrate only on the (unknown) proportion of those whose involvement is based on paid compensation.

Data collected by INDEPENDENT SECTOR and the Gallop Organization suggest that much larger numbers of persons are involved in nonprofit, voluntary, and philanthropic activities as volunteers. In 1987, 45 percent of all persons over age 14 in the United States reported working in some way to help others for no monetary pay during the previous year. That number is down from a high of 52 percent reported in 1981 (U.S. Bureau of the Census, 1989). Seventy-one percent of all American households reported making charitable contributions in 1987, with 20 percent donating less than $100 and 14 percent donating more than $1,000 (U.S. Bureau of the Census, 1989).

Another category of philanthropic activity is measured by the number and size of foundations whose goal is to assist or support social, educational, religious, or other activities deemed to serve the common good. According to data published by the Foundation Center, the number of foundations in the U.S. increased from 21,967 in 1981–82 to 27,661 in 1986–87. Total foundation assets increased from $47.6 billion in 1981–82 to $115.4 billion in 1986–87. In this same period, total gifts received by foundations increased from $2.4 billion to $4.6 billion, and total grants awarded increased from $3.8

billion to $6.7 billion. One of the implications of these increases, however, is that smaller portions of foundation wealth are being paid out. The proportion of assets paid out in grants actually fell in this period from 7.9 percent to 5.8 percent.

Nonprofit Action and Unproductive Labor

Before proceeding further, we might ask to what extent it is possible to identify the theoretical origins or conceptual basis of the concepts outlined previously. At first glance, the concepts used in the study of nonprofit groups appear to be derived from direct experience and recent practice; none of the broad range of legal, economic, political, or social "grand theories" or formative doctrines of any of the social sciences makes any mention whatsoever of nonprofit organizations or a nonprofit sector. In contrast with de Tocqueville's ([1862] 1945) references to associations, nonprofit groups appear at first glance to be an invention of the mid twentieth century.

Yet upon closer examination, the theoretical (as distinct from the practical) origins of the concept of nonprofit action can be traced to the neglected half of a dichotomy made by Adam Smith ([1776] 1981) in *The Wealth of Nations*. In that work, Smith distinguished between "productive" and "unproductive" labor.

> There is one sort of labor which adds to the value of the subject upon which it is bestowed; there is another which has no such effect. The former, as it produces a value, may be called productive; the latter, unproductive labor. Thus the labor of a manufacturer adds, generally, to the value of the materials which he works upon, that of his own maintenance, and of his master's profit. The labor of a menial servant, on the contrary, adds to the value of nothing. Though the manufacturer has his wages advanced to him by his master, he, in reality, costs him no expense, the value of his wages generally being restored, together with a profit, in the improved value of the subject upon which his labor was bestowed. A man grows rich by employing a multitude of manufacturers; he grows

poor by maintaining a multitude of menial servants.
[p. 430]

This distinction between productive and unproductive labor is, in all likelihood, the theoretical source of the contemporary distinction of profit-making and nonprofit endeavors. It is entirely consistent with Anthony's distinction of type A and type B nonprofits previously presented. It is also consistent with Hansmann's distinction (1981b, 1987) of "commercial" and "donative" nonprofit groups.

Although Smith's concept of unproductive labor applies to the class of nonprofit organizations that rely on donations, we should not conclude that Smith (an "unproductive" moral philosopher) meant to be critical of unproductive labor. Smith said, "The labor of some of the most respected orders of society is, like that of menial servants, unproductive of any value, and does not fix or realize itself in any permanent subject, or vendible commodity, which endures after the labor is past and for which an equal quantity of labor could afterwards be procured" ([1776] 1981, p. 432).

That Smith had many of the activities later labeled as nonprofit in mind when he spoke of unproductive labor is clear from his references to "the declamation of the actor, the harangue of the orator, or the tune of the musician" ([1776] 1981, p. 431). Smith also affirms the basic quality that led Anthony and Young (1984) and others to associate nonprofit groups with services: the intangible, immaterial character of what these groups produce. Like the services of actors, orators, and musicians, the services of nonprofit groups, Smith said, perish in the very instant of their production.

Once he introduced the distinction between productive and unproductive labor, however, Smith, like most of the economists who followed him for the next two hundred years, devoted his attention exclusively to productive labor. One of the few notable exceptions to this pattern was the American institutional economist John R. Commons, who also noted the nonmarket character of unproductive labor. Commons ([1934] 1961, p. 180) said, "The physician or surgeon, the lawyer, statesman or politician, the minister or priest, the teacher, the musician or actor, the scientist, the domestic servant, the housewife, were 'unproductive' because the usefulness of their labor did not appear in a commodity which could be saved and sold on the markets, or exchanged directly for other commodities or for the labor of others."

Commons was more interested in the implications of the economic value of unproductive labor than in the discussion of nonprofit groups. He said that "the only way in which the value of such services could be measured was in terms of money, as wages or salaries, or in terms of the commodities directly exchanged for them. For this reason, labor itself could be treated only as a commodity, whose value was its exchange-value. Personal services had exchange-value, but their use value appeared only in the happiness of other people and there were no units of measurement, like tons or yards, which could measure happiness" ([1934] 1961, p. 180). His argument is often echoed in later discussions of the economics of services, wherein the point is made that because of the inability to measure the productivity of nonprofit services, employment and wages must be used as proxy measures of productivity (Stanback, 1979a).

Commons, it should be noted, does not make any distinction between commercial and nonprofit ventures or declare further interest in the matter. Yet his line of reasoning is of critical importance to the nonprofit question. Commons remarks that "a hundred and fifty years of economic theorizing has puzzled over the problem of giving a decent status to these personal services" ([1934] 1961, p. 181). Even though we now have over two hundred years of such theorizing, his basic point remains the same. Commons says, "If they are use-values how can we measure them except by the dollar? But the dollar measures their scarcity-value and not their use-value" (p. 181).

The theory of nonprofit economics that emerged in the 1980s placed this issue in a different perspective. In general, the nonprofit economics literature skips over the distinction made by Smith on the strength of near-unanimous acceptance of an operational simile in which the economic performance of nonprofit organizations is analyzed as if they were profit-oriented organizations. Weisbrod (1988, p. 67) views unproductive labor as volunteer labor—which is a largely operational concept, the definition of which he terms "vague and inconsistent" (See also Wolozin, 1975; Stinson and

Stam, 1976.) Volunteer labor in this sense represents a narrowing of Smith's concept ([1776] 1981), which embraces all endeavors that do not generate revenue, and Commons's concept ([1934] 1961), which speaks of "intangibles." The vagueness and inconsistency noted by Weisbrod are probably related to the unresolved issues raised by Smith and Commons.

It is unlikely that these conceptual problems can be resolved within economics alone. Any economic concept of volunteer labor as the action associated with the production of nonprofit services and the implicit diadic concept of leisure as the action associated with consumption of those services will remain vague and inconsistent. Modern social science's understanding of the unproductive labor to which Smith alludes, the intangibles to which Commons refers, and the volunteer labor cited by Weisbrod is bound by important constraints that are not explicit in the domain of economics. The term *leisure*, which also figures prominently in what follows, has a very narrow and restricted meaning in economics and is virtually ignored in other social sciences. (However, see Rybczynski, 1991, and Dumazedier, 1968.) One can no more ignore these constraints and understand nonprofit activity than one can construct an economics of energy that ignores the laws of thermodynamics.

Voluntary Association

The concept of a nonprofit sector has been of interest primarily to public officials, lawyers, accountants, and public and association administrators. Despite the nonprofit sector's theoretical anchor in economics, economists remained largely indifferent to nonprofit activity until the early 1980s. Social workers, sociologists, fundraisers, administrators of volunteer programs, and others have tended to emphasize voluntary association concepts for denoting approximately the same phenomenon (Babchuk and Schmidt, 1976; Caulkins, 1976; Kramer, 1966, 1973, 1981; Lanfant, 1976; Lenkersdorf, 1976; Perlstadt, 1975; Ross, 1977; Rose, 1954; Smith, 1974).

Current use of the terms *nonprofit* and *voluntary* in nonprofit and voluntary action studies suggests a possible connection between nonprofit and voluntary. The name of the Association for Research on Nonprofit Organizations and Voluntary Action

(ARNOVA), for example, suggests just such a link. Yet the terms *nonprofit* and *voluntary* are hardly synonyms. There are important, if subtle, differences between the two, including different theoretical origins and different points of emphasis. Most important, the emphasis on social behavior evident in the voluntary action tradition can be seen as complementary to the unresolved definitional concerns of the "unproductive labor" approach to nonprofit organization. We can begin to see this more clearly by examining various definitions of the term *voluntary associations.*

Definitions emphasize interests or purposes held in common (Banton, 1965; MacIver and Page, 1949; Rose, 1960). Norbeck (1972) suggests the existence of a broader category of "common interest associations" of which voluntary associations are a subcategory. Cavallaro (1983) identifies the study of "participatory" voluntary associations, marginalized deviant groups, and political studies of pressure groups to be three of the five most predominant current approaches to the study of social groups.

Laskin (1962), Kerri (1972), and Berelson and Steiner (1964) add that common purposes are usually pursued as part-time, unpaid activities. Smith (1966, p. 483) also notes the lack of payment and adds the additional element of absence of physical coercion. Sills (1965, p. 363) makes explicit a connection to leisure by defining voluntary associations as "spare-time participatory associations."

Smith (1972b, 1974) identified five basic categories of voluntary action: occupational or self-interest; consumatory or self-expressive; philanthropic/funded; issue/cause oriented; and service oriented. James (1987) and York and Lazerwitz (1987) see religious involvement as a major point of entry for voluntary action.

These definitions are also very close to the meaning of the anthropological concept of *sodality,* which Hill (1970, p. 15) defines as "nonresidential associations having corporate functions or purposes that serve to integrate two or more residential units," including warrior societies, ceremonial societies, kachina societies, and ritual groups. Smith and Freedman (1972) also briefly discuss sodalities in their review of the voluntary association literature.

Anheier (1990) distinguishes countries by the legal and constitutional environment of nonprofit organizations. He sees civil law countries, such as France, Germany, Austria, and Italy; and common law countries, including Britain, Canada, Australia, and the United States. A second demarcation is between these capitalist–free market countries and previously socialist countries such as Poland, Hungary, and Russia. A third distinction is between developed and underdeveloped countries, and a fourth distinction is between countries in the Christian and Islamic traditions.

The theoretical origins of the voluntary association are somewhat more clear cut than those of the nonprofit organization. These origins are usually tied explicitly to the nineteenth-century French social analyst Alexis de Tocqueville, whose observations on the unique and distinctive role of associations in life in the United States are cited by advocates of pluralist democracy. At approximately the same time as Alexander Hamilton was warning Americans against the dangers of factionalism, de Tocqueville ([1862] 1945) articulated the doctrine of associations as "mediating institutions" between the individual citizen and the state.

As Peter Dobkin Hall (1987, p. 24) notes, de Tocqueville's original formulation was an explicitly political one. De Tocqueville, he says, "did not view private voluntarism as an amusing carnival midway of private intentions, but as a fundamental part of a national power system. At its core there was, as he observed, 'a natural and perhaps a necessary connection' between civil associations and the political associations through which citizens combined to influence the state." In this important sense, the views outlined in this book are fundamentally Tocquevillian. To the model of nonprofit organizations as components of a service economy noted earlier, I must add this view of associations as components of civil society. Many view voluntary association as a means for attaining important ends associated with the larger issues of what it means to be human. Adams (1986) argues that voluntary association is an individual and interactive way of life suitable for achieving freedom, friendship, justice, truth, progress, and other goods.

Arnold Rose (1954, pp. 62–66) makes a compatible distinction between two types of voluntary associations: "expressive" and "social influence." He says that expressive groups "act only to express or satisfy the interest of their members in relation to themselves," and social influence groups "wish to achieve some

condition or change in some special segment of society as a whole."
This dichotomy has since been supplanted by the apolitical
distinction between expressive and instrumental purposes, a distinction that seemingly removes any trace of the essential insight by
de Tocqueville noted above (Gordon and Babchuk, 1959; Bonnett,
1977; Palisi and Jacobson, 1977). The citizen participation movement is grounded in the democratic aspirations expressed by de
Tocqueville and has generated a good deal of research and practical
interest among nonprofit and voluntary action scholars (Barker,
1979; Faramelli, 1976; Flynn and Webb, 1975; Gluck, 1978; Heshka
and Lang, 1978; Klobus-Edwards and Edwards, 1979; Molnar and
Purohit, 1977; Ostrom, 1978; Paris and Blackaby, 1979; Rosenbaum,
1977; Salem, 1978; Schulman, 1978; Sharp, 1978; Stinson and Stam,
1976; Van Til, 1975; Walker, 1975).

The theoretical Achilles heel of the concept of the voluntary
sector appears to include two points. First, as in the case of the
adjective *nonprofit,* the idea of a voluntary sector seems to connote
a set of discernable establishments and a level of formal organization that may at times prove misleading. By itself, this objection can
be easily overcome. The term *sector* does not have to mean a set of
industries, establishments, or formal organizations exclusively. It
can also mean category, type, division, genre, or even territory (as
in the American sector in postwar Berlin). As with the concept of
the nonprofit sector, however, asserting the existence of a voluntary
sector also introduces the problem of typology. However, fewer efforts have been made at exhaustive classification and census of the
voluntary sector than of the nonprofit sector. In fact, many researchers regard such an exercise as essentially pointless.

One of the major recent stumbling blocks to voluntary sector
theory has been the multiple connotations of the term *voluntary,*
which seems to refer to all behavior that is uncoerced. Does this not
mean, for example, that unconstrained buying and selling in the
marketplace is part of the voluntary sector? One of my colleagues
is fond of pointing out that sex between consenting adults is usually
voluntary and asks if that means that sexual intercourse should be
included in the voluntary sector. Although the question may be
frivolous, the underlying issue of definition is not.

Furthermore, there is the complex question of the relationship between the nonprofit and voluntary sectors as posited here. Are these two conceptions completely independent, overlapping, or identical? Because usage of these terms divides so neatly along disciplinary lines, the issue has generated remarkably little interest or attention.

However, the view that the two concepts overlap has received increased attention recently. The terms *independent sector* and *third sector* were both coined, for example, to seek a compromise between adherents of the labels *nonprofit* and *voluntary*. New labels arrived at through committee compromise, however, fail to resolve underlying theoretical issues, and entirely new issues raised by these labels threaten to create further distractions. For example, in an open society, we can also consider markets and families to be independent. Several sources have already asked whether there are really four sectors, rather than three, and at least one author has asked whether there are four or five sectors (Smith, 1991).

Tallying the organizations in the voluntary sector is an even more daunting task than tallying nonprofit organizations or employees in philanthropic organizations because of the ease with which voluntary groups are formed and members move into and out of them. Indeed, it could well be argued that the best approach to the voluntary sector might be to tabulate the average number of groups and associations in which populations are active at any given time. In general, however, data of this type are spotty at best.

Smith (1991) differentiates voluntary action into an organized corporate realm (which corresponds closely to the nonprofit sector) and an informal sector of associations, clubs, groups, and organizations that have never incorporated or sought tax-exempt status. Such an approach extends the scope of the third sector considerably, while rendering it considerably more difficult to measure exactly. One frequently cited estimate of the scale of the informal sector is the proportion of the adult population reporting in any given year that they do volunteer work.

Each of the various concepts of the nonprofit and voluntary sectors has its uses. It is even possible to define them so as to emphasize their overlapping characteristics. For example, a nonprofit sector can be defined using the nondistribution constraint. The sector would consist of corporations bound by legal or ethical con-

straints on the distribution to shareholders of surplus revenues that
arise from the corporation's activities (that is, "profits"). Or, the
nonprofit sector could be extended to include unincorporated organizations *ethically* committed to the nondistribution constraint. Extending the nonprofit sector in this way brings it much closer to the
notion of a voluntary sector.

   Whether the voluntary sector is defined to include nonprofit
corporations or restricted to informal organizations, it can be defined as those clubs, associations, groups, and related organizations
characterized largely or exclusively by noncoercive membership,
free and unconstrained participation, and involving leisure rather
than paid employment. It may also be desirable under some circumstances to denote a *club sector* along the lines Smith (1991) suggests,
in which membership rather than participation is the key delimiter.
A *nongovernmental sector* can be defined as including those organizations or institutions that are outside the political state and function independently of state oversight or direction but interact with
the state frequently enough to justify differentiating them from the
state (Pifer, 1983). The modern welfare state in the United States and
elsewhere frequently incorporates such a nongovernmental sector
(Kramer, 1981). An *independent sector* is presumably one able to
function autonomously and without external interference or involvement. A *third sector* is simply the nonbusiness, nongovernmental side of public life outside the family (O'Neill, 1989).

Conclusion

Modern nonprofit and voluntary action studies, as exemplified by
the Association for Research on Nonprofit Organizations and Voluntary Action are occurring at the intersection of two distinct but
related research traditions. The nonprofit tradition can be traced to
Adam Smith's concept ([1776] 1981) of unproductive labor and is
animated by a central concern for what might be termed the appropriate uses of the surplus product of an affluent society. In contrast,
the voluntary tradition can be traced to de Tocqueville's concept
([1862] 1945) of intermediate institutions and is animated by a central concern for the individual and social consequences of uncalcu-

lated and uncoerced participation in organized social endeavors within civil society.

These two concerns are connected in numerous ways in the ongoing social reality from which they have been abstracted. At present, however, the traditions of nonprofit organization studies and voluntary action studies are upheld along largely disciplinary lines, with only a few genuine cases of crossover. In the chapters that follow, I make a preliminary attempt to sketch the outlines of a "fusion" perspective known as the theory of the commons, which seeks to reconstruct voluntary action as unproductive labor (or leisure action) and broaden the conception of nonprofit organizations to include both formal and informal (or communal) organizations.

A New Approach:
The Theory of the Commons

> In democratic countries, the science of associa-
> tions is the mother science; the progress of all others
> depends upon the progress it has made.
> —Alexis de Tocqueville

In the first issue of the *Journal of Voluntary Action Research,* Smith and others (1972) presented definitions and conceptual issues of voluntary action theory and research in a list of "major analytical topics" identified earlier in 1972 at a planning conference of the Interdisciplinary Voluntary Action Task Force. In that same article, Smith and others asked, "Can there be a theory of voluntary action, or must/should we pay major attention to theories and models about one or another aspect of voluntary action without attempting to put it all together for the moment?" (1972, p. 6). Clearly, the latter course proved the prudent one, and "the moment" lasted for twenty years.

Two decades later, voluntary action theory and its cognate, nonprofit theory, even with the various extensions identified in the preceding chapter, are still insufficient for clarity of understanding, policy, or practice. Simon notes, for example, that tax policies "have been unaccompanied by a coherent theory of intervention or by empirical support for intervention" (1987, p. 94).

Because the ground on which an adequate theory of non-profit and voluntary action must be constructed is an explicitly interdisciplinary one, the task of theory building should begin at an elementary level with the statement of assumptions. In this chapter, a number of key assumptions will be identified and some of the fundamental concepts of such a theory will be defined. In succeeding chapters, further empirical and theoretical investigations of the implications of this theoretical approach will be explored. I will conclude this book with a number of propositions.

My approach is to attempt to identify a set of interdisciplinary "first principles" rather than the more conventional residual approach, which, according to the introductory editorial statement of *Voluntas,* treats the voluntary sector "as what is left over once government and commercial agencies, and probably also the 'informal sector,' have been put to one side." Especially important in defining the sector in this way is value for comparative studies in the international domain (Anheier and Knapp, 1990).

I am not primarily concerned in this book with all nonprofit organizations, all members of the legal category of nonprofit corporations, or all members of the subcategory of tax-exempt corporations. My primary concern is with eleemosynary or donative associations, organizations, and groups engaged in unproductive or volunteer labor, whether or not they are incorporated, recognized by the state, tabulated in national data, or made up of paid employees. This broad category of social organizations will be called *commons* for reasons that follow, and generalizations about these organizations will be said to constitute the theory of the commons.

Initial Premises and Assumptions

The following discussion sets forth nine basic assumptions upon which the theory of the commons is premised. Some of these assumptions are explicit alternatives to commonly employed assumptions set forth about the nonprofit and voluntary sector and as such may be controversial. Others are straightforward and noncontroversial.

Social Action

One of the most interesting and challenging characteristics of non-profit and voluntary services is their intangible character. Thus, a basic assumption of the theory of the commons is that nonprofit services and unproductive labors are composed of social action, or "substantively meaningful experience emanating from our spontaneous life based upon preconceived projects" (Schutz, 1970, p. 125). As Max Weber (1968, p. 4) puts it, "In 'action' is included all human behavior when and insofar as the acting individual attaches a subjective meaning to it." Ignoring or explicitly rejecting profit orientation, said by some to be the defining characteristic of nonprofit action, constitutes such a subjective attachment of meaning.

Action, in this sense, is social insofar as subjective meaning attached to it by acting individuals "takes account of the behavior of others and is thereby oriented in its course" (Weber, 1968, p. 4). Philanthropy as action for the good of humanity, charity as action for the good of others, altruism as action in the interest of others—all involve social action in this sense. Thus, the various organizations and structures of nonprofit and voluntary action will present predictable, recurring, and institutionalized as well as idiosyncratic patterns of social action (Billis, 1991).

Affluence

Coherent, self-aware actors in nonprofit organizations and voluntary associations, who are capable of social action, are aware that they are acting outside of the institutional contexts of markets, households, and the state. Under ordinary circumstances, overriding ethical considerations of philanthropic, charitable, and altruistic purposes discourage people from seeking personal gain and mandate that people in the commons deny, downplay, or ignore their own self-interests. The appropriateness of such self-denial, however, is conditional upon the absence of any immediate threats to the safety, security, health, or well-being of those people involved. (One cannot, for example, ethically demand of starving people that they take time out from the pursuit of food to aid others who may be ill or homeless.) We might ask, Under what circumstances is such self-denial reasonable? An answer to this question is offered by the condition of affluence.

Bona fide participation in the commons is available only to

the affluent: those people whose individual and group survival and reproduction are sufficiently assured so that their own self-interest is not their paramount concern. Only those whose basic needs for survival and reproduction have been met are in a position to rationally choose or reject self-interested behavior. It is unreasonable to expect that people who are starving, under siege or assault, or threatened with extinction should rationally choose to ignore their own interests or that any society or association can have a legitimate interest in encouraging them to do so.

Substituting an assumption of affluence for the customary economic assumption of scarcity has major implications for future research in voluntary and nonprofit action (Neal, 1984). In the theory that follows, it is assumed that a commons can emerge only where the fundamental problems of material, human, and social reproduction have been, at least temporarily, overcome (Wolff, 1970). Under conditions of affluence, when the problems of material, human, and social reproduction are overcome, even momentarily, the choice of whether to engage in maximizing profit or some other nonprofit activity is, itself, a rational choice. In the United States, the creation of a tax-exempt, nonprofit 501(c)(3) corporation signifies the creation of a commons, and individuals knowingly accepting the legal obligations of board membership for such an organization indicate a willingness to abide by its standards.

Authenticity

The theory of the commons also assumes that actors operating in nonprofit and voluntary settings are *authentic*; that is, they are what they appear to be to informed others also operating in the same context (Etzioni, 1968). Affluent actors who seek to pursue their own self-interest in the commons or whose individual or organizational goals include maximizing utility are operating under false pretenses and are subject to penalty or expulsion from the commons. Norms of authenticity may not be universally or consistently invoked, but when they are invoked, the result is usually consistent and convincing, as in the collapse of various empires of television evangelists in the past decade. State charity fraud statutes throughout the United States seek to enforce such norms of authenticity.

Theoretically, people who adopt a self-interested (or profit-oriented) posture at any time are assumed to remove themselves from the commons. Such behavior is treated as evidence of deviance, and invoking the profit orientation to justify or sanction such deviance serves no useful theoretical purpose. This simple assumption is intended to focus clearly upon the issue of the basic nature of the commons. In the real world, members of a commons often appear to be unable to enforce the norm of authenticity, and the practical problems of enforcing it are often left to the coercive powers of the state. It is not clear whether this inability to enforce the norm results from the weakness of particular group norms or inherent limits on common social action.

Although it may appear to be somewhat pretentious or moralistic, the norm of authenticity points up the fundamentally ethical core of common social action and encapsulates numerous examples of actual empirical practices in the commons. For example, professional oaths in helping professions usually prohibit placing the professionals' own interests above those of the clients, and scientists in most disciplines are subject to severe sanctions for falsifying research data or results. Thus, although its enforcement may be complex and problematic, there is little doubt of the importance of the assumption of authenticity in nonprofit and voluntary action.

Continuity

Charitable, philanthropic, and altruistic action and other common action is also associated with consistent life-style choices. The experience of others in nonprofit and voluntary action is an ongoing one, characterized by past, present, and future and a sense of connectedness between them. The experience of continuity offers a basis for explanation and prediction. As Schutz (1970, p. 7) points out, "I trust that the world as it has been known to me up until now will continue further and that consequently the stock of knowledge obtained from my own experiences will continue to preserve its fundamental validity. . . . From this assumption follows the further and fundamental one: that I can repeat my past successful acts."

The ongoingness of common experience and the social nature of the commons mean that desirable purposes and goods can also have inevitable intergenerational aspects. Because individuals involved in many types of commons will be of different chronological ages, decisions of ongoing groups will as a consequence inevitably take on an intergenerational character as old members die and new ones are born or socialized into the group. Intergenerational continuity is an important characteristic of religious commons, for example, where organizations and practices often stretch over decades, centuries, and millennia.

Continuity in nonprofit and voluntary action is often experienced in the form of tradition. I (and others) will continue to exist in a known and knowable world through the repetition of time-honored ceremonies and habitual and familiar ritual acts. The continuity of present experience may also be experienced as rational. We will act in the appropriate manner because it is reasonable, predictable, or productive of desirable consequences to do so. Occasionally the experience of continuity even takes the form of transformative, "inexplicable," or other charismatic experiences.

Practical questions of an intergenerational nature often arise with respect to the appropriate division of an individual's estate between heirs and the commons. Legal issues of this type are among the oldest, most long-standing, and thorniest of issues of the law as it relates to common goods. These issues were a fundamental concern of the 1601 Statute of Charitable Uses in Great Britain, for example, and also a major concern of Islamic law (Gray, [1905] 1967; Coulson, 1978). Recruitment of new members and the quest to keep and restore particular heritages figure large in the decision making of many commons.

Rationality

We shall assume that actors in the commons, engaged in acts of philanthropy, charity, and altruism, act rationally in the sense of observable consistency between the intentions they announce to themselves and others and the results they hold up to be successful outcomes. The rationality of actors in the commons is a practical rationality, concerned with the exercise of reason in solving the problems that arise in the conduct of daily affairs. It is often also a prosocial rationality, devoted to solving problems primarily affecting others, engaging in various forms of presentation, and obtaining the resources necessary to carry out these pursuits.

The rationality of the commons is not merely a matter of moment-to-moment consistency of thought or behavior. The term *rational* refers, instead, to the philosophical sense of having (and following) a life plan (Rawls, 1971). Practical rationality, in this context, involves the day-to-day decisions that must be made in consistent pursuit of a life plan.

As Suzanne Langer (1967, pp. 273–274) notes, "Our standards of rationality are the same as Euclid's or Aristotle's—generality, consistency, coherence, systematic inclusion of all possible cases, economy and elegance in demonstration—but our ideal of science makes one further demand: the demand of what has been called 'maximum interpretability'. This means that as many propositions as possible shall be applicable to observable fact."

Near-Universality

Commons are assumed to be near-universal cultural forms, known in some manner in most, possibly all, human cultures (Brown, 1991). But the degree to and exact ways in which the theory of the commons transcends the U.S. cultural context and history remain to be determined. Research has already shown that commons exist in a variety of countries and cultures. See, for example, studies of Ghana (Gray, 1976), France (Lanfant, 1976), Jamaica and the Caribbean (Fletcher, 1977; Gray, 1976), Norway (Anderson and Schiller, 1976; Caulkins, 1976; Hallenstvedt, Kalela, Kalela, and Lintonen, 1976; Kvavik, 1976; Moren, 1976), and Mexico (Lenkersdorf, 1976).

Nonprofit corporations and philanthropic foundations are the distinctive products of Anglo-American legal traditions. U.S. voluntary associations are the unique inventions of an open society devoid of a long heritage of intermediate institutions and intent upon creating an open society. Both nonprofit corporations and philanthropic foundations are members of a larger class of related groups, organizations, and institutions to which the name commons is applied.

In all known cultures, self-defining collectives of people voluntarily associate and act jointly outside of markets and households and independent of the state in pursuit of common purposes. Even among itinerant hunter-gatherers and farming and fishing cultures, leisure time not spent in subsistence activities can be devoted to group participation in common activities: Construction of kivas and other spirit centers; organization of spirit quests and initiation rites; and donations of beads, feathers, shells, drums, and other valued objects to dance and ceremonial activities are just part of the broad range of common endeavors.

The issue of whether commons, like families, are found in absolutely every human culture ever known or, like markets and states, are found in most cultures is an empirical question. Until it can be answered, anecdotal evidence suggests that there is good reason to assume universality, as we shall see in the following chapter.

Autonomy

Organized action in the commons is assumed to be autonomous in the sense that actors in the commons are capable of acting independently and exercising both individual and group self-control. Such autonomy may merely be assumed or may take institutional form as freedoms of speech and association. Under repressive conditions, people may deliberately seek this autonomy by engaging in covert actions or secret societies.

Actors in the commons are assumed to be able to create and sustain autonomous social worlds. Although this idea is most evident in the case of certain social movements and religious zealots, it is also implicit in everyday clubs and associations of bird watchers, stamp collectors, and peace or environmental activists (Cavan, 1977; Cummings, 1977; Ross, 1977). The ability to act with others to create and sustain an autonomous social world is one of the most fundamental characteristics of nonprofit and voluntary action.

Intrinsic Valuation

The proper way to evaluate an autonomous common world is assumed to be on the basis of the values arising within it. This as-

sumption is consistent with those found generally in qualitative
social research, symbolic interactionism, and ethnomethodology
(Mead, 1965). Following Garfinkel, the theory of the commons re-
fuses to give "serious consideration to the prevailing proposal that
efficiency, efficacy, effectiveness, intelligibility, consistency, plan-
fulness, typicality, uniformity, reproducibility of activities—i.e.,
that rational properties of practical activities—be assessed, recognized, categorized, described by using a rule or standard outside
actual settings within which such properties are recognized, used,
produced and talked about by settings' members" (quoted in Mitchell, 1978, p. 143).

Ordinary Language

An assumption related to that of intrinsic valuation is that a satisfactory theory of nonprofit and voluntary action must be stated in
language that philanthropic, charitable, and altruistic actors can
recognize and understand. While the subjects of a theory are not
accorded veto power or monopoly control in interpreting the cor-
rectness or applicability of the theory, their views may be taken into
account. Thus, the language regularly used by charitable, philanthropic, and altruistic actors may also be employed in theories of
their actions. Terms such as *endowment, benefit, gift, patron, legacy, heritage,* and *treasury* are among those borrowed from common
usage and applied in the theory of the commons.

Terms and Concepts

On the basis of the previous assumptions, we can now look more
closely at the basic vocabulary of the theory of the commons. It should
be clear to anyone who examines the issue closely that new ways to
speak and think more clearly about nonprofit and voluntary action
are needed. The very first necessity, therefore, is to identify some terms
and concepts that are both clear cut and faithful to the observable
realities of action in this arena. In particular, we need an adequate
summary term to describe the range of nonprofit and voluntary action
usually grouped together in law, statistics, and tradition and to set it
apart in a general sense from other human endeavors. In the follow-

ing discussion, a set of related terms are set forth as fundamental to an understanding of nonprofit and voluntary action. These terms are *benefit, benefactory, commons, endowment, civilization, socialization, technique, search, treasury, collection, repertory, regime,* and *patronage.* Together, they provide a basic theoretical language for discussing nonprofit and voluntary action.

Benefit and Benefactory

The largest, most important, and most definitive subclass of nonprofit organizations are those 501(c)(3) nonprofit corporations that are exempt from federal taxation on the basis of their charitable purposes. Such organizations are part of a larger class of service organizations in which no tangible product is produced, marketed, or sold and no individual or group of owners or stockholders should legitimately expect to profit. In the voluntary tradition of social services, such entities have been known as *agencies.* Theoretically, this term is a legal one, intended to highlight the role of these organizations in acting as agents for the interests of others. Such organizations also correspond closely with the type B organizations, engaged in unproductive labor, that were discussed in Chapter One.

The term *benefactory* is used here as a play on the economic terms *factor* and *factory* and is intended to highlight the central role of deliberate and organized distribution of benefits. A benefit can be defined as an advantage, useful aid, or financial help (Gifis, 1991). Benefit, in general, involves enhancing or advancing the interests of any person or group by increasing wealth, health, well-being, safety, or security. A benefactory, then, is any network of organized social relations established for the purpose of aiding, assisting, helping, improving, supporting, comforting, enabling, or in other ways benefitting other persons or groups. Those people who act to enhance the interests of others have traditionally been called *benefactors,* and recipients of such advantages or gains have been termed *beneficiaries* or *clients.* In addition to benefit, *benefice* is another traditional term for the advantages conferred.

A good deal of the conceptual work to define nonprofit and voluntary social agencies in a manner compatible with this concept of benefactory has already been done. Etzioni (1963) laid part of the groundwork for the contemporary notion of a sector of benefactories when he distinguished normative compliance from coercive (state) and remunerative (market) compliance. It is fairly easy to conclude that while markets emphasize personal gain and loss, and states address public goods for all, nonprofit and voluntary agencies are primarily concerned with functioning as agents of one group (often termed patrons) who dispense benefits to another group (clients or beneficiaries).

Use of the term *benefactory* directly links the role of agent (in which the nondistribution constraint plays a vital role) with the tendency in organizational literature to categorize nonprofit organizations by the types of benefits they produce. Blau and Scott (1962) identified four types of organizations based upon their beneficiaries: (1) mutual-benefit organizations, whose primary beneficiaries are their members; (2) business concerns, whose primary beneficiaries are owners; (3) service organizations, whose primary beneficiaries are their clients; and (4) commonweal organizations, whose beneficiaries are the public at large.

Smith (1991) extended this conception to the nonprofit/voluntary sector with his identification of four beneficiary classes: owners, public, clients, and members.

Obviously, charities such as soup kitchens or free counseling centers would be benefactories in this sense. However, the term can also be extended to encompass churches, symphony orchestras, experimental theatre groups, dance companies, museums, galleries, and all types of artistic and athletic events in which a performance or presentation by one group (actors, athletes, priests, political candidates, and others) has as its purpose enhancing the interests of other people (congregations, audiences). The purpose of the benefactor might be to "save," inform, entertain, startle, "actualize," or in any way benefit others. For example, catharsis, or the benefit of emotional release for the audience, is the principle motive behind the Aristotelian theory of Greek tragedy.

Based on the assumptions of autonomy and authenticity discussed earlier, two tests can determine whether or not an organization should be considered a benefactory. First, there is the test of authenticity: is the potential benefactory what it appears to be, or is it merely a front for some other type of nonbenefactory? This is the test ordinarily applied by legal authorities in prosecution of charity scams and telephone solicitation "boiler rooms," in which false charitable claims are made. Second, there is the test of purpose: does the structure of the organization identify classes of benefactors and beneficiaries, and are the goals or purposes of the possible benefactory actually designed to benefit individuals or groups other than the benefactors?

As organizations, benefactories are distinct from firms, government bureaus, and families. If we follow the logic of Blau and Scott (1962) and Smith (1991), benefactories are also intrinsic, extrinsic, and mixed. *Intrinsic benefactories* include self-help groups, social and recreational clubs, membership associations, fraternal societies, trade associations, and employees' beneficiary associations, which focus their benefits upon members. *Extrinsic benefactories* include charitable organizations, foundations, civic associations, legal aid societies, and other groups that focus their benefits upon nonmember clients. *Mixed benefactories* engage in both intrinsic and extrinsic benefactions. Most churches, for example, combine ecclesiastical and missionary efforts.

The distinction between revenue-oriented and nonrevenue nonprofit groups, discussed in Chapter One, can also be applied here. Type B benefactories like churches, free museums and community theaters, nonrevenue intercollegiate sports and amateur athletic associations, settlement houses, and soup kitchens can be distinguished from type A nonprofits like hospitals, museums and theatres charging admissions, nursing homes, fee-based social service agencies, intercollegiate football and basketball teams, and other revenue-based groups in which the level of involvement or activity is metered by the revenue received.

Particular benefactories (most notably voluntary associations) have been viewed as falling into two additional major types of function: purposive and expressive (Gordon and Babchuk, 1959; Rose, 1954). Purposive organizations are goal oriented; that is, devoted to solving particular and often clearly identifiable problems from among a repertoire of known and workable solutions. Expressive benefactories are those devoted primarily to presentations: exhibitions, performances, dramatizations, rites, ceremonies. Once again, mixed benefactories would combine purposive and expres-

sive elements. The unique combination of religion and social service of the Salvation Army, for example, has been confounding and
infuriating those researchers devoted to a solely purposive and instrumental interpretation of charitable work for decades.

Commons

The concept of benefactory as employed here corresponds with
many uses of the generic term *organization*, albeit with an explicit
emphasis on the dispensing of benefit to designated target groups.
It necessarily implies a second level of relations between the benefactors (or patrons), beneficiaries, and those who may be acting as
benefactors to the benefactor. For example, government agencies,
foundations, the United Way, and other groups provide grants to
service agencies so that they may, in turn, provide grants or services
to clients. For membership associations and intrinsic benefactories,
this relationship involves a strictly internal division of roles: the
relations of members to themselves. Researchers in the sociological
tradition of social psychology have often treated this as a problem
of ephemeral, or short-term, situation-specific roles (Zurcher, 1978).
Williams and Ortega (1986) found, however, that memberships in
(and presumably the benefits of) different types of voluntary organizations are not interchangeable. For extrinsic benefactories, the
issue involves complex questions of who is in the organization, the
nature of interorganizational relations, and ultimately the nature of
community organization.

    A concept is needed to denote the complex of organized re-
lations between benefactors, intermediaries (defined as beneficiaries
who benefit others as a condition of their own benefit) and end
beneficiaries. This complex of intrinsic and extrinsic organized relations is one of several related meanings I will attach to the term
commons.

    The main characteristics of what I intend by the concept of
commons are encompassed by the Greek term *koinonia*. According
to the historian M. I. Finley (1974b), the ancient Greeks had five
prerequisites for koinonia: (1) participation must be free and uncoerced; (2) participants must share a common purpose, whether
major or minor, long term or short term; (3) participants must have

something in common that they share such as jointly held resources, a collection of precious objects, or a repertory of shared actions; (4) participation involves *philia* (a sense of mutuality, often inadequately translated as friendship); and (5) social relations must be characterized by *dikiaon* (fairness). This five-part definition encompasses all of the major elements sought by advocates of nonprofit, voluntary, independent, and third-sector terminology and does so in a simple and elegant manner.

If it is defined in this manner, the commons is an explicitly interdisciplinary concept that links under a single rubric the separate concerns of the nonprofit organization and voluntary labor perspective and the voluntary action perspective, which is concerned with associations and groups. Definitions of groups tend to emphasize stable patterns of interaction and feelings of unity and shared consciousness that parallel the shared purpose and mutuality in the definition of koinonia/commons (Smith and Preston, 1977; Vander Zander, 1977). Defining organizations as groups "deliberately formed to achieve a specific goal or set of goals through a formalized set of rules and procedures," Smith and Preston (1977, p. 536) connect purpose with a specific set of means. Uncoerced participation is ordinarily indicated by placing the word *voluntary* before the word *group, organization,* or *association.* Two of the five elements of the commons are not ordinarily inherent in definitions of group or organization. The treatment of jointly held resources is an explicit economic concern. Dikiaon as fairness or justice (Rawls, 1971) can be interpreted as an explicitly political concern. Thus, any set of related social acts characterized by uncoerced participation, common purpose, shared resources, mutuality, and fairness can be characterized as common, and social organizations and institutions in which such norms predominate can be called commons.

A commons can be thought of as an economic, political, and social space outside the market, households, and state in which associative communities create and reproduce social worlds. Associative social worlds are composed of the images, meanings, and sense of reality shared by autonomous, self-defining collectivities of voluntarily associating individuals. Table 2.1 systematically compares the five key characteristics of the commons with the characteristics of markets and states. Market participation is free and

Table 2.1. Comparison of Commons, Market, and State on Five Dimensions.

	Commons	Market	State
Participation	Uncoerced	Uncoerced	Coercive
Purpose	Shared (common goods)	Maximization (private goods)	Authoritative (public goods)
Resources	Common	Private	Public
Reciprocity	Mutuality	Quid pro quo	Equity
Social relations	Fairness	Caveat emptor	Law

uncoerced, just as it is in the commons, while the potential for coercive participation (as in military drafts or prosecution of tax evaders) is a fundamental characteristic of states.

While shared purposes, goals, and objectives are characteristic of commons, maximization of profit or utility is the presumed universal purpose of markets. Authoritative allocation of values is the fundamental defining purpose of the state (Easton, 1965). Private ownership of property is the basic expectation of the market, and universalistic state conceptions of public goods (such as beaches, roads, and national parks) are characteristic of market and state. Common resources held jointly and allocated collectively are characteristic of commons. Existing economic theory makes a fundamental distinction between market goods and services and the special characteristics of public goods. An additional category called *common goods* will be introduced later in this work.

A basic characteristic of social action in commons is the norm of mutual reciprocity. Participants in markets and states feel no such mutuality. Instead, market participants are usually governed by the norm of quid pro quo (give and take), and concepts of the democratic state place emphasis on equity—in particular, the equality of citizens before the state. Social relations in the commons are governed by the basic norm of fairness. Market relations are governed by caveat emptor (let the buyer beware), and social relations in the state are governed by law (including rules, as in the Weberian model of bureaucracy [Weber, 1968]).

Norbeck (1972) presaged the approach to the commons introduced here when he advocated "common-interest associations" as a broad, cross-cultural classification under which voluntary associations would be a subcategory. The Japanese common-interest organizations examined by Norbeck met some but not all of the five criteria for commons noted above: membership was not voluntary and governance was not democratic, yet participants appeared to have shared purposes, joint resources, and distinctive norms of mutuality and fairness.

As commentators since Adam Smith and Alexis de Tocqueville have noted, commons include some of the most intrinsically interesting of human endeavors. These endeavors include religious celebrations, ceremonies, rituals, and observances; dialogue and contemplation; basic scientific research; literary criticism and hermeneutics; the arts; amateur athletics; counseling and psychotherapy; and care of abused or neglected children and adults, the dying, and the disadvantaged. We might even include political activities such as electoral campaigns, legislative or administrative advocacy, political parties and caucuses, labor unions, and trade associations in this list, insofar as their immediate goals are noncommercial.

Commons in art, religion, philosophy, and athletic games are found in diverse forms in all human societies. In addition, achievements in these commons are frequently among the elements cited as hallmarks of the attainment of high civilization. Thus, the philosophical schools of Plato and Aristotle and the temples and amphitheaters of ancient Athens are intrinsic to our understandings of the Greek origins of Western civilization (Matson, 1968). Similarly, the patronage of the Medicis must be recognized as a fundamental factor in the Italian Renaissance (Acton, 1967).

Wherever and whenever commons are found, we see the coordinated social action of benefactors, intermediaries, and beneficiaries. Indeed, commons are inherently social. The existence of a community—a plurality of mutually interested and interacting persons—is a fundamental precondition of religion, athletic games, ceremonies, art, science, social service, and all true commons.

The essential character of commons rests in their role in the presentation and dramatization of profound symbols of community; that is, in the affirmation of the most fundamental human values of the community through human communication (Goodman and Goodman, 1960; Hillary, 1963; Warren, 1963). No civilization can afford to ignore or deny this role of the commons without trampling underfoot its most sacred values. To see a U.S. Fourth of July celebration only as an activity of state, for example, is to miss much of its fundamental character as a celebration of the nation— itself a kind of commons.

Commons are not places any more than are markets or states. Commons consist of sets of complex social acts that are basic, universal, and not reducible to more fundamental categories of social behavior. The mutual, collective purposes, ends, or objectives that participants in these complex acts share (regardless of their rationality or irrationality as perceived by outsiders) constitute the common goods that are the real economic products of the commons.

Significant common acts include worship, contemplation, help, inquiry, self-expression, and play (the latter often dignified as leisure, recreation, or athletics). Each of these acts is a fundamental human activity at least as basic as production, consumption, or exchange and not reducible to them. Any theory of economics that reduces common goods to the basic categories of production, consumption, and exchange is reductionistic and misleading.

Although a commons is not primarily a physical place, it may include a place, as in the case of temples and other common spaces. A commons can be any social space for interaction within a community. Common space may be a committee room, a conference center, a restaurant dining room, or almost any other public or private space. It may also be the social space of a newspaper, scientific journal, or electronic bulletin board. The commons can be anywhere in the community where the baseline assumptions discussed earlier are played out.

Social actors throughout history have known that there is public space outside the marketplace and the state. The public space of the commons is not predominantly a space for buying and selling or of ordering and forbidding. It is a space for talking and listening (dialogue) and for seeing and being seen (presentation). This use of public space should be evident to anyone who has ever attended an association meeting, given a speech to a public gathering, or in any way participated in an associative community. It is evident as well by the frequency with which community terms such as *fellowship, congregation,* and so on are used in describing such communities.

It is useful, therefore, to locate the commons alongside the marketplace and the state, with its distinctive concerns for the authoritative allocation of values. The metaphor of the commons is particularly appropriate in the context of U.S. history. Important historical cities as diverse as Boston, New Haven, Philadelphia, and Santa Fe have commons even today. The town square is a major feature in many smaller communities as well. Similarly, most associations have an annual meeting or conference whose function, at least formally, illustrates the potential for open dialogue in the commons.

Commons are fundamentally "universes of discourse." They are composed of groups of people who understand one another, speak common languages, and evolve specialized terminology and language over time. Such discursive universes are a type of commons whose shared understandings have become known as cultures (Urban, 1991), communities (Schwartzman, 1992), or paradigms (Berger and Luckmann, 1966; Bernstein, 1983; Kuhn, 1962). In this sense, *philosophers, librarians, physicists, Roman Catholics, philatelists, joggers,* and *social workers* are all terms for such commons, and *realism, information science,* and *Copernican cosmology* are the names of particular paradigms.

Commons tend to be organized both informally, through use of common languages and a common worldview, and formally, through associations and other noncoercive groups. The structure of a commons consists of a community of one or more benefactories and related basic institutions. Two such institutions are most basic: language and education.

Common language is essential because without it meaningful common activities would be literally impossible. Certain elementary types of "trading," tool making and tool use can be observed among primate species. And there are recorded instances of human economic activity between communities that could not communicate in words, such as the "silent trade" between Ghanaian and Arab traders during the Ghanaian Era in Africa (A.D. 3–1200). However, the existence of all types of common activities on a significant scale requires substantial language ability. This is particularly the case with commons in which the community functions as a reference group to set and reinforce attitudes and values, a process that occurs primarily through the medium of spoken and written language.

Another set of institutions basic to the commons are those necessary for the education, training, and socialization of participants. Because knowledge, as the combination of available meanings and information, is a key element in the commons, ways and means of passing knowledge among members of the community and from one generation to another are basic to any commons. Ways of passing on knowledge include the socialization rites by which primitive youths are initiated into the mysteries of tribal dance and legends, the apprenticeships of medieval cathedral builders, and the management training programs of the modern private nonprofit settlement house.

In the United States, ongoing associations of all types tend to be incorporated because of the explicit tax concessions and limits on participant liability offered by incorporation. Incorporation, however, represents a legal adaptation in a particular society and not a fundamental defining characteristic of commons. Even within the Anglo-American tradition stemming from the Statute of Charitable Uses, a great deal of voluntary common action occurs outside the formal limits of incorporation, and many incorporated and unincorporated organizations perform similar functions.

There is a danger in overstating the importance of corporations and seeing commons primarily in terms of sets of discrete benefactories. Commons also constitute associative social worlds, which have two important characteristics. First, collectively, participants in associative social worlds are free to order their behavior as they choose, so long as their actions do not threaten others or the community as a whole. Second, participants are free to leave at any time to join another social world (such as another association, the social world of the marketplace, or the private social worlds of the household). In associative social worlds, such action occurs all the time. For example, lodge or fraternity members may become inactive and take up the church choir or political campaigning. Nozick (1974) has defined the ability to leave a social world as one of the characteristics of his utopia.

Democratic self-governance has evolved as one of the basic characteristics of the autonomous commons, in which participants are free to leave if they wish. The model of the self-governing association is characterized by a special vocabulary. *Bylaws* are rules adopted by a group to regulate its own actions. Under common law, in the absence of any other law to the contrary, the power to make bylaws rests with the constituent members of the group (Gifis, 1991). *Minutes* are the record of official proceedings of an organized group. Legally, the self-governing association can be either incorporated or unincorporated, tax paying or tax exempt (Oleck, 1980).

Meetings are official gatherings, sessions, or assemblies of the group. *Plenary* means full, complete, entire, or unqualified. A *plenary session,* such as an annual meeting, is a meeting that is open to the full or entire membership. *Articles of incorporation* are the legal instruments that create nonprofit and other corporations. Articles are sometimes also called charters. A *charter* is usually a document issued by a government establishing a corporate entity. The term derives from the practice of medieval monarchs of granting charters specifying certain rights, privileges, and powers (Gifis, 1991).

A *committee* consists of "a person or persons to whom the consideration or determination of certain business is referred or confided" (Gifis, 1991, p. 82). The *board of directors* or *trustees* is a special committee, elected by rules or procedures held by the group to be fair and usually spelled out in the bylaws or articles. In most state law, boards are held responsible for the overall management of the affairs of the association or corporation (Oleck, 1980).

Endowment

Another key concept in the theory of the commons is that of the *endowment,* or the set of resources (potentials for action) held jointly by a commons. The term *endowment* is taken directly from historical and contemporary usage. The concept of resource endowments is linked by definition to the central concept of the commons. One of the components of the definition of the commons offered earlier is the conception of a "fund" of common, or shared, resources. In any commons, that fund or pool of shared resources is its endowment. The term *endowment* has been used in this way in English at least since the Middle Ages.

The term *endowment* is used to specifically include what are today called foundations. The term *foundation,* as the name of a special type of managed endowment, does not figure importantly in the vocabulary of the commons. In medieval usage, the term originally referred to the creation of an endowment. In both medieval and modern times, a founder, often the first donor and ongoing patron, was afforded a special place in the commons, which is seldom seen today.

The specialized accounting of the nonprofit sector is known as *fund accounting* (as in public accounting, where common funds are also held). Unfortunately, in some financial circles this robust and useful term has taken on specialized connotations not of a fund or pool of shared resources generally but of such funds only when their use is restricted in some way. Thus, a college's endowment or an endowed chair of a professor means for some only those particular restricted funds.

It is important to note that we can restore the broader historical usage of the term *endowment* without disrupting in any way this more restrictive meaning. We can also restore some of the derivations of this term, including *dowry* (meaning gift, as in the dowry of a bride, certainly, but also in the more generic sense of any gift or donation, including the creation of a restricted endowment) and the archaic verb *dower* (to give). Later in this chapter, I shall further refine the concept of endowment by identifying various types of resources, including treasuries of financial resources, collections of tangible objects, and repertories of acts that can be learned.

Legally, an endowment is "a permanent fund of property or money bestowed upon an institution or a person, the income of which is used to serve the specific purpose" for which it was created (Gifis, 1991, p. 158). The legal concept of endowment explicitly links the dimensions of common purpose and resources and involves mutuality and fairness as well. An endowment defined in this way is a type of *trust,* or real or personal property held by one person for the benefit of another. This explains why nonprofit board members are sometimes called trustees, for they hold legal title to property in trust for another. Such persons have fiduciary obligations under the law, which are created by their accepting the trust, to act primarily for the benefit of another in matters connected with the undertaking. To violate those obligations is a *breach of trust,* or "violation by a trustee of a duty which equity (that is, justice) lays upon him, whether wilful and fraudulent, or done through negligence, or arising through mere oversight and forgetfulness" (Gifis, 1991, p. 54). This idea is closely related to the *cy pres doctrine* that "equity will, when a charity is illegal or later becomes impossible or impractical of fulfillment, substitute another charitable object which is believed to approach the original purpose as closely as possible (Gifis, 1991, p. 116).

An endowment may be created by a *gift,* or voluntary transfer of property made without consideration or for which no value is received in return. Legally, these may be individual or *class gifts;* that is, gifts to a body of persons, uncertain in number, all of whom receive equal or other defined portions of the gift. A gift may be *inter vivos* (between living persons) or *causa mortis* (in anticipation of death) as in a will. An *inheritance* is an estate distributed to heirs according to the laws of descent and distribution. A *bequest,* or gift of such property, is contained in a will. *Property* is, simply, "every species of valuable right or interest that is subject to ownership, has an exchangeable value or adds to one's wealth or estate" (Gifis, 1991, p. 380). Property, in the legal sense, can be *incorporeal* (with no physical reality) or intangible (with no value in itself, but merely representing value). The usual term for tangible goods is *commodities.* In each of these cases, we are dealing with valuable resources that make up the endowment of a particular commons or benefactory.

The concept of personal endowments is a closely related concept, borrowed directly from psychological research, that can be used to highlight the personal resources and individual skills that members of a commons bring to a joint effort. It has been used in exactly this way, for example, in studies of minority issues in mental health (Lorenzo, 1989), creativity (Shainess, 1989), instinct (Schneider, 1988; Gutmann, 1982), intelligence (McGlashan, 1986; McGee and Brown, 1984), personality (Huang, 1984), and motherchild bonds (Kestenbaum, 1984). Piechowski and Cunningham (1985) address the "psychological endowment" of artists. Erikson

(1985) speaks of the "sensory endowment" of artists, as well as of the possibility of expanding sensory endowment through education. Kodym and Kebza (1982) employed the concept in a manner completely consistent with the use of repertories as endowments. They studied "musical endowment and talent," which they say involves special components (including auditory and rhythmical components, memory, harmony and counterpoint, tonal feeling, and musical thinking) and general components (including cognitive processes, volition, and motivation). Five particular types of musical endowment that they identified were technique, singing, teaching, conducting, and composing.

The concept of endowment also figures large in physiological psychology, psychoanalytic psychology, and genetic studies. The "genetic endowment" (Lidz, 1976) of an individual has been related to a number of phenomena, including aggressive and violent behavior (Eichelman, 1985), aphasia (Gainotti, Nocentini, Sena, and Silveri, 1986), and delinquency (McManus, Brickman, Alessi, and Grapentine, 1985).

Civilization

Hill's treatment (1983) of what he calls the "concept pool" offers a useful pointer to the concepts of civilization and paradigm as human endowments. The full connotations of the term *endowment* in the theory of the commons become clear only in light of the concept of civilization. Every commons is endowed with a dowry of jointly held resources, some created by its benefactories; some received from markets, states, and households; and some handed down from benefactors of previous generations (and thus constituting its heritage). For example, the rituals and practices of *The Book of Common Prayer* are part of the endowment of the Church of England, and the collection of books in a college library are part of the resource endowment of the school.

Some portion of every endowment consists of public goods for the simple reason that any good that is available equally to everyone will be as available in the commons as it is elsewhere. Thus, the Library of Congress is part of the resource endowment of every U.S. school, thanks to the interlibrary loan system. Current economic arguments notwithstanding, however, the production of public goods is not a fundamental objective in most commons. Members of religious groups, lodges, fraternities, sororities, and other social groups do not indiscriminately seek to share participation and mutual relations with every other social organization but only with others of similar affiliation (and presumably similar outlook).

I shall employ the term *common goods* for the goods shared in commons. Private goods can also be made available to the commons by donation. The bulk of common goods, however, are characterized by the rather remarkable fact that while they may not be universal in the same sense as public goods, they are treated as universal within the commons. This is one of the most difficult concepts to realize or implement when money and market goods enter the commons. Perhaps some examples will help.

The system of metric measurement is a common good. Metric measurement is not yet a public good in the United States because it is not indivisible, in that some people can practice it while others cannot, and it is not universal. Members of the human species are not born with intrinsic knowledge of the metric system, nor is such knowledge universally available to everyone. Indeed, the majority of people in the United States still struggle with even understanding metric measurement and many simply do not try to understand it. Yet in scientific communities in which any type of exact measurement is important, the metric system is a common good. It is in precisely this sense that metric measurement (indeed, mathematics as a whole) is an important component of the endowment of modern science, and presumably a part of its legacy to future scientific development.

In this same sense, the astronomical observations and calculations of a great many ancient civilizations were part of their endowments, but important parts of this legacy have been lost to us. This point can be generalized to the level of entire civilizations. Living civilizations consist of a great many such legacies, whose monetary value is truly priceless (that is, valuable but not for sale and consequently without price). These legacies may be more numerous than we can count and sometimes we even take their very existence for granted, but their impact upon our daily lives is important nonetheless.

The particular legacy of Western civilization that we call humanism, humanitarianism, or, more recently, the much derided secular humanism, is another such resource endowment that is especially important in the modern private nonprofit world. Virtually every contemporary benefactory—including those religious institutions that explicitly reject certain values that they deride as humanistic—relies upon the rich resources of the humanist/humanitarian legacy to realize those common goods that are most important to it.

I am not suggesting here that commons play a unique role as producers or creators of civilization. Civilizations represent the total product of all institutions of which they consist, and it is a matter of historical interpretations which contributions were most important and valuable.

It is the role of the commons in preserving, restoring, and utilizing the heritage of a civilization that is unique. Commons apply resources of our heritage to solve what might be called the puzzles or mysteries offered by a particular cultural heritage—whether religious, scientific, or modern-day attacks upon social problems. Thus, scientific research paradigms do not just include formal theories but also include a complex array of associated (and mutually reinforcing) research evidence, techniques and methods, tacit assumptions, and practical ways of doing things.

The value of a particular endowment may be realized only in dramatizing, presenting, and thereby preserving it. This is as true of jazz musicians seeking to preserve their legacy in after-hours jam sessions as it is of the concert halls, museums, and theaters of the culture industry. The endowment of the Latin language was irreversibly transformed when it ceased to represent the resource of a living language. Until the advent of writing, literature, myth, and lore could only be preserved through the oral tradition of retold tales. In a similar way, prior to visual recording techniques and systems of choreographic notation, dance could only be preserved through actual regular performance.

At one level, we might speak of the transformation of social surpluses of wealth, power, and status into culture through two distinct dimensions: problem-solving and expression. The former is most likely to be associated with the creation or discovery of new cultural values (artifacts and symbols as well as larger complexes of value embodied in art, music, literature, and science), while expressive modes are more likely to be associated with the affirmation of established cultural and civilized values through ritual, ceremony, and other forms of presentation. Endowments for problem solving and expression can be combined in many ways. The endowment of any science, for example, involves both an established endowment of settled procedures (its own "scientific method") and agreements about novel problems to which they can be applied.

As part of the overall social surplus, the sum total of the values of a civilization (its social capital, so to speak) may include a great many artifacts that are neither purely privately held nor universally accessible. It is that portion of a civilization which we can call its endowment. In a larger sense, a civilization itself represents a common endowment as it is passed down from one generation to the next.

Socialization, Technique, and Search

The endowment of any civilization is not a static thing. The acts of creation, preservation, presentation, and restoration can be very costly in numerous ways. Tremendous investments of time and energy are necessary in many ongoing cultures simply to transform the heritage of the past into meaningful contemporary terms and to continue it as a legacy to the future.

A good deal of the social action of sustaining cultural continuity occurs within the commons. Much of that action consists of three fundamental processes: *socialization,* or learning; *technique,* or performing learned skills and demonstrating repertories and thereby revitalizing them in the present; and *search,* or consciously seeking to solve established problems or identify new ways of doing things. The learning and presentation of repertories, which often take routine disciplines or ritual forms, can constitute an important study in itself. For example, Van der Veer (1989) examines how members of the Ramanandi order in northern India create and use their abilities and potentials to totally transform basic attitudes and emotions in a discipline of detachment.

Socialization, technique, and search are fundamentally important processes in any commons, market, or state. Socialization is a social and psychological process related to voluntary participation. The role of socialization in the formation of commons and in the admission of new participants to commons has not been widely explored, however.

Technique is one of two ways of bringing value in from the heritage to the current situation. An accumulated set of learned techniques that is possessed by a person or a group is a special set of meanings or values that can be called a *repertory*. For example, founding a musical or theater group often hinges upon identifying seasoned performers with an established repertory who are able to act upon and to teach their techniques. The same can also be said for a monastic order, an athletic team, or a research laboratory. The particular techniques may involve problem solving, such as knowledge of how best to carry out aspects of scientific research, social work, or artistic creation. Or they may be techniques of presentation, as in concerts, rites, and performances. In both cases, however, the techniques in question are clearly subordinate to the larger common goods with which they are associated. The value of the cantor is established and maintained within the repertory of the synagogue, and the value of the choreographer within the repertory of the dance company. Techniques are units of larger meaning complexes, and their value in the commons is intimately connected with the meanings associated with the common goods that they render.

Search is the primary way in which information is brought into the commons. Philosophical contemplation, scientific research, and artistic creation are important forms of search, as are most forms of religious activity, such as vision quests and other quests for more profound religious experiences, and some types of athletic activity. Some search techniques involve searching the immediate environment, while others seek to invoke and revitalize a common heritage. Value brought into the commons through search is value closely associated with innovation, novelty, and change, as compared to the close association between technical values and tradition, stability, and order.

Treasury

A *treasury* is generally the best known and most clearly understood set of common resources held by a benefactory. Treasuries consist of closely measured funds of identifiable assets; that is, resources that can be measured by accounting systems and reported in financial statements of an association or corporation. Although such funds are not as frequently labeled treasuries today as they once were, it is still conventional to refer to the principal officer of an association or private nonprofit corporation responsible for managing assets as the treasurer.

In an economy driven by money, most benefactories appear to have at least a minimal need for a treasury. In many of the contemporary commons in U.S. communities, treasuries are used to purchase many types of resources from the market, such as technical and professional labor, supplies and equipment, and space. Treasuries seem to have been important in nonprofit institutions long before the modern age, however. In addition to the ark of the covenant, the original temple at Jerusalem contained a temple treasury (de Vaux, 1965). The treasury is also a standard feature in the architecture of Greek temples (V. Scully, 1991).

The most conventional mistake people make in identifying the resources of a benefactory is to look only at the monetary resources of its treasury because these are the most easily identified and most closely measured types of resources. Therefore, we may overlook or understate the resources of most commons. To avoid this error, we need some way to systematically denote, categorize, and signify other facets of the resource endowments of benefactories. The theory of the commons incorporates two additional terms already in widespread use: *collection* and *repertory*.

Collection

Many benefactories maintain an extensive collection of objects that are essential in rendering their shared purposes or common goods. The *collection* of any benefactory consists of the physical objects held or controlled by it as part of its endowment. Collections are

many and varied. Historical and contemporary benefactories often
maintain collections as part of their ongoing programs. For
example, churches and religious organizations of all types commonly retain collections of sacred icons, artwork, musical instruments, sacramental vessels, and other objects used in religious rites
and ceremonies. Museums and archives exist for the explicit purpose of being repositories of collections of artifacts, manuscripts,
and other objects of archeological, historical, or artistic value.

Many different types of benefactories maintain collections.
Every library has its book collection and every medieval cathedral
and monastery has its reliquary and collection of statues. Theater
companies have collections of makeup, costumes, scripts, and sets
created for previous productions. Athletic associations, unions, and
clubs typically have collections of sports equipment and paraphernalia associated with their particular interests.

Such groups offer interesting case studies of the divisions
between personal property and common goods. Members of a soft-
ball club may own their own gloves, for example, while the team
collectively owns a set of bats and bases. Libraries are collections of
books, and modern libraries also have highly diverse sets of other
information-bearing objects—professional journals, archaic manuscripts, films, microfilms, microfiche, audiotapes, videotapes, compact disks, and other media of information and knowledge.

Libraries hold one of the most common forms of collections
in the modern commons. The very idea of a library, which presumes
commons of writers and readers knowledgeable of the same languages, is one key to understanding the role of collections in the
commons. To view a library collection solely as a treasury and to
attempt to maintain an inventory of it, in the sense of a current
running estimate of the combined economic value of the collection
in money terms, illustrates the problems involved in the economics
of the commons. While a great many fascinating and highly technical economic and accounting issues are raised in such a case, large
numbers of librarians, readers, and writers harbor deep suspicions
that such an approach misses the fundamental point of making
money available to library collections.

Collections are not simple analogues of the inventories of
raw materials and unfinished goods that occur in productive firms.

While superficially resembling the inventories, plant, and equipment of productive firms, the collections of benefactories are really quite different from them both in purpose and in scope. Most important, items in collections are seldom acquired with the intention of processing and reselling them. Thus, questions of their enduring market value are almost never of any continuing interest once the objects have been acquired. What is important about items in a collection is usually only information of their existence, whereabouts, condition, and uses. Ordinarily, it should be sufficient for a benefactory to maintain simple records of a collection and to avoid extensive and misleading inclusions of collections among the monetary assets of its treasury.

Sometimes the connection between a particular collection and civilization is especially clear cut. This is the case for a collection of the Haeinsa Temple, a Buddhist complex of shrines and temples in the mountains near Taegu, Korea. The temple possesses a set of 80,000 woodblocks for printing the entire Buddhist canon. These printing blocks were carved during the Mongol invasion of the 1230s. In the evolution of the West, the Library of Alexandria, with its collection of Greek philosophy, literature, and science, played a comparable role in preserving knowledge of the ancient world (Forster, 1961; Préaux, 1967).

Recently, a major crime wave has been directed at plundering art artifacts from the museums, churches, and archeological sites of Italy, which is estimated to have the largest national collection of artworks in the world, totaling in excess of one million items (Rowland, 1991). Thefts of art and artifacts in Italy averaged more than fifty-five a day in 1990.

Italian police have estimated that Italy has 3,400 museums and archeological sites (700 of which are state run), 100,000 churches, 40,000 castles and forts, and 900 important town centers. Rome alone has 333 churches, more than 80 convents and monasteries, and 83 museums, not counting the 18 in the Vatican. Italian churches, archeological sites, and even museums have not traditionally kept detailed inventories, so the problems of even tracking stolen works have been extraordinarily complex. Because of the absence of institutional collection lists, dockets of stolen items reported to the police constitute virtually the only records of collections in many instances. The absence of collection lists is a rather extreme example of the way in which preoccupation with treasuries and financial accountability leads commons to ignore or neglect the more elementary question of logs or lists of collections of precious objects.

Repertory

The resource endowment of a commons that is the most difficult of all to deal with is the intangible *repertory*—the symbolic gestures, rituals, and ceremonies of religious bodies; the skillful, nuanced performances of actors, singers, musicians, and other performers; the occult body of specialized knowledge and practical wisdom, whether scientific, magical, religious, artistic, political, or otherwise, that communities have built up over years, decades, and in some instances centuries.

No one can expect to put a price on such knowledge and add it to the treasury. How can we put a monetary value on, for example, the astronomical knowledge of the Druids or the Maya, the subtle reasoning of a philosopher, or the skillful intervention of a caseworker? Yet efforts to assess the resource endowments of many types of commons are incomplete unless we take such resources into account.

The term *repertory*—already in use by actors and musicians to describe the range of accomplished performances of an ensemble or company—may be applied to the intangible endowments of many other commons as well. A repertory is, in this sense, any set of acts that an individual or group is prepared to perform. It may be the set of discrete but related skilled behaviors necessary to rescue a community of disaster victims or the set of unique patterned motions and utterances that compose a performance of *Hamlet*.

Repertories are often built up of sequences of related problem-solving strategies. Some repertories involve straightforward applications of if-then reasoning: if the victim is choking then perform the Heimlich maneuver. This maneuver and numerous others constitute the repertory of emergency medical technicians.

Repertories may involve ordinary, conventional behavior or extremely high levels of skill, judgment, and timing that only members of the repertory company are able to master through the dedication of a lifetime. Yet the point remains—the stock of solutions in the repertory of problem-solving actions constitutes one of the principle forms of resources available to a benefactory.

Although we may be unaccustomed to thinking of them as resources, performance repertories are also among the key resources of the commons. They often constitute the uniqueness and relative advantage of the commons that money cannot buy. This is as true of charitable and religious organizations as it is of artistic performances and athletic competitions. For example, the twelve-step method of Alcoholics Anonymous describes a repertory that is distinctive and unmistakable.

Although the term *repertory* is perhaps most widely used and understood in the arts, even in this context the underlying problem-solving connotation should be apparent. Each new production and each performance represents a new problem to be solved. It is in the problem solving of the live performance where the excitement of the performance is to be found.

Professional benefactories are set apart from amateurs by differences in repertories. For example, a brilliant actor, musical performer, dancer, or surgeon can perform movements and introduce nuances of performance that others are simply unable to duplicate. When a new type of service for intervening with alcoholics or people with Alzheimer's disease is developed, the greatest interest is always in the repertory of new skills and techniques that may be involved.

Resources specifically associated with capturing power and demonstrating authority also clearly involve repertories. The endowment whose repertories encompass skills of political intelligence gathering, the exercise of influence, and ample amounts of legitimacy and authority is likely to make significant additions to its treasury and collections, and further expand its repertories.

Economists, accountants, and managers have shown virtually no interest in repertories as key resources of nonprofit corporate benefactories. Contemporary financial statements and annual reports not only fail to list estimates of the value of repertories, they usually even fail to note their existence. Such are the exigencies of contemporary concern with the accountability of nonprofit groups. Estimating the full or true value of any endowment should require at least a simple listing and description of its repertory of skills and techniques.

Regime

As noted earlier, the nonprofit and voluntary action community has been preoccupied in recent years with the question of suitable delineations of the nonprofit sector in relation to government, business, and even the informal sector. This preoccupation has produced a theoretical and conceptual impasse that consists of equal measures of straw man, deus ex machina, and genuine puzzlement. The literature on this topic leads to the paradoxical conclusion that making distinctions between market, state, and commons serves only to point up the interrelations and connections between these sectors.

According to Ostrander, Langton, and Van Til (1988), we need new ways of thinking about the interdependence and interaction of the state, for-profit organizations, and nonprofit organizations. It may be possible, however, to use existing concepts in new ways to produce what represents, in effect, such new ways of thinking. One approach, for example, is to use the interdisciplinary model of urbanism, with its distinction between core and periphery, as a matrix for spelling out the links between sectors.

The concepts of core and periphery as they have evolved in urban and regional theory can be used to distinguish the defining, or central, characteristics of the sectors from other peripheral functions that they may serve. Thus in the traditional terms of the theory of civil society, the recognized core of the state involves those coercive powers usually identified as police powers. It is a conventional axiom of political theory that legitimate governments may justly deprive others of their liberty and property through the exercise of these powers. Yet modern governments also clearly involve a variety of public (that is, tax-supported) functions in which coercion is replaced by compassion, community, or some other public virtue.

This distinction is well illustrated by the child welfare field, where the core coercive powers associated with child custody, adoption, and prosecution of child abuse and neglect coexist with peripheral compassionate purposes of other child welfare services. The public utilities of local governments (sewer and water, for example) and national park campgrounds are just a few of the many peripheral commercial services sold or leased by governments.

Similarly, although the core of the market-oriented business and commercial sector may indeed be profits, we can hardly overlook the conclusion that some activities at the periphery of this sector assume the qualities of the commons and the state. Thus, the traditional company town and the modern corporation frequently assume important measures of coercive influence over the private lives of employees. The country store, the proverbial soda fountain, the neighborhood Mom and Pop grocery store, and the neighborhood bar are among the many examples of commercial establishments that have blended a profit orientation with more communal functions.

Part of the current enigma of the firmlike, Type A, or commercial nonprofit organization may involve a similar core transformation, or the historical evolution of what were thought to be commons (such as nonprofit hospitals, nursing homes, and childcare centers) into quasi-commercial enterprises that are clearly businesslike in orientation and operation. In other cases, both modern and medieval commons have evolved essentially coercive powers. Such powers may be exercised in cooperation with the state, as in the case of nonprofit child welfare agencies or services for the elderly charged with quasi-regulatory responsibilities. Or, similar powers may be exercised in direct opposition to the state, as in the case of terrorist groups and organized crime families.

At their core, families and households serve as essential primary groups, but at the periphery, they may assume coercive powers (as in patriarchal, tribal, and other ascriptive societies), commercial functions (as in family businesses), or even associational characteristics. Members of a number of large kinship networks, for example, have formed "family reunion" associations solely to support periodic clan gatherings.

The hybrid types that emerge from distinguishing the core and periphery of state, market, household, and commons represent a step beyond the straightforward consideration of isolated ideal types. Such hybrids still speak only to the internal organization of each sector. An additional distinction is necessary to encompass relations across sectors.

The political concept of regime can be broadened and usefully applied for this purpose. A *regime* may be said to be a network of related formal and communal organizations across sectors. We already have names for some such combinations. *Democracy* is the term we ordinarily apply to a regime in the control of elected officials. Oligarchy, fascism, and monarchy are other types of regimes.

The conventional use of the term *regime* in political studies emphasizes primarily those regimes in which the state figures prominently as a core. Thus, for example, Lowi (1969) has characterized "interest group liberalism" as a regime, and the Frankfort School has addressed authoritarianism (Adorno, 1950). *Capitalism* is a term applied to any regime with market-oriented enterprises in its core, as opposed to *state socialism*, a term that defines a regime with state-controlled enterprises at the core, or *barter economies,* a term that typically implies strong common elements. *Welfare state* and *mixed economy* have frequently been used to denote regimes in which the core is shared by market, state, and, perhaps, commons. The term *welfare state* conjures up one type of core regime (regulated mixed economy) to its adherents and quite another (state socialism) to its critics. The literatures on participatory democracy, coproduction, and collaboration also conjure up quite distinct core regimes. At the heart of the Reagan revolution was the vision of a market-centered, family-centered regime, with a restricted state and a vibrant commons on its periphery.

As a regime may be said to consist of a specific set of relations between commons, markets, states, and households, a civilization may be said to consist of a set of relations between regimes. Medieval Western civilization, for example, was built upon the primacy of a particular set of religious commons, and modern Western civilization is to a high degree built upon the civil society model of the supremacy of the constitutionally limited nation-state (Cohen and Arato, 1992).

Patronage

The core of the commons, as noted earlier, consists of social relations between patrons, agents, and clients. *Patronage* occurs between a *patron* (someone with some type of good) and a *client* (someone who is seeking that same good). Such relations are often cast in explicitly hierarchical terms of superiority and subordination: for example, the relation of the teacher and the student (one with more knowledge and one with less), the master craftsman and the apprentice (one with more skill and one with less), or the political boss and a benefice seeker.

Publics (as the term is used in behavioral political science) are aggregates from which both patron and client classes are organized. *Memberships* are patrons who constitute their own publics. In the commons, the term *patronage* suggests stable relations between a group or class of patrons and groups or classes of intermediaries or clients. Patronage may at various times embrace the support, sponsorship, legitimation, financing, or protection of common goods. Patrons are called givers, donors, supporters, benefactors, helpers, philanthropists, and a range of other names. In Western civilization, patronage can be found in ancient, medieval, and modern times. Patronage is also evident in many other civilizations as well.

The central focus of patronage theory in the commons is on voluntary (uncoerced) hierarchies—of power, influence, wealth, status, information, knowledge, or other resources—and the circumstances leading to the emergence and continuation of inequalities in this sense. This focus accounts in part for the strong emphasis on negation in terminology of the commons. The absence of kinship as a requirement of association membership, for example, points up the nonfamilial nature of the commons as a pure type. Apparent exchange asymmetries (or the absence of fair and equal exchanges by buyers and sellers in a competitive environment) for grants of all types point up the nonmarket nature of the commons. The absence of legitimate control or domination by a single actor (the "monopoly of force") points up the nonstate nature of the commons.

Patronage relationships may be seen in different ways by different parties; relations can be seen as coercive, remunerative, or normative by either party. Thus, for example, Samuel Johnson's loud literary protestations about what he perceived as his exploitation tell us nothing about the attitudes or intentions of his patron, Lord Chesterfield.

Note that many patronage relationships are asymmetric in another sense: they do not involve equitable exchange in its traditional sense. The teacher who gives knowledge, information, or skill to a student does not receive the student's ignorance in exchange. The patron who gives money to a charity or directly to the poor presents a much more complex case. Although the patron may not expect an equitable return, some reciprocation in terms of recognition, status, and gratitude may be involved. The current view that all common relations involve exchanges is thus one requiring a good deal of close examination.

Conclusion

Ordinary English contains a robust vocabulary for speaking of nonprofit and voluntary action. Terms like *benefit, benefactory, commons, endowment, socialization, technique, search, treasury, collection, repertory, regime,* and *patronage* provide a conceptual matrix for denoting and explaining nonprofit and voluntary action. Moreover, they provide a vocabulary that places emphasis where many have argued it belongs—on the uncoerced cooperation of peers. For the most part, we may talk of issues and matters of common concern by using long-standing English terms like *commons, beneficiary,* and *endowment.* In other cases, there are no existing terms for important ideas, and we need to apply well-understood principles of language construction to coin terms like *benefactory.* In both cases, the robustness of our language serves us well.

3

The Evolution
of the Commons
in Western Civilization

If people living in democratic countries had no right and no inclination to associate for political purposes, their independence might be in jeopardy, but they might long preserve their wealth and their cultivation: whereas if they never acquired the habit of forming associations in ordinary life, civilization itself would be endangered.

—Alexis de Tocqueville

Two points made in the previous chapter require additional comment. One is the suggestion that the concept of the commons is broader than and encompasses the concepts of nonprofit organization and voluntary association. The other is that the commons that may be related in varying degrees to the U.S. nonprofit organization are basic to Western civilization and are found in many other civilizations and cultures as well. The group portrait of commons that begins to emerge in this chapter is based upon cursory review of a broad range of historical sources. It suggests a view quite different from the one inspired by de Tocqueville's vision of the uniqueness of the United States that is found in much of the current nonprofit and voluntary action literature.

The need for a more complete and detailed historical understanding of the commons has long been recognized. In 1972, a planning conference of an interdisciplinary voluntary action task force identified "the nature and development of voluntary action from early times to modern society (history of voluntary action)" as one of a number of major analytical topics of voluntary action theory and research (Smith and others, 1972). Since that time, historical and cross-cultural understanding of facets of the heritage of nonprofit and voluntary action has expanded substantially (Bauer, 1990; Bremner, 1988; Hall, 1987; Seibel, 1990, and others). At the same time, the conceptual impact of expanding historical insight upon the main body of nonprofit and voluntary studies has been limited, as witnessed by the apparent belief among many nonprofit and voluntary action scholars that the U.S. voluntary association and nonprofit organization are unique U.S. inventions. The priority placed on the concepts of heritage, collection, and repertory in the preceding chapter makes it clear that in the theory of the commons, the beliefs, rituals, ceremonies, and other practices of a civilization, which are built up over time, represent a major set of resources in the contemporary commons.

Some aspects of the long history of nonprofit and voluntary action have been acknowledged. Chalmers (1827) wrote a monograph on the problem of endowments from which the use of the term in this work is derived. An article on philanthropy in the 1917 *Encyclopedia of Religion and Ethics* included sections on Chinese, Indian, Greek, Roman, Jewish, early Christian, and modern philanthropy (Hastings, 1917). A work by Chambers (1917) is still one of the most encyclopedic sources available on the long history of charity and almsgiving. It includes ten sections, each written by an authority on that period: primitive, biblical, Buddhist, Christian (early, medieval, and modern periods), Greek, Hebrew, Hindu, Jewish, Islamic (the reference is to Muhammadan law), and Roman. References to classical sources are woven into the text, and a selection of additional references follows each section. Bruno (1944) cites and discusses selected references that cover Oriental, Egyptian, Hebrew, Greek, and Roman concepts of charity.

In this chapter, I will examine selected aspects of the evolution of commons in the United States within the framework of the heritage of Western civilization. The core of this history is largely the heritage of beliefs and practices that evolved from the ancient world of the Mediterranean, expanded in medieval Europe, and were transported to the Americas, where they took new and distinctive shape. This core has an incredible number of counterpoints that also need to be developed, but the restricted space here and my limited vision preclude me from considering them all.

A civilization and its main features—cultures, languages, technologies, arts, religions, games, and sports as well as the organizations that tend bodies of knowledge, including philosophies, religions, and sciences—conform in important respects to the characteristics of commons. Successful civilizations, in contrast with empires and totalitarian regimes, evoke in very fundamental ways a level of voluntary compliance from those who inhabit them. One can be ordered to write music or watch the stars, but the highest levels of human achievement associated with the triumphs of any civilization cannot be coerced. Moreover, the resources of language and culture as well as the fundamental sense of purpose, mutuality, and "fellow-feeling" and basic standards of justice and fairness are all implicit in what we mean by a civilization. The distinct forms these commons take in modern liberal democracies are variants on much larger, older, and broader themes.

Civilization is as much a product of human effort as any other aspect of economic, social, and political development. The total social product of a society is not simply measured by its gross national product. The development of any component of civilization beyond its present state is dependent upon how people use the social product of society. This is as true of the cultural achievements of a civilization as it is of material products.

Civilization and Social Surpluses

Focusing on civilization in this way allows us to point up the critical role of social surpluses and the leisure classes who control them in the relation between the economy and the commons. For example, connections can be shown between the leisure-time cultural

activities and the associational activities of workers in Europe between 1590 and 1914 (Yeo and Yeo, 1981). The real product of any
society is formed in its leisure as well as its labor and includes its
sciences, arts, literature, music, philosophies, and religions as well
as the techniques and practices of daily living that make up its way
of life and the many other artifacts that together compose its
culture.

Of course, a portion of the social product of all societies must
be devoted to assuring the survival of members of the society and
the continuation of its basic infrastructure of social institutions.
Action to assure survival and social reproduction is the real meaning of the term *labor* in an economic tradition running from Aristotle to Adam Smith and Karl Marx (Arendt, 1958). Another portion
of the social product, together with the natural resources controlled
by the society, provides the basis for organizing future production.
In an affluent society, several broad alternatives emerge for use of
the remaining social product after the basic survival needs of the
society are assured. Surpluses that might be directed back into increased production can also be employed to support personal leisure
or dedicated to the pursuit of public goods as diverse as the building
of empires, providing of public welfare, defense of civil rights and
liberties, or construction and maintenance of highways. A third
option, even in relatively poor economies at levels of development
barely above subsistence, is support for the unproductive labor of
distinct leisure classes—priests, scholars, poets, scientists, artists,
musicians, and others.

Prehistory

Preliterate cultures do not leave documents and "lost" civilizations
do not leave audiotapes or videotapes. Therefore, we typically know
a good deal more about the material aspects of prehistoric cultures
than we do about their intangible symbolic practices, beliefs, and
social structures. Nonetheless, within the limits of the existing evidence, it is quite plausible to suggest that many ancient civilizations knew and practiced the uncoerced participation, sharing of
purposes and resources, mutuality, and fairness we associate with
the commons (Lieberman, 1991). The anthropologist Adolph

Bandelier's novel, *The Delight Makers* ([1890] 1971), offers a convincing picture of clan associations and kiva societies within the complex community life of early communities in the southwestern United States. In all likelihood, commons reach deep into the past of many preliterate cultures, which suggests that caring, concern, and community are anything but signs of modern progress. Indeed, the selfishness and greed found in primitive societies by Colin Turnbull (1972) are more likely the products of social disorganization than the "brutish nature" projected upon the past by social theorists in the tradition of Hobbes.

Commons are at least as ancient as markets and states and may, in fact, predate both. Artifacts suggesting unproductive labor, for example, are evident in the remains of a great many sites from the Neolithic and earlier. The earliest hunter-gatherers making the transition to agriculture did not just fashion available materials into productive tools like axes and digging sticks. They used the same knowledge and skill to develop tools for painting on cave walls; carving images; and making prayer sticks, totems, and other religious objects.

Moreover, primitive life was seldom the unrelieved struggle for survival that we think it was. Sahlins (1972) has argued that primitive man may have had relatively large amounts of leisure time, punctuated by occasional periods of hunting and gathering to assure survival. This fits the portrait painted by Herman Melville in his early novels *Typee, Omoo,* and *Mardi* ([1846, 1847, 1849] 1982), based on firsthand observations of Polynesian life.

With even minimal levels of affluence, people can have some leisure. It is quite plausible that from an early date most primitive humans had leisure. It is also plausible that portions of their leisure went into the unproductive labors of religion, games, decorative arts, myths, storytelling, and other common goods. Preliterate peoples must have spent substantial amounts of leisure time developing, learning, and performing myths, rituals, and ceremonies to produce the artifacts that have already been discovered and to sustain the legends and traditions that have come down to us.

Commons can arise under conditions of even relatively modest affluence. None of the required elements of a commons assumes high levels of social and economic development. An indicator of the

extent of prehistoric leisure is the presence of one or more classes
free of the necessity of producing their own food (Lenski and
Lenski, 1978). To the extent that such unproductive classes are
found, the potential exists for the emergence of characteristic prehistoric commons: temple cults, priests, and shamans. When a distinct leisure class emerges to devote itself to unproductive
endeavors, a commons of some type is almost certainly present. To
the present day, all classes are possessed of varying degrees of leisure, from the complete idleness of the courtier and industrial-age
plutocrat to the sabbath (day of rest) of agricultural peasants and
laboring classes.

Evidence of the existence of commons among prehistoric societies is made clearest through studies of ritual. Initiation rituals
are a nearly universal form of commons among prehistoric peoples.
For example, Shaw (1991) studied a ritual of the Samo people of the
East Strickland plain of Papua New Guinea, called *kandila,* which
is an elaborate three-day initiation ceremony that takes two years of
preparation. Any people on the brink of subsistence would be unable to tolerate the kind of sustained "wealth" of leisure time and
surplus resources needed to organize and carry out rituals over such
extended periods of time.

Some portion of primitive commons may have evolved out
of the projection of family life into the community. Marriage feasts
and bridal dowries are consistent evidence of levels of affluence. The
same can be said for funerals and elaborate grave sites. Existing
knowledge of these aspects of primitive cultures offers detailed and
elaborate testimony of their role in creating and sustaining the social solidarity of communities. We recognize the similar potentials
of nonprofit institutions such as charities, the arts, and religious
groups for creating and sustaining modern community solidarity.
Yet we have largely ignored the obvious functional parallels between primitive and modern commons.

Ritual feasting is another common activity widely evident in
primitive societies. Feasts are, by definition, the creations of affluent
peoples and show many of the signs of mutuality, pooling, and the
voluntarism of the commons. Typically, participation in ritual
feasting would be voluntary (at least, any coercive pressures to participate are likely to be subtle and not overt) and mutual, with

shared purposes and resources and would include implicit or explicit rules of fairness (order for receiving food and so on).

In some instances, conspicuous display of wealth was a central function of the feast. The display of wealth may also have been an element in evolving distinctions between the concepts of public and private. For example, Wilson (1989) examines how the development of permanent settlements during the Mesolithic period and the division of space into public and private areas encouraged tendencies to both conceal and display wealth. Display in this sense approximates the concept of presentation in the theory of the commons. Thus, the emergence of patronage in the commons signifies a series of major historical shifts in such displays of wealth, virtue, and so on. Patronage of temples, public spectacles, and other commons constitutes a historically significant shift away from conspicuous displays of wealth in the grandiose private consumption of ritual feasting and toward the substitution of common goods.

The significance of ritual and its connections to common goods is not limited to prehistoric and primitive cultures. The distinctive patterns of ritualized friendship among ancient Greeks may be directly related to the patterns of patronage and philanthropy that were developed in ancient Greek civilization (Hands, 1968; Morris, 1986; see Herman, 1987, for a description of ritualized friendships in ancient Greece). Among contemporary societies, Japan is noteworthy for the continuing importance of similar rituals and ceremonial and symbolic behavior. Jeremy and Robinson (1989) conclude that ceremony and symbol are much more important in all aspects of Japanese society than they are in the contemporary West. One should expect, as a result, to locate the Japanese commons in its tea ceremonies, serene gardens, and roadside Shinto shrines as well as more familiar forms of ritual and symbol.

Understanding of U.S. nonprofit and voluntary action might also be considerably advanced by closer examination of its ritual aspects. Mary Jo Deegan (1989) uses dramaturgical theory to examine U.S. ritual behavior in settings such as football games and singles bars. Lincoln (1989) explores ways in which myth, ritual, and classification hold societies together and how in times of crisis, they can also be used for social reconstruction. These and other perspectives on ritual should readily be applicable to a broad range of nonprofit and voluntary action in commons.

Two of the most universal categories of material artifacts of the ancient world are *stelae* and *temples*. Even simple stela and surviving ritual objects suggest the existence at one time of skilled stone masons, wood-carvers, and builders who were not exclusively engaged in tool making. Temples suggest not only the existence of architects and builders but also of classes of acolytes and priests.

The gigantic stone statues of Easter Island must have had some type of religious or ceremonial significance, as did the rock temples of Petra (one of which was made famous as a backdrop in the movie *Indiana Jones and the Last Crusade*). Collins (1988) recently identified the iconography and ritual associated with relief sculptures inside the cave temple of the Hindu god Siva on Elephanta, a small island in the harbor of Bombay, India. Meanings and rituals this elaborate and detailed imply leisure to develop, sustain, and understand them. They also imply common projects involving large numbers of people acting jointly. Thousands of such examples survive from prehistory.

Various of the identified structures of prehistoric Northern Europe, including Stonehenge, are thought to have been the monuments of Stone Age craftsmen. Egyptian rulers constructed a series of vast desert pyramids whose ritual significance is not entirely clear. Various ancient Mesoamerican peoples constructed elaborate "urban" temple complexes, whose functions and uses are still not well understood (Childe, 1950; Hardoy, 1968; White, 1963). In eastern North America, various woodland native American populations developed their own unique forms of earth mounds, some of which are sculpted into fantastic animal shapes.

We are inclined to view such structures as the constructions of enslaved peoples laboring under tyrannical rulers. But the precision and spirituality we see in these structures suggests that they were the products of voluntary labor, possibly inspired by religious ecstasy. We already know that similar enthusiasms played a role in the human sacrifices of Aztec and Maya temple cults that used some of these structures.

The debates over the functions of these structures point toward the existence of ancient commons of one type or another.

Whether these various monuments served primarily religious purposes, as some people would have it, or scientific (astronomical,
mathematical, and calendrical) purposes, as others have suggested,
is not especially important when we realize that both religious and
scientific purposes are subsumed by the concept of the commons.
These were the projects of civilized and affluent leisure classes, and
by their very existence, we can infer the existence of distinct types
of commons in the prehistoric world.

Further studies of prehistoric rituals and monuments under
the rubric of the commons may shed some interesting light upon
current interest among nonprofit and voluntary action scholars in
the institutional relationships between the market, state, and commons. Archeological and anthropological studies of the village peoples ("Pueblo Indians") of the American Southwest, for example,
point toward a civilization of settled communities lacking a political state until very recent times. Evidence also points toward the
existence of elaborate and extensive networks of voluntary associations (for example, kiva societies and clans) in these communities
and a monumental architecture of great subtlety and aesthetic orig-
inality, linking kivas and pueblos into an organic whole with nature (Scully, 1975). We find among these same village peoples
extensive and elaborate mythologies (for example, the Hopi Way),
rituals (for example, corn dances), and ritual objects (for example,
kachinas). The assertion that some measure of affluence and leisure
are essential for commons but that great wealth is not essential is
well illustrated by the rich commons of these village peoples, which
arose out of the meager social surpluses of communities forced to
scratch a living out of the "dry farming" of the southwestern desert
region.

Civilization and Urbanization

However pervasive commons may have been in prehistory, the urban revolution and the development of cities was certainly a hall-
mark in the evolution of commons. Arnold Toynbee argues that the
presence of a leisure class is consistent evidence of a civilization
(Toynbee, 1967). The agricultural and urban revolutions at the
dawn of civilization must have had profound implications for com-

mons, especially by dramatically increasing the possible activities of urban leisure classes freed from subsistence living. We see not only dramatic increases in the size and scale of monuments in the cities of Mesopotamia, the Middle East, China, and elsewhere but also the proliferation of entirely new unproductive urban occupations and professions: priests, artists, scholars, and performers (athletes and actors). In pre-agricultural and pre-urban cultures, performers of ritual and builders of monuments were most likely part-time amateurs who devoted their leisure to such pursuits, as we say, after work. In cities, we see the emergence of leisure class occupations.

Spates and Macionis (1986–1987) believe that the key to understanding cities as a major social phenomenon is to examine them in a historical, cross-cultural, and interdisciplinary context using major theories for analysis. The basic approach taken in the remainder of this chapter is to examine the growth of civilization and urban development through the theoretical lens of the theory of the commons.

The existence of urban temples suggests surpluses of food, spices, and other substances to be used in sacrifices and ritual observances. We can also say that monuments and temples probably imply a patron or group of patrons. Such patrons are generally necessary for financing, legitimacy, protection, labor supply, and other purposes. Sometimes, we know who the patrons of temples were—Solomon, Asoka, Agamemnon, Cleopatra, Pericles, Alexander the Great, the Ptolemies, and others. In other cases, we can only infer such patronage.

Thus, we can surmise that there may have been patronage by the rulers and at least an elemental commons associated with the ziggurat in the city-state of Ur in ancient Mesopotamia, for example, even though we know almost nothing about the religion practiced there. We know somewhat more about the role of royal patronage in the construction of the Egyptian pyramids, although we still know little about their use. The First and Second Temples at Jerusalem are particularly important in this respect because they are important in the development of both Judaism and Christianity. We also know a good deal about the construction, financing, organization, and cult practiced in the Temple as well as the relationship of the Temple to other subordinate Hebrew temples (de Vaux, 1965).

The patterns of urban commons of the ancient Middle East are also repeated elsewhere. When the imperial Chinese capital of Changan grew into the largest city in Asia during the eighth to ninth centuries, it had an estimated population of one million people and more than one hundred Buddhist, Taoist, Zoroastrian, and Nestorian Christian temples among its institutions (Wright, 1967).

One of the contested points in the theory of civilization involves the role of writing. Is writing the central indicator of the rise of civilization? And did writing emerge for largely utilitarian, business purposes or for some other reason? In Asia, perhaps more so than elsewhere in the world, writing attained not only a utilitarian but also a common importance very early in its development. Scribes and scriptoria have also been part of the division of labor of even minimally affluent literate societies from very ancient times. During the so-called Dark Ages of Western civilization, virtually the entire canon of ancient Greek and Roman texts was maintained—and recopied from one generation to the next—at a handful of isolated Irish monasteries (DePaor, 1958).

Athens

Ancient Greek and Roman civilizations both incorporated distinctive philanthropic practices and institutions (Finley, 1974a; Hands, 1968; Gold, 1982, 1987; Wiseman, 1982). In fact, classical Greek commons were so extensive that it would require an entire monograph to cover the subject completely. In this discussion, I can only hope to mention some of the highlights of Greek commons and link them to our principal concern with the theory of the commons.

The evolution of the ancient Greek commons is a record of the emergence of distinctive patterns of philanthropy and associations within the Homeric leisure class of prehistoric Greece, the transformation and diffusion of aristocratic practices in the democratic context of the Athenian polis, and the rediscovery of these practices in the classicism of the West in the eighteenth century. The exact origins of the earliest Greek philanthropic practices are unknown. They probably parallel to a considerable extent the prehistory of primitive common practice noted earlier. According to Parker, "[G]ift giving was perhaps the most important mechanism of social relationships to Homeric society" (1986, p. 265). Homeric and classical Greek giving was an expression of peer-oriented "reciprocal friendship" and mutual aid among aristocrats quite unlike modern notions of philanthropy and charity. Homeric gift giving may well have been a form of the ancient mutual aid in villages as it emerged in the new circumstances of an urban elite with vastly increased wealth and power (Finley, 1974a; Hornblower, 1986). In this respect, it resembles the emergence of an American philanthropic elite in the plutocracy of the United States in the nineteenth and early twentieth centuries.

Gradually, reciprocal norms of Greek village gift giving may have evolved into the ritualized aristocratic patronage obligations known as *liturgia* (Finley, 1974a; Hornblower, 1986). Pericles is credited as the founder of classical Athens, by virtue of his role as patron of the Parthenon and other structures of the Acropolis (Bowra, 1967). Pericles' patronage was accomplished by redistributing funds contributed by other Greek city-states for war against Persia (Boardman, 1986). Although the method and the size of funds was somewhat unique, Pericles' act of patronage was not. Hornblower (1986, p. 127) concludes that "aristocrats such as Cimon and Pericles, by their political and military leadership, brought in the public wealth which subsidized the buildings and sculptures of Phidias, Ictinus, and Mnesicles on the Acropolis; and by making available their private wealth for public purposes, they financed the festivals and dramatic productions which gave classical Athens its attractive power. (This was the liturgy system, a tax on the rich which conferred prestige when taken beyond what was obligatory). Pericles' first known act was to pay for Aeschylus' great historical opera, the *Persae*. We know this . . . from a list carved on stone." The archaic Greek ethical model of philanthropy (or *liturgia*) as obligatory at a minimal level and as conferring status at higher levels appears to have important ramifications that have not yet been discussed in the context of the commons.

The Peloponnesian War of 431 B.C. destroyed the power and influence of the original aristocratic class of Athens and undermined its philanthropic activity. However, the citizens of the emergent democratic city-state followed the example of the aristocratic obligations of patronage and reciprocity, with notable result.

Hornblower (1986) credits Athenian democracy and aristocratic patronage of culture (*paideia*) as important in the emergence of
Athens as the premier Greek city-state. Classical Greek patronage
extended very broadly to include construction and operation of vast
numbers of temples; comic, tragic, and choral theatres; public hospitals; oracles at Delphi and elsewhere; sporting events and games
at Olympia; and a broad range of other community affairs (Finley
and Pleket, 1976; Levi, 1986). These were not public (in the modern
sense of tax-supported) events or facilities but were instead supported, as in the past, through the liturgical system of patronage.

Liturgical patronage, however, was not the only feature of
the Greek pursuit of common goods. Many modern forms of association also have counterparts in Greek life. The democratic political organization of the polis was essentially an association of adult
males (Murray, 1986). As such, it was one of several major forms of
association prominent in Athenian life. The *symposium* was a kind
of private drinking club. Every male Athenian citizen belonged to
a *phratry* (from which the modern term *fraternity* derives). Originally aristocratic warrior bands, phratries were involved in all the
main stages of a man's life and were the focus of his social and
religious activity (Murray, 1986). There are, in fact, certain intriguing similarities between the Athenian phratries and the kiva societies of the American Pueblo Indians and other similar urban male
associations. The probable emergence of such brotherhoods from
essentially military origins might take many other forms as well.
For example, the *syssitia,* or mess groups of Sparta, were the basis
of the entire social and military organization of that city-state.

In ancient Greece, the civil society of the commons was largely dominated by males. Greek deities of both genders were abundant,
but women participated socially in commons only tangentially and
occasionally.

In Athens, there were also aristocratic religious groups called
gennetai, whose members claimed descent from common ancestors
and monopolized the priesthoods of important city cults. *Gymnasia*
were not merely physical facilities, as today, but also the sporting
clubs who used them. As Murray (1986, p. 209) notes, "There were
benefit clubs and burial clubs and clubs associated with individual
trades and activities. There were religious and mystical sects and

intellectual organizations such as the philosophical schools of Plato and Aristotle.''

The philosophical schools of ancient Athens also belong within the profile of what we are calling commons. Plato's Academy existed for centuries as an educational common. Like so many other commons prior to the modern democratic era in philanthropy, the Athenian schools probably had rich aristocratic or royal patrons. Plato was, quite probably, a wealthy man who began the Academy within his own household a few miles outside of Athens. As such, either he may have been his own patron or he might have had help from others.

Aristotle, however, was not independently wealthy and required philanthropic patronage to launch his own philosophical school. He was trained at the Academy and later set up his own philosophical school, the Gymnasium, with the help of Philip of Macedon, father of Alexander the Great, whom Aristotle had tutored. Aristotle may have left Plato's Academy after being passed over as Plato's successor. In any case, other philosophers also set up schools, and philosophical schools became numerous enough in classical Athens that it is reasonable to suggest a regional concentration of schools.

It is important to remember that Greek philosophical schools were not all merely centers for contemplation and Socratic dialogue. Aristotelian science was akin to modern scientific fieldwork, and the Gymnasium may have had something of the air of a modern nonprofit research laboratory or institute. At one time Aristotle may have had over a thousand researchers in the field throughout the Mediterranean region. The logistics of support for such an army of investigators would challenge the resources of any modern nonprofit organization.

Another offshoot of the Athenian philosophical movement that was of great importance to the rise of modern science centuries later was the diffusion of the concepts of science and philosophy. Ancient libraries and scriptoria at Alexandria, Toledo, and other sites collected and duplicated an astounding wealth of knowledge and information and kept it alive for hundreds of years. Under the Ptolemies, Greek rulers installed in Egypt by Alexander the Great, the Greek city of Alexandria in Egypt became headquarters of what we might today call a private university—a scientific and philosophical complex centered on the famous Library of Alexandria (Forster, 1961). In this setting, important discoveries regarding Euclidean geometry, solar and astronomical calculations, and detailed knowledge of animal and plant taxonomies were preserved and passed on. Later, monastic libraries and scriptoria in Cordoba, Celtic Christian Ireland, and elsewhere forged the essential links between the knowledge of the ancient and modern worlds. The modern world would know nothing of Greek philosophy, science, medicine, drama, or poetry without these links. Each of these institutions was, in all probability, an endowed institution, with one or more wealthy patrons and a class of attendants and functionaries devoted to its operations in a manner not inconsistent with modern nonprofit research libraries and laboratories.

Public recognition and affirmation of the patrons of these institutions must have been an important consideration. The previously discussed ethics of liturgia would suggest as much, as would the frequency with which patrons were memorialized on stela. Meritt, Wade-Gery, and McGregor (1939) collected a four-volume catalogue of English translations of the inscriptions on all of the various Athenian tribute stelae that had been located to that point.

The Hellenistic Age

The Hellenistic Age generally refers to the period after the classical age of Athenian Greece and to the process of the dissemination of Greek culture throughout the Mediterranean region. An important element in this diffusion was the continuing norm of aristocratic responsibility for patronage of at least some Greek commons. Most Hellenistic cities, for example, had temples and amphitheaters that housed subsidized productions of Greek drama. And the Hellenistic period was "the golden age of Greek science," particularly astronomy and medicine (Barnes, 1986, p. 381). It seems reasonable to assume that as Greek arts and sciences were disseminated, the practices of support for them (liturgia and paideia) were disseminated with them.

According to Price (1986, p. 349), "We know most about [Hellenistic] patronage in Alexandria, where the Ptolemies' record was important but limited: the literature they patronized did not produce major talents in history and philosophy. They had an alphabetical list of pensions, a museum and two libraries. They had a serious need for a royal tutor to teach the little princes and a royal librarian to preside over the growing arsenals of books. Long-term patronage was for useful industry: tutoring, science, the library and textual scholarship."

Price summarizes the character of Ptolomeic patronage:

> All the [Hellenistic] courts had libraries, even on the Black Sea, but Alexandria's are the most famous. Followers of Aristotle had settled in that city with memories of their master's learned society and great collection of books. Probably they suggested the idea of a royal museum and library to the first Ptolemy. The royal library was probably attached to the colonnades and common room of the museum and served more as a vast arsenal of books than as a separate set of reading rooms. Nearly half a million book-rolls are alleged to have been stored inside, while another 42,000 are said to have lived in a second library attached to the temple of Serapis.
>
> Why did the kings bother? As the Aristotelians had no doubt explained to a willing Ptolemy I, libraries and scholarly studies kept a king abreast of man's understanding of the world. The Ptolemies had had good tutors and they did not lose interest in learning. . . . Royal extravagance inflated these tastes, and when others entered the race, book collecting became a mad competition. [1986, pp. 340–341]

Hellenistic cities also developed a distinctive variation on gymnasia in which sports training was combined with libraries and lectures (Price, 1986). Another form of Hellenistic association, a variant on symposia, were societies in which members would dine and patronize recitals (perhaps a kind of early dinner theater). It is possible that other Hellenistic cities may also have developed additional innovative commons in this period.

In ancient Greek culture and during the Hellenistic period in particular, another form of association familiar to modern readers was developed and refined: military federations or leagues of cities were a common feature known to the Greeks and used for common defense. It was from such a league, for example, that Pericles purloined the funds used for the Athenian Acropolis. Another multicity association, known as the *Delphic amphictyony,* long served as an international panel that controlled the affairs of the shrine of Apollo, home of the famous oracle of Delphi, with its power to declare sacred wars (Hornblower, 1986). Such leagues took on renewed importance with the decline of Athens as the single most powerful center of Greek culture.

The ancient Greeks appear to have had a broad and subtle grasp of the potentials and possibilities of commons and common goods and applied their knowledge to a broad variety of situations. Ancient Greece also represents an important historical point of evolution from the prehistoric commons to the modern association. An important, but largely unanswered, question is whether the Homeric Greeks developed the basis of Greek commons on their own or learned them from other earlier cultures.

Rome

While cities from Ur to Athens incorporated common elements from the very earliest times, perhaps no city in human history is more reflective of the range and diversity of the commons than is Rome. From the days when it was the center of the Roman Empire, through its medieval role as the center of Christianity, and down to the present day, Rome is a city built on grants (Boulding, Pfaff, and Hovrath, 1972). It is also a city in which leisure figured importantly (Balsdon, 1969).

Rome constitutes a unique exception to generalizations about the economic basis of city life. Rome was never at any point in its history an important manufacturing or trading center (Girouard, 1985). The economic foundations of the city have, from the earliest times, been built on tribute and devotion, donations and pilgrimages, and the "unrelated business income" of the farms and factories of imperial and papal holdings. "Its dual role as the capital of western Christendom and the successor of Imperial Rome made [the medieval and modern city] a center for politics, finance, education, science, art, archaeology, tourism, entertainment and pleasure, as well as religion" (Girouard, 1985, p. 132). In Rome, perhaps more than in any other city, the commons holds the dominant position over market, state, and (due to the large number of influential celibate religious orders) the family.

Rome is as important as Greece for philanthropic, charitable, and other common innovations. Waltzing (1895–1900) produced a four-volume study of Roman associations and corporations. Medieval and modern Western fund-raising practice, built upon a Christian religious and ethical basis, originated in Rome. In A.D. 321, Constantine permitted donations and bequests to the church, and from then on substantial ecclesiastical endowments began to grow in the city and throughout Christian Europe.

In classical Rome, we see the evolution of a system of patronage quite different from the Greek pattern, a difference with implications for all of medieval Europe. In both aristocratic and democratic variations, Greek patronage stressed the "horizontal" obligations of the giver to peers. By contrast, the Roman emphasis, particularly during the Middle Era, was upon the "vertical" obligations of *clientela*, which stressed the obligations of the recipient to the giver. On this basis, clientela were to become traditional, often inherited relationships of dependence of one person on another and the principal integrating factor in Roman society of the Middle Republic (Crawford, 1986).

According to Gold (1987, p. 5), "Ancient and modern notions of patronage are quite different. There was indeed no one word in Greek or Latin for 'patron'; the Latin *patronus* means quite specifically an advocate or the former master of a freedman. A supporter of another man in any situation was often called simply . . . *amicus* [or friend]." Gold, whose principal interest is the analysis of literary and poetic patronage, notes also that an understanding of Roman politics is not possible without an understanding of the Roman concept of clientela.

Other important Roman innovations were the *annona civica* (civic foundations) and *fideocommisia* (trusts) that figure importantly in Roman law (Johnson, 1989). Roman trust law is an important, if not well understood, topic for contemporary nonprofit and voluntary action research for a number of reasons. German, French, and other European commons have grown up within the tradition of Roman law, while U.S. and British commons have grown up within the tradition of English common law (Anheier, 1990). Roman law is most important, however, as the base from which the religious commons of medieval Christianity evolved.

Purcell summarizes the role of the commons in Rome and the rest of the ancient world in this way:

> The reciprocal relations of benefaction, competition and prestige among those who controlled the resources of the ancient world are found throughout antiquity, from the aristocracies of the archaic Greek cities to the Roman Emperors. In these relations were included the whole range of ancient cultural activities, from architecture and utilitarian building to the patronage of literature, music, and painting—also to the entertainments of the circus and the amphitheatre and the religious festivals which were the setting of almost all of these forms of display. This characteristic aspect of ancient society produced a type of bond between the élite and the peoples of the cities which was unique— a major source of the stability and continuity which we associate with the Greek and Roman world.
>
> Unfortunately, ancient culture had never rid itself of its uneasy companion, warfare. In the end this aspect came to be dominant. . . . At that point the end of the ancient world was in sight. [1986, p. 590]

Arabic Civilization

It is conventional in American treatments of the development of Western civilization for a discussion of medieval civilization to follow directly after a discussion of ancient Greece and Rome. Most of us are only dimly aware of the Arabic urban cultures that arose out of the mixture of classical and Islamic influences in the Arabic world during the "Dark Ages" of Western Europe and made important contributions to logic, mathematics, science, and other fields (see, for example, Netton, 1991).

This civilization evolved distinctive forms of Arabic urbanism in a group of cities stretching from Marrakesh in the west to Baghdad in the east and from Cordoba in the north to Mecca in the south (Arberry, 1967; Hourani, 1991). This was a world of affluence and high culture and a world in which commons figure in important ways.

The urban centers of the Arabic world are a key link in the chain of commons stretching from the ancient worlds to the present. In general, however, the subject of the Arabic commons is too little understood and too little documented outside specialized scholarly circles to explore thoroughly here (Bishai, 1973; Blanchi, 1989). What is clear, however, is the impact of Islam on the Arabic commons. Indeed, two of the five pillars of Islam speak directly to common goods. One of these is the common institution of the pilgrimage, or sacrificial journey to a sacred or holy place for a purpose such as purification or enlightenment.

In the development of Islam, the city of Mecca (the hometown and base of the prophet Mohammed) rapidly emerged as the premier sacred site and has remained the focus of Islamic pilgrimages. Even today, Mecca remains closed to non-Moslems. The faithful Moslem who is affluent enough to afford it is expected to make at least one pilgrimage to Mecca in a lifetime. An Islamic (or other religious) pilgrimage meets all of the criteria of the commons, and is, in the context of world history, an important and distinctive form of common good. Yet there are no studies of the economics, social organization, history, or other aspects of the pilgrimage as a form of common action.

The second Islamic commons to be noted here is another of the pillars of Islam—the distinctive set of charitable practices associated with *zakat,* or Islamic charity. Closely related to this is the distinctive Islamic foundation, or *waqf* (Hourani, 1991; Coulson, 1978; McChesney, 1991; Simsar, 1940). Although the history of Islamic commons may be well known to Islamic scholars (the majority of whom write in languages not widely known in the West), scholarly study in English of this topic would represent a significant contribution to our further understanding of the commons in its full multicultural and historical context. What we do know suggests that more is to be found. Simsar (1940) discusses a waqf in Turkey that survived from the sixteenth into the twentieth century. Moreover, the waqf is not the only indication of common activity in Moslem countries. Al Din Khairi (1984) found evidences of gift exchanges among family and friends in modern-day Amman, Jordan. Daniel (1970) reviews modern American philanthropic efforts in the Middle East since 1820.

Medieval Europe

Several important types of commons are found in the history of medieval Europe. These include synods and conferences; cathedrals, monasteries, and universities as medieval commons within the dominant Christian civilization; chantries, or prayer groups; the medieval systems of charity; defense and sport organizations, the emergence of synagogues and Jewish communities as alternative commons in the same civilization; and gilds, fairs, and holidays.

Synods and Conferences

In contemporary religion, the term *synod* is used by some Protestant denominations (Lutherans, for example) to describe a commons that is both a league or association of associations (or congregations) and an annual conference held by members of the association for purposes of dialogue and debate. Other Protestant denominations have other terms for the same phenomenon. Methodists, for example, use the term *annual conference* to refer both to the annual convocation and the association of all those who convene. Within the Roman Catholic church, such convocations are much less frequent but serve similar purposes. The last Vatican Council was convened in the 1960s and is still famous (infamous, in some circles) for its revisions of doctrine and ritual.

The Christian precedent for such events was the remarkable series of assemblies held in Rome, Corinth, Nicea, Caesurea, and other Mediterranean cities in the earliest Middle Ages (Marty, 1959; Chadwick, 1990). At these convocations, the fundamental structures of the Christian biblical canon and the distinctive doctrines of

Christianity were agreed upon. It is a matter of faith for most Christians that these convocations were guided by divine inspiration. These assemblies, sometimes involving hundreds of participants, resemble modern religious, scientific, and professional conferences in many ways.

Christianity took shape as a coherent religious organization within the dialogue of these convocations. Even more remarkable to the modern analyst accustomed to thinking of early Christian congregations as small, beleaguered bands of the faithful is the fact that attendance at many of these synods numbered five hundred or more bishops or local leaders. These convocations are in all respects commons.

Cathedrals

By the eleventh century, the combined forces of urbanization and trade created sufficient concentrations of common wealth and architectural insight to enable Europeans to construct, maintain, and operate the Gothic cathedrals. These imposing edifices were not, for the most part, the product of states, like castles and palaces, nor utilitarian structures, like the marketplaces of Ghent and Flanders. They were essentially the product of private religious associations— the archdioceses of such cities as Canterbury, Rheims, and Paris. Indeed, the Gothic cathedrals of Europe may represent the most dramatic and concrete examples ever constructed of the expressive and presentational principles of the medieval commons.

A major cathedral is a much more complex organization than the simple assembly or membership association of a local parish. Medieval and modern cathedrals (which must incorporate associations devoted to preservation or restoration as well as other traditional organizations found in cathedrals) constitute a bewilderingly complex pattern of overlapping, competing, cooperating, and functionally specialized associations and groups. Societies devoted to the care and maintenance of many different altars, chapels and chantries; choirs; fundraisers; and gilds of the numerous crafts uniquely associated with cathedral construction (for example, stonemasons and makers of stained glass windows) are just a few of the many associations in the cathedral. Separate associations and gilds may also be responsible for staging particular festival or hol-iday observances; maintaining bells, musical instruments, banners, and flags; and overseeing crypts and cemeteries. Contemporary auxiliaries are devoted to conducting tours and giving historical lectures, and there is no reason to doubt that similar groups existed in the Middle Ages, particularly given the importance of cathedrals as destinations in medieval pilgrimages.

Medieval gilds, societies, and confraternities are voluntary associations to one degree or another and conform to the other criteria of the commons. Complexity and division of volunteer la-bor are as much characteristic features of organizations in cathedrals as they are of modern local governments. Because of this diversity, it is inaccurate to think of cathedrals as single organizations. The many associations affiliated with a cathedral resemble the nonprofit sector of an entire modern community more closely than they do an organization in the modern sense.

Furthermore, there is an important intergenerational aspect to cathedrals as commons. Many cathedrals (perhaps most) took fifty to one hundred years or longer to finance and construct. The last Gothic cathedral built, the National Cathedral in Washington, D.C., was completed in 1990, but construction was frequently halted until additional funds were raised. Murray (1986) traces campaigns for the construction of the French Troyes cathedral from the thir-teenth to the mid sixteenth century. Because the time needed to build a cathedral exceeds the working life (and frequently the entire life) of single individuals, enduring, intergenerational organiza-tions for training and apprenticeship are an essential characteristic of cathedral organizations.

Monasteries

The monastery is another type of medieval commons that was im-portant in the growing wealth and influence of medieval Christian-ity. The original Christian monastic movement among Coebic monks in the Egyptian desert and the solitary Celtic monks of fourth-century Ireland was largely individualistic in character. (*Coebic* is derived from the Greek *Koinos*, which means common [Lawrence, 1989].) Medieval monasticism gradually took on an increasingly communal organization, and through the eleemosynary practices endorsed first by Constantine, the great medieval monastic orders—Benedictine, Cluniac, Dominican, Franciscan, Jesuit, and others—were built. These orders amassed wealth unparalleled in private associations until the rise of the modern business corporation. Medieval monasteries may have controlled as much as one-third of the wealth of medieval Europe at one time (Gray, [1905] 1967).

Western monasticism did not develop indiscriminately. The orders displayed their own unique and distinctive patterns of organization and authority. Monastic order was premised upon rules, or constitutions, laid down by founders, which consisted of manuals of conduct such as the Rule of Benedict of Mercia or the Rule of St. Augustine, and the *patronus* of leaders (abbots) authorized to enforce the rules (Ross, 1974a).

Few monasteries functioned as independent associations. They were instead incorporated in complex leagues or federations of superior, subordinate, and equivalent institutions called *orders*. Quite similar patterns are evident in the organization of medieval Buddhist monasteries in Japan during roughly the same time period (Lohmann and Bracken, 1991).

The Cluniac order was founded on observation of the Rule of St. Benedict of Nursia. The Cluniac reformation began in A.D. 910 when Duke William I (the Pious) of Aquitaine endowed the monastery of Cluny in Burgundy. The Cluniac order is significant in part because of its role in the emergence of self-governing monastic communities. Duke William granted the land in perpetuity and said the monks were free to pick their abbot without secular influence (Previté-Orton, 1924–1936).

Monasticism as a social movement remains in a much diminished form today, in large part because of its active suppression by England, France, Germany, and other countries when they were rising as nation-states (Gray, [1905] 1967; Woodward, 1966).

Universities

A third major component of the medieval commons are the universities that began to become important in the twelfth century. Universities at Paris, Bologna, Oxford, Cambridge, and elsewhere were founded in this period and were devoted to learning and science within autonomous and self-governing communities. Medieval universities carried on common traditions in philosophy and science, with important connections to the Greek philosophical schools and the urban Moslem schools of Baghdad, Ahman, and other Arab cities (Hourani, 1991).

One of the medieval donative practices that holds a certain mythic importance among contemporary college faculty members is the practice at the University of Paris in the thirteenth century of students paying faculty directly for lectures. The organization of the University of Paris into faculties of theology, philosophy, law, and medicine is also important in the history of modern professions, and these professions are an important form of modern commons (Douglas, 1967).

Chantries

A unique form of medieval commons virtually unknown in the modern nonprofit, voluntary, philanthropic world was the *chantry*. Frequent, but ambiguous, references to chantries are scattered throughout the medieval historical literature. Sometimes the term is used to mean a specific association or group of monks devoted to the constant offering of mass or repetition of prayers (Warren, 1985). Other references are to specific rituals or observances (Lawrence, 1989), and in other cases, the term appears to refer to a place: a chapel or alcove devoted to prayers for specific individuals (Wood, 1955).

Modern students of commons will note at least two important characteristics of chantries: Many chantries took the form of highly specific and restricted endowments of particular monasteries, or even individual monks, not fundamentally unlike modern endowed chairs in universities. Such endowments came in many forms: outright gifts, revenues from particular properties, and the full range of feudal obligations. Secondly, chantries appear to have dealt with a range of philanthropic self-interest and altruism similar to modern motivations. Chantries were sometimes established out of very direct expressions of religious self-interest (to offer prayers for the souls of the founder or his family) and in other cases they were established for very broad conceptions of common good (prayers for universal peace or for the cessation of plagues; prayers for the souls of unbelievers everywhere).

Medieval Systems of Charity

Modern social welfare scholars are only beginning to fully understand the common organization of medieval charity. We can locate medieval systems of charity approximately at the convergence of Greco-Roman philanthropic practices and associations with Judeo-Christian ethics in the Middle Ages (Morris, 1986). Out of this convergence of values, a substantial network of distinctively medieval charities arose. This network included not only monastic hostels for the refuge of travelers and household almoners in castles and monasteries but also a broad range of urban charity associations.

Many of these associations were formed in reaction to specific plagues and epidemics or religious movements and survived for long periods of time by acquiring permanent endowments or by combining their charity work with a range of other social and recreational activities. For example, in Venice, a network of charitable confraternities, or *schuole,* grew up in the thirteenth century as an offshoot of the flagellant movement. Through bequests, many of the associations acquired large amounts of property, and by the fifteenth century, some were extremely rich. Each was affiliated with a church or religious house but eventually acquired its own buildings. Although they spent the majority of their income on charity, most had resources left over for feasting and pageantry (Girouard, 1985).

The associations were by no means restricted to Venice or Italy. The number and range of studies of medieval charity are growing steadily, and with these studies comes an increasingly complex picture of activity over longer and longer periods of time. Flynn's *Sacred Charity: Confraternities and Social Welfare in Spain 1400-1700* is a study of medieval and early modern charitable activities and lay religious culture among Spanish Catholics in the city of Zamora. Norberg (1985) examines relations between rich and poor residents of the French city of Grenoble over two centuries and gives particular attention to the charitable activities of residents.

Rubin (1987) examines demographic and economic factors underlying charity in Cambridge, England, and the forms in which it was
offered.

In an age when travel was often difficult and dangerous,
giving hospitality, food, and shelter to travelers was afforded a
much higher status as a charitable endeavor than it currently enjoys.
Heal (1990) explores changes in the ideals and practice of the social
virtue of hospitality from 1400 to 1700. Medieval monasteries, in
particular, frequently extended hospitality to travelers.

Another of the components of charity in the medieval period
were organized responses to the social consequences of urban
plagues and epidemics. Shortly after 1350, for example, the Black
Death cut the population of Florence roughly in half (Girouard,
1985). Other estimates suggest that the Black Death may have reduced the entire population of Europe by 25 percent in a single year.

Defense and Sport Organizations

Some of the more unusual commons in medieval Europe were the
"tower societies" in Italian cities in the twelfth century. These associations consisted of families living together in neighborhood
complexes of buildings and bound together by articles of association that specified how the complex was to be shared.

The first such articles of clan association date from 1177.
Many clan associations constructed private towers (essentially urban castles) for defensive purposes. These groups constituted *protective associations* as that term is used in Chapter Six, and are at
least distantly related to modern street gangs. At one time, the phenomenon was widespread on the Italian peninsula. In Bologna, for
example, there is evidence of the existence of nearly two hundred
such towers built between the twelfth and fifteenth centuries (Girouard, 1985).

The articles of association of Italian tower societies may represent a much broader phenomenon of explicit social contracts for
protection and mutual aid drawn up by local communities. One
would expect to find similar artifacts for the Hanseatic League and
autonomous city-states, for example. In the United States, the line
from the Mayflower Compact to the modern suburban neighbor-

hood association is clear and direct. Such local associations are not limited to the West. In the sixteenth century, Confucian scholars in Korea advanced the science and art of public administration by codifying traditional understandings of village and clan association into "village codes" that included explicit provision for social welfare (Hahm, 1991).

Archery companies of the civil militia used common grounds near city walls to practice with longbows (often under the patronage of St. Sebastian) or crossbows (under the patronage of St. George) (Girouard, 1985). The Society of the White Bear originated in Bruges in 1320 as a jousting society. Jousting was the most expensive and prestigious sport of the Middle Ages. Another Bruges society, the Poortersloge was, "in modern terms, the Polo Club as well as the Conservative Club of Bruges" (Girouard, 1985, p. 98). It was also not unusual for medieval bridges to be built with donated funds, and they sometimes contained chapels, complete with a staff of priests, and were maintained either by endowments or collections of user fees (Girouard, 1985).

Inevitably, the patterns of donation and the duration of foundations in Roman law meant that the Church eventually became the biggest property owner in every medieval European city. And by the late Middle Ages, endowed ecclesiastical buildings were the finest and most impressive in most cities (Girouard, 1985). It was this pattern of economic hegemony that was a principal target of emerging nation-states, beginning in the sixteenth century. Henry VIII's seizure of English monastic properties in 1538 was only the best known of several major conflicts between the state and medieval commons that signaled the end of medieval commons, per se. Henry also seized monastic properties in Ireland (Bradshaw, 1974). Monastic property was also seized in France, Germany, China, and elsewhere at various points. The takeover of Buddhist monastic properties by the Japanese government in the Meiji Restoration of 1868 may well have been the latest example of a worldwide trend toward supremacy of the nation-state over the medieval commons (Lohmann and Bracken, 1991).

However, the pattern of the medieval Christian commons was more complex than simply official Church ownership of properties. Some of the more fascinating and variegated commons were the various Christian lay organizations that were formed for diverse charitable purposes. In medieval Bruges, these organizations took the form of communes. Girouard (1985, p. 92) describes these communes as "the distinctive settlements of the Beguines and the Bogards, communities of poor spinsters or bachelors working together at spinning or weaving under a religious rule. . . . [T]he outer areas were, on the whole, the poor ones, and as a result the hospitals, almshouses and pawnshops were to be found there." In a somewhat similar vein, Bilinkoff (1989) discusses the economic and social history of sixteenth-century Avila in Castile as a center for many influential religious mystics and reformers. Like modern social movements, medieval communes frequently combined the major features of a commons with shared residential living. More typical than such communes were religious confraternities of middle- and upper-class members of the laity.

Commoners were as active, if on a smaller scale, as members of the upper classes in forming, rebuilding, or enlarging foundations. Many chapels were dedicated to the use of gilds, fellowships, and other organizations or to the saying of masses for individuals who were usually buried in them. The bequests of these individuals endowed a variety of functions, for it was accepted that education, health, and everything else that today would be put under the heading of social services were the province of the Church. (Girouard, 1985). Some hospitals (the label itself is a generic medieval term for charitable institutions of all types) were run by lay confraternities such as the Order of the Holy Spirit. The order was founded by Guy de Montpellier in the late twelfth century and endorsed shortly thereafter by Pope Innocent III, who gave it a headquarters in the hospital of Sto Spirio in Sassia in Rome (Girouard, 1985).

Russell-Wood (1968) divides medieval associations into two categories: artisan groups and confraternities. Artisan groups (*jurés, scuole,* or *Zünsste*) served primarily as professional or craft associations. The first are the famous medieval gilds. Members were obliged to attend mass in the group's church and the annual celebrations in honor of the patron saint, according to Russell-Wood. Mutual aid to members might include dowries or alms, and some groups maintained their own hospitals. Confraternities, by contrast, were for members of all classes who wished to perform acts of charity. Confraternities were governed by boards of elected directors who served one-year terms, and benefits to the needy might include dowries, alms, prison aid, hospital treatment, or burial. Some confraternities specialized in a single function, such as the confraternity of St. Leonard at Viterbo, which operated a famous Portuguese hospital, or the confraternity of St. Giovanni Decollato of Florence, which specialized in accompanying condemned people to the scaffold and burying their bodies. Such medieval confraternities operating under the generic name of *misericordia* were imported to Brazil and other Portuguese colonies in Central and South America in the fifteenth and early sixteenth centuries (Russell-Wood, 1968).

Synagogues and Jewish Communities

Any picture of medieval commons would be incomplete without considering the role of medieval European Jews. Throughout the history of Western civilization, Jewish congregations existed as independent commons in Europe and the Middle East, with none of the official stature or broad cultural support of Christian churches or Moslem mosques and often in the face of official opposition, hostility, and active anti-Semitism (Goldberg and Rayner, 1989). The synagogues of both Christian and Moslem medieval cities were clearly private, nonprofit endeavors. Further, the Jewish communities supporting these synagogues are major examples of the concept of the commons as it is used in this book.

Jewish schools and institutes were found in many cities and were supported by patrons in a manner similar to Greek philosophical schools and early Christian and Moslem ones. In one of these schools in Cordoba, a twelfth-century Jewish scholar, Maimonides, was responsible for codification of an eight-level hierarchical classification of "degrees of charity" (Cass and Manser, 1983). Comparative study of the eleemosynary schools of Greece and Rome; the Moslem, Christian, and Jewish schools of the Middle Ages; and similar schools found in the Jain, Confucian, Hindu, and Buddhist religious traditions should yield important insights into the universal and historical qualities of commons.

Fairs and Holidays

One of the seeming anomalies of the contemporary classification of nonprofit corporations in most state law and tax policy in the United States is the inclusion of fairs, carnivals, and festivals as nonprofit activities. Even more curious to the modern eye may be the suggestion that holidays and the organized activities associated with them, such as Carnivale in Rio and Miami or Mardi Gras in New Orleans, also constitute commons (Orloff, 1980). Neither suggestion would have appeared at all unusual in medieval times, which were filled with all manner of fairs, festivals, pageants, and celebrations.

Fairs, carnivals, and festivals were often associated with market days in medieval Europe. The right to hold a market or fair was one of the most valuable privileges acquired by religious institutions in medieval cities (Girouard, 1985). Several of the religious houses of medieval Paris were granted the right to hold fairs by French kings. One of the most famous and longest lasting of French fairs was the six-week Foire de St. Germain, held by the Abby of St. Germain-des-Pres. It acquired its own permanent buildings and, like most fairs, had its own court and jurisdiction during its six-week run (Girouard, 1985).

The economic importance of medieval fairs is well known. Braudel (1986a, 1986b) argues that the entire system of long-term trade in the medieval economy of Europe at one time hinged upon a circuit of annual fairs held in the Champagne valley. In the thirteenth century, the twice-annual arrival of the Genoese and Venetian fleets into the ports of Bruges and Flanders brought about the decline of the Champagne fairs (Girouard, 1985).

Fairs were also typically associated with feast days. They were thus occasions for miracle plays, football matches, horse races, tournaments, animal fights, fireworks, clowns, jugglers, processions, and banquets (Girouard, 1985).

Many traditional medieval festivals continued in most European cities into the eighteenth century. Indeed, some, such as the Pallio in Ciena, have continued to the present. Fairs, such as St. Bartholemew's in London, gradually became more important as recreation and leisure activities as their commercial significance declined. Eventually, "puppet shows, plays, rope-walkers, wax-works, menageries, fire-eaters, jugglers, and Punch and Judies took over," giving the term *fair* its current meaning (Girouard, 1985, p. 184).

Examination of modern holidays should not be limited just to the standard set of days off from work. Uncommercialized religious holidays (such as Good Friday, Passover, Ramadan, or Kwanzaa), national holidays observed by ethnic groups (for example, Latvian Independence Day, Simon Bolivar's birthday), and other similar common group observances probably reflect more clearly than legal holidays the significance of holidays as defining events in the constitution of commons.

Gilds

Gilds and religious confraternities were among the most widely distributed forms of voluntary association in the Middle Ages (Ross, 1983). Thrupp (1965) sees the history of gilds as important to three separate issues that still concern nonprofit, voluntary, and philanthropic studies: (1) whether freedom to associate is an inherent right or a concession of the state; (2) the role of gild-type associations in transcending kinship loyalties and what she terms "the elementary bonds of kinship" (p. 184); and (3) the nonpolitical nature of social control exercised by gilds.

Thrupp compresses the long and complex development of medieval gilds into five phases.

Phase 1. In the early Middle Ages, associations in the "barbaric" kingdoms of northern Europe were allowed to function unchallenged by weak monarchies. Feud rather than royal authority was the principal source of compliance, and gilds functioned as protective associations and alternatives to lordship, by protecting property, discouraging violence, and offering mutual aid, common forms of worship, and decent burial to members.

Phase 2. Beginning with Charlemagne, monarchy and papacy both asserted claims as the sources of legitimacy of gild association. Free fraternal associations were permitted among the laity, while autonomous public authority in town government was permitted through explicit chartered concessions.

Phase 3. Towns eventually permitted the differentiation of citizen communities into occupational gilds serving both private and public ends. Gild officers emerged as semipublic officials (analogous, perhaps, to contemporary "community leaders" in the nonprofit community). The fund-raising activities of medieval gilds in supporting the cults of patron saints and major festivals represent an important connection between ancient liturgia and modern philanthropy.

Phase 4. In the sixteenth and seventeenth centuries, gilds became enmeshed in systems of state-regulated privilege, with noneconomic associations in Protestant states surviving only through sectarian organization. The gulf between artisan and mercantile gilds widened. Gild offices fell increasingly to merchant entrepreneurs and fraternities of wage workers were actively suppressed.

Phase 5. Between the seventeenth and nineteenth centuries, the system of gild organization died out in Europe. Voluntarily or through revolution, states abandoned systems of gild privilege and gilds either atrophied or were abolished. The fact that de Tocqueville observed the lively state of associations in the United States in this period, which followed the demise of the gilds and was prior to the rise of the vigorous European trade union movement, may account to some degree for the tone and direction of his observations.

It would be a mistake to assume that the mutual aid functions of the gilds disappeared entirely with the demise of the gild system. Voluntary mutual insurance funds such as those associated with ethnic mutual aid in the United States were also widespread in Europe by the end of the nineteenth century. They only disappeared with the advent of social insurance programs in the modern welfare states (deSwaan, 1986; Kropotkin, n.d.).

Byzantium

Prior to the division of Christianity into the eastern, or Byzantine, and western, or Roman, realms, the Byzantine Empire had already created some major commons. Possibly the single most impressive and inspiring Christian monument (now a mosque) was Santa Sophia in Constantinople, constructed in the early fourth century.

Also important in the transition from the ancient to medieval world was the empire of Byzantium controlled by Rome's challenger to the east, Constantinople. Usually noted in the social science literature only as a symbol of bureaucracy, the Byzantine Empire created an incredible range of philanthropic and charitable operations, including *gerocomeia* (homes for the aged), *xenones* (hospices), *ptocheia* (orphanages), *xenotapheia* (cemeteries), and homes for the blind and houses of correction for reforming prostitutes (Constantelos, 1968; Geanakoplos, 1985; Morris, 1986; Lewis, 1988). Some of the earliest evidence of specialized charitable institutions occurred within the Byzantine Empire. A renowned asylum was founded by St. Basil in Cappadocia in 369 C.E. It was said to be a miniature city, with special housing for each kind of need, including housing for blind people (French, 1932).

By the beginning of the fifteenth century, the Byzantine Empire was reduced to a city-state of less than 100,000 in Constantinople and its immediate surroundings. When the city was taken over by the Turks in 1453, there was a major transformation of its common institutions from Christian to Moslem by the Ottoman Turkish state. The name of the city was changed to Istanbul and large numbers of Greek residents were expelled and replaced by Turks from Anatolia. Markets were transformed into bazaars, and Christian religious buildings were converted to Moslem use.

Interestingly, strategic use of one of the central elements of the commons—the endowment (or the foundation, or trust fund)—was a major element in the radical transformation of the city. Much of the property in Istanbul was converted to religious endowments (*waqf* in Arabic, or *vakif* in Turkish) to support Islamic mosques, schools, and other institutions (Brunn and others, 1983; Runciman, 1967). The Waqfizah of 'Ahmed Pasa is a Turkish endowment of the sixteenth century that is said to have continued at least into the 1940s and that could conceivably still be in existence today (Simsar, 1940).

The Renaissance

The Italian Renaissance of the fifteenth century was brought about in no small measure by a dramatic upsurge in wealth because of increased trade by the Italian city-states and the eleemosynary transformations of considerable portions of that wealth into commons. Although the economic growth of Florence was less dramatic than that of Venice and Genoa, the Renaissance was an exceptional period in the history of Florence, in large part because of three generations of a single family of patrons (the Medicis) and their incredible list of clients (Acton, 1967).

The Medicis were not exclusively patrons of the arts. One of the architectural masterpieces of Renaissance Florence subsidized by Cosimo de' Medici is a children's home, the Ospedale degli Innocenti. In *Charity and Children in Renaissance Florence,* Pavitt (1990) argues that this facility came about partly because a shift in public opinion led rich Florentines to begin to give less to religious orders and more to institutions addressing specific social needs. Such private charity was already well known in Florence before the Renaissance. For several centuries prior to the Renaissance, the cities of northern and central Italy had been hotbeds for organizing lay confraternities. Venice, Milan, and Florence are said to have had hundreds of such confraternities (Hale, 1967; Russell-Wood, 1968).

Patronage of individual artists and charity were not the only forms of common activity of Renaissance Italy. Palisca (1989) discusses the Florentine Camerate, an informal interdisciplinary group that prefigures some of the royal societies and academies discussed later. The Camerate met in Florence during the latter part of the sixteenth century at the palace of the scholar and music patron Giovanni Bardi.

Reformation Europe

The transition from medieval to modern in the commons is not nearly as distinct and abrupt as similar transitions in states or markets. There is nothing in the history of the commons to correspond with the rise of the modern nation-state or the rise of capitalism and the industrial revolution. Nevertheless, transformations of the state and market left their mark upon the evolving commons, as did the Protestant Reformation, the Counter-Reformation, rationalism, science, humanitarianism, and the European conquest of the Americas. Common traditions of participation, shared purposes and resources, mutuality, and fairness reaching deep into the ancient and medieval worlds have been modified but not fundamentally transformed in the modern world.

The Protestant Reformation of the sixteenth century is often regarded more in terms of changed beliefs and religious values and changes in markets and states than in terms of its impact upon commons. Commons figure prominently in both the Protestant Reformation and the Catholic Counter-Reformation. While the emerging Lutheran, Calvinist, and Episcopal churches largely substituted one form of ecclesiastical authority for another, later groups, including the Puritans, Quakers, Anabaptists, and Methodists, contributed very directly to the evolution of group-centered common authority, whose implications for nonprofit and voluntary action are widely suggested but nowhere clearly explicated (Brinton, 1963).

Something of the emerging differences in commons can be seen in the contrast of Amsterdam and Rome in this period. Sixteenth-century Amsterdam was a Protestant city devoted primarily to commercial activity. The city had no monasteries, cathedral, great castle, university, or college of any great importance and the public squares were devoted primarily to commercial activity. Similarly, there were no jousts, masques, or giant processions on feast days. Yet Amsterdam exhibited a great deal of common activity, some of which illustrates the historical relationship of municipal institutions and the commons (Girouard, 1985). Among the associations of Amsterdam was the civic guard, a civilian militia that had grown out of medieval gilds of longbowmen and crossbowmen and that had taken on as much social as military significance by the sixteenth century.

When Amsterdam became officially Protestant in the seventeenth century, hospitals, orphanages, almshouses, prisons, schools, inns, and a lending bank that had been operated by religious orders came under control of the city council. The city council also handled food and fuel distribution to the poor and operated the house of correction. There were few beggars and little serious poverty in sixteenth-century Amsterdam. Solid sewage and garbage were collected by the city and sold for fertilizer, with revenues supporting the city orphanage (Girouard, 1985).

Counter-Reformation Rome offers a marked contrast with Amsterdam. Operas, plays, and other entertainments were frequent in lavish dinner parties at colleges and palaces. Since there were no permanent opera houses or theaters, public performances were staged on carts or platforms in the streets during feasts and festivals. Bullfights and tournaments took place in public squares. The Vatican library, one of the greatest libraries in the world, was freely available to all. There were no museums, but the collections that filled the galleries and courtyards of the villas were almost all open to visitors, as were the gardens of the villas. Antiquities donated to the Palazzo dei Conservatori formed an open collection, which was housed after 1645 in a building beside Michelangelo's courtyard and which became the world's first public museum (Girouard, 1985).

Rome has long been an important center for pilgrimages. During the sixteenth century, a number of new commons, hospitals and hospices, and at least seventeen confraternities were devoted to pilgrims. The number of pilgrims rose to new heights in the last decades of the century. In 1575, the number of pilgrims visiting Rome was probably about 400,000. By 1600, there were probably more than 500,000 pilgrims coming to Rome (Girouard, 1985).

Classicism and the Age of Reason

An important line of development in European commons was a social movement for founding academies and institutes. This movement provided much of the organizational basis for the Renaissance as well as the spread of science in the seventeenth century and the Age of Reason in the eighteenth century.

Academies of Art, Science, and Literature

During the fifteenth century, groups with an interest in classical literature and art began to meet in Italian cities and villas in the countryside. Many called themselves academies in self-conscious emulation of Plato's philosophical school. Members met to compose, write, and read their own poetry; read and discuss the classical authors; read addresses on ethics or other subjects; act plays; or perform music. Initially, these academies had no organization and no special buildings of their own. By the sixteenth century, they began to organize formally and develop rules. Membership grew, and some of the groups acquired buildings. Academies began to specialize in law, sculpture, painting, language, archeology, natural history, chemistry, and even "leisure arts" like fencing, riding, dancing, playing cards, and shooting. In the sixteenth and early seventeenth centuries, such academies spread throughout Europe and sometimes acquired powerful patrons. Kings and rulers began to take an interest in the academy movement and to patronize what thus became "royal academies."

Academies or societies for the cultivation and development of German and French culture were set up in 1617 and 1635, respectively. Louis XIV of France became a major founder of academies. He founded the Académie de Danse in 1661; the Académie de Musique, which was in effect a royal opera company, in 1666; the Académie Royale des Inscriptions et Belles Lettres in 1663; the Académie Royale de Peinture in 1667; the Académie Royale des Sciences in 1666; and the Académie de l'Architecture in 1671.

Anyone familiar with the development of modern science is aware of the role of academies and scientific societies in early scientific research in physics, chemistry, and biology. In the seventeenth century, Rome, Paris, and London became major centers of academies of scientific research and discovery. An informal scientific academy, the Accademia dei Lincei, was founded in Rome in 1603 but collapsed after Galileo's prosecution by the Inquisition in 1632.

The associational character of such academies in many different societies and cultures is unmistakable (Ellsworth, 1991). The French Académie des Sciences gave royal patronage to a group of scientists including Descartes and Pascal. Similarly, the Royal Society for Improving Natural Knowledge was founded in London in 1660 and given a charter by Charles II in 1662 on the basis of an informal group that was first organized in London in 1645 (Girouard, 1985, pp. 206–208). Lux (1989) traces the brief history of the

Académie de Physique de Caen, a scientific institution founded in 1662 but forced to close in 1672.

European academies and royal societies of architecture also exercised important influences on urban design in the eighteenth century. L'Enfant's original plan for the Washington Mall, for example, called for it to be "a place of general resort . . . all along side of which may be placed play houses, rooms of assembly, accademies and all such sort of places as may be attractive to the learned and afford diversion to the idle" (Girouard, 1985, p. 253). Hauptman's plan for rebuilding Paris and the Ringstrasse in Vienna are other examples of the same trend.

Commons in the Americas

Little is currently known of the commons of the indigenous populations of the Americas before the arrival of the Europeans and their African slaves. As discussed earlier, what we do know is intriguing. Aztec and Maya societies may have incorporated a variety of leisure class groups and occupations. Among the Maya, in particular, these groups appear to have achieved subtle and sophisticated knowledge in astronomy, mathematics, and other fields. Pueblo life in the North American Southwest incorporated sodalities as well as clans based on kinship (Hill, 1970). Among plains and woodlands peoples, bands were organized into confederations and both were treated as voluntary membership organizations, open to all (Brandon, 1961).

No one avenue of dissemination single-handedly explains the remarkable growth of the American commons in the centuries following the European colonization. The Portuguese imported confraternities (misericordia) to Brazil in the late sixteenth century (Russell-Wood, 1968). Scottish immigrants to Boston formed the first ethnic mutual aid society in 1657, initiating a trend that continues today for virtually every ethnic, racial, or nationality group (Bremner, 1988; Trattner, 1989). A French religious order founded the first American orphanage in New Orleans in 1718 (Trattner, 1989). Residents of Williamsburg, Virginia, and Philadelphia founded early mental hospitals (Trattner, 1989).

Indeed, what de Tocqueville ([1862] 1945) observed in the

1840s was at least partly the result of the transplanting of traditional European commons to the New World. This process occurred in two distinct ways. First, immigrants of all types brought with them traditional patterns of ecclesiastical organization and mutual aid. Thus, Puritans, Quakers, Anabaptists, Catholics, and the people of other religions coming to America followed established organizational principles and practices. Indeed, the ability to do so was one of the much-remarked-upon (and sometimes overstated) qualities of life in the New World.

Throughout the colonial period and well into the nineteenth century, a number of important commons in the Americas were shaped by conscious emulation of European models. Spanish and Portuguese colonists in Central and South America sought to found cities on European models (Picon-Salas, 1971). New England Puritans, Virginia planters, and Dutch colonists in New York and New Jersey all adopted church-based relief committees as the basis of colonial welfare systems. Only gradually did the New England Puritan towns move to more civil welfare administration. Although religious voluntary associations date from the earliest settlement of New England, more secular associations of charitable and mutual aid societies, fire brigades, lodges, and professional societies emerged later, mainly in Boston (Brown, 1973).

Throughout the nineteenth century, Boston Brahmins, southern planters, emergent community elites in most communities, and finally the newly rich plutocrats of the industrial age consciously emulated European aristocratic models in a number of important ways. One of the most interesting for this study is the deliberate emulation of beau monde patronage in the manner that dates back to the Athenians. This nineteenth-century emulation of European models is the point of origin of many "class" (as opposed to "mass") aspects of contemporary commons. One of the most obvious is the two-tier approach to fund raising, which emphasizes different approaches to large and small donors.

Such elite practices probably seemed both ordinary and unworthy of comment to de Tocqueville. The aspect of commons in the United States that this French aristocratic observer found most fascinating was the vast extension of the participation, patronage, and social action of the commons to the middle and lower classes.

Both the phenomenon and de Tocqueville's reaction to it are thoroughly understandable in hindsight.

The Protestant political culture of the early United States, with its emphasis on individual initiative and private action and its lack of the many complex institutional layers of the *ancien regime,* must have provided nearly ideal conditions for the proliferation of independent common associations. The chronic labor shortages of the colonial era meant relatively high wages for workers, who as a result would have had both disposable income and leisure time to devote to common action. Yet these contextual conditions do not themselves explain the democratization of the commons observed by de Tocqueville.

For this we need only look to the English, Scotch, Irish, German, Dutch, and other northern Europeans who made up the majority of U.S. residents in the areas visited by de Tocqueville. Most nineteenth-century U.S. residents immigrated from cultures with broad repertories of associational and common practices not only for the elites but also for the middle class. Culturally, these immigrants were already armed with many organizational skills that they could call upon as needed. From the very start these skills were used in organizing fire companies, mutual aid societies, local governments, and an array of other associations (Brown, 1978). Later, the religious fervor of the Great Awakening and the patriotic fervor of the American Revolution combined to call forth these organizing skills.

Closely related to this was the rapid growth during the revolutionary period of a number of anti-Calvinist religious sects that emphasized democratic equality rather than the election of the few (Brown, 1971). During much of the nineteenth and early twentieth centuries, fraternal organizations serving both civic and quasi-religious functions were an important means of social integration for the middle and lower classes, particularly in predominantly rural areas (McWilliams, 1973). They have since diminished considerably in importance (Babchuk and Schmidt, 1976, 51).

Into this environment, de Tocqueville came as an observer from a culture that remained heavily Catholic and statist, and whose citizens were relatively inexperienced in the skills of the commons. The French Revolution had actually brought an outright ban on

private associations, and that ban remained in effect into the twentieth century. (The reader may recall from Chapter Two how few
references there are to French associations, and that all of those mentioned are either royal or aristocratic in nature.) Small wonder that
what de Tocqueville saw struck him as novel and unprecedented.

The growth of commons in the middle and lower classes is
also clear and traceable in the phenomenon of voluntary cemetery
associations. The New Haven Burying Ground in Connecticut,
created in 1796, was the first voluntary, nonprofit cemetery company. Mount Auburn Cemetery, founded on seventy-two acres ten
miles outside of Boston in 1831, incorporated a planned landscape
of lakes, winding roads, and vistas in a setting that appealed to the
American sense of the picturesque (Biemiller, 1991; Sloane, 1991).

Polite Society

A status revolution in seventeenth-century European cities that has
had important implications for the development of the modern
commons was the emergence of the distinctive socioeconomic leisure class known as "polite society," beau monde, or "the elite"
(sometimes simply "society"). Consisting essentially of loose associations (communities) of the idle rich, society in this sense assumed
important roles in defining standards of taste and trends in fashion
in the emerging urban marketplace. Courtiers, land-owning families residing in the city, and "the urban establishment"—wealthy
businessmen, lawyers, judges, and others—made up the core of society in most European cities. The resulting informal association
was tremendously important for the shops, clubs, racecourses, coffeehouses, theaters, restaurants, and other commercial establishments its members frequented.

Members of European society gradually took on roles reminiscent of the Greek aristocrats discussed earlier in their sponsorship and patronage of philanthropic and charitable projects for the
entire community. Newly emerging economic and commercial
elites in American cities since the nineteenth and early twentieth
centuries self-consciously modeled themselves on the European
beau monde and in this way set down patterns of behavior and

expectations that continue to exercise major influences on fundraising, the composition of boards of directors, and special events.

Modern fund-raising theory is, to a considerable extent, built upon the model of beau monde society. A successful fund-raising campaign is expected, for example, to identify a chair who is a member of elite society and willing to solicit donations from other members (Seymour, 1966). One of the most distinctive common institution of society in many contemporary communities is the charity ball. Indeed, the debutante ball or cotillion at which young women are "presented" to society is still conducted in several U.S. communities. Debutante balls are, at least nominally, charitable events (however, see Odendahl, 1989). *Town and Country* magazine features a regular monthly listing of such events in U.S. cities.

The contemporary commons in the United States is still a peculiar blend of the beau monde influences, which de Tocqueville must have found so ordinary as to not require comment, and the associations of the ordinary citizens that drew his special attention.

Conclusion

From Homeric Greece to contemporary America, the history of Western civilization offers a continuous parade of many different types of commons, some of which were discussed in this chapter. Two things should be evident from this cursory historical overview. First, common institutions and associations, such as liturgia, symposia, gymnasia, and philosophical academies, were as characteristic of ancient Greece as of modern Los Angeles. It may be as accurate to hypothesize common behavior (religious enthusiasm, perhaps) in the ancient world of Babel, Ur, and Egypt as it is to attribute the construction of ziggurats and pyramids to oppressive totalitarian rulers. In Roman law, in Byzantine and Arabic cities, in medieval Europe, and in the practices of diverse ethnic groups immigrating to the Americas, we find many manifestations of what is a continuous and unbroken aspect of Western civilization.

Second, in almost all of its divergent European and American branches, Western civilization is characterized as much by donation, association, foundation, and other manifestations of commons as it is by the institutions of market, state, or family. And whether through diffusion or indigenous development, other civilizations that have come into contact with the West (most notably the Arabic civilization) also show clear evidences of their own common institutions.

Much work remains to be done in presenting a more complete historical portrait of the type called for by the Interdisciplinary Voluntary Action Task Force in 1972. Fortunately, much of the necessary evidence for at least a schematic view is already scattered throughout the existing body of historical writing, and the initial challenge is to extract the information.

4

The Varieties
of Common Action

We make associations to give entertainments, to found seminaries, to build inns, to construct churches, to diffuse books, to send missionaries to the antipodes; in this manner, we found hospitals, prisons, and schools.

—Alexis de Tocqueville

Numerous commentators have observed the relative absence of social theories of nonprofit and voluntary action beyond the level of simple description. For example, in their review of voluntary association literature, Smith and Freedman (1972, p. 1) concluded that "the term theory has to be applied to the study of voluntary associations with care, since very little theory, in any strict sense of the word, has yet been developed in the field. There is no grand, all encompassing, and generally accepted theory of voluntarism, or even a respectable middle range theory." Regrettably, this assessment is still largely true today, although a number of additional provocative hypotheses, definitions, and propositions have been advanced in the interim.

Unfortunately, too many of these hypotheses continue to be guided by an oversimplified metaphor of profitable exchange that is characterized by utilitarian exchange, dualistic transactions between benefactors and beneficiaries, very narrow and short-term notions of self-interest, and simplistic cost-benefit calculations. In the remaining chapters of this book, I will attempt to build an alternative conception of social exchange as it relates to the central issues of social organization, the state, the economics of common goods, and charity.

Benefactories and Social Exchange

I have suggested benefactories as the characteristic form of organized endeavor in the commons and have identified three principal roles in the commons (donor/patron, beneficiary/client, and intermediary/agent). And I have suggested repeatedly that the positive consequences (benefits, or common goods) arising out of beneficiary action draw upon the resources of the society or community (in the quite distinct forms of surplus wealth and leisure and the cultural heritages of accumulated civilization).

It remains now to ask, on what basis do organized benefactories arise out of the spontaneous behavior of any of the individuals involved? More specifically, Why do people organize commons? Why do they create formal organizations? Why do they create legal organizations?

Why Organize?

Why would reasonable people who were members of families; were able to buy and sell in the marketplace; and were assured of at least minimal affluence, protection, and civil order by the state be interested in engaging in the social action of the commons? For the simplest answer to this question, I turn to the definition of a commons offered in Chapter Two: an aggregate or plurality of persons, aware of shared interests or purposes, might wish to associate with one another to discuss the depth and range of their common interest; to pool their resources (whether to use the resources directly in furthering their common purposes or to seek additional resources); to reinforce or sustain their feelings of mutuality; or to establish procedures assuring fair treatment of one another.

Overall, the most satisfactory single answer to the question of why people would organize a commons is simply that they wish to associate with one another for some particular reason. Thus, the terms *associate* and *association* are probably the best general descriptors of the process of common organization. If people join together informally and without the benefit of any affiliation agreements or formal rules, we would ordinarily characterize their association as a group. Such characterizations cover not only peer, friendship, mutual aid, and support groups and other elementary associations but also many other types of informal organization occurring within work settings and bureaucratic organizations.

We might further inquire as to why it is that people wish to associate with others. One widely held answer is that people associate because it is profitable (in terms of gains, benefits, or satisfactions) for them to do so. Such explanations are frequently useful, as in the case of business firms and their nonprofit analogs. In the case of commons, however, profit-oriented explanations are usually atomistic and reductionistic; they reduce the central fact of association (which is inherently interactional) to a set of unrelated, individual motives—and in the process dissolve the very thing that is to be explained. Further, in the case of benefactories as defined here, such an approach is nonexplanatory, because it implicates the original definition: persons associating in benefit-conferring associations are motivated by the desire to confer benefits. Finally, the range of gains, benefits, and satisfactions evident in commons is so vast and diverse that reducing them to a single impulse of any type seems arbitrary and unsatisfactory.

The question of why people associate in commons is probably beyond the scope of conventional social science inquiry. It is ultimately part of the larger philosophical issue of what it means to be human. To the extent they are relevant, explanations grounded in gains, benefits, or satisfactions can be subsumed within a larger class of explanations in terms of problem-solving and presentation as discussed in Chapter Seven.

Why Create a Formal Organization?

Even in those cases where satisfactory answers are forthcoming as to the question of why people associate, there is still the related question of why any group of people voluntarily sharing a sense of common purpose, common resources, and a sense of mutuality and fairness would find it necessary to formalize their relationship. What circumstances would make members of a group sufficiently dissatisfied with the present level of organization of their group to change it into a more formal association? A formal organization may be said to be an association with one or more of the following traits: formal affiliation procedures, whether in the form of memberships, dues, or any other form of distinction between participants and nonparticipants; a formal division of labor and accompanying status differentiation; and written, stated, or agreed-upon rules for common action.

Participants might choose to associate formally for a number of reasons. They might seek to advance or publicly affirm their common interest or purpose, whether to proclaim their identification with it, to seek to attract others to join with them, or for some other mutually agreed-upon purpose. They might also choose to associate formally because some aspect of less-formal interaction may prove problematic (for example, the relationship between the group leader and another participant chosen to act as leader in his or her temporary absence). They may choose a formal association to prevent or deal with false claims of membership or participation by nonmembers that are detrimental to the group's interests or purposes. Furthermore, they may wish to prevent or minimize misunderstandings about the interpretation of shared purposes (for example, the doctrinal and theological controversies of religious groups) and about the handling of shared resources (for example, the management of dues and shared facilities). Or they may formalize rules and roles to create or enhance a patina of authority for justice where none otherwise may exist. When associates bring with them clear shared models of status and authority, no formal structure may be needed to resolve such practical questions as speaking order, veto powers, and so on. For example, the eldest, best-educated, or most powerful member or the best hunter may by mutual consent carry the greatest authority. However, when (as in new groups) such norms may not yet have been fashioned or (as in pluralist groups) two or more equally plausible but conflicting norms exist, formal ratification of agreed-upon rules may be the wisest course.

When the decision is made to formally organize, some arrangements must also be made for formalizing the informal leadership of an association. The most common term for the formalized leadership group of any type of commons today is the *board of directors,* a term derived from the corporate model. Inherent in formalizing the division of labor is the problem of oligarchy, which we might think of as the creation of a preferred, more selective, or narrowly defined commons within an existing commons. To some analysts, the problem of oligarchy is inevitable (Michels, 1949).

Why Incorporate?

Why would any group that already had formal affiliation, a formal division of labor, and stated rules seek the additional step of legal incorporation or other similar legal protections or state sanctions such as in the Islamic waqf? This question has two general answers. First, the social bonds of mutuality or affiliation may not be sufficiently strong or satisfactory in all cases. Thus, less-trusting affiliates of an association who are unconvinced of the protections of the association's own operating rules may demand the additional protection of the nondistribution constraint. Second, members of the group may desire a relationship or status (tax exemption, a grant, or contract) with some external entity that is conditional upon legal incorporation. For example, for a large number of existing nonprofit social service agencies, incorporation was a necessary precondition to qualifying for various grant programs from which they seek funds.

The characteristics of a commons—uncoerced participation, shared purposes and resources, mutuality, and fairness—can be manifested at any level of organization: informal association, formal association, or incorporation. Thus we can expect to find related commons at any of these levels.

A Partial Typology of Benefactories

It is an easily observable social fact that people do choose to associate with one another in benefactories of all types. One approach, there-

fore, would be to set forth at least a partial inventory of different
types of easily observed benefactories. The discussion that follows
makes no claim of being exhaustive. Yet it is clear from reviewing
the items that the range of benefactories goes well beyond the usual
categories of voluntary association and nonprofit organization as
those two terms are ordinarily understood and includes many other
types of social organization, collective behavior, and gathering.

Associations

By far, the most widespread form of organized commons is the
association. An *association* is any group of persons not related by
kinship ties, not engaged in profitable exchange (buying and selling from one another), and not engaged in the exercise of coercive
control who affiliate, join together, or regularly interact with one
another in some organized or predictable manner. Thus, in the
broadest sense, a business firm is also a type of association. In the
firm, however, the shared objective of profit seeking may lead participants to place constraints on nonowner participation, limit
sharing of purposes and resources, substitute a labor-management
hierarchy for mutuality, or discount fairness as an element of social
relations. Therefore, we are only concerned in what follows with
associations demonstrating all five characteristics of commons.

Common associations are called groups, clubs, societies, and
many other labels. According to Finley (1974b, p. 32) "Obviously,
no single word will render the spectrum of *koinoniai*. At the higher
levels, 'community' is usually suitable, at the lower perhaps 'association', provided the elements of fairness, mutuality and common
purpose are kept in mind." The "krewes" (clubs) of costume and
float makers who constitute the traditional backbone of Mardi Gras
in New Orleans and Carnivale in Rio are clearly associations, as are
the Pueblo kachina societies, the pan bands of Trinidad, inner-city
and suburban "pickup bands" of musicians, and street gangs
(Grady, 1991).

Agencies

For purposes of the theory of the commons, an *agency* is an association in which volunteer or employed agents, who are usually not

members of the patron class, are designated by patrons or their representatives (for example, a board of trustees or a designated staff) to act for the benefit of clients, who are also generally not members of the patron class (Kramer, 1966, 1981). Agencies carry out their actions without fees, user charges, or other revenues from clients metering the level of the activities.

Legally, agency is action on behalf of another (Fama and Jensen, 1983). In this sense, most state nonprofit laws enable boards of directors to employ paid agents to conduct their affairs (Oleck, 1980). In a social agency, the legal notion has been generalized and institutionalized into a commons of patrons, agents, and clients. The organized social agency as commons encompasses a structured set of relations between patrons, clients, and paid staff intermediaries that emphasizes the dual roles of intermediaries as agents of patrons and trustees for clients. The agency as a social organization is defined by the unique nature of authoritative communication and dialogue between these classes of participants that results from such dual responsibilities. As a communications network, the typical social agency can be construed as a "node" linking two distinct "information streams." In social agencies, conversations and information regarding client needs, wants, and desires intersect with various information regarding available and esoteric resources for solving problems and improving the life of clients (Lohmann, 1990b).

The conventional, indeed archetypal, form of social agency is *group trusteeship*, in which the agency operates for a stated common good under the control of a group of trustees. This is the normative model of agency assumed by most nonprofit corporation statutes, the "stewardship" assumption of nonprofit accounting, and the assumption in the IRS tax-exemption process. Recent research evidence, however, suggests that this model may be honored more in the breach than in the observance (Middleton, 1987).

The model of group trusteeship requires a board of directors, entrusted with the management of the affairs of the organization, and implies a constituency, or community, of interested others to whom the board is, in some manner, accountable. The role of the principal paid agent, principal operating official, or staff director receives minimal attention in the traditional model. This is in glaring contradiction with the realities of the managerial revolution that has occurred in the nonprofit world in recent decades.

One of the more challenging issues of conventional organizational analysis in nonprofit and voluntary studies involves the proper treatment of nonprofit corporations that depart from the norm of group trusteeship. For example, the problem of organizational oligarchy made famous by Robert Michels ([1915] 1962) is one significant departure. The commons controlled by a single key decision maker is another (whether control is exercised by a board member or officer, executive director, principal patron, staff member, or even, conceivably, a client). Such key figures place themselves in a position that might be called *solo trusteeship*.

Achieving such a dominant position in a common organization is not always simply a matter of the exercise of power. Board members, staff members, clients, and others involved may simply acquiesce to such a locus of control rather than resisting or contesting it. In other instances, a high degree of interest and involvement on the part of a single individual, coupled with disinterest or apathy by others, can produce the same result. For whatever reasons, recent research has documented that solo trusteeship has become extremely pervasive in, perhaps even characteristic of, common agencies contracting with the state (Bernstein, 1991b; Herman and Van Til, 1988; Middleton, 1987).

It is increasingly difficult to simply dismiss solo trusteeship as a deviant and undesirable departure from the norms of association and governance. In fact, the history of modern social welfare reform (to take but one example) is punctuated by examples of such solo practitioners, often with spectacular results.

Possibly the single most widely known charitable institution of the present century is Hull House, founded by Jane Addams in Chicago in 1889. Addams (and her collaborator Ellen Gates Starr) did not found Hull House in the approved manner by forming a board of directors (Lohmann, 1990a). In fact, the settlement house was in operation for six years before a board of any type was formed; even then there is scant evidence in the minutes that the board considered more than a handful of program policy issues during Addams's lifetime.

Addams overturned the conventional wisdom regarding appropriate divisions of labor and terms of office by serving as treasurer, president *and* chief resident for ten years, and retaining the latter two titles continuously until her death in 1935. It seems somewhat presumptuous to conclude from this that Hull House was poorly managed and the suggestion that it was an ineffective organization simply lacks ordinary credibility. What seems more likely is that in Hull House we have a particularly dramatic and historically important case of a solo trusteeship. Just as in the case of less-celebrated instances, however, the facts of solo trusteeship do not fit our theories of the "proper" methods of organizing and running such an organization.

In examples large and small, the issue of nonprofit service organizations dominated by a single individual is, as Young (1987) suggests, partially an issue of entrepreneurship. It is also, as Bernstein (1991b) demonstrates, an arena in which many games must be played in order to reconcile the normative dissonances that arise. Yet in no sense can we summarily dismiss nonprofit corporations posing as nominal associations but controlled by a single individual or very small group of individuals as oddities, highly unusual, or socially undesirable. They are a phenomenon that deserves further serious study in their own right. Our theory must eventually catch up with the practice, rather than vice versa.

Campaigns

A campaign is another particular form of association characteristic of commons. A *campaign* can be defined as a time-limited, goal-oriented, single-purpose commons, in which a relatively small core of organized participants seek to reach out to and enlist the appropriate participation of a broader mass of potential participants (Van Vugt, 1991). Campaigns may be carried out for a bewildering variety of purposes. Medieval crusades were campaigns (Riley-Smith, 1991). So are certain other types of military action. Although military campaigns generally lack the degree of voluntarism usually associated with the commons, there are two important exceptions. Militia and all-volunteer armies and guerrilla and insurgency movements possess many but not all of the characteristics of common campaigns. Crusades and military actions are not generally the main concern here, however, since they represent rather extreme examples of the common tendencies of the campaign. Three other types of campaign are of much more central interest in examining the general social organization of commons: political, fundraising, and community organizing campaigns.

Campaigns are probably best known in contemporary terms as political and fundraising organizations. In politics, campaign organizations are often maintained separately from party organizations. In fundraising, the same tends to be true of capital campaigns and various other major fundraising ventures, including telethons, United Way campaigns, and so on (Van Doren, 1956).

General understanding of campaign organization is not well developed. Etzioni's (1968) analysis of the "active society" was a step in that direction. Campaigns typically involve the common pursuit of projects, or shared programs of action. Thus, civic improvement projects, reforms, and other similar ventures almost always take the structure of a campaign.

Although it may be customary to think of campaigns as organized subunits of formal organizations, there are other instances in which the formal organization (bureau, committee, association) is a subunit of a campaign. In major social change episodes, specific identifiable campaigns often provide the structure of more amorphous movements. Thus, in the operation of the Civil War–era Sanitary Commission, the West Coast campaigns and in particular the San Francisco campaign stand out as particularly successful fundraising episodes (Bremner, 1980). Each of the major organizations involved in the U.S. civil rights movement conducted its own campaigns, with their own organization, strategy, tactics, funding, and objectives. The Southern Christian Leadership Conference, for example, carried out major campaigns in Albany, Georgia; Birmingham and Selma, Alabama; Chicago; and Memphis. The 1963 March on Washington was a campaign organized and carried out by a coalition of major civil rights organizations (Fairclough, 1987).

Common Places

One of many interesting aspects of the commons is the existence of specific places dedicated to or set aside for common action. There is no satisfactory term in the English language to characterize such places generically, although there are a large number of specific terms: *fraternity house, lodge, grange hall, clubhouse, temple, church, kiva,* and many more. Some people refer to some of these places (museums, for example) as *institutions,* leading to unending confusion.

The largest and most clearly defined class of such places are temples, each with its association of priests and ritual specialists. The term *temple* is unsuitable for this entire class of common places, however, because of its explicitly religious connotations. Each of the world's major (and many minor) religions uses dedicated buildings and natural spaces as common places. Even the quasi-mythical Celtic druids, about which relatively little hard factual information exists, are associated with their sacred groves (Chadwick, 1971; Herm, 1975).

Terminology for common religious places is highly variable. In Jewish tradition, a temple is the site of sacrifices, while *synagogue* is the term for a gathering of the people (de Vaux, 1965). In the Islamic world, a mosque is a space for common prayers. Christians have a bewildering variety of terms for their common places: *churches, chapels, cathedrals, houses of prayer, meeting houses, campgrounds, revival centers,* and more. Another large class of common places are monuments, shrines, altars, stelae, and various pilgrimage sites.

Because of the enduring legacy of classicism in civil society, a great many American common places have been given Greek or Latin names such as *academy, coliseum, gymnasium, forum, auditorium,* and *lyceum.* A unique form of common place that has been important in India is the ashram, or religious retreat. The ashram is associated with Mohandas Gandhi and the Indian democratic revolution because it was so clearly the staging area from which the revolution was discussed, legitimated, organized, and led (Mehta, 1976).

A controversial public policy doctrine of common places as sanctuaries has generally received insufficient attention. Churches have frequently sought special status as sanctuaries, from the tenth-century Peace of God movement through the martyrdom of Thomas Becket to contemporary Latin American liberation theology and the domestic sanctuary movement sheltering illegal aliens (Lorentzen, 1991).

For purposes of a formal model of the commons, it is useful to distinguish discursive common places (literally, places of discussion) from presentational places devoted to ritual and other forms of presentation. A forum for public debate is functionally distinguishable from a theater or concert hall used for presentations. In certain cases, common places, like Carnegie Hall, can serve multiple purposes.

In addition to being one of the great cultural establishments in the United States, Carnegie Hall in New York City represents an interesting historical case study of a major U.S. common place (Bernstein, 1990). Carnegie Hall, like Hull House, the Russell Sage Foundation, and certain other charitable and cultural establishments, served as a transitional link between earlier patterns of philanthropy and contemporary ones.

The place of Carnegie Hall in U.S. cultural life and its status as a commons are beyond question. Pyotr Tchaikovsky conducted at the opening festival. Ignacy Paderewski, Sarah Bernhardt, Lillian Russell, Frederick Douglass, Antonin Dvořák, Arthur Rubinstein, Theodore Roosevelt, Booker T. Washington, Victor Herbert, Albert Einstein, Frank Sinatra, and The Beatles are among the thousands of important figures in music, literature, philosophy, politics, religion, and science who have appeared there in concerts, speeches, and other presentations in the past century.

Carnegie Hall is not simply a performance venue. The building (and the institution) also embrace a maze of practice rooms, studios, and hallways. The American Academy of Dramatic Arts was housed at Carnegie Hall for sixty years.

Prior to 1960, Carnegie Hall existed as a privately held, tax-paying company, whose annual operating deficits were absorbed personally by a series of owner-patrons. In this sense, Carnegie Hall is an important link with the past, and the personal patronage that enabled it to exist bears more than a little resemblance to the Greek pattern of liturgia and the religious, literary, and artistic patronage of the medieval and Renaissance European nobility. In such cases, legal organizational forms are absent and taxes, ownership, and liability are vested in an individual or group of individuals who function as patrons of the commons in a particularly personal way.

The initial patron of Carnegie Hall was its namesake, Andrew Carnegie. In 1889, Carnegie contributed $1.1 million toward the construction of a music hall in New York City. However, as was his custom, Carnegie contributed only a portion of the total cost of creating Carnegie Hall. He refused to endow the hall, believing this to be the responsibility of the beneficiaries of his gift. The remainder of the cost was therefore borne by a newly created Music Hall Company of New York (a joint-stock corporation), largely through mortgages on the land and building. The architect and suppliers of the new building were paid in stock in the corporation. The budget for construction and equipment was set at $763,531, $550,000 of which was mortgaged. The budget included $20,000 for decoration and $18,000 for 2,500 seats. Purchase of the land (eight and a half lots) was financed with an additional mortgage of $300,000 from the Bowery Savings Bank, but records of the price of the land have been lost (Bernstein, 1990).

Carnegie continued in his role of patron throughout his life, making up annual operating deficits of $25,000, so that by the time of his death he had contributed nearly $2 million to the hall. After his death, the role of principal patron for Carnegie Hall was assumed by Robert E. Simon, a Manhattan realtor, who purchased the hall from the Carnegie estate in 1925, reportedly for $2.5 million. His son inherited the hall ten years later and held it until it was sold to the city of New York in 1960. The Simons, father and son, were of course not the only patrons of Carnegie Hall. Many other people gave substantial sums in donations over the years, principally to support the many programs undertaken at the hall (Bernstein, 1990).

Only after nearly seventy years of existence under this classical form of patronage did Carnegie Hall take on a more conventional nonprofit form. Apparently, the beneficence of this form of private patronage was eventually exhausted, and in 1960, the Carnegie Hall site was to be sold to a private developer for the construction of what was described as a "red brick skyscraper" (Bernstein, 1990, p. 65). The violinist Isaac Stern assumed a distinctly modern, middle-class role of patronage and spearheaded a committee to save

Carnegie Hall. The city of New York eventually purchased the hall for $5 million and leased it to the newly created nonprofit Carnegie Hall Corporation for $183,600 a year. The city purchase required explicit enabling legislation by the state legislature.

In 1990, roughly 60 percent of the operating costs of the hall were recovered in rents, which ranged from $6,300 on weekdays to $7,200 on weekends. (Ushers, rehearsal time, and ticket printing were extra.) The remainder of the operating budget was made up with a variety of grant income from foundations, the state and federal government, and private donations (Bernstein, 1990).

Repeated efforts to have the facility designated as a tax-exempt educational institution have failed. New York State nonprofit law was apparently quite unclear at the time the hall was built, and creating a modern tax-exempt establishment of this type, particularly one generating substantial sums in ticket revenues, was a complex task. When the Russell Sage Foundation was created in 1907, the founders elected to seek a special act of the New York legislature to cut through the vagaries of state law, and the founders of several other important national foundations chose the same path.

The issue of local taxation of commons has long been particularly important in New York City because the headquarters of a large number of national charitable and philanthropic establishments are located there, and all of them seek exemption from local taxes. In essence, Carnegie Hall operated for roughly seventy years as a private business and faced significant tax liabilities: $10,000 in the first year alone. By 1925, the facility was valued at $1.85 million and the tax bill was $49,765 (Bernstein, 1990, p. 74).

In choosing to function as personal patrons of Carnegie Hall for over thirty-five years, the Simons were important modern exemplars of the operation of a critical portion of the theory of the commons. Under a condition of sufficient personal affluence (how much exactly is a matter of no importance), they were able to ignore or resist what must have been abundant inducements to maximize their profits.

Committees

One of the most universal and, at the same time, one of the most difficult forms of common social organization is the committee. Not only do we find committees in community life (that is, in the commons and the public sector) but we also find business and corporate committees as infiltrations of the commons into the commercial world of the marketplace. Sometimes we can even find committees in family life—for example, in extended families engaged in the "production" of family reunions or other family rituals. Many family foundations that do not have paid staff members may carry out more mundane aspects of their business that do not require official trustee action through informal committees.

At some level, participation in a committee is inevitably voluntary. One can be coerced to be a committee member, baited with various inducements and threats, and still retain a large measure of discretion over one's conduct in committees.

Conferences

Another highly important form of the social organization of the commons is the conference. According to Mead (1965), a conference is a meeting of individuals called to engage in a discussion with the aim of accomplishing some limited task within a restricted period of time. Other terms for approximately the same phenomenon are *convocation, convention,* and *synod.* Mead (1965, p. 215) identifies the conference as a "Euro-American invention" and cites such precedents as royal societies, the long tradition of intellectual controversy within eastern European Judaism, and the Quaker meeting. Conferences are not totally a western practice, however. Robert Redfield (1953) cites a 1930 study by H. J. Spinden that presented evidence of a convention of Mayan astronomer-priests at Copan nearly 2,000 years ago at which agreement among the conferees was reached on various calendar revisions and a general plan for measuring time.

Many professional groups that assume a nominal associational form are, in fact, fundamentally conferences in which membership fees are synonymous with conference registrations. Conferences can be defined as periodic commons in which members or participants convene to discuss, debate, and resolve common problems and issues or adopt common positions. The conference type of commons is particularly important in religious, scientific, labor, and other commons where the legitimacy of a single conclusion or the adoption of a unified position are important.

Following the conference, members typically expect to go their separate ways and guide their actions in the interim until the next conference on the basis of positions adopted at the conference. Whether it is political candidates guided by a platform adopted at the party convention, scientists designing new research on the basis of findings presented at a scientific conference, or religious delegates at a synod, participants in a conference expect to receive guidance for their postconference action.

There are few forms of organized commons that display the dialogue basic to all commons more clearly and distinctly than the conference. The purpose of a conference is talk in all forms: speeches, discussion, debate, negotiation. One attends a conference to speak and to listen, to be heard and understood, and to understand.

No other type of commons displays more clearly the underlying relationship between such dialogue and the involvement and commitment of participants. It is because one understands, speaks, and is understood by one's peers; because one's questions can be assigned proper importance; and because one's doubts can be seen as well founded that one truly is a physicist, social worker, Methodist, folklorist, Republican, or feminist. It is in conference that theologies are hammered out and scientific paradigms shaped and molded. Conferences signal the existence and the resolution (or abandonment) of social problems and preferred policies.

Unfortunately, most work on conferences in nonprofit and voluntary studies to date has addressed only the pedestrian and mundane aspects of conference organization. Much more work needs to be done on the role of this distinctively important form of commons. One area that is particularly promising is the examination of the conferencelike aspects of democratic parliaments, congresses, councils, and other legislative bodies. The manner in which the authoritative actions of the democratic state are produced out of the dialogue of legislative conferences is one of the most amazing and profound examples of the commons as a general form of social organization.

Cooperatives

Both general and specific social processes of cooperation have been important in understanding nonprofit and voluntary action (Argyle, 1991; Elkin and McLean, 1976). Producer and consumer cooperatives are a fundamental and distinctive form of benefactories in which economic functions are mixed with social cooperation (Ben-Ner, 1987; Wertheim, 1976). Cooperatives have been important in rural development in the United States and elsewhere (Attwood and Baviskar, 1989). Clayre (1980) uses them to define the third sector as a political economy of participation and cooperation. In nineteenth-century France, cooperative bakeries, groceries, and other consumer cooperatives were used to finance labor activism. In contemporary Egypt, cooperatives are part of the challenge to political authoritarianism (Blanchi, 1989). Jones and Moskoff (1991) identify cooperatives as an important step in the rebirth of a nonstate economy in Russia.

Co-ops have long been a feature of certain U.S. campuses, and student cooperative bookstores continue in operation after decades. Co-ops are frequently found in U.S. agriculture, including co-op grain elevators, feed and supply stores, electrical suppliers, and milk- and other commodity-producing cooperatives (Attwood and Baviskar, 1989). More recently, consumer groups, proponents of organic foods and holistic health treatment, and a broad range of "new age" and environmental groups have also found the cooperative an advantageous form of economic and social organization (Furlough, 1991). Some researchers have even suggested that university departments and hospitals might be regarded as cooperatives (Hunter, 1981; James and Neuberger, 1981; Pauly and Redisch, 1973).

The similarities between nonprofit corporations and cooperatives are highly suggestive but largely unexplored (Jones and Moskoff, 1991; Oleck, 1980). Those analyses that have been done have not been incorporated into the corpus of nonprofit and voluntary action studies (for example, Clayre, 1980). Yet contemporary nonprofit and voluntary action theory would be hard pressed to deal adequately with cooperatives or the enduring cooperative movement.

Discipline

A *discipline* may be defined as a genus of commons, composed of several distinctly identifiable species. The term itself is applied most commonly to academic disciplines, or fields of study that may have common intellectual history, problems, and methods; shared theory; and other features. It applies equally well to religious orders, which by tradition share the discipline of common rules, and professions, unions, and gilds, which seek to extend the discipline of self-governance of an association to the members of an entire occupational group (Northrup, 1965; Snow, 1959; Van der Veer, 1989). In general, terms like *order* and *discipline* point to underlying problems of social control and normative compliance, which every viable commons must resolve.

Academic Disciplines. In many respects, academic disciplines (as opposed to the formal associations representing those disciplines) conform to the form of social organization I am characterizing as a commons. Scientific disciplines like physics and biology, humanistic disciplines like literature and art history, and "interdisciplines" and multidisciplinary fields like gerontology, peace studies, and nonprofit and voluntary action studies conform to most of the characteristics of a commons.

Philanthropic foundations in the United States have played an important role in the development of several disciplines. Stanfield (1985) discusses the Laura Spellman Rockefeller Memorial, the Rosenwald Fund, and The Carnegie Corporation and their support of the sociologist Robert Park. Sontz (1989) identifies a similarly important role for philanthropic foundations in the growth of gerontology.

Universities may be organized into departments by discipline, but most modern universities also feature a variety of centers, institutes, and programs whose participants, in effect, form commons that do not conform to the existing formal organizational structure of the university. Indeed, nonprofit and voluntary studies is such a program because it draws scholars from dozens of different academic disciplines.

Since membership in commons is voluntary, commons are

much easier to form, sustain, and change than any type of formal organizational entity, and therein lies what may be the most profound, enduring, and chronic problem of organization in the modern university. New commons are continually being formed out of the interests and enthusiasms of faculty members. Such commons constitute an ongoing challenge and headache for those responsible for the formal organization of the university. It is no easy task deciding when new groups that are organized around, for example, gerontology, women's studies, or peace studies should be given formal recognition, budget authority, and other accoutrements of formal organizational status.

In general, it is communication and dialogue within the framework of the discipline, imposed by adhering to agreed-upon methods and procedures of search, problem solving, and presentation, that characterize disciplines. Another way of saying this is that shared intellectual or theoretical problems or shared problem-solving methods are at the core of more scientific disciplines, while shared aesthetic or other criteria for the assessment of performances of various types are at the core of many humanistic disciplines. Professional disciplines like law, medicine, engineering, and social work tend to place emphasis on both common problems and performances.

In the past century, many new disciplines have formed. Wilson (1990) studied the evolution of American philosophy as an academic discipline. Silva and Slaughter (1984) discuss the formation of the American Economic Association (1895), the American Political Science Association (1903), and the American Sociological Society (1905) and their displacement of the American Social Science Association. Numerous other studies of the formation of disciplines are also found in the social science literature.

Orders. The term *order* can have several meanings. It is frequently used to describe the principles, characteristics, or social behavior that give predictability and coherence to social processes (for example, social order) or to describe the objectives or results of social control. Modern attention to the Hobbesian problem of social order arising from unconstrained self-interest has been a major preoccupation of contemporary sociology.

Orders as religious, fraternal, chivalric, or other commons have received relatively little attention in the nonprofit and voluntary action literature. Yet for more than 1,000 years in the history of Western civilization, various Christian monastic and lay orders were principal forms of commons, and many continue in existence today. Much the same can be said for the Islamic world, where various orders were long the principal basis for the civic organization of Islamic cities and the political organization of Islamic states (Hourani, 1991). An understanding of Islamic orders may be one key to understanding the organizational dynamics of resurgent Islamic fundamentalism in Iran and elsewhere (Ayubi, 1991).

Both Christian and Islamic orders are forms of social organization closely associated with normative compliance structures and traditional authority. Whether such orders are an archaic form of social organization and new and contemporary forms of order will arise remains to be seen.

The modern labor movement refers to the necessary discipline as solidarity, which typically involves appeals to the collective economic self-interest of a group or class of workers. Solidarity can represent an important form of coercive economic power in strikes, boycotts, or other actions.

At the same time, growing numbers of occupations are adopting professional modes of organization. The choice between professional and trade union modes of organization has been particularly clear-cut between the "professional" National Education Association and the "union" American Federation of Teachers.

Etzioni (1969) has referred to the rise of the "semiprofessions." Far from consisting of a single organization of modern professions, like academic disciplines, religious orders, and communities, semiprofessions are frequently composed of complexes of many related organizations with overlapping memberships. This may include incorporated national or international associations such as the American Medical Association or the National Association of Social Workers, separately incorporated state or local chapters of a national group, and vast complexes of related groups with varying degrees of autonomy. These may include accrediting bodies, public authorities such as licensing boards and regulatory agencies with various ambiguous relations to the professional body. They may also include professional schools and training programs and separately incorporated journals with editorial boards composed of recognized members of the profession.

Emphasizing solidarity and the economic and political functions of gilds, unions, professions, and other related forms of occupational organization (such as businessmen's associations) tends to downplay their coexisting roles as commons. Mutuality arises from shared experiences and outlooks and the common repertories of professional nomenclature and jargon, and distinctive standards of fairness arise from peer review and professional community. Both mutuality and distinctive standards of fairness are important common dimensions in most types of occupational association.

Unions and Professions. Medieval gilds have at least one important connection with modern trade unions and professions: All three types of organization are commons-like organizations organized for the mutual, collective, or common occupational or employment interests of their members. Full-scale examination of the common characteristics evident in the existing literature of labor and professional studies would be a task far exceeding the limits of the present inquiry. The intent here is only to suggest that unions, professions, and other forms of occupational association fall at least partly within the broad topic of the commons.

The traditional division of the medieval university into schools of medicine, law, theology, and philosophy point to the early existence, if not necessarily the political or economic importance, of professions. Even as the rise of the modern state led to the demise of the medieval gild, working conditions for labor in the industrial revolution led to the development of new types of what were often called "working men's associations." In the United States in the twentieth century, we have seen the rise, followed by the more recent decline, of trade union membership.

One of the more interesting aspects of trade unionism (which it shares with the more recent civil rights, women's, and other movements) is the use of familial terms and imagery to symbolize the common bonds of members. Thus, many unions are explicitly named "brotherhoods," and in racial, ethnic, and gender organizations members refer to one another as sister and brother. Such usages point to a persistent problem of commons: How to hold the loyalty of members to common purposes in the face of strong oppositional forces such as coercion, individual self-interest, or kinship loyalties.

Fiestas

A major class of common social organizations with both historical and contemporary significance are the numerous fairs, festivals, fiestas, parades, fireworks displays, and other similar events that have marked the Euro-American landscape at least since the Middle Ages (MacAloon, 1984; Orloff, 1980; Steinberg, 1989). The number of such events occurring annually in the United States, and the number of organizations sponsoring them, probably is between 5,000 and 10,000.

Almost all modern U.S. festivals have a nonprofit corporation at or near their core. Outside the United States, rotating systems of individual patrons (known in Central America as *mayordomos*) that are similar to the Athenian model may be of greater importance than nonprofit corporations are (Smith, 1977).

Frequently, healthy doses of entrepreneurial profit seeking, civic boosterism, and diverse other manifestations of self-interest, promotion, and aggrandizement are associated with many festivals and similar events. Undoubtedly, festivals are good for business. Yet the fair boards, chamber of commerce committees, veterans' organizations, and other civic groups and quasi-governmental bodies that act as official sponsors of such events seldom account for the full range and scope of these events.

Virtually every large city and most of the smaller ones have their mardi gras, winter carnival, strawberry festival, or rose parade. And seldom are these activities solely restricted to the association or corporation sponsoring the event. The millions of people filling the streets of New Orleans at Mardi Gras, Miami and Rio for Carnivale, and Ciena and other Italian cities for Pallio are not simply crowds. Whether we look at the traditional African-American "Indian tribes" of Mardi Gras, the motorcyclists of a local Shriners' organization performing in a street parade, the neighborhood and block clubs that sponsor competing horses and jockeys in the pallios, or the pan bands of Trinidad, we see the same thing. Most genuine festivals are, at one level, composed of clusters or networks of groups, clubs, and associations whose primary reason for organizing is to see and be seen in the festival.

Presentation—to see and be seen—is as fundamental an object of the festival as talking and listening is of the conference. Children take their 4-H projects to an agricultural county fair to be seen by all and critically evaluated by judges who award prizes to the best entrants. In a considerable number of the over 3,000 counties in the United States, the annual fair or festival is formally titled an *exposition*, a term that highlights the presentational (expository) quality of the event. Seeing and being seen is not a characteristic limited to the associations and organized segments of a festival, however. In a manner reminiscent of emerging beau monde society discussed in Chapter Three, promenading, or strolling the grounds for the primary purpose of seeing or being seen, is an important characteristic for everyone who attends such an event.

Many anthropological studies of feast days and festivals are available. For example, Sherman and Sherman (1990) discuss the ritual significance and political economy of feasting among the Samosir Batak of Sumatra.

Foundations

Both the term *foundation* and the concept of the foundation date back at least to the Romans and probably to the Greeks (Johnson, 1989). The modern foundation is a financial instrument, sanctioned by the state, with a governing organization (usually a committee or board of trustees) and with or without an accompanying staff organization. In certain important respects, the modern American philanthropic foundation is as much an intellectual product of Andrew Carnegie's Gospel of Wealth (Carnegie, [1889] 1983) as it is a product of the income and inheritance taxes. Carnegie's doctrine of the moral obligation of the rich to give voice and additional moral weight to aristocratic and plutocratic actions stretches back at least to the Greeks.

In a sense, the modern American foundation with its paid professional staff is also a product of both John D. Rockefeller's employment of Frederick T. Gates as his philanthropic advisor and the creation of the Russell Sage Foundation. In the Carnegie view, philanthropic patronage is the personal obligation of the rich. In the Rockefeller and Sage examples, which are certainly the norm for at least the largest foundations, the obligation has been transformed into an obligation to turn over to expert and professional agents a large measure of practical control for the dispensing of funds.

Robert Payton's characterization of philanthropy as private action for the public (or, in our terms, common) good offers a particularly apt characterization of the modern foundation. Because they are essentially private institutions engaged in public affairs, foundations have been a target of social critics at least since Eduard Lindeman's study (1936).

Journals

In a number of important cases, periodical publications ordinarily called journals (or professional journals or trade journals) are associated with sciences, disciplines, professions, or other commons or independently develop into a type of commons on their own. For example, Survey Associates, which was for more than forty years a membership association, published *Survey* and *Survey Graphic*, the leading magazines in the field of social reform for over four decades until their demise in the early 1950s (Chambers, 1971).

In a few cases, the social organization of those who produce and control the journals can be transformed into an important and independent commons. This is particularly the case with various reform caucuses and change-oriented endeavors. Thus, for example, the writers and editors of the *Partisan Review* gave voice to a political, intellectual, and artistic movement in postwar New York, just as writers and editors of the *Village Voice* did in the 1960s and those of the "little magazines" did in the 1920s. *The Masses* and *The New Republic* both served in this way as centers of political commons associated with the movement of social liberalism.

It is not entirely unheard of for commercial magazines to attempt to create a journal commons. *Rolling Stone* and *Playboy* are mass-circulation publications that have endeavored to cast themselves into a reformist mode vis-à-vis rock music as a platform for social change and hedonism as a life-style (the notorious "play-boy philosophy" of publisher Hugh Hefner).

In eighteenth-century England, the journalism of Addison and Steele gave political voice to public opinion formed in the English coffeehouses. In nineteenth-century America and Europe, newspapers were frequently the organs of particular political parties, factions, or splinter groups.

In the United States, ethnic groups have frequently tried to discover or retain a sense of common identity through the medium of journals. Spanish-speaking, Jewish, and black communities retain important journalistic outlets in many major metropolitan areas, for example. Most ethnic groups in the United States have had, at one time or another, newspapers or magazines directed toward them, and many such publications continue to exist today.

Parties

Political parties of all types (including, to some degree, Nazi, Fascist, Communist, and other totalitarian parties that hold monopoly control of the state and a position as the dominant institutions of a society) conform to a considerable degree to any definition of commons (Gluck, 1975; Kayden and Mahe, 1986; Van Doren, 1956).

In terms of the theory of the commons, the defining characteristic of the political party may be that it is, quite literally, an embryo state; that is, the distinctive purpose of the political party is to seek control of the state and to reshape the state to its view. Party commons, then, must be seen as important political staging areas for the formation of states in democratic societies. Sometimes (as in most U.S. elections), the process of state formation is typically routine and occurs almost unnoticed. In many cases, new parties struggle for long periods with only limited success (Garcia, 1991; Valelly, 1989). In parliamentary systems, the dominance of a new party may lead to formation of a new government. In other cases, the rise of a party can have broader revolutionary implications. In colonial India, for example, parties like the Madras Native Association were important ingredients in the country's emergence from colonialism to political autonomy (Suntharalingam, 1967).

In democratic politics, parties must capture control of government through the electoral process. A prior issue, however, is an internal organizational one of capturing control of the party apparatus (Schlesinger, 1975; Schwartz, 1990). Thus, the creation of an enduring party leadership and the recruitment and support of party candidates for elective office are major focuses of party activity (Goldman, 1990).

The connection between political parties and other forms of association are subtle and complex. In the United States, this issue is frequently discussed in terms of the distinction of parties, interest groups serving various political functions, and nonpolitical civil associations. This distinction is the basis, for example, of limits on lobbying imposed on tax-exempt 501(c)(3) organizations by the Internal Revenue Service. The line between political and civil associations, however, is a complex and variable one. The particular histories and political traditions of much of Latin America, for example, often mean that virtually all forms of civil association are politicized. Thus, most Latin American nations operate with multiparty systems in which there are very few nonpolitical civic associations.

Pilgrimages

Religious and other pilgrimages, or sacred journeys, are one of the most fascinating and enduring forms of commons, despite their relative absence in modern American life (Neville, 1987; Nolan and Nolan, 1989). I have already discussed the cities of Mecca and Rome as the foremost destinations for Islamic and Christian pilgrims. The pilgrimage was an important part of medieval Christianity, as shown, for example, in the group of sojourners portrayed by Chaucer in *The Canterbury Tales*. Pilgrimages have also played an important role in Hinduism. The river Ganges is one of the many Hindu pilgrimage sites. Also worthy of note here is the frequency with which U.S. Jews travel to Israel and U.S. ethnic groups travel to Europe, Africa, and Asia. Senior citizen travel tours may be the closest approximation in U.S. society to genuine pilgrimages.

As a commons, the pilgrimage may be most similar to the campaign and the committee in its time-limited, goal-oriented, and single-purpose nature. Neville (1987) argues that the Catholic custom of pilgrimages to sacred shrines has been replaced in Protestant culture by camp meetings, church homecomings, family reunions, and grave decorating ceremonies.

Research Institutes

The term *institute* has many different shades of meaning, yet almost all of them share connotations of common association for research, knowledge building, or dissemination of knowledge. A research institute is a commons devoted to scientific investigations. Perhaps the most distinctive form of institute is the freestanding institute, which is not part of any other host institution. The National Geographic Society, publisher of a highly successful periodical, is an example of such. In the economic vernacular, many research institutes might be characterized as "researchers' cooperatives."

Two other distinctive research institutes are the Consumer's Union, a nonprofit consumer group that also produces a monthly periodical reporting its findings in the area of product research, and the Brookings Institution, which has been publishing independent policy research for more than fifty years (Peschek, 1987). The Urban Institute is another more recent policy research institute with an admirable track record.

Secret Societies

One of the more intriguing forms of commons is the *secret society*, in which membership, resources—perhaps including patrons, rituals, common goods, and objectives—or other details are intentionally held in confidence among members for reasons of protection or group solidarity. Simmel (1906) and Wedgewood (1930) both conclude that membership in secret societies adds to social prestige because of the belief that members are in possession of special knowledge not available to nonmembers.

Another major category of secret societies are those whose membership and activities remain secret to avoid publicity or detection by the state. Some of these secret societies, such as the Mafia and other crime families, remain secret in order to engage in criminal activities. Yet other secret societies may carry out an organized program of political opposition. Two of the more enduring and infamous examples of such societies in U.S. history are the Ku Klux Klan and the American Communist Party.

Other quite different examples of secret societies opposed to state action are the contemporary sanctuary movement, dedicated to sheltering illegal aliens from Central America, and the abolitionist Underground Railroad, devoted to aiding escaping slaves prior to the Civil War. Fitzgerald (1989) focuses on Alabama and Mississippi in a study of the Union League, a nineteenth-century secret society led by a coalition of blacks and whites whose goal was the promotion of political participation among black freedmen.

Wars and warlike conditions inevitably encourage various secret and semisecret resistance movements. Virtually every European country occupied by the Nazis during World War II had an organized resistance movement. A more recent example of such a movement was the Kuwaiti resistance movement, which operated throughout the 1990–1991 Iraqi occupation of Kuwait. For such groups, maintaining secrecy may be the key not only to effective operations but also to survival.

By their very nature, some types of secret societies are associated with myth and mystery. College fraternities and sororities are organized as rather harmless secret societies, with all manner of secret rituals, oaths, paraphernalia, code words, and the like. The linguist and novelist Umberto Eco has recently revived the myth of a secret society in *Foucault's Pendulum,* which is a tale of the alleged secret society of the Knights Templar, supposedly reaching back to the time of the Crusades. Secrecy surrounding the Freemasons has long made some people suspicious of the group (Rosenzweig, 1977). Demott (1986) examines the history of the Masons, their place in the formation and preservation of the United States, the philosophy of the fraternity, and their place in contemporary life. Chrisman (1974) reports on the structure and ritual system of a fraternal secret society he calls the Badgers.

By their very inaccessibility, secret societies generate continuing interest. Secret societies are often at the center of conspiracy theories of various sorts. Secret cabals of Jewish bankers, for example, have been a common feature of anti-Semitic propaganda for hundreds of years, and conspiracy theories of capitalist domination are standard fare on the political left.

Science

Another category of commons at the opposite pole from secret societies are sciences. The term *science* is used here in the sense of a group of interacting investigators or researchers engaged in the investigation of research issues or questions that they share in common, ordinarily through the use of shared or agreed-upon methods of inquiry (Barnes, 1986; Fisher, 1980; Olesko, 1991).

Recent work in the philosophy and sociology of science has emphasized the social processes of cooperation and competition in the evolution of scientific knowledge (Hull, 1988; Latour, 1987; Lux, 1989; Wilson, 1990). Uncoerced participation is a central characteristic of any commons claiming to be a science. One traditional meaning of the term *science* might be interpreted as the interests of a group gathered around a common set of interests. Thus, there are those people who hold that philosophy, philology, and rhetoric are sciences in this sense. The defining characteristic of science in the modern sense is the public criterion of "intersubjective testability"; that is, the methods used to investigate a question as well as the findings must be subjected to the common scrutiny of peers and colleagues.

In our civilization, the predominant category of support for science is actually support for applied research and development—the discovery of new techniques and applications of basic knowledge to product development. Particularly important are the categories of military, biomedical, and engineering research and development.

Research and development fits in well with the market model of microeconomics. However, the other basic category of scientific work—often called basic or fundamental science—involves alleged cultural or "amenity" benefits that are, like other community services, considerably more difficult to measure than the benefits of research and development or impossible to measure exactly.

The benefits of "practical" scientific ventures, such as constructing a newer, safer automobile or curing a particular disease, can be measured fairly exactly. But basic scientific work often has an impracticality and lack of precise outcomes that is very similar to other common goods. It is as hard to place a utilitarian gloss on such fundamental scientific issues as astronomical research involved in locating the edges of the universe or the search for prime numbers as it is to determine the economic value of art or religion.

Writing in *Scientific American,* Lederman (1984) estimates that perhaps 95 percent of all public support for scientific research is directed toward applied research and development and 5 percent is directed toward fundamental science. Such figures, however, are seriously skewed by the economic importance of defense-related research and development and can easily lead us to undervalue the fundamental importance of basic science to Western culture and society over the past three centuries.

Lederman (1984, p. 41) does set forth a familiar "cultural" argument for fundamental science, irrespective of its payoff. He says, "Society must care about science in the same way as it must care about its other creative intellectual activities, such as art, music and literature. Science, like art, manifests its deep cultural influence when its basic principles or its way of viewing the world is appropriated and applied to a larger social context."

There are, he says, two distinct cultural effects of fundamental science: the cultural appeal of science, which has attracted some of the best minds in society, and the role of fundamental science in maintaining the esprit de corps of the scientific community. Even these effects, however, relate closely to an economic view of the world. The first criterion offers a "human capital" argument for fundamental science, and the second corresponds closely with the human relations approach to management and its argument that good morale improves productivity. In basic science, as in most contemporary human services, we have grown accustomed to a kind of duplicity: we value activities as ends in themselves while at the same time justifying them in largely economic terms.

Conclusion

Researchers interested in nonprofit and voluntary action studies have shown great interest in some types of common social organizations, such as the association and the nonprofit social service agency. They have, on the whole, shown remarkably little interest in many other types of common organization, including some of those discussed in this chapter and other additional forms of organization discussed in the chapters that follow. These tendencies have resulted in a somewhat constricted view of the true range of the commons and the neglect of many valuable opportunities for increased understanding of the mechanisms of social bonding, participation, commitment, compliance, and the host of other issues that have interested researchers. One can only hope that future research efforts are addressed more broadly in an effort to capture the full range of common social organization.

The Economics
of Common Goods

A people among whom individuals lost the power of achieving great things single-handed, without acquiring the means of producing them by united exertions, would soon lapse into barbarism.

—Alexis de Tocqueville

This chapter explores several implications of the theory of the commons for the emerging field of nonprofit economics. In particular, three basic issues are addressed: (1) the commons as unanalyzed economic phenomenon, (2) an expanded concept of volunteer labor, and (3) common goods as an alternative to public goods, marketable goods, and services as measures of nonprofit and voluntary action. All of these issues are addressed within the perspective identified as endowment theory.

Modern economics, according to a widely accepted definition by Lionel Robbins, is the study of the allocation of scarce means among alternative ends (Robbins, 1963). Economics is both an empirical and a normative science dealing with decision making and practical action. Recently, a number of economists and scholars in related fields such as law, management, and accounting have begun to address nonprofit economic issues (Wagner, 1991; Weisbrod, 1977, 1988; Hansmann, 1981b; Weinstein, 1980).

Their principal project has been to explain the existence and relative advantage of the nonprofit sector within conventional utilitarian rational choice models and microeconomic assumptions like production, maximization, and optimality. The doctrine of relative advantage figures importantly in nonprofit theoretical approaches. A recent debate in the economic literature, for example, focuses on whether not-for-profit hospitals return more benefit to society than for-profit hospitals (Arrington and Haddock, 1990; Bays, 1983; Cleverley, 1982; Pauly and Redisch, 1973). Another similar debate has been raging for years in the field of aging over the effects of ownership on nursing homes (Idson and Ullmann, 1991; Krivich, 1990). Analysis of the economics of the arts has been another major interest in this area (Baumol and Bowen, 1968; Edwards, 1983; Moore, 1968; Nelson, 1983).

There are at least two economic theories of the nonprofit sector: *market-government failure theory* and *voluntary failure theory* (Winkle, 1990). The first theory suggests that the nonprofit sector develops when both market and government fail to provide needed services. Hansmann (1980, 1981b, 1987) offers a close analysis of the phenomenon of "contract failure," which emphasizes the residual role of the nonprofit sector in compensating for the deficiencies of market exchange under conditions of information asymmetry. Weisbrod (1977, 1988) characterizes government as providing public goods only at levels demanded by the median voter; therefore, people with demands higher than the median are underserved by government and must look elsewhere.

Salamon (1987a, 1987b) reverses Weisbrod's formula and suggests that it is the nonprofit sector, not the government, that is likely to respond first to people's needs. He says that government is likely to compensate for the deficiencies of the nonprofit sector, instead of vice versa. Salamon identifies four general types of philanthropic failures leading to governmental action: insufficiency of resources, particularism, paternalism, and amateurism.

Each of these approaches represents a type of failure theory in which relative advantage is the anchor for explaining one set of social institutions in terms of their dissimilarity to another set. In a chapter in *The Nonprofit Economy* entitled "Options Among Institutional Forms," Weisbrod (1988) is particularly explicit about the nature of this theoretical project. Elsewhere, I have expressed doubts about the value of this style of argument by negation (Lohmann, 1989).

Nonprofit economics grounded in failure theory treats non-profit organizations by analogy with (as if they were) the profit-oriented firms of microeconomics (Crew, 1975). Adam Smith's distinction between productive and unproductive labor, discussed earlier, is ignored or overturned in the contemporary concept of volunteer labor (Weisbrod, 1988). Such an approach is defensible in the analysis of revenue-generating nonprofit firms like hospitals; nursing homes; and some museums, theaters and concert halls, where clear-cut prices are exchanged for recognizable products. However, the rationale for treating "unproductive" (nonrevenue) membership clubs; donative charities; and a broad range of other religious, scientific, or artistic commons as if they were commercial firms is highly questionable. Yet because of the widespread commitment of nonprofit economics to the market firm analogy, no other economic models of the commons have received serious consideration. A major project confronting nonprofit and voluntary action researchers, therefore, is to begin the construction of a genuine economics of common goods premised on more plausible and relevant assumptions.

Some interesting work along these lines has already been done (see, for example, Frohlich and Oppenheimer, 1984; Gassler, 1990; Krishnan, 1988; Steinberg, 1987; Sugden, 1984). Wagner (1991) provides an economic analysis of collective goods and the "share economy" in terms quite consistent with the analysis of common goods and the commons offered in this work. Clayre (1980) offers an economic analysis of the political economy of cooperation and participation.

Inadequacy of Current Economic Theory

An adequate economic model for analysis of the commons ought to begin by studying actual common economic institutions, like donations and endowments, and by adjusting or suspending three conventional economic assumptions: scarcity, production, and maximization. The economics of common goods does not require rejecting the concept of scarcity entirely. However, acknowledgment of the moral and rational consequences of affluence or social surplus is important.

The most important form of scarcity in terms of its impact upon common action might be called *existential,* or weak, scarcity; that is, the recognition that all human resources and potentials are finite. This scarcity is the basis of the need to make choices in human affairs generally.

Existential scarcity is morally distinguishable from *triage,* or strong, scarcity. Scarcity that threatens the existence or well-being of some or all members of the community has interested economists since Malthus. Self-interested action to assure survival under conditions of triage is justified on both moral and rational grounds. Although we might praise the altruist who sacrifices her life to save others, neither reason nor ethics demand such sacrifices of anyone.

It is the voluntary choice involved in altruism or other common goods that gives them their special character. Not only is self-interest justified under conditions of triage but productive efforts are also morally preferable to leisure pursuits and efficient production is preferable to inefficiency. Thus the scarcity, production, and maximization assumptions are bundled with self-interest to make a morally resilient position, the anchor of which is threat to survival or well-being (see Arendt, 1958, on the distinction between labor, work, and action).

Under conditions of affluence, when productive surpluses are sufficient and survival is not threatened, the powerful rational and moral arguments linking triage scarcity and self-interest lose much of their power. The distinction made between instrumental and expressive (or, as they are called in this work, problem-solving and presentational) actions in the voluntary action tradition does not attempt to shoulder the heavy moral burden that scarcity places upon the dichotomy of self-interest and altruism in the rational choice tradition (Smith, [1776] 1981). In a world of affluence, it is easy to lose sight of the moral compass represented by the economic norms of maximization and optimality: In a "triage" world in which it is a certainty that resources are insufficient and not all can survive, productive labor to assure survival carries greater moral density and is a seemingly clear rational choice over leisure.

Under conditions of affluence, we discover new rational and moral grounds for leisure action. Self-interest loses its privileged position as an obligation, and self-interest and interest in others become equally plausible choices. When our survival is not endangered, it is no more rational to act for our own or our group's advantage or gain than it is to be indifferent or even averse to profit seeking. In other words, under conditions of existential scarcity, people are fully free to allocate any additional increments of leisure in their control to self-interested or other-interested endeavors as they see fit.

Similarly, production is not a morally preferable form of social action under existential scarcity. Furthermore, the recent line of thought that equates all types of human behavior with production must be explicitly rejected in the case of the commons (Alhadeff, 1982; Becker, 1976). At the very least, nonprofit economics should attend more closely to the productive means arising out of shared purposes and the intangible outputs of information, meaning, and understanding that are nearly universal in the commons.

Attending to these issues inevitably brings us to recognize that service production in the commons cannot be distinguished from consumption. As authorities since Adam Smith have told us, service production and consumption are aspects of the same act; therefore, the distinctive economic action of the commons is some form of "coproduction." In contrast to most treatments of nonprofit production, Rudney (1987) discusses the treatment of nonprofits as consumption in macroeconomics. Although analyses of volunteer coproduction by Brudney and England (1983), Spiegel (1987), and others have been primarily concerned with policy and practical issues, the extension of these analyses to nonprofit economics of the type called for here should be straightforward.

Coproduction of intangible commodities (services, in the noneconomic sense) is ordinarily contemporaneous with the consumption of those services. The term *rendition* is used here to denote such simultaneous production and consumption. This usage is consistent with conventional usages and highlights the significance of aspects of presentation, discussed previously in Chapter Two. In a religious observance, for example, we might note the traditional rendition of ritual prayers, and at a scientific conference, we might listen to the rendition of research results in the context of prior work.

If the surrounding theoretical matrix sustained by scarcity and production is removed, maximization—whether in terms of profit, surplus, or attainment of some other value—loses its privileged position as an economic end of common action. The failure to recognize the legitimate limits of production and the application of the norm of maximization to commons can produce amusing or reductionistic conclusions such as the conclusion that rational individuals engaged in religious endeavors are seeking to maximize their salvation. In the language of variable analysis, religious salvation, like many other common ends, is not an interval variable and thus is not amenable to the kind of degrees or increments of attainment implicit in the concept of maximization.

The fundamental question that forms a plausible starting point for an economics of the commons is how and why societies choose to allocate portions of surplus social product to ends other than increased production, household consumption, and public goods. Robert Paul Wolff (1970) suggests that all of classical economics be viewed as an attempt to provide theoretically sound answers to the questions of who gets the surplus of physical production, how those people get the surplus, and what they do with the surplus. Current economic perspectives tend to view only three uses of surplus wealth as practical ones: surplus wealth can be reinvested in capital expansion, spent on higher taxes to support the continued further expansion of the state, or spent on growing mountains of consumer goods. From this perspective, it is mere common sense that nonprofit firms are engaged in a form of production rather than expansion of the state or consumption.

An economics of common goods might suggest a fourth use for surplus wealth: the application of social surpluses for the rendition of common goods. Investment in civilization sounds terribly pretentious, and yet this is precisely the idea often expressed in statements of the purposes of commons. Advancement of civilization was a stated mission in the papers incorporating Hull House. A 1985 advertisement for the National Corporate Theatre Fund in *Newsweek* magazine read "We're Looking for More Corporations to Invest in Laughs . . . Tears . . . Magic. . . . Your investment in the National Corporate Theatre Fund will bring an enormous return, not in dollars . . . but in laughter . . . tears . . . magic."

Calling corporate or any other donations "investments" and suggesting that returns on these investments are measurable in non-dollar terms is at one level a clever and devious advertising ploy. What rational investor would seriously consider laughter and tears a return on an investment? Yet, at another level, the underlying message of this ad is entirely compatible with the thrust of widely shared visions of the commons. The challenge for a genuine economics of common goods is how to take the objectives of the commons—religious, scientific, social, political, athletic, and other—seriously on their own terms and not treat them as rather odd, intangible, and inefficient forms of productive enterprise (Segelman and Bookheimer, 1983).

The leisure classes who studied Greek philosophy, fashioned the Christian Bible, practiced liturgia and zakat, formed medieval hospitals as well as associations and societies devoted to art and science, and engaged in the other common activities of human history drew upon the "capital" of their heritage—the art, ethical principles, philosophical and scientific knowledge, and other accoutrements of civilization—and left their own legacy of "surpluses" for others to learn from, adapt, and utilize. Such common endeavors, whether in the past, present, or future, are as real and consequential as any material production. Yet they require a distinctly different theoretical language. This is the challenge of an economics of common goods.

Volunteer Labor

One of the theoretical perspectives exercising considerable influence in contemporary nonprofit economics is the model of nonprofit activity as the private production of public goods through volunteer labor (Weisbrod, 1988). In this model, volunteer labor is a primary input, or factor of production, and public goods are the principal output. Both concepts require some further examination.

An initial distinction of great importance is between free labor as that concept has traditionally been dealt with in economics and volunteer labor. The freedom of free labor is the very special quality of being able to bargain in labor markets for wage rates. (Indeed, in competing for employees, nonprofit organizations are more clearly enmeshed in markets than in any other single case.) Nonprofit employees are free laborers in the important sense that they are not conscripts or slaves, even though they are paid.

By contrast, the term *volunteer labor* refers to unpaid or donated work. Volunteer labor involves not only services delivered by unpaid service workers but also the donated services of board members, fundraising soliciters, and others.

The services, or donations of time, of patrons also appear to constitute a form of volunteer labor, as do the acts of prosocial behavior reviewed in Chapter Nine. Altruism, empathic responses, disaster and bystander behavior, political parties, interest groups and other forms of civic action, support and mutual aid groups, and all of the various forms of common behavior discussed in this work constitute volunteer labor insofar as they have economic implications for the allocation of resources. Thus, in its fullest context, volunteer labor is nothing short of the individual contributions to the social action that creates and sustains civil society. Voting and other expressions of democratic citizenship are also forms of volunteer labor. When we take out the social action of the marketplace and the state and the private behavior of the household, what remains is volunteer labor.

The Problem of Measurement

The concept of public goods arose within the subfield of economics known as welfare economics, or normative microeconomics (Sassone, 1982). Pigou's famous "measuring rod of money" (1932) is one of the fundamental reasons often cited for the desire to apply economic reasoning to the analysis of nonprofit economic decision making. Some people presume that money is the one obvious measuring instrument available in social life.

The limitations of such a perspective should be obvious for the commons, where monetary data are largely unavailable and the flow of money only "meters" the flow of important resources in fee-based and other revenue-generating activities. The absence of a stable metering relationship has led, among other things, to the necessity of distinguishing between "outputs" as products and "outcomes" as results in various nonprofit approaches (Anthony, 1978; Elkin and Molitor, 1984; Staw, 1984).

In considering the application of the measuring rod of money to nonprofit economics, I am reminded of the observation by Robert MacIver (1926, p. 19): "There are things we can measure, like time, but yet our minds do not grasp their meaning. There are things we cannot measure, like happiness and pain, and yet their meaning is perfectly clear to us." Certainly, one of the most difficult aspects of common goods economics is activities that we cannot measure but that are nonetheless perfectly clear to those engaged in them. This problem inevitably raises the issue of the extent to which the economic analysis of commons is value-free, or whether economists engaged in analysis of the commons should be construed as reform caucuses seeking to capture or control commons externally through analysis.

Values and the Analysis of the Commons

Amatri Sen (1970, pp. 56–57) takes issue with the premise that welfare economics can be value-free:

> Welfare economics is concerned with policy recommendations. . . . It is obvious that welfare economics cannot be "value-free," for the recommendations it aims to arrive at are themselves value judgements. In view of this it must be regarded as somewhat of a mystery that so many notable economists have been involved in debating the prospects of finding a value-free welfare economics. . . . For reasons that are somewhat obscure, being "value-free" or "ethics-free" has often been identified as being free from interpersonal conflict. The implicit assumption seems to be that if everyone agrees on a value judgement, then it is not a value judgement at all, but is perfectly "objective."

It is preferable, Sen says, to make a distinction between objectivity, or being value-free, and unanimity of judgment (consensus or agreement). He goes on to divide value judgments into two classes. "A value judgement can be called 'basic' to a person if the judgement is supposed to apply under all conceivable circumstances, and it is 'non-basic' otherwise. Nonbasicness of a judgement in someone's value system can sometimes be conclusively established, but the opposite is not the case, and to take a given value judgement to be basic, is to give it, at best, the benefit of the doubt. It seems impossible to rule out the possibility of fruitful scientific discussion on value judgements" (1970, pp. 59, 64).

One of the principal uses of the public goods theory is reliance upon *Pareto optimality* as an allegedly value-free criterion for the evaluation of common action. Using Pareto optimality, an alternative that one can choose in making a decision is said to be optimal when it does not detract or take away from the welfare of any member of society and it enhances the welfare of at least one member. Pareto optimality is a standard criterion in economic analyses of the nonprofit sector.

There is, Sen (1970, p. 22) notes, good reason not to be overly committed to the single criterion of Pareto optimality as an ultimate standard for assessing decisions. Sen says, "There is a danger in being exclusively concerned with Pareto-optimality. An economy can be optimal in this sense even when some people are rolling in luxury and others are near starvation as long as the starvers cannot be made better off without cutting into the pleasures of the rich. If preventing the burning of Rome would have made Emperor Nero feel worse off, then letting him burn Rome would have been Pareto-optimal. In short, a society or economy can be Pareto-optimal and still be perfectly disgusting."

Collective Choice Theory

In recent years, a growing interdisciplinary group of economists, analytical philosophers, sociologists, and others, seeking to resolve some of the problems discussed above, have collaborated on a project usually known as *collective choice theory*. Rigorous logical analyses of gifts, charity, cooperation, and other common goods have been a central preoccupation of this group (Ireland and Johnson, 1970; Sen, 1970; Hechter, Opp, and Wippler, 1990; Knoke, 1990). Sen (1970) says that the theory of collective choice belongs to several economic and noneconomic disciplines, including the theory of the state, the theory of decision procedures in political science and ethics, the theory of justice in philosophy, welfare economics, planning theory, and public economics.

The basic goal of collective choice theory is to formulate models of rational collective, as opposed to individual, decision making. Some highly interesting results have emerged from this project. The concept of public goods that has emerged from this work has proven highly useful in the analysis of public policy and is often applied to nonprofit economics as well (Weisbrod, 1988). Much of the work on the free-rider problem (which will be discussed shortly) has also emerged from work in this field.

In collective choice theory, no distinction is generally made between productive and unproductive labor, but the dichotomy between public and private goods is treated as fundamental and exhaustive (Knoke, 1990). Other researchers using this paradigm have sought to identify a third category of goods, often called collective goods, or shared goods. The term employed in this work for the third category is *common goods,* which will be discussed further later in the chapter.

A *private good* is one whose benefit can be restricted to those who have paid for it (Heath, 1976). A private good is "a good whose subject and object is the individual. It could be enjoyed and possessed by an individual. Its primary aim is the satisfaction of the individual's desire and interest" (Udoidem, 1988, p. 100). By contrast, a *public good* is one that, if available at all, must be available to everyone regardless of whether they have paid for the good or not. Thus a public good possesses two properties: it is indivisible and universal. As a result, it costs no more to provide a public good to all people than it does to provide it to one person, and any one person's enjoyment of the good in no way infringes upon or interferes with the enjoyment of others. Thus we speak of public goods as indivisible and universal and private goods as divisible and particular (Heath, 1976; Knoke, 1990; Olson, 1956).

The Free-Rider Problem

One of the principal theoretical implications to arise from collective choice theory to date is the *free-rider problem.* The free-rider problem can be described in this way: rational consumers will know that all people benefit uniformly from public goods regardless of their contribution and, therefore, be inclined to contribute only when it makes a difference to the overall success of the venture. They will contribute when the stakes involved are the presence or absence of the public good, since the size of the public good is a matter of indifference.

Olson (1956) notes that if three special conditions are absent, rational, self-interested individuals will not act to achieve common or group goals. The special conditions he notes are, first, selective incentives (private goods within the public good that stimulate group action); second, a disproportionate distribution of the public good so that some members of the group benefit more than others and are thus induced to encourage the participation of other members; and third, a small number of members needed to provide the public good.

Selective incentives must be selective in such a way that group members benefit while nonmembers do not. When this is not the case, they function instead as disincentives, or costs. Protection of job security for union members is a selective incentive. Similarly, a large landowner may find that the benefits to him for a new highway will be so great that he will mount a campaign for it even though it is a public good from which all will benefit.

Free-riders are those people who benefit from public goods without paying for them. Strictly from the standpoint of individual utility, everyone has an equal disincentive against contributing to the cost of the public good unless he or she can be assured that all others will also contribute. Otherwise, those people who pay risk subsidizing the nonpaying free-riders.

Although the free-rider problem is very real, complex, and difficult to deal with, it is an important question for theory only to the extent that actors are rationally self-interested. To the extent that sharing of resources and purposes, mutuality, and fairness are the defining characteristics of a situation, the impact of free-riding will be minimal. If the participants in a commons become rational individuals in this narrow sense and begin calculating their individual utilities, the fundamental, defining condition of social order in the commons would appear to have broken down.

Grant Economics

Another approach with interesting implications for common goods economics is *grant economics* (Boulding, 1973; Boulding, Pfaff, and Horvath, 1972). Kenneth Boulding is generally credited as the creator of the grants economics approach. In an engaging work called *The Economy of Love and Fear* (1973), Boulding suggests that human motives other than desire for profit, and particularly two motives he calls love and fear, deserve consideration by economists. He associates these motives with two types of unilateral transfers, or grants, which he calls patronage and tribute.

In keeping with this theme, Horvath defines *grants* as "a broad assortment of subventions (subsidies, bounties, favoritism) on the one side, and a broad assortment of tributes (underpayments, extortions, dispossessions) on the other side" (1982, p. 458). Horvath (p. 458) says that a grant is "an unmatched transaction where the net worth of one party—the grantor—diminishes while the net worth of the other part—the grantee—increases." Grants, in this sense, correspond closely with the concept of gifts, as that concept will be developed in Chapter Seven. However, some of the expanded possibilities of reciprocity found elsewhere in the literature may be lacking in Horvath's dualistic view of exchanges.

An important issue raised by grant economics is whether or not the twin bonds of love and fear, and the resultant grants of patronage and tribute, adequately account for the kinds of exchanges that arise in nonprofit and voluntary action. I sense that they do not and were not intended to. In Boulding's analysis (1973), they are presented primarily as illustrations of the many possible motives that may be associated with grant transfers. They are suggestive, therefore, of two compatible approaches: further identification of other companion motives and identification of a general summary concept that ties together all such motives, for example, utility. A related question is whether or not love and fear may be said to constitute utilities in an economic sense so that the formal logic of the utility-maximization model can be applied to them.

Regardless of these types of questions, grant economics has blazed some pioneering trails in examining the kinds of rational choice models that may be most appropriate for the study of nonprofit and voluntary action theory. It is also slowly finding its way into the literature of nonprofit and voluntary studies (Galaskiewiscz, 1985). Given the insights we can find in grant economics, we should ask whether or not other parts of modern economics can make similar contributions to an understanding of the economics of nonprofit and voluntary action.

Common Goods

One of the most powerful criticisms of the application of the public goods orientation to nonprofit or voluntary action is that most commons fail to fit the definition of a public good; church services, lodge meetings, food pantries, scientific meetings, amateur athletic events, and most other commons are available to some people (members and participants) without being available to all. Thus, they fail to meet the criterion of indivisibility, which is one of two defining characteristics of public goods.

Yet many of the desired or preferred ends or objectives of common action are clearly not private goods either. They cannot be fully alienated and controlled exclusively by particular individuals without ceasing to be what they are. There is an undeniably other-oriented quality to any religious ritual, scientific finding, or artistic expression, for example. Yet this public quality of many, perhaps most, goods of the commons stops well short of the universality demanded of public goods. The mathematical standing of calculus, for example, is not conditional upon its universal understanding or acceptance. It is sufficient that calculus be understood and accepted by mathematicians, who constitute a disciplinary commons, as noted in Chapter Four. Calculus is, in a way, what I am calling a common good.

The concept of the common good has been used frequently in democratic political theory and discussions of social problems (Ford Foundation, 1989). For example, Jordan entitled his 1989 study of the relationships of the political implications of citizenship, morality, and self-interest *The Common Good*. Sherover (1989) proposes time, freedom, and the common good as the central concepts of a free society. Riley (1986) discusses the transformation of the theological notion of God's "general will" to save all men into a political concept of the citizen's general will to place the common good above his particular will as an individual. He ascribes a pivotal place in this transition to Rousseau. The use of the concept is also not entirely unknown in political economy. For example, Raskin (1986) and Daly and Cobb (1989) incorporate the concept of the common good into their economic and social critiques. Raskin's model makes explicit a place for nonprofit institutions in what he calls "zone four" of a reorganized economy.

The concept of common good is ultimately traceable to Aristotle, who said that politics is the science of the provision of good for everyone, and to Plato, who identified the common good with the political virtue of the entire community (Udoidem, 1988). St. Augustine insisted that "the bond of a common nature makes all human beings one," and he therefore defended peace as the common good (Udoidem, 1988, p. 91). Thomas Aquinas declared the common good as the end of law and government (Udoidem, 1988).

In all of its many connotations, the notion of the common good is central to the idea of a democratic community in which a plurality of people share, without coercion, their experiences, outlooks, or purposes in some way. The democratic community of all citizens who have voluntarily accepted a dominant protective association is one expression of such mutuality. Internal democracy within organizations in democratic states is ordinarily seen as a microcosm of the larger social condition (DeVall and Harry, 1975; Petersen, 1976).

Udoidem (1988) provides an excellent introduction to the concept of the common good in social and political philosophy. He says, "A good is common when it is available, accessible and desirable by all" (p. 90). Udoidem says that a common good combines two aspects: it is ordinary, simple, and natural as opposed to extraordinary and complex, and it is available and accessible as opposed to being scarce and difficult to achieve.

Udoidem's idea is similar to, but stops short of, the explicit universality and indivisibility of public goods. Also, it does not account for the affinity between the state as a dominant protective association and the other associations in a democratic society, whether they are political or civil. In this context, it seems desirable to distinguish public and common goods along familiar lines. Thus

Figure 5.1. Typology of Common Goods.

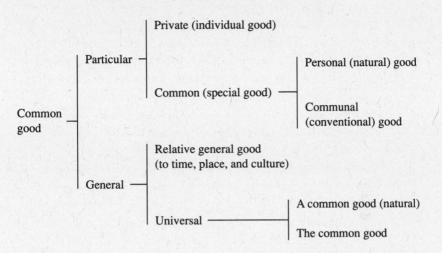

Source: Udoidem, 1988. Reprinted by permission of the University Press of America.

the public goods of the state are those that are universal and indivisible, and the common goods of the state are those particular to identifiable commons. Essential to this distinction is the further distinction between *a* common good, which may be the province of any association, and *the* common good (or public good), which is the unique province of the democratic state as the dominant protective association (Simon, 1962). In support of this view, Udoidem (1988) offers a branching diagram (Figure 5.1).

Udoidem says that a natural common good is "a good with which man is naturally endowed," such as rationality, authority, or autonomy (1988, p. 100). In that sense, mutuality of the type that arises in groups out of the sheer proximity of persons probably constitutes a natural common good. "A good that is achieved through human effort is said to be a conventional good. . . . Such goods include language, law, community, state, peace, etc." (p. 101). Conventional goods thus come very close to what I call nonstate common goods.

Maritain (1972) highlights the distinction between public goods and common goods:

That which constitutes the common good of political
society is not only the collection of public commodities and services—the roads, ports, schools, and so
forth, which the organization of common life presup-
poses; a sound fiscal condition of the state and its
military power; a body of just laws; good customs and
wise institutions, which provide the nation with structure; the heritage of its great historical remembrances,
its symbols and its glories, its living traditions and
cultural treasures. The common good includes all of
these and something more besides—something more
profound, more concrete, more human. . . . It includes the sum of sociological integration of all the
civic conscience, political virtues and sense of right
and liberty, of all the actuity, material prosperity and
spiritual riches, or moral rectitude, justice, friendship,
happiness, virtue and heroism in the individual lives
of its members. For these things are, in a certain measure, communicable and so revert to each member,
helping him to perfect his life and liberty of person.
They all constitute the good human life of the
multitude.

Udoidem's conception of a common good comes close to my
use of the term *common good*: "A common good that is achieved
through human effort (for example, language) though universal to
its particular community, is relative to time, place and people"
(Udoidem, 1988, p. 104). By contrast, his conception of *the* common
good comes closest to the economic meaning of public goods: "The
common good in human society is that which all human beings,
whether as individual or as a group, seek" (p. 108).

Udoidem concludes that "one can argue that if the common
good is a thing that is to be desired and pursued by all in the
community, whether as a group or as individuals, the means or
what it takes to achieve it must be something that is common to all"
(1988, p. 119). I might add that this holds true whether the community in question is an entire democratic polity in pursuit of the

common good or a particular common in pursuit of its own particular common good.

Conclusion

The emerging discipline of nonprofit economics has convincingly extended microeconomic models of productive enterprise to a considerable portion of the most organized and established forms of nonprofit and voluntary action. Tax-exempt nonprofit corporations that generate revenue through ticket sales or fees charged for services, such as orchestras, opera companies, hospitals, nursing homes, and various types of social service agencies, appear to be particularly amenable to this approach. Although a number of complex issues remain, rather substantial progress has been made in integrating these nonprofit establishments into the main body of economics.

By contrast, contemporary economists have largely ignored large portions of the commons. There are no economic analyses for example, that seek to step outside the familiar (but arbitrary) limitations imposed by the scarcity, production, and maximization assumptions and deal with allocative decision making under conditions that approximate those found in empirical commons.

Likewise, analyses of club theory can be found scattered in the rational choice literature, but there are no empirical studies of the economics of joining or participating in real membership associations (Badelt and Weiss, 1990; Buchanan, 1969; Cornes and Sandler, 1986). There are no adequate economic analyses of professional conferences, academic or professional journals, academic disciplines, sciences, or professions. Similarly, the economic analysis of forums and other common places has received virtually no attention. The lack of studies on common places is particularly curious in light of the evident materialistic biases of economic theory and the extensive record of the discipline in dealing with rents, properties, construction costs, and related matters.

Fernand Braudel's three-volume economic history of Europe in the sixteenth to eighteenth centuries (1981, 1986a, 1986b) offers many sound beginning points for examination of the economics of fairs and festivals and other commons. Mark Girouard's two volumes (1985, 1990) also offer many concrete examples of historically significant European commons.

The modern foundation is the subject of increasing attention, albeit within the bounds of the crippling economic maximization paradigm discussed in this chapter. In many respects, the foundation (together with the treasuries of membership associations and agencies that do not charge fees) represents the core problem of a bone fide economics of the commons. On what rational basis does an individual or group of stewards (managers, treasurers, and so forth) in control of an endowment (whether through inheritance or gift) allocate it (including any legacies to future use)? The youthful area of nonprofit economics, still hardly a decade old, has yet to deal directly with this important question.

6

The Politics
of the Commons

If each citizen did not learn, in proportion as he individually becomes more feeble and consequently more incapable of preserving his freedom single-handed, to combine with his fellow citizens for the purpose of defending it, it is clear that tyranny would unavoidably increase together with equality.

—Alexis de Tocqueville

An important focus of recent nonprofit and voluntary action studies has been the attempt to account for the range of relations between commons and states. Scholars have sought to identify a distinctive political view of nonprofit action (Douglas, 1987); to deal with specific policy issues or domains (Simon, 1987); and to deal with a range of general issues involving changes in state-commons relations, called privatization (Netting, McMurtry, Kettner, and Jones-McClintic, 1990), coproduction (Brudney, 1987), or some other label. Masterson (1979), for example, discusses Scotland's system of "official voluntarism." A Tocquevillian view is clearly evident in attempts to deal with institutions that mediate between individual, community, and state (Ben Zadok and Kooperman, 1988; Kerri, 1972). Another recent line of inquiry involves accounting for the genesis of the nonprofit sector in the structural weaknesses and deficits of state or market. Pluralism and the mixed economy concept focus on a division of labor between political states and other social institutions (Johnson, 1988). Weisbrod (1988) treats the relationship between commons and states as a competition between proprietary, nonprofit, and public sectors over which sector can deliver services most efficiently. Douglas (1987, p. 44) chooses to deal with "nonprofit organizations carrying out a public function." Within the voluntary sector view, another widely cited work locates voluntary agencies "in" (part of) welfare states (Kramer, 1981).

Many nonprofit and voluntary scholars have been interested in the state as a situational precondition or environmental cause of various nonprofit or voluntary phenomena. Contemporary nonprofit and voluntary action theory fails to capture the equally important role of commons as staging areas for the formation of democratic states and for organized challenges to existing authority, from the mildest of reforms to revolutions. The necessary connection between civil and political associations through which citizens influence the state, noted by de Tocqueville ([1862] 1945), is the cornerstone of understanding the role of associations, interest groups, and all manner of commons in the formation of the democratic polity (Newton, 1977).

Contemporary theory is extremely limited in its ability to anticipate or explain political change and its impact upon nonprofit and voluntary action. Foundations, associations, parties, interest groups, social movements, and other commons are often involved in change efforts, as well as in efforts to resist change (Delgado, 1986; Stanfield, 1985; Stephenson, 1991). For example, the Ku Klux Klan and various nativist associations in U.S. history resist change. Ostrander, Langton, and Van Til (1988) argue that the classical dichotomy between public and private sectors is neither accurate nor useful and that new conceptualizations of the reciprocal relations of the state, market, and commons are needed.

A balanced view of the reciprocity between commons and states should emphasize the generative role of commons in forming states and in maintaining continuity and change within the state, as well as such familiar roles as that of volunteers as coproducers of services and of states as purchasers of nonprofit services. This

need for a balanced view is as apparent when examining the political competition of opposition parties and reform caucuses within
ruling parties as when examining broader reform movements,
reform-oriented interest groups, and revolutionary parties. What is
needed is a conception of the state that highlights its reciprocal and
interdependent relations with the commons. In some cases, for example, evidence suggests a role for commons as alternative or substitute expressions of state powers (Brown, 1978; Johnson, 1975;
Bennett-Sandler, 1978).

This chapter sets forth a refinement of the distinction between public and common goods introduced earlier and presents a
conception of politics as a distinctive preoccupation of urban leisure classes. It identifies parties and interest groups as components
of the commons along with other types of association and addresses
issues of problem solving and presentation through their associations to freedom of speech and assembly and political ritual.

In *Mapping the Third Sector*, Van Til (1988) identifies several "spanning and mediating" propositions thought to be especially useful in examining the reciprocity of commons and state.
Three of these are particularly useful: (1) careful attention needs to
be paid to the role of the corporation as it relates to voluntary
action, (2) all associations are in part voluntary in aim and principal, and (3) voluntary associations (those in which the principal
of shared commitment predominates) may be either productive or
destructive in relation to democratic values and societal stability.

These three propositions are important for understanding
the state-commons connection. Modern corporations—whether
nonprofit, commercial, or public—are, in important respects, associations, but they are also creations of the state. As legally recognized "artificial persons," corporations simply could not exist
without positive action by the state.

The democratic state, based on the principal of popular sovereignty, is itself a unique and distinctive kind of commons—an
association of citizens pledged to civil participation, shared resources, and norms of justice in pursuit of common goods. In many
respects, nationalism may supply one of the most powerful of all
modern sources of mutuality. The democratic state possesses coercive powers of ordering and forbidding like other states, but it also

contains unique constraints upon state action, particularly against its own citizens. The U.S. Bill of Rights, in particular, places important constitutional constraints upon the state in its relation to citizens and the commons. In this chapter, I will address the critically important role of the First Amendment in setting forth a theory of the connection between state and commons in which the elements of dialogue and association figure critically.

The state, like the market, the family (or household), and the commons, is an ideal type. By the term *state*, we generally refer to the potential and real exercise of coercive authority—collection of taxes, enforcement of laws (for example, police powers), imprisonment and execution, and the ability to wage wars. In the classic view, the state is characterized by a monopoly of force (Weber, 1968). In modern nation-states and federal (or federated) states like the United States, Canada, Australia, Germany, the European Common Market, and the fledgling Russian Federation, which replaced the Soviet Union, coercive state powers are shared or distributed among a federation of several related authorities with ultimate sovereignty vested in the people. (Recall the importance here of the supremacy of the elected Boris Yeltzen over the party-designated Mikhail Gorbachev in the Russian revolution of 1991.)

The state as a coercive ideal type is not synonymous with government, the public sector, the political system, or the polity, and we must be cognizant of these differences. Modern government is not exclusively preoccupied with the exercise of authoritative or coercive powers. Some functions of modern government (for example, funding of sciences, arts, humanities, and some social services) are exercised by government bureaus that are virtually components of commons and not engaged in anything like the coercive exercise of state powers (Rourke, 1977). Lowi has mounted a powerful argument for the demise of authoritative state action in the rise of what he calls "interest group liberalism" (Lowi, 1969). To some extent, this and other arguments that modern states are unable to act decisively or effectively may be expressions of Karl Marx's vague prediction of the decline of the state.

State as Dominant Protective Association

What is the relation between the state and commons, market and family? "One of the hardest tasks in defining the sector is deciding where to draw the boundaries between voluntary, for-profit (commercial), and government agencies, and between formal and informal activities" (Anheier and Knapp, 1980, p. 8). The interdependence of the state and the third sector is one of the consistent themes of recent work. Hall (1987) says that the Filer Commission (1975) attributed an unwarranted degree of autonomy to the nonprofit sector. Wolch (1990) used the term "shadow state" to describe a body of nonprofit organizations that are technically independent but depend on government support and perform duties previously reserved for the welfare state. Concentrating on nonprofit service vendors offers an accurate, but incomplete, portrait of the interrelationship between states and commons.

Weber located the study of the association (*verein*) "in the gap between the politically organized or recognized powers—state municipality and established church—on the one side and the natural community of the family on the other" (1972, p. 20). In a similar vein, Robert MacIver (1926) treats government and corporations as associations. Etzioni's (1963) distinction between coercive, utilitarian, and normative compliance focuses the issue on the distinctive types of relationship that characterize each sector.

In an evocative phrase, Robert Nozick defines the state as the dominant protective association in a community or society (1974, pp. 15–17). The state in this sense consists of elected and appointed public officials engaged in the enforcement of protection or justice, and the associated auxiliaries that assist public officials in coproducing the conditions of civil society.

Nozick's emphasis on the dominant position of the state among authorities covers the same ground as Max Weber's (1968) "monopoly of force" definition of the state, without being sidetracked by the issue of whether or not the state must have an outright monopoly of force. Nozick (1974) argues that Weber's view can be reconciled with even a profoundly libertarian view of the limited state. Nozick is certainly not the first person to draw this connection between associations and states. The Benedictine view of the monastery was that of a little state, and Neibuhr's conception of a religious sect emphasized an ethically grounded constitution (Bestor, 1970).

The model of the state as the dominant protective association has two fundamental criteria. First, a state must be the only generally effective enforcer of prohibitions against the use of unreliable enforcement procedures by others. Thus, members of an association can expect to be protected by the state from efforts by organization officers to extort unreasonable dues from them. And nonmembers may be protected from coercive efforts to force them to join an association. Second, a state must protect noncitizens in its territory whom it prohibits from using self-help enforcement procedures on its clients. Thus, Latin American drug dealers, Arab terrorists, and illegal immigrant street gangs constrained by the state from using their own enforcers to protect themselves in business dealings in this country still are entitled to Miranda rights upon arrest.

This conception of the state as the dominant protective association is also a remarkably concise definition of some aspects of the modern welfare state. Many of the social welfare functions assumed by the modern state constitute attempts at the protection of vulnerable, disadvantaged, victimized, and helpless people. Many activities of the modern welfare state, such as protective services, child labor laws, wage and hour laws, and nursing home regulations, fall clearly within a dominant protective framework requiring the exercise of legitimate force.

However, many other social welfare activities, and in particular most forms of social service delivery, do not involve the exercise of coercive force. Many of these activities involve common goods and the kind of government bureaus embedded within commons discussed in the previous chapter. As such, they are part of the welfare *state* only in a very weak and imprecise sense of that term. They involve activities that can easily and readily be contracted out by the state to various nonprofit organizations. Theoretically, attempts to hire nonprofit organizations to carry out state regulatory and enforcement powers would be unsuccessful. This may account for some of the complexities one encounters in the contemporary social service contracting environment (Bernstein, 1991a, 1991b).

What is at issue in this definition of the state is the specification of the proper limits of the state. Libertarians are inclined to see as legitimate only a highly restricted state that protects primarily property rights. Social democrats are inclined toward an expanded role for the state. On the basis of Stalinism, Nazism, Maoism, and the many lesser "total states," we can dismiss the option of totalitarianism as acceptable in any way. Thus, the central issue raised by this definition is over the meaning and extent of the limits on the state.

Nozick (1974) does not define the state as the only protective association, as implied by the monopoly view, but simply the dominant one. Alternative protective associations are of several types. Some are clearly legitimate; insurance companies, for example, offer various forms of nonstate protection against accident, theft, death, and other risks, and they are generally subject to state regulation. Various neighborhood associations, mutual aid societies, and ethnic organizations give some forms of protection to their members.

Some types of protective associations are clearly illegitimate in that they attempt to usurp or counter the protective functions of the state. Crime families and gangs, posses and vigilante groups, and revolutionary and terrorist groups fall into this category. Some mutual aid, ethnic, and neighborhood protective associations such as the Jewish Defense League, urban street gangs, and the Black Panthers can also be treated as illegitimate protective associations by local authorities.

The legitimacy of some protective associations is unclear or problematic within the state. One such category of groups are protest groups that are committed to nonviolent civil disobedience in the tradition reaching from Thoreau to Gandhi to Martin Luther King. Another category are "radical" communes and cults (for example, "snake-handling" religious cults and the People's Temple cult in Jonestown, Guyana) that seek total escape from civil society to voluntarily engage in practices that the state finds intolerable breaches of protections it offers to all citizens. Yet another category are private militias and private (nonstate) paramilitary organizations.

States Emerge from the Commons

If we look at public programs subsidizing the creation and continued operation of various nonprofit corporations, we will probably conclude that the state creates the commons. It is probably sounder, on the whole, to step back and view the state as arising out of the commons than to see the state as engendering the commons. Certainly, this viewpoint is more accurate in the long-term history of civilizations. Anthropological literature reviewed by Smith and Freedman (1972), for example, supports the conclusion that commons probably predate the state in human evolution and the rise of civilization. The social science literature includes many examples of religious and ceremonial groups and other commons in societies and cultures lacking the rudiments of a political state. It is also true in the immediate sense that the issues that constitute the current agenda of the state are readily influenced by common action (Thielen and Poole, 1986).

Another more important basis for the logical priority of commons over states is theoretical. States or governments may enact and fund programs that create nonprofit service deliverers, as in the case of the community action program of the War on Poverty, or may purchase such services. However, we can probably trace the origins of such state-run programs back through the political parties, interest groups, and legislative campaigns of the commons that preceded and prompted state action.

The African nation-state of Liberia presents a clear example of a political state emerging from a commons. Liberian political, economic, and social institutions are largely extensions of the values of the American Colonization Society, which began its campaign for the return of African-American slaves to a newly created African nation in the 1820s (Beyan, 1991; Franklin, 1980). Other political revolutions, whether the American Revolution of 1776, the Russian Revolution of 1917, or the Chinese Revolution of 1949, also illustrate the process of the creation of entirely new states from the commons of revolutionary political parties. The connection between voluntary associations and the formation of states is also particularly clear in the emergence of the state of Israel partly from the planning that took place in voluntary associations (Eisenstadt, 1972; Loewenberg, 1991).

The social behavior associated with the establishment of a democratic state has a good deal in common with the establishment of any paradigm. Implicit, consensual, and shared beliefs, assumptions, and values—known in the modern democratic political arena as public opinion—are of critical importance.

Many different possible configurations of state and various interest groups have been identified. Constellations in which the state is relatively weak and interest groups are representative of a broad spectrum of policy positions are ordinarily designated by the label of *pluralism*. Control of the state by a small cluster of powerful interests is usually called *oligarchy* (Michels, 1949). Meier (1982) has labeled a configuration in which the typical pluralist relations between interest groups and the state are reversed as *corporatism*.

In a democratic system, the relationship between state and commons is open to continuous renegotiation. In a very real sense, it can be argued that democratic elections are the "midwives" through which various party, factional, and interest group commons gain legitimate mandates to rule and are transformed into legitimate elected governments. Thus states are created and empowered to act by candidates and parties, by the platforms and issues in the commons of political campaigns.

Commons can also have important and sometimes unexpected roles in implementing and enforcing state action when the state is not strong and the commons are strong. For example, the Elizabethan Statute of Artificers (1562) made the system of apprenticeship mandatory for certain occupations, but the uncertain powers of the Elizabethan nation-state were insufficient to enforce apprenticeship upon employers without the aid of the powerful medieval craft gilds (Abbott, 1938).

States as Producers of Common and Public Goods

The state, as the dominant protective association in a society, is often said to be uniquely concerned with the creation or production of public goods, frequently on a monopoly basis. The argument here is that the concept of common goods can be used to introduce a necessary corrective to the overgeneralized notion of public goods. Functioning states are also concerned with creating common goods in response to the demands of interest groups with which they are allied.

Public goods, as defined earlier, are goods that are indivisible and uniformly available to all. The list of public goods would include national security, public highways, clean air and water, and so on. Contemporary analysts of the public and nonprofit sector have tended to ignore the restrictive implications of this definition when they prove inconvenient. As a result, the term *public goods* has been overgeneralized to apply to virtually all possible relations between government and any nonprofit or voluntary entity. Such, for example, is the case with the view of nonprofit corporations in general as "private producers of public goods" and the definition of philanthropy as "private action for the public good."

The underlying political formula involved is a straightforward one: partisan advocates of social services, the arts, professions, science, and virtually any common interest seek various short-term political advantages by claiming that their common interests are, in fact, matters of vital public interest. Such claims are ordinarily preludes to appeals for the exercise of public powers or public subsidy of common goods. When successful, these appeals often result in the creation or modification of a commons in which a public bureau (for example, a licensing board, funding agency, or regulatory agency) is a participant.

Most nonprofit organizations clearly do not produce public goods. The claim that the arts or social services directly benefit everyone uniformly and indivisibly is demonstrably untrue, simply by virtue of the fact that many people never even attend artistic performances or receive services and could not possibly benefit directly from such organizations. The goods of these ventures are both divisible and nonuniformly distributed and thus fail both of the tests of a public good. This does not mean, of course, that such programs, services, and benefits are not goods or that they are not preferred by a majority of the population and not just those who benefit from them. It does mean, however, that the large body of analysis and theory of public goods by economists, policy analysts, and political scientists and others does not apply to these goods.

Claims that such goods are public goods are often propped up with various claims of "indirect" benefit. Not only does this idea present a major theoretical complexity, it usually also results in claims that cannot be verified. Unverifiable claims have certain strategic political advantages but do not, however, make for sound theory.

Many, perhaps most, of the claims for subsidy forced upon the state by scientific, professional, educational, religious, charitable, and other commons tend to be appeals by various leisure classes for tax-supported patronage of particular common goods valued by those leisure classes. There is almost never clear-cut majority support for (and seldom even majority understanding of) such common goods. Instead, the public tolerates or is indifferent to these common goods and is sometimes alienated by them. There are no theoretical grounds in democratic theory for such systematic satisfactions of minority interests. Therefore, nonprofit and voluntary organizations producing these common goods will feel compelled to go on appealing to specious public interests in their demands for public subsidy until other grounds for subsidy are found. And legislators and bureaucrats in control of restricted funds of this type will feel compelled to continue honoring such requests, at least for those leisure classes in a position to exert their claims most forcefully.

Nonstate Protective Associations

What can be said about protective associations that do not achieve dominance as states? One overtly political role for such groups is within majority coalitions, where they function as interest groups (Anderson and Schiller, 1976; Kvavik, 1976; Levitt and Feldbaum, 1975). Another role for such associations is as opposition groups, loyal or otherwise. Far more interesting for the theory of the commons, however, is the modern emergence of nonstate private protective associations. Although it would be easy to focus on private militias of security guards and mall police under this rubric, such services are generally organized as commercial ventures and are outside our interest here. Other less obvious, but equally interesting, examples of nonstate protective agencies fall within the domain of the commons.

One of the most interesting subcategories of this class of associations includes those organizations that seek to enforce common goods (and even, in some instances, public goods) through strictly voluntary compliance of a group of members or clients. For example, groups such as the American Society for Testing and

Materials and the American National Standards Institute voluntarily establish product safety and quality standards for voluntary acceptance by manufacturers. Such groups may be subsidized by manufacturers, or, like the Consumers' Union, they may be subsidized by donations from consumers and publish test results in the public domain.

The number of voluntary protective associations is large and the range of their standards broad. Examples include the American Welding Society's technical standards for welding beads, the American Red Cross's standards for the safe handling of blood products, and the familiar seal of acceptance of the American Dental Association on oral hygiene products. They also include the full range of ethical standards and practices of professional groups such as the American Medical Association, the American Bar Association, the National Association of Social Workers, and the National Society of Professional Engineers.

Some of the first nonstate protective associations to emerge, of course, were the various voluntary charitable and philanthropic societies. Stereotypes notwithstanding, such charity work is not entirely a matter of benign good deeds. The various societies for protecting animals and children, creating domestic violence shelters, and so forth are often engaged in creating private protective associations in areas where state action is inadequate or not forthcoming. The Underground Railroad and the more recent sanctuary movement devoted to sheltering illegal aliens from Latin America, as well as covert organizations devoted to parental "kidnapping" in defiance of court orders or societies devoted to assisting people in committing suicide, are all examples of such groups. In each case, the group takes action in support of a common good that is ignored, discouraged, or opposed by dominant state interests.

This list by no means exhausts the possibilities for nondominant protective associations, however. Also included here would be the full range of secret societies and groups devoted to overthrow of the established order. It is at this point that interest in the commons merges with traditional interests of the law of civil liberties.

Civil Liberties and the Commons

It is in the ever-present possibility that those in power will use their control of the state to harass, intimidate, or suppress their rivals or enemies that we find the normative basis of support for civil liberties associated with the commons. Several commentators in the nonprofit and voluntary action literature have commented (incorrectly) on the centrality of associations in U.S. political life and the absence of an explicit constitutional basis of a right of association. In fact, no less than four freedoms related to the right of association are found in the First Amendment: religion, speech, assembly, and redress of grievances. Although it may be argued that there is no separate right of association, the related civil liberties to assemble for peaceful purpose, speak freely, and seek change in public policies that are defined in a long series of Supreme Court rulings rather clearly outline such a right. Furthermore, those rights—together with voting rights—have been consistently interpreted in a manner that is consistent with the doctrine of popular sovereignty.

In the modern democratic political arena, we get an exceptionally clear portrait of the underlying basis of the creation of the state through processes of interaction, discussion, and debate. The First Amendment to the Constitution says "Congress shall make no law respecting an establishment of religion, or prohibiting the free exercise thereof; or abridging the freedom of speech, or of the press; or the right of the people peaceably to assemble, and to petition the Government for a redress of grievances."

According to Emerson (1964, p. 2) "freedom of association has traditionally been conceived as 'an independent right possessing an equal status with the other rights specifically enumerated in the first amendment.'" Yet, Shiffrin (1990, p. 221) notes, "The associational aspects of the first amendment have never been adequately explored." Emerson (1970, p. 292) cast the same point more broadly when he remarked, "Strangely enough, the fundamental structure of [First Amendment] rights has never been fully explicated by the Supreme Court and stands today in a state of great uncertainty."

Although legal scholars have generally dealt with the First Amendment solely in terms of individual rights, Shiffrin (1990) advocates analyzing political dissent in commons rather than as a strictly individual matter. Shiffrin notes that dissent is often construed in strictly individualistic terms as self-expression, self-realization, or individual autonomy. Yet, in seeking to realize their goals, Shiffrin says, dissenters seek to persuade others, form associations of like-minded individuals, and in general promote "engaged association" to advance social change.

According to Shiffrin (1990, p. 92), dissent is a fundamentally nonprofit idea: "Dissenters do not 'sell' ideas in the manner depicted in the marketplace metaphor." People talk, exchange ideas, and quote one another. "One could *impose* a market model on this process," Shiffrin says, but dissenters generally "seek something other than the monetary profit of a commercial transaction."

The theory of the commons provides a lattice for understanding the fundamental interconnections between the seemingly separate freedoms of the First Amendment and their associative implications. For example, religion is a major type of commons particularly in need of protection from the state in the wake of the Reformation and Counter-Reformation. Such protections remain current to offset the ever-present impulses of religious zealots, which may arise in any open and pluralistic society. Free speech (which in the preceding chapters I have called dialogue) is a fundamental basis for the discovery, organization, and presentation of common goods of all types. People identify what purposes they share by discussing their dreams and aspirations as well as their hopes and fears and coordinate their actions through sharing of strategy and tactics.

Association in common places (which the Constitution calls peaceable assembly) is fundamental to the uncoerced discovery of shared purposes, sharing of resources, and group process that is mutual and just. Prior to the development of communications technology, assembly, or, perhaps less archaically, "getting together," was the single most effective and efficient means of facilitating common dialogue. The importance of assembly is in no way diminished by the development of the telephone, television, computer, and other communications technologies that have revolutionized and extended the ways in which people can assemble and interact.

Indeed, it would appear initially that freedom of the press is the only component in the First Amendment not directly and obviously related to all the others and the commons. We might regard this as a historical anomaly and evidence of a former connection to the commons now broken. There was a strong tendency for eighteenth-century newspapers to be partisan vehicles of political groups, parties, and movements rather than the "objective" business institutions of today.

Right of Assembly

There is a significant body of First Amendment constitutional law bearing on the shape and form of the commons in the United States. My purpose here is not to review those findings in any detail but merely to highlight the relevance of First Amendment freedoms of assembly, speech, religion, and redress of grievances as major normative concerns for the theory of the commons. Oleck (1980) offers an extensive introduction to legal issues relating to the freedom to associate.

Despite the patina of individualistic rhetoric that surrounds discussions of these rights, nonprofit, voluntary, and philanthropic organizations figure prominently in First Amendment cases. Religious groups such as the Jehovah's Witnesses, civil rights organizations in the 1950s and 1960s, and museums and theaters are regularly involved in First Amendment cases arising out of attempts to impose limits or restrictions on their activities (Lewis, 1991; also see Emerson, 1970, beginning on p. 292, for a dated but interesting discussion of such cases).

Such legal cases should be of greater interest to nonprofit and voluntary action researchers than they have been, in part because they involve setting the real normative limits of common action in U.S. society. In addition, constitutional cases often involve issues that are both controversial and complex. Dworkin (1977) presents a rationale for dealing with "hard cases." Usually, such cases tend to provoke strong responses and conflict and involve issues that are intrinsically complex and difficult to resolve. Many such cases, for example, have arisen in the wake of the labor and civil rights movements. Others come in the context of state efforts to suppress various extremist political organizations, including the American Communist and Nazi parties, the Ku Klux Klan, and others.

In 1939, the Supreme Court explicitly examined the issue of the freedom of assembly implied by the Constitution and concluded that such freedom applies not only to meetings in private homes and meeting halls but also to assemblies in public streets and parks

(*Hague* v. *C.I.O.*, 1939). It found that although licensing laws can be used to protect public order or public safety, such laws may not be used for purposes of prior censorship.

The right to assemble is not absolute, however. Authorities may make reasonable time, place, and manner restrictions on public assemblies. The First Amendment does not give a person the right to communicate "one's views at all times and places or in any manner that may be desired" (*Heffron* v. *International Society for Krishna Consciousness,* 1981). In another case, the court set down guidelines by which private shopping centers may restrict leaflets, picketing, and other First Amendment exercises, but state and local officials may also legally obligate the owners of such centers to permit their use for peaceful political purposes.

One of the controversial questions raised by the civil rights movement was the issue of whether the right of peaceful assembly included the right to intentionally violate a law nonviolently. In *Walker* v. *Birmingham,* the court held that it did not, although the dissenting opinion of four justices insisted upon a right to defy peacefully an obviously unconstitutional law. In a later case the court distinguished between regulating the time, place, and manner of public assemblies for legitimate reasons such as public safety and unwarranted efforts to prevent particular groups from meeting or speakers from speaking (*United States* v. *Mary T. Grace,* 1983).

There is an undeniably political rationale underlying the freedom of assembly. In 1958, for example, the Court said, "It is beyond debate that freedom to engage in association for the advancement of beliefs and ideas is an inseparable aspect of the 'liberty' protected by the Constitution" (*NAACP* v. *Alabama,* 1958). The court concluded that unless the state could show some compelling public purpose, it may not force a private association to hand over its membership lists (*NAACP* v. *Alabama,* 1958).

Whatever their other legal ramifications, such precedents bear directly upon the distinction between public and private much sought after by nonprofit and voluntary action researchers. From this doctrine, we might reasonably conclude that in the absence of compelling public purpose, the affairs of any common are private (that is, common only to the participants, who are in turn able to determine collectively who may be a participant).

Freedom of Speech

The emphasis on the formative role of dialogue in the theory of the commons points up the critical role that freedom of speech plays in the formation and continuation of genuine commons. Although they have been generally taken for granted or neglected by non-profit, voluntary, and philanthropy scholars, speech rights are almost certainly more fundamental to the formation of commons than nonprofit corporation statutes or tax exemptions. At the same time, speech rights are as inherently social as the freedom of assembly. While cases routinely concentrate upon the rights of speakers, the speech act itself is an inherently social one, so that a speaker speaking inevitably implies an audience listening as well. Freedom of speech issues are usually tested against several well-known standards.

The standard that the Court has applied to freedom of speech cases for more than half a century is the Holmes-Brandeis "clear and present danger test": "whether the words are used in circumstances and are of such a nature as to create a clear and present danger that they will bring about substantive evils that Congress has a right to prevent." This is the constitutional basis of the famous curb on the right of an individual to falsely shout *fire* in a crowded theater. It is also the basis for the suppression of various "radical" political organizations and the protection of others.

A somewhat less-stringent criterion for the protection of free speech is the "dangerous or bad tendency test," which stems from English common law and also has been the doctrine of the Court at various times (for example, in *Gitlow* v. *New York,* 1925). Although the practice had not been subjected to First Amendment testing at the time this book was written, federal restrictions on the ability of nonprofit (and other) service providers to discuss abortion options with Medicaid clients would probably be defended on the basis of the "dangerous or bad tendencies" standard.

A third standard used by the Court in the past is that freedom of speech holds a "preferred position" among freedoms in the United States, which comes close to being an absolute right (Burns, Peltason, and Cronin, 1984).

Freedom of Religion

At first glance, it might appear that freedom of religion is somewhat redundant with freedoms of assembly and speech. If religious devotees are free to assemble and speak freely, why is a separate freedom necessary? Yet, freedom of religion is not simply about freedoms to assemble, speak, and listen. There is an essential element of practice and action associated with freedom of religion. From the vantage point of the theory of the commons, religious freedom is also about freedom of presentation; ritual and ceremonial practices figure prominently in freedom of religion concerns.

Freedom of religion might be subject to two general doctrines. On the one hand, the "no-preference doctrine" would prevent the state from aiding any particular religion but allow public religious activities that indicate no preference for a particular religion. A major difficulty with this approach in a society as pluralistic as ours is whether any type of meaningful religious doctrine or practice can be nonpreferential. Instead, the Supreme Court has generally preferred the "wall-of-separation doctrine," which forbids the government to aid, encourage, or support any and all churches or religious activities (Burns, Peltason, and Cronin, 1984). This wall of separation doctrine raises a large number of important but insufficiently examined issues in the nonprofit sector.

Redress of Grievances

In many respects, some of the most interesting recent political history of the commons is that involving what are often called protest movements. Whether we examine the labor movement, the civil rights movement, the women's movement, the environmental movement, or the recent resurgences of political conservatism and social traditionalism, coalescence around a perceived problem, or grievance, and a plan of action, or redress, is one of the most frequently encountered forms of common political action. Even in highly repressive regimes, commons may emerge as protest movements, revolts, riots, or in other more peaceful forms. And, inevitably when protest movements develop, the common rhetoric of shared purpose, shared resources, and mutuality is likely to be heard.

Conclusion

This chapter is not in any way intended to be a full or complete discussion of the major issues of political theory and law to which it alludes. Adequate conceptualization of the democratic political state must attend to the state as a kind of political association. Nozick's (1974) conception of the state as the primary protective association makes this connection and also corrects for some of the inadequacy of Weber's "monopoly of force" conception. The issues involved, however, reach well beyond the definition of the state.

Nonprofit, voluntary, and philanthropy scholars seeking to consider the commons as well as the nonprofit firm will be drawn unavoidably into the fundamentally dialectical relationship of the state and the third sector. Many nonprofit firms that are essentially creatures of the state make up an important portion of the third sector. At the same time, other nonprofit commons, including political parties, interest groups, political campaigns, and common endeavors of many different types are critical to the formation and continuation of the state. Limits on lobbying by 501(c)(3) corporations outline a gossamer boundary between these divergent dynamics.

A far more substantial and meaningful boundary is represented by the First Amendment freedoms of assembly, speech, religion, and redress of grievances. Political states do have an important impact upon the formation and continuation of nonprofit corporations through such vehicles as incorporation statutes, tax policies, and purchase of service contracting. Yet, First Amendment freedoms tend to place substantial restrictions, both individually and as a whole, on the ability of the state or others to interfere with the free and uncoerced definition of common purposes, pooling of shared resources, expression of mutuality, and promulgation of internal standards of fairness inherent in the rendition of common goods.

7

The Role of Gifts
and Other Exchanges

The most democratic country on earth is that in which people have, in our time, carried to the highest perfection the art of pursuing in common the object of their common desires and have applied this new science to the greatest number of purposes.

—Alexis de Tocqueville

This chapter will concentrate on some of the elementary forms of behavior or volunteer labor through which commons are built up within the broad confines of social exchange theory. It will look toward breaking out of some of the arbitrary constraints imposed on nonprofit and voluntary action research by the market model of mutually profitable exchange. To explore this topic, I will use the concept of the benefactory, previously introduced in Chapter Two.

Social exchange theory has had an enormous importance for nonprofit and voluntary action studies (Homans, 1961, 1968; Blau, 1967; Blau and Scott, 1962). American social exchange theory has its conceptual origins in attempts by George Homans and his colleagues to discover what Homans called the elementary forms of social behavior (Homans, 1961). This approach has been subjected to extensive criticism and analysis (Heath, 1976; Mitchell, 1978). It does, however, impose an interesting and seemingly rigorous model on the study of the commons, and organizational researchers have been attempting to explore the research possibilities suggested by this model (for example, Saidel, 1989). Unfortunately, attention has been limited to the most marketlike common organizations and those with the closest ties to the state. The resulting studies have left many organized commons like those discussed in Chapter Four completely out of the picture. Without making any claims about the exhaustive or universal nature of the list, this chapter identifies a number of forms of exchange, organization, and interaction that appear to be the building blocks upon which many forms of commons are built.

Common Goods Exchange and the Gift Map

Common goods exchanges, or the voluntary and uncoerced social acts of patrons and beneficiaries in which purposes and resources are shared, mutuality is built up, and fairness is assumed, are the irreducible units of social, economic, and political behavior in the commons. The model of the gift (or benefit) freely given by a benefactor to a beneficiary offers a starting point for analysis of all types of common goods exchanges.

Much of conventional exchange theory follows grant economics in treating gifts as unilateral transfers, in contrast to the two-way exchanges of buyers and sellers in the marketplace. Such an approach is reductionistic in deconstructing all types of gift exchanges to unilateral and unidirectional transfers in single-round exchanges and masks other equally important types of common exchange.

An alternative model has already been suggested in the preceding chapters: in common goods exchanges, groups of affluent persons, who are temporarily not at risk in terms of their basic needs, voluntarily forego their own self-interest and associate with others to define mutual purposes and pool resources. In the process, they develop a sense of mutuality within group-determined standards of fairness and justice. Not all affluent people choose to act this way or to act this way all of the time, nor are they obligated to do so. And all people do not act rationally all of the time. How-

ever, affluent people acting rationally may on some occasions favor
the interests of others over their own. When they do, at least four
distinct types of common exchange can be noted: patronage and
tributes, gifts, potlatches, and offerings. More can be said about
each of these without the need to preclude the possibility of additional types.

Patronage and Tributes

Quite possibly the simplest form of common goods exchange is the
simple unilateral transfer of a tangible substance, message, or other
meaningful object (the gift, benefit, or benefice) from one subject
(the giver or donor) to another (the receiver or beneficiary). I shall
follow Boulding, Pfaff, and Horvath (1972) and refer to this type of
unilateral transaction as patronage and tribute. However, I shall
depart from Boulding's (1973) suggestion that patronage is exclusively positively charged (love) and tribute is exclusively negatively
charged (fear). The two terms suggest an almost infinite variety of
hierarchical opposites—higher and lower, richer and poorer, older
and younger, knowledge and ignorance, and so forth. In each case,
patronage involves a unilateral transfer, or gift, in one direction and
tribute in the other.

Patronage and tribute exchanges commonly involve interaction between at least two parties of manifestly unequal status. Because they involve manifest inequalities does not necessarily mean
that tributes are always objective or rational exchanges or that the
hierarchies are static, rigidly defined, or mutually exclusive. Gifts
between lovers, for example, often assume the form of mutual tributes. And parental support of children has many features in common with other forms of patronage.

It is of central importance to note the risky nature of reciprocity with patronage and tributes. Whether the tribute is to a
powerful ruler, a lover, parents, children, or some other person,
equitable exchange, a contract, or obligations of reciprocity are not
ordinarily part of the understanding in tributes.

An important question for nonprofit and voluntary studies
involves the extent to which prosocial helping behavior and various
forms of organized charities constitute tribute. The distinction be-

tween unreserved giving and gifts in anticipation of return figures prominently in the distinctive fourth-century positions of St. John Chrysostem and St. Ambrose discussed by Morris (1986). It is also important in the "degrees of charity" of Maimonides (Cass and Manser, 1983).

Possibly the earliest intermediaries in tributes were the priests and temple cults of ancient religions. Regardless of other differences, a major characteristic of most religious observances is the intermediary or intercessional role of the priest, shaman, magician, or soothsayer between the worshipper/giver/subject and the god who is the recipient of tribute. In Buddhist ethics, the issue of assuring that gifts given to the intermediary actually "reach" the intended recipient is a major concern of the ethics of tribute (Lohmann and Bracken, 1991).

One of the consistent historical and contemporary themes of the evolution of the commons in Western civilization is the multifaceted role of the state as patron of diverse common goods. Patronage in U.S. politics has a dubious reputation. Since the Progressive Era, the idea of political patronage has been widely condemned even as it continues to be widely practiced in U.S. public life. One of the principal effects of dismissing all forms of patronage as undesirable and objectionable is to leave virtually no means to discuss major aspects of the relation of state and commons. Terms like *aid, assistance, grant,* and *support* all have their proper and specific uses, but *patronage* remains the most satisfactory generic term.

In the context of the commons, *patronage* is the giving of either protection or support (Gifis, 1991). Political sinecures, favoritism in the awarding of public contracts, and protection from prosecution are forms of patronage, but so are commissions of works of art and architecture, grants, awards, honors, and recognitions. Rather than ignoring or rejecting the idea of patronage outright, it is preferable to distinguish *merit patronage,* patronage distributed on the basis of some defensible principle of merit, from mere *favoritism.* Such a distinction might hold, for example, that federal aid to urban areas or to the poor is patronage justified on the basis of merit (in this case, need). Indeed, it is just such a distinction that advocates of "positive discrimination" in affirmative action policies claim to be making.

From this vantage point, it is not the fact of patronage per se but the justification of the merit associated with it that is the key issue. A distinction between merit patronage and favoritism along these lines is entirely consistent with the arguments for rejecting false public goods already discussed. Thus, there is a legitimate recognized public interest, in the form of an educated citizenry, in universal free public education as a public good but no similar public good for higher education. Instead, public support for higher education is in the form of distinct common goods outlined by the National Endowments for the Arts and Humanities, the National Science Foundation, and other governmental agencies closely allied with distinct, identifiable commons.

Ironically, the growth of government since the end of World War II has also meant vast increases in merit patronage programs, largely without corresponding changes in public attitudes toward patronage. The currently operative system of interest group liberalism (Lowi, 1969) is notable in part as a way of reconciling the resulting cognitive dissonance: partisans of any particular and localized interest tacitly agree not to challenge the special privileges enjoyed by others so long as those others do the same for them.

Gifts

Tribute can be distinguished from gifts in the ordinary meaning of this term by the norm of reciprocity. Tribute is given with no expectation of receiving a gift in return, but people expect reciprocity when they give gifts (Gouldner, 1960). Thus, if I give you a present for your birthday, it is typically with the expectation that you will do the same for me on my birthday. Reciprocity, in other words, is encoded in the gift situation and establishes a fundamental equality between giver and recipient that is not characteristic of either patronage or tribute. For example, after a period of time, those people who fail to respond in kind to our holiday greeting cards may be removed from our mailing lists.

In what remains the classic study of gift giving, the French anthropologist Marcel Mauss (1967) defined the gift as given, received, and returned; that is, a new gift is given by the original recipient to the original giver and so on, ad infinitum. Indeed, it is this continuous, ongoing quality of gift giving that is the basis for interpreting gifts as a key to social integration and solidarity. In giving and receiving, individuals establish, symbolize, and demonstrate their ongoing relations and mutual obligations.

The logic of the giving-receiving-giving pattern explains many aspects of common behavior as well as some of the dilemmas of the nonprofit field. For example, this logic can be used to offer a more benign explanation of one of the favorite shibboleths of critics of modern charities. It seems to be almost a law of charity that a gift given (whether in the form of an individual donation or an institutional grant) will be followed up by a later request for, as we say, continued funding. The almost unanimous conclusion of the self-interest theorists is that this request is clear-cut evidence of self-interest on the part of the recipients. Moreover, such self-interest can easily be seen as evidence of greed if one comes to dislike the recipients or question their motives. The message seems clear enough: "I, the donor, did good in my gift to you. You have no right to suggest I have any further obligation to give you another gift!"

If we view the matter exclusively from the donor's perspective, it does indeed appear to involve self-interest or greed. However, if we examine the matter from the vantage point of the other parties to the exchange as well, quite another perspective arises. For example, intermediaries who receive gifts may have a reaction that is quite different and entirely consistent with a reciprocal gift perspective. The intermediary is likely to say, "You gave me a gift on the condition that I use it to help others. I continued the cycle and gave help to others (which was our gift to them—yours and mine). Now, simple reciprocity says that unless I receive another similar gift, the chain of reciprocal giving is broken, and I am the victim of bad faith!"

Thus, it would appear that norms of reciprocity based on gift theory are at the heart of a conflict in values that is of overriding importance in the modern commons. In many practical cases, we simply lack an adequate normative basis on which to resolve the seeming conflict between interpretations of donor and intermediary. (I will leave aside entirely the equally important issue of donor and intermediary expectations upon recipients. For example, in exchange for food stamps, how much right does the state, as donor, have to prescribe the recipient's eating habits?) In general, while it is quite clear that very real norms of reciprocity do in fact exist, it is equally clear that they are inadequate in a number of cases.

Potlatches

In its narrowest sense, the *potlatch* is a distinctive ceremonial gift-giving institution of traditional Tlingit culture on the Northwest Pacific coast (Kan, 1986). More generally, the term *potlatch* can serve to identify a broad form of reciprocal gift giving involving serial reciprocity, of which the Tlingit potlatch is a noteworthy example.

In the potlatch, reciprocity is trilateral, as opposed to the closed system of reciprocity of gift giving. A person who receives a gift in the potlatch is obligated to further giving, not simply to the original giver but to others. This form of exchange might be paraphrased as the message "Here's my gift, pass it on!" The potlatch form of giving is, logically at least, eventually extended to embrace the entire community. Both the self-interest and social status of givers are involved in the potlatch. Examples of the potlatch are numerous, from the grand patronage of the temples and ceremonial events of ancient Greece to the *mayordomia* of Latin American villages (Smith, 1977).

Something like the potlatch exchange shows up in some surprising places. The practice in the United States of granting tax-exempt status to various nonprofit charitable organizations, for example, can be interpreted as a potlatch in which an original gift (freedom from taxation) is given by the state to nonprofit organizations in expectation of a return gift to various deserving client groups. In typical potlatch fashion, the process does not stop there, however. The distinctive rhetoric of U.S. social and economic policy also anticipates further steps to this gift, in the expectation that those clients benefited by such services will eventually be transformed into productive workers who will contribute to increased social product and who will become tax-paying citizens. They are expected to eventually pay tribute to the state, which will continue the tax-exempt status of charitable organizations and the entire cycle.

Thus, one possible avenue toward resolving the conflict of values noted earlier is to bring the recipient into the picture. If a donor makes a gift to an intermediary who uses that as a basis to make a gift (as anticipated by the donor) to a recipient, what are the accumulated expectations on the recipient? Is the first part of the transaction a gift and the latter part of the transaction tribute? In that case, we can say the recipient has no explicit obligation to reciprocate. If so, on what basis did the transformation from gift to tribute occur? If not, in what form can the recipient be expected to respond with a suitable gift? Many of the answers to the current quandaries of nonprofit charity theory rest upon the answers to these questions.

Offerings

Offerings can be said to be given, received, and eventually returned to the giver, but not by the receiver (Strong, 1983). Interestingly, this type of exchange is the basis of the Judeo-Christian concept of charity; the traditional Christian concept of almsgiving has been interpreted as offerings to a generous and loving God. It is also the basis of the Buddhist concept of *dana,* in which donations to the Buddhist monks are interpreted as gifts to Buddha, who can be expected to respond in kind (Dharmasiri, 1989; Goodwin, 1987; Strong, 1983). For example, a gift is given to a beggar or a monk who receives it but is in no position to reciprocate; divine reciprocity comes instead.

Because of the overt religious connotations involved in offerings, exchange theorists have been inclined to discount offerings or view them as simpler gift, tribute, patronage, or potlatch transactions. Yet the grounds on which theorists redefine offerings as they are interpreted by various commons is highly problematic. Mauss (1967) captures the exact sense of offerings in his suggestion that alms are not really given to the poor but are actually offerings to gods, deities, or spirits, who in turn grant that the obligations that were sacrificed to them should be given to the unfortunate. In the same vein, the Bible quotes Jesus as telling his disciples that whatever is done to the poor, weak, and helpless is done also to him.

Because we may be accustomed to thinking of offerings as ceremonial or ritual acts, the concept of the offering as an elementary common exchange may be a difficult one to accept. Offerings, whether sacred or secular, involve exchange among unequals that are linked to a long chain of serial reciprocity in which the most exalted being, whether human or supernatural, holds the penultimate position. This is the sense of offerings in the example given by Mauss (1967). However, offerings should not be mistaken for, or reduced to, simple tributes because the various sacred beings assume an intermediary rather than an object role.

Thus, offerings involve serial, triadic relations rather than the simple diadic relations of tributes and gifts. Rather than involving only the giver, receiver, and gift, offerings also involve intermediaries who handle the exchange—whether ceremonially or ritualistically or in more prosaic reality. The idea of offerings also appears regularly, for example, in modern, scientific professional guises as well. It is said of the practice of medicine, for example, that physicians treat illnesses (make offerings of medicine), but only God heals (grants the benefit of health).

Free-Riding

Free-riding can be defined as an elementary form of common goods exchange characterized by acceptance of a benefit not offered. Since the introduction of the term by Hardin (1968), the concept of free-riding behavior has become a given in a considerable portion of nonprofit economic, management, and organizational studies. It is interesting to note, therefore, that findings from several studies suggest important parameters of the free-riding phenomenon.

A study of 212 undergraduates concluded that individuals are more likely to avoid socially responsible behavior when they are in groups than when they are alone (Wiesenthal, Austrom, and Silverman, 1983). Yamagishi (1986) presents an explicitly social-psychological approach to the problem of public goods and concludes that members of a group who have realized the undesirable consequence of free-riding and the importance of mutual cooperation will cooperate to establish sanctions that assure other members' cooperation instead of trying to induce other members into mutual cooperation directly. Such an approach virtually cries out for connection with various findings in the area of the social psychology of opinion leadership.

Rich (1988) concludes that there are countless examples of successful collective effort that cannot readily be explained by reference to formal or informal sanctions against free-riding. Most solutions to the free-rider problem ignore the importance of a sense of community, which is a common good as Rich (p. 14) defines it: "the recognition that one's own interests are intimately bound to the capacity of an identifiable group to satisfy their interests."

Taken together, these findings point toward the tentative conclusion that although free-riding is certainly an important element of the psychology of the commons, it is hardly a fixed and immutable characteristic of voluntary group action. In fact, a good deal of work remains to be done on specifying more precisely the conditions under which free-riding occurs. It is quite plausible, for example, that free-riding occurs primarily, or even exclusively, under conditions of "normative dissonance"; that is, when the social norms regulating participation, approval and affirmation, sharing, and the other dynamics of common action are weak or conflicting.

Rich (1988) singles out three conditions affecting the likelihood of free-riding: (1) sufficient recurring interaction so that participants have an opportunity to form expectations about the behavior of others, (2) conditional cooperation, or being willing to cooperate only if others are also willing, and (3) common goods that are clearly defined and that exceed the individual's cost. He goes on to suggest that it is not the total number of people in the group that is relevant to determining whether or not a group can supply itself with a common good but rather the size of the subset of members who can see the relationship between their interests and the group's capacity for joint action and are willing to pursue a strategy of conditional cooperation.

Acts of Common Good

The everyday meaning of the term *gifts* is of tangible objects—baseball bats and electric trains and fur coats—given and received for birthdays, holidays, and special occasions. It is worthy of note that a synonym for such gifts is *presents,* a term that subtly calls attention to the act of presentation. However, as already discussed, most common goods consist primarily or exclusively of intangible social acts rather than tangible objects.

Acts of common good are by their very nature notoriously varied, which brings us back again to the issue of classification raised in Chapter One. We can find people praying, acting, writing, singing, and working together to aid those victimized by all manner of threats and perils. We can also find them meeting together in groups for all manner of purposes—doing research, playing games, and engaging in a myriad of other pursuits that are voluntary, mutual, and fair pursuits of common ends with shared means. Yet we have great difficulty conceiving of the entire class of common goods and seeing any natural divisions of such goods as a class.

Empirically, this difficulty may be because most of us are normally only involved in a small spectrum of the entire class of common goods, and our preoccupations are with our fellow participants and the concerns we share with them. Theoretically, such narrow vision leads to the kind of fractured and partial views of the commons to which we have grown accustomed. I shall attempt to deal explicitly with the major categories of organized commons in Chapter Eight. For the moment at least, we can forsake typologies of common actions and instead reduce the vast inventory of possible common actions to two principal categories: discourse and presentation. Information and meaning and problem solving will also be discussed in the context of these categories.

Discourse and Presentation

Commons, benefactories, and common goods consist of the social acts of persons in time, and as such there is an inherent subjectivity, unpredictability, and spontaneity about them that can be downplayed but that cannot be arbitrarily ignored in the name of objective science. Common goods are ephemeral human creations in that they cannot be stored or saved for later distribution. They are thus distinctly part of what Simon (1981) calls the "artifice," or the humanly constructed order, of civilization. Unlike technology, equipment, and products, however, the artifacts of the commons are almost entirely symbolic rather than material.

In general, the symbolic artifice of the commons can be divided into two broad categories of action: *discourse,* or the use of complex verbal symbols to assert things through a process of successive understanding and aggregation of separate meaning units (Langer, 1967), and *presentation,* consisting of rites (or rituals), ceremonies, and myths (Morgan and Brask, 1988; Langer, 1967). Most of discourse can be subsumed within the pragmatic problem-solving model.

Discourse is an important element of action in all commons. Indeed, common language may be the original commons. Discussion, debate, dialogue, and argument are all forms of discourse. One contemporary indicator of the importance of discourse is the stress such issues as speaking order and other discursive issues have in constitutions, bylaws, *Roberts Rules of Order,* and other common governing documents. Discourse is the basis upon which the five defining elements of a commons are linked; free and uncoerced participation and fairness can only be realized, shared purposes and resources identified, and a sense of mutuality and affiliation built up through talk, dialogue, communication, and exchange.

An equally important form of action in common goods, and one that is somewhat more complex to grasp than discourse, is presentation. Understanding presentation is particularly important in understanding the artistic, religious, and emotional content of common goods. The approach I take here follows Langer in defining presentational symbols as direct presentations of objects that speak directly to sense and lack intrinsic generality. Presentational symbols have no adequate permanent units of meaning; therefore, their meanings are grasped only through their relation to larger patterns, structures, or fabrics (Langer, 1967).

Because of their importance in discourse and presentation, symbols are the building blocks of common goods. Symbols in discourse require elements of both practical context and novelty (Langer, 1967). These symbols are most commonly encountered in activities of a "practical" or problem-solving character (in the Deweyian sense), such as social service, social action, competitive athletics, science, or philosophy.

Presentational acts tend to be of four types: rites, ceremonies, dramas, and games. *Rites* are prescribed sets of words and actions used without variation and believed to have symbolic powers to produce certain desired effects. Common rites vary widely, but include religious rites and an undetermined number of other practices (Smith, 1972a). The use of parliamentary procedure introduces a degree of ritual and predictability to common gatherings.

Ceremonies are special occasions in which explicit rules of behavior govern the performance of members (Rose, 1958). Such ceremonies in the commons include commencement and award ceremonies. Annual meetings and business meetings of large associations tend to take on a ceremonial quality as well.

Dramas are complex social acts that may involve several types of ceremonies in dealing with problems such as victimization and redemption, sickness and healing, and so forth (Brissett and Edgley, 1990). Many nonprofit problem-solving activities in social services and some types of scientific activity constitute dramas in this sense. Thus, problem and solution may be knitted together by a fabric of meanings spelling out the normal or typical steps in the problem-solving drama. *Games* are strategic social acts of a more or less routine nature (in which everyone knows the rules). Committee meetings, conferences among experienced individuals, and budget decisions often constitute games in this sense.

Information and Meaning

The signs that are the building blocks of discourse and presentation can be organized in several different ways. Among the most important behavioral characteristics of such constructions are practical context and novelty, which correspond closely to what is ordinarily meant by information and meaning. Discourse always requires these two distinct elements: verbal or practical context (or knowledge) and novelty (what the speaker is trying to point out or express) (Edelman, 1977). Knowledge can thus be defined as the quality of order and predictability in symbols.

Information is generally acknowledged to be a critical factor in all types of community service practice. In social casework, for example, the interview has long been held to be the central process, and information gathering, or assessment, and strategic use of information, or intervention, are usually regarded as fundamental dynamics of the interview. In social group theory, theories of group formation and dynamics often revolve around the information that group participants have or learn about one another. In community organization, the knowledge-is-power dynamic has long been critical, and information is often seen as one of the key variables separating the disadvantaged from various powers and elites. Simon (1976) first identified information as a critical variable in the effectiveness of decision making in administration.

In general, this approach makes information and meaning measurable by placing it in the context of that which is and is not presently certain. It also systematically integrates time as a critically important factor in common goods, in terms of both the time involved in searching for information and the time needed for separating information and meaning. What is presently known and meaningful (for example, is the client currently employed?) is alterable, and information must be collected again and again. Thus, we cannot in this context speak of information or meaning absent an explicit time frame. At the same time, the value of information and meanings is also alterable. For example, the fact that the client is not employed today was established at an identifiable cost. If the client is employed tomorrow, the meaning of today's discovery may be lost, and the question arises of whether the cost of information gathering was justified.

The distinction between information and meaning also implies that three particular types of action are critically important to the theory of common goods. One of these is *search,* which is action by which information is obtained. Search is likely to proceed along any of a number of lines, including trial and error, problem solving, and planning. *Technique* denotes any act in which existing meanings are employed. Socialization, or *learning,* involves the acts by which techniques (including search strategies) are disseminated. The categories of search, technique, and learning can be employed to classify virtually all types of common repertories, whether the performance repertories of the concert musician, the roles of the actor, or the skills of the human service provider.

It is important to ask to what extent can we treat discourse and presentation as the basic elements of tributes, gifts, potlatches, and offerings? Discourse and presentation are important elements in tribute. It is standard at awards banquets, convocations, and numerous other common events to "pay tribute" in the form of speeches of recognition and commemoration or to present plaques, awards, and other mementos to those whose actions in the common good are deemed praiseworthy or exemplary in some way.

Discourse and presentation as forms of gift giving in the commons are only slightly more complex. Much of the rhetoric of grantsmanship (or, the ways in which people talk about grant activities) incorporates recognition of reciprocal gift exchanges. If you will give me an award of money, I will help you achieve the purpose you desire: cures for cancer, solutions to social problems, greater knowledge, or whatever. The negotiations constitute a complex dialogue and we even speak directly of the "presentation" of findings. In fact, this very pervasive rhetoric may mask the existence of a potlatch rather than ordinary gift reciprocity.

I have already discussed tax-exempt status as an example of potlatch giving. Serial patronage of philanthropic projects, in the manner of the Greek *liturgia* or the Latin American *mayordomia*, is another major example. In both cases, a gift is given or a benefit conferred in explicit consideration of the serial award of that gift to yet another. In all such cases, serial conversations occur in which the "middle party" (agent or intermediary) must form a common bond based on purpose, mutuality, and fairness in separate diadic relationships with patrons and clients. In the one case, we speak directly of budget "presentations" by community service agencies. In the latter case, the purpose of interviews with clients is ostensibly for clients to "present" their needs and wants to those same intermediaries in quest of the transferred benefit.

Offerings are sometimes mistakenly associated only with religious observances. Anyone who has ever given a speech or presented an academic or scientific paper representing his or her very best efforts to a group of respected and valued peers should also have an intuitive grasp of the offering exchange. Under such circumstances, one may "give my best effort" (or, more colloquially, "give it my best shot") in the hope or expectation that others will do likewise. When they do, the return of the offering is characteristically not associated with any particular individual. In religious terms, it is seen as a divine gift. In more secular terms, such common offerings frequently engender words like *synergy, actualization,* and *gestalt* and phrases like *greater than the sum of its parts.*

Problem Solving

Discourse and presentation are thus the elemental forms for organizing action in the commons, and that action conforms consistently to the logic of gift exchange. The question that arises is, to what ends does such talking and showing lead in gift exchange? What, in other words, is the purpose of common discourse and presentation?

In the context of the microeconomic model as it is frequently applied to nonprofit endeavors, the answer to these questions is simple: people speak and display themselves and their actions and creations in order to gain advantages and rewards for themselves. The assumptions stated in Chapter Two, however, explicitly rejected self-interest and maximization of profit as motives. To briefly restate the matter, when people are acting authentically in a manner consistent with the stated objectives of diverse commons, they frequently claim that they are not merely attempting to serve their own ends. And they do not appear self-interested to objective observers. The main interest of the theory of the commons is in creating a systematic theoretical statement of the commons that explores the implications of that position.

The pragmatic model of problem solving is the formal theoretical backbone of a good deal of common activity. Virtually all contemporary problem-solving approaches begin with, or are traceable to, the problem-solving model of John Dewey (see Bernstein, 1971). The view that one solves problems by defining them, identifying alternatives, assessing the alternatives, and choosing among them is so universal in social welfare, extension, and other voluntary action fields as to be considered virtually a natural attitude.

To Dewey (McDermott, 1973), Mead (1934), and the other pragmatists, the way we experience problems is universal for individuals and groups. Recognizable problems erupt into the flow of normal (that is, nonproblematic) personal or group experience and divert attention away from other things. In experiencing problems, we redirect our attention, temporarily or permanently, from other concerns and focus on the problem. An important aspect of the meaning of solving a problem, therefore, is the redirection of attention away from the problem and toward other concerns.

When we experience a problem, we commonly have a sense of things being out of the ordinary and often have an urgent wish to do something. As a result, the events of becoming aware of a problem and being no longer aware of the situation as a problem per se (and only as a past experience) offer a convenient way to delimit the boundaries of a problem from an individual standpoint.

Thus, in at least a limited sense, we experience a problem in a time interval between an initial "horizon of indifference," prior to which there was no problem, and a later "horizon of indifference," after which the problem is recalled only as a memory. In the terminology of endowment theory, after its resolution, the problem itself has become part of our heritage. Knowledge gained in recognizing and resolving problems may in this way become part of our resource endowment for solving future problems. This is in fact the much-prized attribute of experience and practical wisdom that many social work practitioners prefer over theory.

Common problem solving, which leads to a stable solution, or what might be called "a solution in place," often corresponds closely to the gift exchange model as well. From the perspective of gift exchange, well-defined and well-understood problems are as much a part of common endowments as solutions are. Thus, those cost-benefit approaches that perceive problems as negative valences and solutions as positive valences and problem solving as "neutralization" (for example, cost reduction) are particularly inappropriate for the commons.

The sociologist C. Wright Mills (1959) once made a distinction between troubles and problems that is particularly apt here. An individual or group may have a vague sense that something is wrong without ever identifying or defining the trouble as a problem. Such vaguely sensed problems are more likely to be adapted to and lived with than solved. Yet articulating, clarifying, and defining the trouble into an explicit problem, rather than being seen as an offering, can sometimes be interpreted as a setback or a loss.

The history of family violence in America offers a particularly apt example. What some people have interpreted as an epidemic or sudden outbreak of family violence may actually be our increased awareness of family violence as a result of heightened sensitivity to the problems such violence represents and the deleterious consequences of violence. As understanding of the problem grows, simple acceptance of its consequences becomes more and more unconscionable. Thus, deeper understanding and more clear-cut definition of problems constitute powerful resources for contemporary groups concerned with social problems, environmental issues, and many other matters.

Endowment theory, as noted earlier, is concerned with a pragmatic account of the ways in which communities use resources, including surplus social product and prior problem-solving experience, in the commons. In the problem-solving context, it is time rather than money that is the common measure of problem and solution. Elapsed time is a universal characteristic of all problem-solving ventures, even those conducted outside a money economy such as our own. When problem solving does involve paid employment or other forms of contracted service, some measure of time is typically involved. Money measures such as wages, salaries, and consultations are easily converted into time units as well.

A Buddhist Ethical Perspective

Those familiar with the nonprofit and voluntary sector in the United States are accustomed to the well-known association between Judeo-Christian ethics and various elements of prosocial behavior, including altruistic acts, donations, and other forms of patronage. It may come as somewhat of a surprise, however, that theologians and ethicists in other religious and cultural systems have also been concerned, to one degree or another, with comparable sets of issues (see, for example, Fisher, 1978; Saddhatissa, 1970; Dharmasiri, 1989).

On the basis of a study of Burmese Buddhism, Melfred Spiro (1970) links the Buddhist conception of merit to explicit charitable and philanthropic actions. Merit is the goal of religious action because merit can improve one's karma. Merit is acquired, among other ways, by performing acts of charity and by giving. In the hierarchy of giving, religious giving, such as supporting a monk or building a temple or shrine, brings the greatest merit. To contribute to a poverty-stricken widow or to build a school is considered inferior giving. Although there may be other variations between Burmese and Japanese Buddhism, this order of priority for giving applies in the case of Japanese Buddhism also.

Conclusion

This chapter identifies four distinct types of gift exchange frequently encountered in the commons: tributes, or unilateral exchanges without expectation of return; gifts, or reciprocal exchanges; potlatches, or serial chains of reciprocal exchange; and offerings, which might also be called "broken chain" exchanges, because a gift is given without reciprocity and a return gift comes from another, independent source. No claim is made that these types entirely exhaust the range of possible kinds of gift exchange. They do, however, occur frequently enough to deserve further attention.

Because of the intangible character of these types of common gift exchanges, it is necessary and appropriate to analyze them as conversational exchanges that involve discourse, presentation, and problem solving rather than to deconstruct them into utilitarian exchanges that involve "costs" and "benefits." Building upon these various models of gift exchange, it should be possible to build more complex descriptive and explanatory models of the dynamics of common action that have the symbolic interactions of discourse, presentation, and problem solving, rather than the utilitarian action of profitable exchange, at their core. In Chapter Eight, three implications of this will be explored: charity, self-help, and mutual aid.

8

Charity, Self-Help, and Mutual Aid

> Among democratic nations, all the citizens are in-
> dependent and feeble; they can do hardly any-
> thing by themselves, and none of them can oblige
> his fellow men to lend him assistance. They all,
> therefore, become powerless if they do not learn
> voluntarily to help one another.
>
> They look out for mutual assistance; and as
> soon as they have found one another out, they
> combine.
>
> —Alexis de Tocqueville

Beginning in the second half of the nineteenth century, ethical precepts of charity reaching back to the ancient Hebrews and ethical
precepts of philanthropy dating to the Athenian Greeks were gradually merged and transformed into the modern, organized institutional base of social service. This transformation has important
enduring implications for the commons. In Great Britain and the
United States, this transformation took place largely within the
voluntary sector of private charitable organizations.

Three elements of this transformation are of particular interest to charity theory as a component of the theory of the commons:
the focus on "charity organization," the unprecedented emphasis

on science as an element in charitable practice, and the belief (at least partly false) that personal and voluntary charity must inevitably become a matter of specialized professional practice. Although social work and a number of other specialized helping professions have arisen, the professionalization of charity has not displaced voluntary acts of charity nor caused amateur organized charities to disappear.

Western civilization appears to have been characterized by only three distinct systems of charity throughout its long history: (1) personal charitable practice based upon the ethical obligation to perform other-oriented acts of positive good invented by the Hebrews and adopted in turn by Christianity and Islam; (2) religiously based systems of organized charity associated respectively with Jewish *zedekah*, Christian charity, and Islamic *zakat*; and (3) the public responsibilities of state charities articulated in the locally oriented Elizabethan Poor Law tradition and more recently by the nationally oriented "welfare states." The first of these systems is the basis of altruism theory, as discussed in this chapter. The second system presents a major concern for the social organization of commons. The last of these systems is an important aspect of the contemporary relations between states and commons.

Charity as Ethical Behavior

Within the Judeo-Christian-Islamic heritage, the ethical basis for individual acts of charity has not changed fundamentally in more than 2,000 years. Robert Morris locates the historical origins of Western charity in ancient Hebrew ethics and in the revolutionary ethical concept of an obligation to perform acts of positive good that emerged about 800 B.C.E. (Morris, 1986).

O'Connell (1983) provides a brief introduction to the key biblical references to charity. The unlimited generosity and informed giving advocated by various early church leaders sound entirely familiar to us, as do most of the issues raised in the monastic codes. Whether or not we concur entirely with the order of priority of Maimonides' eight degrees of charity, set forth in the twelfth century, there is little in the degrees themselves to give pause to the modern philanthropist (Cass and Manser, 1983; Morris, 1986).

Anonymity in giving was held in highest regard by the ancient Hebrews. What is sometimes called the chamber of whispers was an institutional expression of this anonymity. A quiet room was set aside in the synagogue into which the individual philanthropist went, unobserved, and left donations for the poor, who went in, also unobserved, to obtain the help they needed.

Principles of donation arose very early in the Hebrew tradition. The tithe as a morally approved basis of redistribution for various purposes was originally an in-kind contribution, in which the tenth part of the yield of the harvest was to be given to the Lord in support of religion and for the relief of the poor. At every harvest, a corner of each field was to be left unharvested for the poor. Every seventh year, fields were left fallow, and the poor were permitted to garner the spontaneous growth during this sabbatical year (Goldberg and Rayner, 1989).

The Jewish ethical tradition of charity was adopted by emergent Christianity with only slight modifications. Throughout the Middle Ages, down to the time of the Elizabethan Poor Law and Statute of Charitable Uses in 1601, organized Christian charity was closely associated with the institutional church. In A.D. 321, Constantine, who had converted to Christianity, "gave license for persons to give or bequeath money to the church. From that time on substantial endowments began to accumulate around charitable institutions" (Marts, 1953, p. 6). Beginning about A.D. 150, Christians began to organize their charity work by creating a church fund in each church, which was supported by voluntary gifts.

Marts (1953) says that deacons dispensed funds to the needy and that, later, districts or deaconries each contained a hostel, alms office, orphanage, and shelter for babies. The first documentary proof of a hospital (established first as a rest room, or *hospitalium*, in the house of a bishop), was of one established in A.D. 369 in Caesarea by St. Basil. Apparently, it grew to be a large institution with different pavilions for different diseases and residences for physicians, nurses, and patients. St. Gregory called it a "heaven on earth" (Marts, 1953, p. 7).

By the fourth century, early Christian doctrine about charity had evolved into two distinct schools of thought, which constitute what might be called "theory X" and "theory Y" of charity. St. John

Chrysostem advocated a position of open generosity, compassion for the needy, and unconstrained giving. He said, "It is the season of kindness, not of strict inquiry, of mercy, not of calculation" (Morris, 1986, p. 103). By contrast, St. Ambrose, St. Augustine of Hippo, and others argued that the poor needed guidance and counsel more than money and that giving should be carefully monitored to assure that funds went only to the truly needy (Morris, 1986).

A similar profile emerges in Islamic zakat, which involves personal ethical obligations much like those incumbent upon Jews and Christians and is venerated as one of the five fundamentals, or pillars, of Islam. Aiding those in need and giving to support Islam is the personal obligation of every Moslem. Furthermore, a substantial network of endowments or foundations (waqfs) grew up in the Arabic world over the centuries (Hourani, 1991). Interestingly, there is little evidence available in English of a system of Islamic charity organization other than the waqfs.

The relationships between Judeo-Christian charity and Islamic zakat is a complex and subtle one. It would be a mistake to assume that zakat has produced an entire western-style set of charitable institutions in the Islamic world. In fact, zakat is usually interpreted as a religious tax rather than an ethical obligation. The basis of zakat as a set of charity-like beliefs and norms originally borrowed from the Jews, however, is unmistakable (Gibb and Kramers, 1953).

We might also note that the Judeo-Christian-Islamic ethical tradition of charity is distinctive but not entirely unique among the world's major religions. Each of the world's major religions appears to have embraced somewhat similar charitable values and practices. For example, by the sixteenth century, charitable practices were incorporated into model Korean village codes developed by Confucian public administration scholars (Hahm, 1991).

Within Buddhism, there is an equally distinctive emergence of charitable norms and practices. About 450 B.C.E., Buddha laid down the essential conditions of Buddhist charity (*dharma*): "In five ways should a clansman minister to his friends and familiars—by generosity, courtesy, and benevolence, by treating them as he treats himself, and by being as good as his word" (Bukkyo Dendo Kyokai, 1983, p. 484). A system of institutional Buddhist charity evolved later. King Asoka, a ruler in northern India, converted to Buddhism and set a worthy example of Buddhist philanthropy by devoting his wealth and influence to supporting Buddhist missions, monasteries, temples, and other institutions. One of the distinctive qualities of Buddhist *dharma* that sets 'it apart from charity in the Judeo-Christian-Islamic tradition is its priorities: gifts to support Buddhist priests and temples are generally "rated" as greater goods than charity for the poor or needy, which are of only secondary importance (Lohmann and Bracken, 1991).

In the West, medieval Christian charity became closely (but not exclusively) associated with the monastic movement. In medieval monasteries, the "rule" was an important document, serving a role that embraced aspects of the modern constitution and bylaws, codes of conduct and professional ethics, and with perhaps part of a rental lease. Two particularly widely adopted and venerable rules were those set down by St. Augustine in about A.D. 397 and Benedict of Nursia roughly a century later.

The Cluniac order was founded on observation of the Rule of St. Benedict. In the Benedictine rule, six rules relate specifically to charitable practices: comfort the poor, clothe the naked, visit the sick, aid those in trouble, comfort the sad, and do not forsake charity. The rule also mandated an office of the cellarer, whose duty it was to care for the sick, children, the poor, and guests (Evans, [1931] 1968; Lawrence, 1989).

There are important connections between monastic rules and charitable practice in the commons. The theological and philosophical writings of St. Augustine are frequently cited as the original source of the concept of common good, discussed elsewhere in this work. In his rule, Augustine touches upon numerous aspects of mutuality, shared resources, need, and community that are of general interest to the theory of the commons but says very little directly about standards or rules of charitable behavior. In rule three, for example, he says, "Among you there can be no question of personal property. Rather, take care that you share everything in common." He goes on to articulate a clear-cut standard of need: "Your superior . . . does not have to give exactly the same to everyone, for you are not all equally strong, but each person should be given what he personally needs" (Van Bavel, 1984, p. 11). Whether one applies them to ancient Greek koininia, medieval Augustinian monasteries, nineteenth-century social movements, or twentieth-century voluntary agencies, the charitable principles and standards discussed by St. Augustine are recognizable and consistent ones.

Overall, the Augustinian approach is largely a statement of general principles. Much attention in the Augustinian rule is devoted to proper attitudes and motives.

The underlying motivations of the Augustinian and Benedictine rules are clearly the same as those assumed elsewhere in the Judeo-Christian-Islamic tradition of charity. Whatever differences of interpretation and emphasis there may be within various subgroups, monasticism was clearly associated with the main body of this tradition of charity. According to some sources, the tenth-century Cluniac reformation, which led to major reforms and revitalization of medieval monasticism, also contributed to significant increases in monastic charitable practices (Cass and Manser, 1983).

Quite a different approach to charity and poverty grew out of the Franciscan movement of the thirteenth century. Following the example of St. Francis of Assisi (and norms of voluntary poverty already evident in the Augustinian rule), Franciscans made a virtue of voluntary poverty even while advocating charity toward the involuntarily poor.

At least from the fourteenth and fifteenth centuries onward, confraternities and lay associations, like the schuole of Venice and the Portuguese misericordia, became common (Russell-Wood, 1968). The Society of St. Vincent de Paul, or Paulist order, was founded in 1845 as an association of Catholic laymen to promote the spiritual welfare of members through works of charity.

Suppression of the monasteries, together with other economic dislocations that led to dramatic increases in poverty, vagabondage, and beggary in England in the sixteenth century, made the sixteenth century a period of "welfare reform" much like the twentieth century. Very little of the ecclesiastical wealth seized in the English suppressions went to the state (Woodward, 1966). Most went instead as state patronage to various friends and supporters of the court, laying what some people believe to be the economic basis of the unique English system of country estates (more than a few of which were located in and still bear the names of abbeys and other monastic buildings).

In the early modern period, state responsibility for the poor began to gradually replace the institutional charities of the medieval church. A variety of methods of punishment, suppression, and relief were attempted by municipal authorities in England, Germany, and the Lowlands (Belgium and Holland). Localism, filial responsibility, and community control of vagabonds and itinerants were prominent among the issues addressed in the Elizabethan Poor Law of 1601, which has had an enduring impact upon Anglo-American welfare practice. The medieval practice of municipal ordinances against begging has recently been revived in the United States. In response to the issue of contemporary homelessness, Seattle enacted an ordinance against "aggressive begging" in 1988, and Atlanta adopted an even more rigorous statute in 1991.

In the Reformation, Luther and Calvin were both relatively hard on the poor—pushing to new extremes the early medieval skepticism of worthiness first identified by St. Ambrose and St. Augustine of Hippo (Morris, 1986). Much of the contemporary work ethic, which has had such an enduring impact on welfare policy, is rooted in Protestant ideas from the Reformation.

In colonial America, the Great Awakening was an important period of religious revivalism and populist humanitarianism from approximately 1725 to 1745. Jonathan Edwards and George Whitefield were the foremost American exponents of this movement. There are suggestions scattered throughout the nonprofit history that the Great Awakening may have been of pivotal importance in the extension of the philanthropic and charitable practices of aristocratic and beau monde society to the lower classes (Bremner, 1988). Elimination of the practice of primogeniture in the American Revolution also had an important effect on breaking up inherited family fortunes in the United States. However, full and complete treatment of the formative influences of the Great Awakening and the American Revolution on the United States commons is not currently part of the repertory of nonprofit and voluntary research.

The first half of the nineteenth century was undoubtedly a renaissance period for the American commons. De Tocqueville was by no means the only visitor to nineteenth-century America who was profoundly affected by what he saw. After her triumphant North American tour in 1850–1852, Jenny Lind is said to have grown tired of the frivolous life of the theater, married her accompanist, Otto Goldschmidt, and devoted the rest of her life to charity (wall notes from an exhibition at the National Gallery, May 1988).

A wealth of utopian and communitarian movements inspired by Robert Owen, the Fourists, and others also date from the mid nineteenth century, roughly the time of de Tocqueville's visit. Although examination of social movements falls outside the scope of this work, the many possible connections of these and more contemporary movements to the theory of the commons should be on the agenda of future research. Kropotkin's (n.d.) term *mutual aid*, for example, continues to be a useful descriptor (often in conjunction with *self-help*) of one set of interests among nonprofit and voluntary action scholars (see, for example, Borkman, 1978a, 1978b).

The Emergence of Charity Organization

A renaissance in charitable practice, on par with the earlier Constantinian, Cluniac, Franciscan, and Protestant transformations, emerged in Britain and the United States after the middle of the nineteenth century and is still spreading throughout the world. The key emphases of this movement are efficiency and effectiveness in the organization of charitable practices. Some rather obvious latent functions are also involved. For example, it is becoming increasingly clear that women in both the Progressive Era and New Deal Washington used associations to further their causes (Muncy, 1991).

Advocates of charitable endeavor first became interested in improving the organization of their efforts, or what are today called service delivery issues. During times of economic distress, large cities like London, New York, and Chicago were faced with literally hundreds of small, independent, and uncoordinated helping associations, and affluent people (particularly those most sympathetic to the doctrines of rugged individualism, social Darwinism, and scientific management) were constantly besieged by appeals for donations. (A somewhat similar condition exists today in the chaos of the "junk mail" appeals from charities.) The solution of that time was to better organize the charities, improve the efficiency of their efforts, and eliminate duplication and overlapping services. Although some of the terminology has been refined, the problem of organization of charities retains a remarkable public vitality even today.

The intellectual basis for this movement toward improved organization of charities also had implications in the other common domains (health care, the arts, sports, and so forth). This broader focus may properly be called "scientific philanthropy." At the heart of scientific philanthropy and its close cousin "scientific charity" are the assumptions that there are rational principles governing philanthropic and charitable practice and that these principles can be discovered and taught. Andrew Carnegie's attempt to articulate a new public standard of behavior for the rich is but one of a number of related attempts at locating such principles of philanthropy evident in the late nineteenth century. Amos Warner's ([1908] 1988) textbook and Kropotkin's (n.d.) study of the biological basis of mutual aid are other examples of this same spirit, as is Frederick Goff's campaign for community trusts, which included a speech to the American Bankers' Association in 1919 (Goff, 1919).

This practical interest in discovering the "principles of social improvement" energized not only the movement to organize charities (and later the social work profession) but also the emerging American social sciences of sociology, economics, political science, and psychology. Social work retains a somewhat unique position in this regard. As one of the original founding disciplines of the American Social Science Association (along with economics, sociology, and political science), social work is unique among the American social sciences in never having proclaimed or developed a "pure" or "basic science" approach. This stance is in marked contrast to economics and political science, in particular. Instead, for most of the current century, adherents of social work have been preoccupied with reinforcing the claims of social work as a practice profession.

The development of social work as a profession (one type of commons, as noted in Chapter Five) and repeated attempts to gain monopoly control over social services have resulted in a series of major transformations within the larger charity commons (Lubove,

1965; Wenocur and Reisch, 1989). In this work, I am not primarily concerned with professional social work. That topic is covered by a large body of literature and is, by the very nature of a professional commons, of interest primarily to professional social workers.

Charitable Volunteering

The perspective of the commons can also be extended to volunteering and voluntarism. Stated simply, volunteer effort is a form of leisure activity and at the same time a form of unproductive labor. The motives for volunteering can be seen as forming a kind of moral hierarchy, something akin to Maimonides' eight degrees of charity. DeLaat (1987) suggests that volunteering should be viewed as a key linkage between sectors. Certainly this is the case with coproduction efforts in which citizen volunteers form or join commons to carry out some of the public works of government (Brudney and England, 1983; Brudney, 1987). It is equally true in the political volunteering associated with parties, campaigns, and the other phenomena of state formation already discussed. Such volunteer labors take the forms of tributes, gifts, potlatches, or offerings already discussed. Nowhere are these four forms of volunteer labor more clear, however, than within the institutions of private (or voluntary) charity.

The majority of this chapter is concerned with the problems of the organization of charities as that phenomenon is ordinarily understood (concern for the poor, social problems, and so forth). Before getting on with that topic, however, let us take one brief digression.

It is fairly common for musicians, actors, and artists of all types to refer to their talent as a gift. Reports of performances thus often fall clearly within the reciprocal cycle of giving and receiving and giving, as these artists "share" their gift with audiences. In an age as conscious as ours of public image and media manipulation, we can safely assume that at least some of those reports constitute deliberate public posturing.

Far more important, however, than what percentage of such reports are sincere and genuine are the underlying norms that these reports point to. Underlying the performances of "great" artists and even the near great is an unmistakable obligation to perform—to share their gift with the world (which ordinarily would make the gift a common good for those interested and willing to appreciate it). This norm—observable in the nonprofit art world of theaters, concert halls, museums, and exhibitions, and also in the lecture tours of scientific and mathematical geniuses—may be of central importance in understanding all types of volunteering and is worthy of further study. For example, the housewife who visits shut-in older people to share her "gift of gab" is engaged in a social act that is remarkably similar in certain respects to the performance of the musician, artist, or scientist.

Volunteering as Volunteer Labor

The psychological dynamics of volunteering have been a stable, long-standing research interest in nonprofit organization, voluntary action, and philanthropy studies (Smith and Freedman, 1972). The perspective of the commons can also be extended to this topic, although some care must be exercised in terminology. Volunteering and voluntarism (or "volunteerism") may be used either in the very broad sense of uncoerced or unpaid efforts of all types or in the more narrow, restrictive sense of a participant in an organized volunteer program. Being a volunteer may be considered the basis of nonprofit organization or voluntary action, unproductive labor, unpaid or unreimbursed effort, uncoerced activity, shared or mutual effort, pooling of resources, an expression of friendship or community, or a quest for social justice. Finally, many types of volunteering for emergency work, volunteer fire departments, and the like are clearly perceived as prosocial behavior.

The mixtures of self-interest and altruism noted above suggest that the concepts of relative advantage and opportunity cost may be useful for understanding volunteering: at a quite fundamental level, there is an important choice implicit in all decisions to volunteer. A person is, in effect, choosing to spend his or her time in the volunteer effort rather than to engage in alternative activities in other sectors: the private activities of the household (reading, watching television, intimate or sexual behavior, household production such as gardening or fishing, state-related activities [paying taxes, voting], or market-related activities [shopping, working at a second job]). The question that arises, therefore, is what are the relative advantages of volunteering which make it more attractive than any of these alternatives? What benefits for themselves and what gifts to others do volunteers perceive for volunteering? The related issue is what opportunity costs are volunteers prepared to pay? What benefits or advantages are volunteers willing to relinquish in order to attain those benefits in return? The prior discussions of tribute, gift, potlatch, and offering and the prosocial mixing of self-interest and other-interest offer a powerful framework within which to address such questions.

In contrast with the social literature on volunteering (Sundeen, 1990) or coproduction of governmental services by volunteers (Brudney, 1989), most of the psychological research on volunteering involves studies carried out with undergraduate student populations. Some of these studies explicitly take relative advantage or opportunity cost into account in the study designs. For example, McCarthy and Rogers (1982) found that student subjects who lost a reward because they agreed to volunteer were less willing to volunteer again than subjects who had gained a reward for volunteer efforts. However, those reward-losers who did volunteer again rated themselves higher in altruism than those who had been rewarded, those who would not volunteer again, and a control group of students not asked to volunteer. This leads to a paradoxical quality in volunteering: the most effective way of inducing altruistic responses may be to provide an extrinsic reward. Yet, this reward may undermine intrinsic motivation and reduce future volunteering.

In an explicitly interdisciplinary (economics and psychology) study, Harvey and McCrohan (1988) compared samples of adult donor-volunteers (givers) with nondonating, nonvolunteering nongivers. They found strong convergence between patterns of volunteering and research findings on tax compliance. Givers were more likely than nongivers to be employed, have higher incomes, have attended college, react positively to fundraising efforts, believe in the agency's program, report benefits to themselves and others from the agency, and see the agency as efficient.

Studies of the costs and opportunities of volunteering suggest a convergence between psychological studies of volunteering as prosocial behavior and the main body of volunteer studies in the nonprofit, voluntary, and philanthropic literature. At the same time, they also suggest major linkages within nonprofit, voluntary, and philanthropic studies between the exchange theory tradition of organizational studies and research on volunteers within the voluntary action tradition.

Types of Charity Organization

Because of the heritage of individualism in Western thought, we have grown accustomed to approaching problems of charity and volunteering from an individual perspective. It should be abundantly clear, however, that volunteer labor is a unique social form of leisure expression. One does not "volunteer" to read a book or mow one's own lawn. Volunteering is a social endeavor, ordinarily done for and in the company of others. The fundamental units of charity are not individual acts as the collective choice theorists believe, but social organizations, the most elementary of which are the self–other diads of tributes and gifts, and the more complex relations of self and others of potlatches and offerings (Knoke, 1990).

In contemporary society, many of the social agencies of the voluntary sector have evolved or are evolving out of the commons and transforming themselves into nonprofit firms through purchase of service contracting (Bernstein, 1991a; Kettner and Martin, 1987; Kramer, 1987). Nevertheless, a large number of nonrevenue charitable commons remain, from soup kitchens to missions, shelters, and settlement houses. In addition to such social service agencies, there has been a resurgence of interest in recent years in mutual aid and self-help organizations and behavior. These concepts, which are also sometimes tied together under the rubric of social support, will be explored in the remainder of this chapter.

Mutual Aid Societies

One of the most fundamental forms of organized charity is the kind of network of reciprocal giving of assistance based on need that is called a mutual aid society. Ideas about mutual aid run deep in American thought. Cotton Mather had an idea for a system of neighborhood benefit societies that Benjamin Franklin seems to have borrowed (Boorstin, 1958). By the early twentieth century, mutual aid was evolving in various new directions. Kropotkin gave the notion of mutual aid a curious Darwinian twist when he sought to raise the principle of mutual aid to a determinant of human evolution (Kropotkin, n.d.). The settlement house movement placed great stress on the encouragement of mutual aid practices in neighborhoods (Addams, 1930). The mental health self-help movement in the United States, which originated with Clifford Beers's book *A Mind That Found Itself* ([1921] 1983), resulted in the formation of a large number of local mental health associations and rivals the much more notable philanthropic crusades of Dorothea Dix.

Ethnic Mutual Aid Associations

Throughout the nineteenth and twentieth centuries, mutual aid associations were closely associated with the immigrant experience in the United States (Jenkins and others, 1988). Such groups continue to be an essential part of the successful adaptation of immigrant populations (Borman, 1984; Cabral, 1978). The fact that such an extremely wide diversity of ethnic groups engaged in similar practices with respect to burial, emergency assistance, and other types of mutual aid is a clue to the great likelihood that such practices did not originate after immigration. In all likelihood, many, if not all, immigrant groups brought such practices with them and subsequently found a uniquely fertile ground for their development in the United States (Kropotkin, n.d.).

The Scots Charitable Society, founded in 1657, was the first of a long series of distinctively American ethnic mutual aid societies founded by immigrant groups in the United States (Bremner, 1988). (However, this organization may be counted as the first mutual aid society only by ignoring the mutual aid practices of the indigenous populations that were living in the Americas when the European invasion began.) The Scots Charitable Society was founded nearly a century before the conquest of the Scottish nation by English forces in 1745. It was probably the creation of immigrants from an independent monarchy with a strong sense of national identity and an acute sense of their minority status in the predominantly English colonies of New England.

Since the founding of the Scots Charitable Society in Boston, associations devoted to providing mutual aid and support for members of particular ethnic groups have been a stable part of the U.S. urban experience (Jenkins and others, 1988). Such associations commonly place a premium on aiding the poor, helping the sick, and burying the dead. Boston was an early center of ethnic mutual aid organizations.

Other early mutual aid societies include the Charitable Irish Society of Boston and the German Society of New York. The Independent Order of B'nai B'rith was organized in 1843 as a mutual aid society for German Jews. Other ethnic mutual aid associations were not exclusively nationality based. They were also organized along religious lines, as was the Episcopal Charitable Society of Boston, founded in 1754 for English immigrants (Trattner, 1989).

A variety of evidence points toward a resurgence of mutual aid and self-help activity based on ethnic, nationality, and language groups following recent increased immigration to the United States and Canada in the past two decades (Katz, 1981). More conferences like that sponsored by the Canadian Council on Social Development in 1992 on this topic are needed to fully articulate the role of mutual aid in initiating and defining common action.

Self-Help Groups

Borman (1984) defined self-help groups as voluntary, self-governing, self-regulating associations that emphasize solidarity among peers, self-reliance, and commitment to the group's common purpose. One of the questions that arises is whether self-help groups are a type of or something different from nonprofit organizations and voluntary associations. In a 1973 study, self-help organizations in a medium-sized city in the Midwest were characterized in the following way: Half were founded within the past two years and two-thirds by stigmatized groups, and the majority of members were from these stigmatized groups. Over three-fourths (85 percent) had formally elected boards, the majority of which met monthly (58 percent). Although 68 percent of the groups had constitutions, the majority (56 percent) had not attained tax-exempt status. (This is not unusual, given the high proportion of new groups.) Seventy-two percent had budgets under $5,000 (Traunstein and Steinman, 1973).

Newsome and Newsome (1983) assume that self-help groups are distinct and suggest giving them a legal status similar to that of nonprofit organizations. It seems more plausible to suggest that groups whose purpose is self-help can fit easily into the existing legal categories of nonprofit corporation or unincorporated association. This conclusion may be somewhat obscured, however, by reliance upon the concept of the nonprofit organization, which lacks legal reference.

Labor organizations, which stress solidarity and mutual self-interest of members, remain one of the most important examples of self-help organizations. Self-help organizations have by no means been restricted entirely to the United States and western Europe. Bouman (1990) updated the anthropological study of Indian credit associations with his study of the economic roles of money lenders, pawnbrokers, and self-help savings and loan associations in India.

There are at least four distinct functional types of modern self-help groups.

- Groups that focus on reorganization of conduct or behavioral change (Weight Watchers, Alcoholics Anonymous)
- Groups that utilize the "natural resources" of interpersonal relationships to reduce stress; ameliorate anxiety; and help people cope with grief, loss, and irresolvable problems (Parents Without Partners, groups for terminally ill patients)
- Defensive groups or mutual protective associations that seek to protect their members from harm, maintain and enhance members' identity and self-esteem, and raise consciousness
- Growth-oriented groups that concentrate upon positive experiences and enhancing personal growth, self-actualization, and so forth of already healthy and secure members

Self-help groups have seldom figured very significantly in recent discussions of nonprofit and voluntary action because of the absence of theory and because a large proportion of them are unincorporated associations that fall outside the established counting and classifying filters. Self-help groups also stretch the conventional boundaries of nonprofit and voluntary association, with the accent on self-help versus helping others. An important variant on social support theory is social network theory, which seems to place emphasis on communication networks rather than organized associations. Goodman and Pynoos (1990) studied a model telephone support program involving peer networks of four or five caregivers in regular telephone conversations. A randomized comparison was made of thirty-one participants in such networks and thirty-five participants who listened to an informational minilecture series. Those in peer networks who gained more information had higher perceptions of social support and higher satisfaction with their support systems.

Several authors have, at least indirectly, suggested links between self-help groups and cults, which can have a major impact on their members' mental health. Nelson (1990) offers a theoretical model of "reentry" for victims of spinal cord injury that appears to describe a general model of the benefits of self-help groups. The four phases Nelson identifies are: buffering, transcending, toughening, and launching. Buffering is the nurturing and protective process of lessening, absorbing, or protecting the newly injured patient against the shock of the many ramifications of the injury and the indignities of being a patient. Transcending involves helping patients recognize and rise above culturally imposed limitations and negative beliefs about people with disabilities. Toughening requires patients to compensate for physical limitations, gain independence, and maintain social interactions without "using the disability." Launching involves exposing patients to the real world, exploring options for living in the community, promoting personal autonomy and decision making, and facilitating the movement of the patient out of the rehabilitation program.

As an exercise in applying the theory developed here, the reader with interests in this type of clinical self-help group might try fitting Nelson's reentry model with the concept of repertory, the various elementary forms of benefactory, and other components of the theory that were previously introduced. It should be clear from the result that self-help groups belong within the range of commons along with nonprofit organizations, voluntary associations, and the many types of common action discussed in Chapter Four. It should also be clear that although the treatment here is very general, the theory of the commons has potential practice and policy implications worthy of further exploration.

Health-Oriented Self-Help Groups

In the past two decades, health has emerged as a common interest around which to organize self-help groups. One major facet of this traditional concern has been the rapid proliferation of self-help groups of people seeking supplements or substitutes for more traditional health care. The range of people and concerns for which self-help solutions have been posed is truly remarkable: recovering alcoholics, former mental patients, people with physical handicaps, people with heart disease, cardiac and stoma patients, cancer patients, bereaved parents, people with multiple sclerosis, obese people, and many more (Butora, 1989a, 1989b; Kobasa and others, 1991; Maton, 1990; Kurtz and Chambon, 1987). Helton (1990) discusses what she calls a buddy system to improve prenatal care.

In a number of instances, the purpose of these groups is to aid caregivers and family members who may be providing care for an ill person. Toseland and Hacker (1985) and Toseland, Rossiter, Peak, and Smith (1990) examined the comparative effectiveness of individual and group interventions for supporting family caregivers of frail elderly people. They found that individual interventions produced more positive effects on the caregivers' psychological functioning and well-being than did group interventions, but group interventions produced greater improvements in caregivers' social support.

Contemporary social support theory is largely an ad hoc, freestanding creation, but several recent writers have begun to explore some of its broader theoretical ramifications (Collins and Pancoast, 1975; Clary, 1987). Their explorations show promise of connecting the theory with the theory of the commons in a number of interesting ways.

Social support can be defined in a manner that brings to mind the expressive/instrumental dichotomy: "significant others help the individual mobilize his psychological resources and master his emotional burdens; they share his tasks and they provide him with extra supplies of money, materials, tools, skills and cognitive guidance to improve the handling of his situation" (Caplan and Killilea, 1976, p. 6). Examination of definitions led Clary to conclude that "it appears that there are only two aspects to social support—emotional support and task-oriented support" (Clary, 1987, p. 59). Likewise Shumaker and Brownell (1984, p. 13) bring to mind the discussion of gifts when they define social support as "an exchange of resources between at least two individuals perceived by the provider or the recipient to be intended to enhance the well-being of the recipient."

One of the most interesting connections between social support and the commons is the dilemma of individual limits and group potentials for action. According to a Czechoslovakian writer, Butora (1989a), self-help is often based on notions of individual self-sufficiency; that is, encouraging individuals to rely on their own strength, knowledge, abilities, and experience. The functions of self-help groups include social and emotional support; defense against feelings of isolation, loneliness, and stigmatization; and provision of information and practices pertaining to a given disease or state. Self-help groups also encourage more active participation of patients in assuming greater responsibility for their own health. Interestingly, these are often the reasons cited for participation in other types of commons as well.

Stewart (1990) is interested in expanding theoretical conceptualizations of self-help groups. Self-help groups, he says, typically lack theoretical grounding. He proposes grounding self-help group theory in psychoneuroimmunological and social-learning theories (neither of which takes into consideration the interpersonal and interactional aspects of such groups).

Other approaches to the theory of mutual aid and self-help groups do emphasize their social character. In some cases, emphasis has been placed on the potential of such groups for social adaptation as well as individual improvements. Maton (1990), for example, adopted an ecological framework in which to interpret mutual help groups.

Conclusion

Preoccupation with issues of professionalism and bureaucratization has created a distorted image of the contemporary world of charitable practice, in which the ordinary charitable responses called forth by the very ancient and deeply ingrained ethics of interpersonal aid are pictured as a mere prelude—a residual action that is only adequate until the experts and professionals arrive. This picture is in serious conflict with the facts of the case as they are understood by many people with problems today. A large portion of those people engaged in charitable activities of all types are not professionals or officials. They are individuals and groups, acting upon traditional norms of personal charity through forms of mutual aid and self-help.

Their actions constitute theoretical as well as practical challenges for nonprofit and voluntary action research. The personal acts of people aiding themselves while aiding others are not easily reconciled with the either-or nature of self-interest as discussed in the nonprofit literature. Nor is the autonomy evident in the self-help movement easily reconciled with traditional professionalism of helping professions like clinical and counseling psychology, social work, psychiatry, and medicine. Self-help and mutual aid organizations are not social agencies per se, nor is the radical individualism of most discussions of self-help easily reconciled with the social nature of the commons. And the national and international networks of self-help groups and mutual aid societies are not easily reconciled with existing models of the nonprofit sector. In these many ways and others as well, self-help and mutual aid groups pose interesting and fundamental challenges to the theory of the commons.

9

Volunteer Labor
and Prosocial Behavior:
The Psychology
of the Commons

> Feelings and opinions are recruited, the heart is en-
> larged, and the human mind is developed only by
> the reciprocal influence of people upon one
> another.
>
> —Alexis de Tocqueville

If the multidisciplinary mixture of existing knowledge in nonprofit, voluntary, and philanthropy studies were a kind of data stew,
the psychological literature that bears on the subject would be the
condiments: not theoretically substantial enough to satisfy in and
of themselves, yet offering an exquisitely broad range of subtle variations and insights with hints of yet more to come. From the
broader institutional perspective of the theory of the commons, the
individualistic assumptions inherent in most psychological research in this area are reductionistic. Yet on certain central questions of motivation and behavior, the richness and complexity of
psychological data offer much-needed correctives to those who
would reduce all motivations in the commons to one (such as a

235

nonprofit analogue to the profit motive) or two (such as Boulding's love and fear).

In this chapter, I shall not address a number of important psychological questions or approaches that have loomed large in the research. Most prominent among these are the whole range of questions raised by the social biology debates. This chapter will not examine any of the interrelated "life science" issues of altruism: the implications of a genetic or evolutionary basis for human altruistic behavior; the emergence and development of altruism; genetic similarity as a basis for selecting friends; ethical reasoning and prosocial behavior in small children; or observations of "altruistic" behavior in ants, birds, chimpanzees, and other animals. Such core sociobiological concepts as kin selection, reciprocal altruism, the genetic basis of altruism, and male-female reproductive strategies need further examination, but not here. In addition, the clinical psychology literatures discussing clinical issues but not reporting research results and literature on such esoteric subjects as the relationship between altruistic behavior and physical attractiveness is also overlooked.

Each of these is an important topic. Indeed, to some degree the very importance of these issues is reflected in the enormity of available literature on the subject. Recently I did a literature search of the *Psychological Abstracts,* for example, and found nearly 600 citations on the question of the prosocial behavior of children for the five years prior to 1990 and nearly the same number dealing with altruism.

Altruism

What I am calling the *theory of altruism* is that portion of the theory of the commons that is most directly related to matters of individual psychology. This topic is ordinarily thought to encompass a number of related issues: altruistic motivation; such specific altruistic behaviors as donating, volunteering, and actualization; and situationally specific behavior such as crisis and disaster responses. I will expand the topic to include such additional issues as learning and the nature of altruistic rationality. Furthermore, the use of the concept of endowment in the theory of the commons can be shown to be anchored in the multiple precedents of psychological research.

One of the fundamental components of psychological interest in prosocial behavior is the measurement of altruistic behavior. Yalom (1982) suggests that altruism involves leaving the world a better place to live in, serving others, and participation in charity. Such a conception is reminiscent of traditional conceptions of philanthropy. Kauffmann (1984) defines altruism in terms of behavior that is voluntary, aids others, and is done without expectation of reward. Such a conception corresponds closely with the dichotomy of altruism and self-interest of nonprofit organizational approaches discussed in Chapter One.

An important difference, however, between contemporary psychological research and nonprofit organizational studies is the manner in which the psychologists have looked at the larger picture and attempted to cast altruism as one type of a broader class of prosocial behavior. According to Kauffmann (1984), prosocial behavior can be related to positive feelings or negative affect, obligatory, associated with the selfish aspects of helping, or compassionate. *Self-transcendence* is a term for the psychological mechanism assumed by the theory that allows individuals to use hedonism and self-actualization in ways that transcend their self-interest (Yalom, 1982).

Hardin (1982) argues that pure altruism cannot persist and expand over time. The principal forms of discriminating altruisms among humans are individualism, familialism, cronyism, tribalism, and patriotism. Hardin argues that universalism (altruism practiced without discriminating kinship, acquaintanceship, shared values, or propinquity in time or space) is not recommended, even as an ideal.

Another major issue is how altruistic behavior is learned. A model of the acquisition of altruism in children developed by Cialdini, Baumann, and Kenrick (1981) might equally well be applied to adults. The model proposed three steps: presocialization, awareness that others value altruistic behavior, and adoption or internalization of the altruistic norm. This model fits in nicely with aspects of the theory of the commons presented in the next chapter. Rushton (1982) reviews the literature on the learning of altruism through the family, mass media, and educational system. He concludes that classical conditioning, observational learning, reinforcement, and learning from verbal procedures such as preaching are all important.

Jankofsky and Steucher (1983–84) argue that altruism is a basic trait of human character and behavior that can be studied in an interdisciplinary context. They say that comparative evaluations over long periods of time and in different socioeconomic statuses (SES) and political structures can be made. Karuza (1983) notes that while a great deal of research has been done on the topics of altruism and helping behavior, the generalizability and impact of this work on applied settings has been limited.

Frohlich and Oppenheimer (1984) investigated interdependent utility elements in three types of interactive preferences, which they termed altruistic, egalitarian, and difference maximizing. When 183 Canadian and U.S. undergraduates were paired anonymously and chose payoffs that would variously benefit themselves and their partner, nonmaximizing and nonself-interested behavior was found consistently. Although attempts to explain the nonself-interested choices by reference to psychological and ideological constructs were unsuccessful, statistical relationships between these choices and partisan political preferences were found.

As we have seen, in one view, altruism is opposed to egoism. Yet Sober (1989) argues that egoism and altruism need not be viewed as diametrically opposite single-factor theories of motivation that view a single kind of preference (self-regarding or other-regarding) as moving people to act. Treating motives as deriving from single causes may explain why hypotheses of altruism and egoism fail to explain observed behaviors. Sober also recommends distinguishing altruistic motivations from altruistic actions.

From another perspective, the opposite of altruism is hedonism. Worach (1980) sought to link use of leisure time (in terms of instrumental activeness and expressive activeness) to the hedonism-altruism dichotomy.

In a 1990 article, Batson suggests that psychologists have for many years assumed (along with the nonprofit organization researchers) that humans are social egoists, caring exclusively for themselves, but that recent research evidence points instead to feelings of genuine empathy for others in need and the capability of caring for them for their own sakes and not out of self-interest (Batson, 1990).

At the same time, numerous studies confirm the importance of ethnocentrism and group membership at various levels as an important intervening effect. Shane and Shane (1989) provide a psychoanalytical discussion of what they call otherhood, or the attainment of the status of other for someone else. In a study of Canadian and Japanese undergraduates, Iwata (1989) found that in both cultures, perception of people was more positive and affiliative/altruistic behavior stronger toward those with whom the subjects had close personal relations than toward those with whom they had more distant relations.

A comparative study of middle-class female Hindu, Moslem, and Christian undergraduates in India found no significant differences in altruistic behaviors (Seth and Gupta, 1984). However, among the similarities found was the fact that all three groups showed a tendency to allocate higher rewards to members of their own group (see also Seth and Gupta, 1983).

As with many other factors, there may also be important differences in altruistic behavior by age, gender, and other variables such as income. In a study of 370 subjects ranging from age five to ninety-five, Weiner and Graham (1989) found that kindness and altruism, pity, and helping behavior were all more prevalent among older subjects, and anger was less prevalent.

In a study of thirty-five men and thirty-five women aged 17 to 68, Mills, Pedersen, and Grusec (1989) found no differences between men and women in their resolution of prosocial dilemmas involving self-sacrifice. However, women used more empathic reasoning with their other-interested choices and attributed their self-interested choices more to minimal conflict and less to concern with the other's interests than men. Gender differences were also found in the subjects' self-reported feelings about their choices.

Ma (1985) identified an altruistic hierarchy. According to Ma, the likelihood of performing an altruistic act depends on the person's relationship with the beneficiary, with probability decreasing in the following order: close relatives; best friends; strangers who are very weak, very young, or elite in society; common strangers; and enemies.

Batson, Bolen, Cross, and Neuringer-Benefiel (1986) reject the likelihood of an altruistic personality. They did, however, find evidence of association of increased helping with three personality variables—self-esteem, ascription of responsibility, and empathic concern. They concluded that the underlying motivations appeared to be egoistic rather than altruistic. They said that altruistic motivation involves benefit to another as an end in itself, while egoistic motivation is an instrumental means to avoid shame and guilt for not helping.

Prosocial Behavior

The concept of prosocial behavior appears to have originated as a general antonym to antisocial behavior (Fedler and Pryor, 1984). Using the example of whistle-blowing as prosocial behavior, Dozier and Miceli (1985) identified a bundle of both selfish (egoistic) and unselfish (altruistic) motives. This idea of mixed motives embodied in a single concept makes prosocial behavior potentially a major leap beyond the fruitless dichotomy of self-interest versus other orientation for nonprofit, voluntary, and philanthropy studies. Bontempo, Lobel, and Triandis (1990) use a different distinction between allocentric persons (those who subordinate personal goals to the goals of others) and idiocentric persons (those who subordinate the goals of others to their personal goals). Both studies illustrate that the concept of prosocial behavior's theoretical value is also to be found in its separation of the issues of motivation and consequences, which are usually confounded in the concept of altruism.

The prosocial behavior concept is one of the products of new thinking about moral behavior and its social and cognitive development, which, together with research and concept formation about positive social behavior, flourished in the 1970s (Asprea and Betocchi, 1981). The renewed emphasis on moral behavior also brought into focus the need to refine the conceptualization and measurement of empathy and altruism, a task that has challenged researchers of prosocial behavior in the last decade (Eisenberg, 1983).

What does the psychological literature identify as the range of prosocial behavior? We can get some idea by looking at the range of substantive topics under study in the 1980s. They include care giving in families (Hall, 1990; Schmitt, Dalbert, and Montada, 1986); interpersonal helping behavior such as helping a graduate student on a research project (Diaz, Earle, and Archer, 1987); whistle-blowing (Dozier and Miceli, 1985; Miceli and Near, 1988); organizational behavior, compliance, and commitment (Brief and Motowidlo, 1986; O'Reilly and Chatman, 1986); public goods (Yamagishi, 1986); charitable volunteering (Daniels, 1985); response to mass emergencies (Lystad, 1985); spontaneous comforting behavior (Samter and Burleson, 1984); sperm donation (Jarrige and Moron, 1982); organizational behavior (Staw, 1984); and helping behavior (Wilson and Petruska, 1984).

What can prosocial behavior be attributed to? Here too the field is somewhat unsettled. Studies have focused on many different factors. However, at least three distinct clusters are evident. One set of studies has examined various personal characteristics associated with prosocial behavior: empathy (Eisenberg and Miller, 1987; Elizur, 1985; Diaz, Earle, and Archer, 1987; Diaz and others, 1985); sympathy and personal distress (Eisenberg and others, 1989); mood (Carlson and Miller, 1987; Shaffer and Smith, 1985); need (Krishnan, 1988); intelligence (Marlowe, 1986); gender (Stockard, Van de Kragt, and Dodge, 1988); aggression (Rutter, 1985); alcohol consumption (Steele, Critchlow, and Liu, 1985); personality (Penner, Escarraz, and Ellis, 1983; Reykowski and Smolenska, 1980); autonomy (Kofta, 1982); moral development (Morgan, 1983; Bar-Tal, 1982; Van Lange and Liebrand, 1989; Tietjen, 1986); and focus on self (Gibbons and Wicklund, 1982). To the extent that such individual factors are critical, individual socialization and learning of prosocial behavior are likely to be extremely important in the advancement of this component of civilization.

Another set of studies has concentrated upon situational characteristics associated with prosocial behavior including: distress (Eisenberg and others, 1989); residence (Amato, 1983); culture (Miller, 1984); religion (Batson, 1983; Morgan, 1983); norms (Schmitt, Dalbert, and Montada, 1986; Tyler, Orwin, and Schurer, 1982); and cost (Staw, 1984; Krishnan, 1988). Such situational studies point up an important role for opportunity and occasion in prosocial acts.

A third set of studies has addressed social processes, including opinion formation (Orive, 1984); performance evaluation (Organ, 1988); groups (Mullen, 1983; Weathers, Messe, and Aronoff, 1984); reciprocity (Krishnan, 1988); cooperation (Van Lange and Liebrand, 1989); social responsibility (Banu and Puhan, 1983); attribution of motives (Schlenker, Hallam, and McCown, 1983); and social responsibility (Banu and Puhan, 1983). These social process studies are perhaps closest in focus and intent to the main body of nonprofit, voluntary, and philanthropy studies and may offer a key point of access for those interested in bringing cohesion between psychological research on prosocial behavior and the study of the commons.

There have been efforts to bring some conceptual order to this mass of variables. Brief and Motowidlo (1986), for example, argue for four individual antecedents to prosocial organizational behavior: empathy, neuroticism, educational level, and mood. They also point to nine contextual antecedents that may be of particular interest to organizational researchers: reciprocity norms, group cohesiveness, role models, reinforcement contingencies, leadership styles, organizational climate, situational stressors, and any additional organizational conditions affecting mood and feelings of satisfaction or dissatisfaction.

Shaffer and Graziano (1983) conclude that many everyday acts of altruism are interpretable as forms of hedonism. They found that moods were associated with increases in the amount of help given if the request was likely to have positive consequences. Furthermore, there was a clear tendency for moods to inhibit the expression of a prosocial act that could have negative consequences for the benefactor. According to Hook (1982), share-the-gain norms are generally stronger than share-the-loss norms.

Gibbons and Wicklund (1982) identify two conditions under which self-focus actually enhanced prosocial behavior. The situation must clearly set off an orientation toward acting on a value of helping, and the person who is called upon to act prosocially must not come to the helping situation with personal preoccupations inimical to thinking about helping.

Empathy is thought to lead to increased helping only under evaluative circumstances (Fultz and others, 1986). Yet, in 1982, Underwood and Moore reported no relation between affective empathy and prosocial behavior on the basis of a literature review and meta-analysis. Five years later, Eisenberg and Miller (1987) explicitly sought to overturn this conclusion with their findings of low to moderate positive relations between empathy and both prosocial behavior and cooperative/socially competent behavior.

Batson (1983) reported a series of three studies in which a distinction was made between two emotional responses to suffering—personal distress and empathy—and two associated motivations to help. Personal distress was hypothesized to lead to egoistic motivation, and empathy was associated with altruistic motivation. In the first two experiments, the hypothesized relations were identified. However, in the third experiment, when the cost of helping was especially high, results suggest an important qualification on the link between empathic emotion and altruistic motivation. Apparently, making helping costly evoked self-concern, which overrode any altruistic impulse produced by feeling empathy.

Staw (1984) recommends treating cooperative behavior in organizations as a form of prosocial behavior. Brief and Motowidlo (1986) call for further investigation of prosocial behavior in organizations and identify thirteen specific kinds of prosocial organizational behavior. They suggest that four areas of research are necessary to advance the study of prosocial organizational behavior: basic dimensions of prosocial organizational behavior; possible personal correlates; organizational conditions, practices, and structures that affect prosocial behavior; and how to increase the incidence of prosocial behavior in organizational functioning. They conclude that the construct of prosocial behavior is value-laden but that some types of prosocial organizational behavior are important elements of individual performance in organizations. Smith, Organ, and Near (1983) suggest that organizational citizenship behavior includes at least two dimensions: altruism, or helping specific persons, and generalized compliance, a more impersonal form of conscientious citizenship.

According to Pulkkinen (1984), research through the mid 1980s tended to focus on prosocial development as well as on the inhibition and control of aggressive behavior. In a review of the literature on families, Rutter (1985) concluded that aggression in family settings is least likely when the individual has well-developed prosocial feelings, enjoys good social relationships, has adequate self-control under stress, experiences high self-esteem, and has effective social problem-solving skills.

In a study of 140 male undergraduates, Weathers, Messe, and Aronoff (1984) found that prior group experiences affected prosocial behavior. Students were more willing to help when they were asked to do so by their former co-worker and when they had had an egalitarian group experience.

Batson (1983) suggests that a function of religion may be to extend the range of limited, kin-specific altruistic impulses that are genetically derived through the use of kinship language and imagery. Such terms as *brotherly love* may provoke and sustain various types of prosocial behavior.

A number of factor analyses offer further light on the nature of prosocial behavior. Walkey, Siegert, McCormick, and Taylor (1987) found three principal factors in an inventory of socially supportive behaviors. The three are called Nondirective Support, Directive Guidance, and Tangible Assistance. Elizur (1985) claims that empathy has four principal components of perception and affective, cognitive, and object relations. Marlowe (1986) located prosocial attitudes within a factor structure of five domains of social intelligence. The other four factors were social skills, empathy skills, emotionality, and social anxiety. Prosocial attitudes were further divided into social interest and social self-efficacy.

Bar-Tal (1982) suggests that cognitive, social-perspective, moral, and self-regulatory skills determine the extent, quantity, and quality of helping actions. Bar-Tal calls altruistic behavior the highest level of helping behavior.

Helping Behavior

Several recent psychological studies have gone beyond the concerns for altruism and prosocial behavior and examined a number of different types of behavior directed at helping others. Studies have looked at various types of socially helpful behavior in such explicit contexts as bystanders observing crisis or emergency situations, various motivations and contingencies inherent in donor behavior, the psychology of volunteering, and various aspects of disaster response behavior.

Bystander Behavior

An interesting tangent on helping behavior arose in the late 1960s with the celebrated Kitty Genovesse case. The young woman was assaulted and killed in front of a large number of onlookers who failed to come to her aid. This incident raised the troubling question of the circumstances under which bystanders would intervene to provide assistance and when they would not, and it led to a number of research endeavors. The issue of bystander behavior is an old and familiar one, dating at least to the biblical parable of the good Samaritan, in which an outsider (the Samaritan) came to the aid of a victim after two members of his own community had ignored his cries for aid.

Two variables that should be of primary importance to a bystander in deciding whether or not to help would appear to be the need of the victim and the cost to the bystander. A review of the recent literature, however, provides inconsistent empirical support for the need of the victim as a variable (Shotland and Stebbins, 1983). Dozier and Miceli (1985) provide a modified version of a bystander intervention framework that traces the decision-making process through five steps: awareness of the event, deciding that the event is an emergency, deciding personal responsibility for helping, choosing a method of helping, and implementing the intervention.

Meindl and Lerner (1983) examined what they called heroic motives—the willingness of undergraduates to confront someone insulting a partner. Rimland (1982) found what he called empirical support for the golden rule by showing that selfish people were less likely to be happy than unselfish people. (Both selfishness and happiness were established as ratings by the subjects' friends.)

In a psychological twist on familiar costs and rewards formulations, Smith, Keating, and Stotland (1989) introduce the possibility of an entirely new level of information exchange based upon sensitivity to the emotional state of the victim and feedback. They suggest that the prospect of empathic joy, conveyed by feedback from the victim anticipating help, accounts for the special tendency of empathic people to help. In an experimental situation, empathically aroused witnesses offered help reliably to a person in distress only when they expected feedback on the result. When denied feedback, they were no more likely to help than their less-empathic counterparts, who were, in any event, unaffected by the availability of feedback in deciding whether to help.

De Guzman (1979) studied bystander responses to a lost passenger among 120 Philippine commuters. Contrary to expectations, urban commuters helped as frequently as rural commuters, and the quality of intervention was found to be better when a pair of bystanders, rather than a lone bystander, were involved (de Guzman, 1979).

Kerber (1984) examined helping in five nonemergency situations and concluded that willingness to help in the five situations was negatively related to costs for helping and positively related to rewards for helping and to personality differences in altruism. He says individual differences in willingness to help may reflect variations in situational perception. In this case, the altruistic person would be an individual who consistently evaluates helping situations more favorably in terms of the potential rewards and costs of providing help.

Moore (1984) cautions that sharing and helping are fundamentally different behaviors and should not be confused. Moore also distinguishes reciprocal altruism from cooperation, mutualism, and nepotism. Eber and Kunz (1984) argue that the desire to help others should be seen in the framework of the maturational achievements of the development of the self.

Donor Behavior

An additional topic that has interested psychological researchers is what might be called donor behavior. Literature on donor psychology deals with a number of different types of donations and the attendant issues they raise. Money, blood, organs, sperm, and children are just some of the objects donated that have been the subject of research (Kessler, 1975; Titmuss, 1970). At times, donations also involve cross-cultural implications; for example, in parts of rural

Mexico, it is apparently traditional for the majority of parents to "donate" their children to the grandparents (Gramajo, 1988).

It would appear that inducements may aid in getting people to donate initially but that other factors are stronger in continued donation. Ferrari, Barone, Jason, and Rose (1985) found that non-monetary incentives significantly increased first-time blood dona-tions among a group of eighty college students of both sexes when compared with a control group receiving altruistic appeals only. Such incentives were not considered effective, however, with repeat donors.

Even major donations may not be psychologically harmful. Sharma and Enoch (1987) found in a study of 14 kidney donors and a control group of 9 nondonors refused on medical grounds that kidney donation does not cause long-term adverse psychological reactions. Parisi and Katz (1986), in a cluster analysis of predonation and postdonation responses by 110 organ donors, identified both positive beliefs (humanitarian benefits and feelings of pride) and negative beliefs (fear of body mutilation and of receiving inadequate medical care in life-threatening situations). Hessing and Elffers (1986–87) identified two potential "death anxieties" operative in the organ donation context: general attitude toward death and fear of being declared dead too soon. These same authors found in a ques-tionnaire survey of 143 students no direct relation between general self-esteem and postmortem organ donation or between physical self-esteem and donation (Hessing and Elffers, 1986–87). A signif-icant relationship, however, was observed between fear of death and donation behavior in students with negative physical self-esteem.

Results of a comparison of 186 blood donors and a control group of 106 nondonors indicate that both the aversive nature of the donation procedure and the donor's motivation exerted consider-able influence on the donor's decision to return and donate again (Edwards and Zeichner, 1985). Additionally, the donor's experience of physical discomfort and fearfulness about the donation proce-dure made the major contributions to the donation's aversive na-ture. Results also reveal significant differences among nondonor, exdonor, and irregular and regular donor groups on several person-ality characteristics, on their motives for donating, and on the com-ponents comprising the aversive nature of the donation procedure.

O'Malley and Andrews (1983) examined the impact of emotions on giving behavior. Happy, guilty, and neutral mood states in ninety undergraduates were compared with responses to an opportunity to donate blood for free, to donate in exchange for $5, or to choose between donating for free or for $5. As expected, there was a significantly higher incidence of helping when the students felt happy or guilty as opposed to emotionally neutral. Contrary to predictions, helping was unaffected by the type of incentive students were offered. However, the type of incentive did seem to influence the postdonation emotions of the students. Students who felt guilty and who donated for money felt significantly less guilty following donation than prior to it, and students who felt happy felt more self-altruistic (kind and generous) following donation when they helped for free. Piliavin, Callero, and Evans (1982) introduce the possibility of an affective addiction to blood donation, through a complex emotional response set in motion by the donor's initial anxiety.

One major focus of the research on donations is adding to the repertory of donor-solicitation skills. Fraser and Hite (1989) found that offers to match funds, paired with legitimization of paltry donations, increased compliance rates and donation sizes and generated greater revenues than either tactic used alone. Two field experiments by LaTour and Manrai (1989) with two thousand community residents manipulated informational influences (through a direct mail letter about donating blood) and normative influences (through a telephone request to donate blood from another resident) and found that both influences interacted to yield substantial increases in donations. Another study found that subjects who approached either friends or strangers with a direct face-to-face request and said that they themselves had just donated were more likely to solicit additional donors than any combination of media publicity, personal letters, and follow-up phone calls (Jason, Rose, Ferrari, and Barone, 1984).

Weyant (1984) found that adding a phrase such as "even a penny will help" at the end of a solicitation request significantly increased the proportion of those who donated. Lipsitz, Kallmeyer, Ferguson, and Abas (1989) found that asking for an additional commitment during a reminder call can appreciably increase blood drive participation rates for college students. On the other hand,

Wiesenthal and Spindel (1989) reported no statistically significant differences in return rates among 209 first-time blood donors who received follow-up telephone contacts using four different scripts and a control group receiving no follow-up contact.

Williams and Williams (1989) did a study of door-to-door solicitation involving 204 households. Their results support the existence of two distinct patterns of the strength of sources of influence on donation requests. They found that if the underlying motive for complying with a donation request was some form of external impression management, stronger influences were likely to have greater effect. If, however, compliance was internally motivated, such as by self-perception, the strength of a source of influence probably will have little or no effect.

Riecken and Yavas (1986) assessed the potential impact of opinion leaders on donor behavior. They concluded that the impact of opinion leaders was greatest when the leader was demographically similar to the prospective donors, actively involved in the topic, and attentive to mass media messages about the topic.

Another major purpose of donations research has been to isolate characteristics of individual donors. One study compared 715 donors of money and time to nonprofit human service agencies with 1,245 nondonors (Harvey and McCrohan, 1988). Donors were more likely than nondonors to be employed, have attended college, be older, have large incomes, have a positive attitude toward the agency's fundraising efforts, believe volunteer training is important, have benefited from the agency, and think the agency is efficient at channeling funds to the needy. Another study of heavy blood donors (for example, those who donated most frequently) found they were predominantly male, older, less educated, effectively reached by direct mail, and motivated by the perception that their blood type is always in demand (Tucker, 1987).

Gender is an issue of some importance in this context. Carducci and others (1989) found a greater willingness to become organ donors among female college students than among their male counterparts. Another study found that Canadian men and women donated about equally to a voluntary blood donor system, but that women were less likely to donate to a market-based blood procurement system (Lightman, 1982).

Age is also an important factor. In a cross-sectional study of people from five to seventy-five years old, which controlled for financial costs, elderly people proved to be the most generous (Midlarsky and Hannah, 1989).

The ethics of various forms of donation are always of considerable concern in nonprofit and voluntary settings. Bouressa and O'Mara (1987) discuss the ethical implications of informed consent of organ donors, brain death, the emotional needs of the competent donor, and the emotional responses of health care providers engaged in retrieving organs. Quigley, Gaes, and Tedeschi (1989) found that any information suggesting selfish motivations on the part of prosocial actors reduced attributions of altruism, charitableness, and benevolence by others, whether or not the actors themselves were aware of the information.

Disaster Response

Unpredictability and sudden onset are important characteristics of most disasters (Cherniack, 1986). Yet even while disasters may occur without notice, community response to them is often both quick and effective. Community relief committees and other forms of voluntary association are important forms of organized disaster response reaching back to the Middle Ages (Lohmann and Johnson, 1991). Lystad (1985) outlines needed research in the area of the mental health impacts of disasters.

Inadequate responses by public officials can lead to decreases in the perceived legitimacy of government (Kronick, 1982). Disasters, particularly ongoing ones like the Centralia, Pennsylvania, underground mine fire that has been burning since the 1960s, can also produce social conflict (Kroll-Smith, 1990).

Motivation for volunteering in disaster situations may be a complex phenomenon. Wolensky (1979) identified six distinct types of volunteers in two types of disaster states, postimpact and recovery. He termed these types egoistic, altruistic, mutualistic, communalistic, decisionalistic, and opportunistic.

In many respects, the volunteer fire department is the quintessential American symbol of voluntary action (Perkins, 1989). Recent work by nonprofit and voluntary action researchers in

Australia, Canada, and elsewhere on organized disaster response points up this area as important and understudied (Britton, 1991). Modern disaster response studies remind us that nonprofit and voluntary action has also long been important during and after floods, landslides, tornadoes, and other forms of disaster. And disaster research points to important international and cross-cultural examples of concerted common action (Kent, 1987). Britton (1991) reviews the implications of many of these studies for voluntary action research.

Edney and Bell (1984) conducted a study in which 180 undergraduates, divided into groups of 3, participated in what the authors called a commons game. The participants had to harvest resources from a shared pool so as to maximize their individual harvests without overexploiting the pool. In one-third of the groups, the group experienced a disaster that resulted in a loss of all their earnings. Only one member experienced the disaster in another third of the group, and in the remaining third, there was no disaster. In this experiment, stealing was about five times as frequent as altruism. However, groups made higher scores and showed more altruism and less stealing when members' scores were tied to the group's score. Paradoxically, more stealing occurred in groups that did not experience ruin. The authors concluded that stealing of this type was in fact functional in preserving the life of the commons but not in improving members' scores.

Conclusion

Psychological researchers have invested a good deal of common effort in the investigation of prosocial behavior. In the process, they have provided a number of important avenues for further exploration by the interdisciplinary community of nonprofit and voluntary action scholars. Most important, the concept of prosocial behavior—even in the present, somewhat uncertain, form in which operationally oriented researchers have left it—appears to be an umbrella concept vastly superior to the altruism/self-interest dichotomy that still permeates far too much of the nonprofit and voluntary action dialogue.

Popular stereotypes notwithstanding, the commons is not

the exclusive domain of altruistic behavior. As psychological studies make clear, those engaged in commons do not all need to wear
hair shirts and take lifetime vows of poverty and total commitment
to altruistic self-denial in order to engage in prosocial behavior or
to participate authentically. The concept of prosocial behavior is a
useful label for the middle ground between the equally anarchic
tendencies of pure and unadulterated self-interest and pure, and
equally anarchic, altruism.

Much of the present psychological literature is limited in
generalizability because of the tendency of researchers to focus heavily on studies of captive populations of schoolchildren and college
students and on the origins and development of moral attitudes
(Poplawski, 1985). These may be important areas in themselves, but
their utility for enriching the nonprofit and voluntary action dialogue is somewhat limited. However, many of those limitations
would be overcome if similar investigations were conducted with
adult volunteers (and nonvolunteer control groups), patrons, and
other common participants and beneficiaries. Some intriguing starts
have already been made in this area in bystander studies, disaster
studies, and certain other areas, but much significant investigation
of this type remains to be done.

(10)

The Values
of the Commons

If people are to remain civilized or to become so,
the art of associating together must grow and improve in the same ratio in which the equality of conditions is increased.

—Alexis de Tocqueville

The 1972 interdisciplinary Voluntary Action Task Force Planning Conference identified the values of voluntary action as a major analytical topic of voluntary action theory and research (Smith and others, 1972). Although the interdisciplinary literature on values offers a bewildering variety of approaches, definitions, and analytical styles, a common central theme is normative analysis of goods, preferences, norms, beliefs, and interests. Based upon the belief, stated in the introduction, that a complete theory of the commons must include a normative component, this chapter is devoted to an exploration of possible common values implicit in the commons. Such a discussion must, of necessity, be offered largely in terms of the metavalues upon which common values are based, since freedom to act in an internally consistent manner is one of the defining characteristics of commons.

This discussion is addressed primarily to the contemporary U.S. context. Its full historical and cross-cultural implications

253

must, of necessity, be left largely unexplored. Nonetheless, comparative value theory may be one of the ways of approaching the spreading, worldwide phenomenon of nonprofit and voluntary action. Schwartz and Bilsky (1990) suggest a common psychological content to human values across cultures. Prosocial motives are one of the eight classes of distinct motivational types they identify. Brown (1991) lists four hundred "human universals," traits and characteristics said to be present in all known cultures, in the intriguing format of a discussion of what he calls "the universal people." Some of these traits, such as gift giving, relate directly to the commons.

Value Theory for the Commons

Commons have been defined here as collectivities in which uncoerced participation, sharing, mutuality, and fairness play an important part. On this basis, it is reasonable to ask what standards of participation, sharing, fairness, and mutuality in the commons may be. In the context of some commons, most notably religious ethics and scientific methodologies, such questions are addressed directly and explicitly. In other cases, predominant economic values such as efficiency, effectiveness, and productivity have been said to be standards. In still other cases, approaches to the issue of values are more indirect and implicit. In general, however, certain recurrent themes are evident.

The discussion in earlier chapters of the pragmatic origins of the theory of the commons bears directly on applications of the theory's approach to values in common situations. As many commentators have noted, pragmatic philosophy incorporates a unique and distinctive approach to values (Bernstein, 1971). That approach may be summarized roughly as the view that values can be tested and verified in much the same manner as facts, that both values and facts are subject to verification in terms of their consequences, and that testing of values and facts is an important step in fully informed action. According to Hill (who refers to pragmatism by Dewey's term, *instrumentalism*):

> Perhaps the greatest contribution of the instrumental-
> ists to economics and the other social sciences is their

theory of normative value. Dewey believed that normative value judgements are instrumental and corrigi-
ble. People have the ability to learn how to derive
values from experience and how to use these values in
the instrumental process of making normative value
judgements and solving practical problems. Moreover, people also have the ability to test and to verify
the truth of value judgements by drawing from experience to evaluate their practical consequences. You
should accept a fact as true only if it relates the various
parts of your experience into an authentic whole and
successfully integrates your past with your future. You
should accept a value judgement as true only if it is
based on a true value and only if it contributes significantly to the instrumental process of solving problems. This process of instrumental verification can
result in a revision and improvement of both values
and value judgements [Hill, 1983, p. 7].

This view is consistent with the previously stated assumptions of the theory of the commons, particularly the assumptions
about the capacity of commons to make and enforce their own
worldviews. Presumably, such worldviews incorporate value judgments and their evaluations of practical consequences.

Since the work of Pierce (1931–1935, 1958), the concept of
community has served as an important marker of common pursuits
in science. According to Bernstein (1971, p. 199), "Pierce's theory of
inquiry stands as one of the great attempts to show how the classic
dichotomies between thought and action, or theory and praxis, can
be united in a theory of a community of inquirers committed to
continuous, rational, self-critical activity." This concept of community is likewise implicated in the pragmatic approach to reality
itself. The pragmatic concept of reality encompasses the concept of
community in a way that has direct consequences for value deter-
minations in the commons.

The real, then, is that which, sooner or later, information and reasoning would finally result in, and which

is therefore independent of the vagaries of me and you. Thus, the very origin of the conception of reality shows that this conception essentially involves the notion of a community, without definite limits, and capable of a definite increase of knowledge. And so, these two series of cognitions—the real and the unreal— consist of those which, at a time sufficiently future, the community will always continue to affirm; and those which, under the same conditions, will ever be denied. Now, a proposition whose falsity can never be discovered, and the error of which is absolutely incognizable, contains, upon our principle, no absolute error. Consequently, that which is thought in these cognitions is real, as it really is. There is nothing, then, to prevent our knowing outward things as they really are, and it is most likely that we do thus know them in numberless cases, although we can never be absolutely certain of doing so in any special case. [Bernstein, 1971, p. 176, quoting Pierce]

The immediate task that faces us now is applying this perspective to the circumstances of the commons in useful ways. In particular, two issues will concern us here. The first is the question of further identifying an appropriate theory of value for the commons, and the second is the related question of the place of need in value judgments made in the commons.

Value and Role Taking

Is it possible in the context of the commons to set forth a limited, institutionally specific theory of value that is of relevance to the particular associational context of the pursuit of common goods? The tentative answer offered here is yes. The conception of a community of inquirers (or what might be thought of as a rational community) set forth by Pierce offers a solid base upon which to suggest that there is a natural, spontaneously occurring, value standard that arises in most human groups and is operational in most common decision-making contexts. We can call this a *com-*

mon theory of value, and state it thusly: things are of value to participants in a commons because they are of value to other persons whom the participants value.

This is the standard of value underlying peer review of scientific proposals and scientific publication, critical reviews of artistic productions, the notion of board members as trustees of the membership found in many member associations, and a host of other specific values found in the commons. This standard may also include the most powerful sanction available to commons; rejection, shunning, or expulsion from the commons of those who disregard or violate common values is one of the most universal practices of religious, scientific, artistic, and other commons.

Common goods are not of value because they allow us to survive, as would be assumed by a labor theory of value. Survival is a precondition of the commons. Nor are they valuable to us because of their usefulness or their exchange value. We value common goods in response to others' valuations. And they, in turn, respond to our valuations, if and to the extent that they value us. This standard is one of the most fundamental implications of the mutuality of the commons.

Principle of Satisfaction

Rational actors operating within a commons and possessed of knowledge of the values of their peers require principles upon which to ground their choices, analogous to the economic principle of maximization, and principles of distribution, analogous to Pareto optimality.

One principle of decision making is the *principle of satisfaction,* which is derived from traditional philosophical concerns with satisfaction or happiness by way of Herbert Simon's satisficing principle of organizational decision making. *Satisficing,* according to Simon (1976), is a rational decision-making procedure to terminate the process of considering all possible alternatives by selecting the first alternative that fully meets the criteria.

Simon may have felt it necessary to use the neologism he did, rather than the simpler word *satisfying,* because of the enduring Benthamite utilitarian associations of satisfaction with pleasure and pain. It is essential to a proper understanding of this criterion that it be stripped of the futile utilitarian legacy of debate over the issue of pleasure and pain. There need be no connotations of hedonism or satiation raised in this connection. Thus, for example, the principle of satisfaction as used by Simon might imply that we need not be familiar with all possible dramatic works to determine that *Hamlet* is the greatest of tragedies. People willing to "join" the commons defined by knowledgeable authorities on drama can note that this is the consistent conclusion of the field. This is, however, a purely voluntary and uncoerced choice for all concerned, and we are completely free to reject the consensus and continuing searching for a better tragedy.

Satisfaction as a criterion for decision making refers explicitly to the intersubjective dialogue of decision makers. Specifically, it refers to the transfer of interest or attention among the actors in a common decision-making situation. It relates directly to contemporary psychological perspectives on attention and perception, and in particular to the pragmatic concept of a problem as articulated by Dewey, Mead, and the other pragmatists. It is also an explicitly behavioral and verifiable criterion.

Satisfaction is attained in the commons when search is suspended and dialogue on awareness and purpose are shifted elsewhere. Thus, the point of rational decision making in the commons is not to attain a maximum of goods (that is, maximization) or even to attain some optimal level of goods but rather to attain a *satisfactory* level of goods. A satisfactory level of goods is a sufficient level of goods so that the problem that prompted the original search can be arrested, and attention can be shifted elsewhere. Actors in the common context recognize when this point has been attained and shift their attention elsewhere. Excessive preoccupation with maximization in the context of commons, therefore, is not a virtue but a serious shortcoming and a form of irrational behavior.

Sometimes the suspension of search and the shift of attention that are implied in the principle of satisfaction occur when needs have been met. Meeting needs, in this sense, is not the basic concept of value that it is sometimes set forth as being for the simple reason that satisfaction may also occur for other reasons.

Principle of Proportion

A second principle involves the specification of a criterion governing distribution of resources within a community and between communities. The term that has been chosen for this criterion is *principle of proportion.* I chose this term at least partially because of its connotations with classical aesthetics (for example, the human scale of classical Greek architecture) and ethics (for example, the Aristotelian golden mean). As employed here, the principle of proportion can be used in a problem-solving context so that the resources used are approximately equivalent to, or in proportion to, the needs met, the problem solved, or the results attained. It can also be employed in a similar vein in religion, athletics, art, and other presentational settings. The principle of proportion has an operational expression fully as coherent as Pareto optimality: resources should be allocated in such a manner that no rational actor with standing to do so will act to gain more resources except from unallocated funds.

The principle of proportion in no way suggests that all actors involved in a situation in which resources are distributed by or among endowments must be fully pleased or happy with the distribution. Given the range of human differences and the plurality of human values, making everyone happy seems as excessive and artificial a standard to apply to nonprofit activities as would be the related standard that everyone should or must "profit" by such transactions. More important in a context of sharing and mutual trust is the question of whether anyone is sufficiently displeased to object. It is in such objections that self-interest begins to overwhelm the shared interests of the commons and mutuality begins to break down.

We can see this principle in operation in contemporary United Ways. Few, if any, such community fund-raising campaigns ever collect all of the contributions they may need or desire, and there may be intense competition for shares of the funds collected and dissatisfaction with the resultant distribution. However, the most common reaction most of the time for most of the competitors in such distributions is satisfaction, in the sense that further seeking after additional funds is abandoned and attention shifts elsewhere.

The effect upon the commons as a whole of a series of such independently arrived at feelings of satisfaction is the condition I am calling proportion. The use of this term is also based upon the common phrases "putting things in perspective" and "putting things in proportion," which are often used to describe this acceptance.

Proportion serves to sanction the equilibrium of networks of common institutions. Where it exists, the rule of proportion functions as a rough-and-ready kind of concept of equity among endowments and accounts for the social order or equilibrium of the commons in a Hobbesian sense. Proportion provides a general criterion for how rational allocative decisions are made in common settings. Like satisfaction, it applies to a broad range of different possible situations, and encompasses proportion grounded in despair of further gains as well as proportion based in contentment or satiation.

Principle of Contextualism

Yet a third principle is also necessary to properly set common decisions within a context of values by which they are to be judged. I have already begun this task with the statement of the emergence of value in role taking. However, the issue of locating an adequate substitute for the misleading model of universal objectivity put forth by utilitarian economics remains. This model might be characterized as the "grandstand model" of objectivity: the decision maker is thought to be much like a spectator in the grandstand with full view of all the action occurring on the field. In reality, no one is ever afforded such a grandstand position with respect to organized decision making, as Braybrooke and Lindblom (1963), Simon (1976), and others have been at pains to point out.

Recently, works in the history and philosophy of science in the tradition of Pierce have pointed up the need for such a criterion in the debate over "scientific revolutions," beginning with Kuhn's famous paradigm shifts (Berger and Luckmann, 1966; Bernstein, 1983; Kuhn, 1962). Such paradigm shifts have major implications for common resources and goods. In major paradigm shifts, any type of resources, from treasuries, collections, and repertories to key or central problems, may be transformed from valuable to worthless or vice versa. Thus, for example, the paradigm shift accompanying the development of printing not only placed new importance on research on the chemistry of ink but also relegated the medieval scriptorium to unimportance except as a historical curiosity.

Anthropologists, archeologists, art historians, theologians, librarians, and others concerned with the value of manuscripts and other artifacts from cultures widely different from our own have had to struggle with this issue as have social workers, psychiatrists, special educators, and others who deal with what are called special populations. Amateur athletics has had its own distinctive struggle with similar issues around the definition of *amateurism* in other, particularly non-Western, cultures.

In each of these many cases, a similar phenomenon is evident: the autonomy of a particular commons is threatened or usurped by the embrace of a larger, more inclusive, or more powerful commons, state, market, or kinship network that insists on replacing fundamental common values with its own. Whether we examine the case of the suppression of Galileo's science by the inquisition or modern conflicts over the works of avant-garde artists, this same dynamic can be seen. Likewise, when we examine religious issues, from the Crusades or the Protestant Reformation to the present impasse over abortion, the futility of attempts of one group to impose its religious values on others stands out. The present issue for the theory of the commons is how to approach such questions from a value standpoint.

We need at least partial relief from the burdens of judgmentalism that a preoccupation with universal objectivity places on the commons without succumbing to the equally oppressive demands of relativism. The pragmatic theory of value cited earlier offers a philosophically grounded, practical basis for dealing with such issues as they occur in the commons.

A pragmatic standard of contextualism that respects the autonomy of common values might be stated as follows: values that are the basis of judgment for decision in the commons—including those allocating common resources—arise in the context of particular commons and can only be assessed within the context of the same commons. This approach constitutes a standard that explicitly takes into account the context in which particular values have developed. The most immediate area of this approach's applicability in contemporary nonprofit, voluntary, and philanthropy studies is with respect to economic issues of allocation and distribution. Consistent application of this standard would suggest that importing value criteria such as maximization and Pareto optimality (or, for that matter, the socialist principle of equal distribution) from the market to the commons is an issue for the actors in a particular commons and not an issue to be decided by general theory.

Perhaps the most interesting possible approach to the study of common values has evolved in the multidisciplinary field of studies of biblical texts. It involves the interpretation of these texts in context—that is, with reference to our knowledge of the social, political, economic, and historical circumstances in which they were written and not from our current vantage point. Gadamer and other European advocates of hermeneutics (see Bernstein, 1983) have broadened and generalized this central idea into a full-flown philosophical position in recent decades. Bernstein (1983) has explored the connections between European hermeneutics and the pragmatism of Pierce and others.

This discussion of hermeneutics is intended to suggest that values that are the basis of judgment of all decisions—including those allocating resources—arise in the context of particular communities or commons and can only be properly assessed within the context of those commons. I shall refer to this notion as the *principle of contextualism* and set it off against the principle of universal objectivity, which is widely endorsed in social science.

Although maximization, production, and optimality may clearly be the group values of researchers conducting investigations, they have not been shown to be the values adopted or endorsed by the commons being studied. Nor are there existing explanations for why such values are superior to those adopted by participants of the commons or why these values should be coercively imposed upon the commons.

The Carnegie Principle

There are other possible general values or principles of the commons that speak directly to various aspects of common experiences.

Many values of possible general interest are articulated in the literature on nonprofit and voluntary action. One of these, the *good Samaritan rule,* is intended to protect volunteers from legal liability arising from actions associated with helping others. Some people would invoke what could be called the *Asoka principle* in some instances and argue that rulers in control of significant resources have a responsibility to create endowments to further the advance of religions. We might debate the relative merits of a *Chrysostem principle,* stated as give unreservedly to the poor, and a *Gregorian-Augustinian principle,* give generously but prudently (Morris, 1986). We might also isolate a *Bonifacius principle,* which states that charity like virtue is its own reward. This view was articulated by the Boston cleric and Puritan theologian Cotton Mather (1966) in his famous essay on philanthropy entitled *Bonifacius: An Essay upon the Good.*

We might also look more closely at the central principles articulated by Andrew Carnegie in his *The Gospel of Wealth* ([1889] 1983). Carnegie's "gospel" is one of those cultural icons that is universally celebrated in public school civics texts and alluded to frequently by scholars but seldom actually read or taken seriously by anyone (Chambré, 1989; Lyman, 1989; Odendahl, 1989).

Andrew Carnegie is familiar to every American schoolchild as the Scottish immigrant steel entrepreneur whose life was a "rags to riches" tale and whose generous beneficence salted the American and English landscapes with public libraries (sixty-six branches of the New York Public Library alone). College and university faculty members also know Carnegie as the initiator of what has become the Teachers Income Annuity Assistance program, and The Carnegie Foundation for the Advancement of Teaching. Residents of the Pittsburgh area know Carnegie also for the museum, auditorium, and collection of the Carnegie Institute; Carnegie Tech (now merged into Carnegie-Mellon University); and the industrial suburb bearing his name.

In all, Carnegie created eleven enduring charities bearing his name in the United States, Britain, and his native Scotland and gave away an estimated $350 million. We are less interested here in his philanthropic actions than in his spoken and printed thoughts on the responsibilities of patronage. Quite independent of his motives, whatever they may have been, Carnegie's actions represent a veritable archetype of modern American patronage, and his gospel offers a possible standard by which to evaluate patronage of all types.

Carnegie recognized the necessity for flexibility in the management of a charitable trust. In his first "letter of gift" to the trustees of The Carnegie Corporation, for example, he wrote, "Conditions upon the earth inevitably change; hence, no wise man will bind trustees forever to certain paths, causes, or institutions. I disclaim any intention of doing so. On the contrary, I give my trustees full authority to change policy or causes hitherto aided, from time to time, when this, in their opinion, has become necessary or desirable. They shall best conform to my wishes in using their own judgement" (Desruisseaux, 1985, p. 11). This statement is an interesting twist on the cy pres doctrine that in new circumstances trustees of an endowment have an obligation to engage in those actions that most closely conform to the wishes of the patron.

The issue to which Carnegie (and the cy pres doctrine) was responding is a serious one in which a good deal of thought has been invested. A number of trusts established by Benjamin Franklin in the late eighteenth century only matured in the 1990s. The problem is not exclusively an American one. Under Islamic law, a number of very ancient educational and religious endowments have endured. The Waqfizah of 'Ahmed Pasa, for example, was a Turkish endowment of the sixteenth century that continued at least into the 1940s and may still exist today (Simsar, 1940).

More controversial than this statement by Carnegie, especially among the higher-income segments of U.S. society, are Carnegie's sentiments on the responsibilities of the rich and his standard of what might be called the "inverse tithe." Carnegie's views, which have always been treated as somewhat eccentric and largely ignored or discounted as philanthropic principles, were set forth in a famous essay entitled *The Gospel of Wealth* ([1889] 1983). His personal performance against this standard is a matter of record.

Carnegie's famous paper on philanthropy was first published as "Wealth" in the *North American Review* in 1889, and later as *The Gospel of Wealth*. Carnegie wrote that "the man who dies thus rich dies disgraced," and he went on to state that the rich were obligated to spend their surplus wealth for the public good. After he sold U.S. Steel to J. P. Morgan in 1901 for $400 million, Carnegie quite literally spent the rest of his life practicing his principles.

We can argue many different interpretations of the motivations of wealthy men such as Carnegie. Perhaps he was actually motivated by a desire to prevent the initiation of an income tax in the United States or to avoid the payment of inheritance taxes. Some people are inclined to interpret all such acts of patronage, large and small, as futile efforts to prop up a faltering system of class domination by capitalists and to forestall revolution by the underclass.

Viewed as an issue of endowment patronage, Carnegie's actions stand alongside numerous other examples of comparable behavior throughout world history. For example, Pericles and King Asoka devoted their resources to philanthropy.

The wealthy in the United States today—many of whom may be arguably less rich than Carnegie—feel very little obligation to follow the precedent set by Carnegie. Indeed, for most of the contemporary rich, Carnegie's problems of selecting trustworthy trustees and not dying rich have been replaced by the quite different problem of maintaining a celebrity image and avoiding taxes.

Unfortunately, the central problem in the practice of patronage today, at least as it is presented by countless tax accountants, media consultants, and others, bears little relation to the entire philanthropic tradition but is instead a perverse variant of profit maximization: how to appear maximally generous on minimal contributions. Corporate executives "on the way up" see service for themselves and their wives on the boards of community charities as tribute to the well-crafted image of corporate leadership. Personal managers of athletes, politicians, and other celebrities of popular culture work hard to create public images of their clients as patrons of charity, culture, and politics. Although every celebrity player in professional sports during the past decade appears to have posed with a handicapped child for a fund-raising poster, actual amounts of their contributions are less regularly publicized. One suspects this may be for good reason.

The contemporary rich in American society—the new beau monde society of oil barons, stockbrokers, rock musicians, and professional athletes, among others—get off remarkably easy in terms of their personal obligations to community services, certainly easier than comparable elites in ancient Athens and Central American villages or urban elites throughout history. This is particularly true in personal (as opposed to purely financial) terms. Tax accountants, media consultants, lawyers, and other retainers have simplified and routinized the contemporary charitable procedures, often to the point of the simple, painless signing of a statement of after-tax income and a few checks. Charitable contributions easily become not an act of personal (or even foundational) patronage at all. They have become merely the afterthoughts of tax calculations, part of an overall plan to maximize after-tax income.

It is easy from this perspective to "flog the rich"—those people who, in F. Scott Fitzgerald's famous quip, "are different from us"—and to develop a campaign of moral smugness and superiority with statements such as those just made above. To counteract this tendency, we can easily characterize middle- and upper-middle-income groups in exactly the same way. With average estimated giving hovering between 2 and 2½ percent of personal income, it seems clear that there is little concern for the kind of patronage of which Carnegie spoke and a motivation primarily to avoid taxes.

The real challenge facing nonprofit fundraising in the United States, therefore, is not management improvement or greater efficiency. It is not economic or even narrowly political (in the sense of campaigns for policy or legal changes). It is more fundamentally practical: specifically, it is the discovery of a modern moral equivalent to the majordomia and the liturgia—the accepted moral norms that create sufficient incentives, if you will, for people to contribute to civilization. The traditional philanthropic practice of naming towns, buildings, rooms, furniture, and even picture frames after benefactors and tax advantages of philanthropic behavior are insufficient to generate the necessary revenues. It is this insufficiency, and not the mismanagement and inefficiency of community services, that is at the heart of the current crisis in philanthropy.

Inflation, technology, and the legitimate wage demands of employees in the community service sector have sent costs skyrocketing, while real contributions (adjusted for inflation) have risen only slightly or perhaps even fallen. To speak of Carnegie's 90 percent contribution or even to fall back to the traditional biblical tithe of 10 percent is almost farcical; most Americans do not even give 5 percent of total income. Many do not even give 1 percent. For the worker who earns $100,000 a year, $10 to the United Way and $100 a year to the church does little except perhaps salve a guilty conscience.

Principles of Conservation and Prudence

Two distinct monetary principles can be applied to common treasuries and perhaps to collections or repertories. Each is a reflection of the mutual obligation participants in the commons feel for one another. One principle is sometimes mislabeled as efficiency, cost effectiveness, or cost efficiency. The other is seldom given a name.

Generally speaking, attempts to apply efficiency and similar concepts to the commons have been largely exercises in metaphysics and have been devoid of empirical content or referents. They usually use an oversimplified engineering metaphor in which efficiency is defined as the ratio of one group of arbitrarily selected situational elements called inputs to another arbitrarily selected group of elements called outputs. Since the directionality of conversation and interaction is subject to some indeterminacy, there are no generally applicable rules and what is input and output is determined on a strictly ad hoc basis. The understanding that because we are dealing with social acts rather than physical substances no underlying assumptions like those of the conservation of matter and energy are appropriate is usually missing. Therefore, there is no particular reason to expect that routine, predictable, or even measurable ratios will result from this effort. No generally recognizable measurements of the efficiency of rendering common goods have emerged from this approach. Thus discussions of efficiency in the commons usually confuse and obscure what are, in fact, two principles of action that actually are quite important in the commons.

Karst (1960, p. 434) calls the first the *principle of conservation* and sums it up as follows: "There remains substantial unanimity on one goal: the greatest possible portion of the wealth donated to private charity must be conserved and used to further the charitable, public purpose; waste must be minimized and diversion of public funds for private gain is intolerable." It should be noted that although Karst uses the term *public* here, his intent is clearly directed at nongovernmental efforts and the term *common* would be more suitable. Trustees of commons who spend excessive sums for purposes unrelated to the rendition of common goods, pay excessively high prices to obtain needed resources, or divert common resources to their own profit are clearly violating the principle of conservation.

The second principle can be called the *principle of prudence,* which is, as Wooster (1952, p. 171) stated it, "to maintain and increase dollar income without excessive risk to principal. Judgment and experience will continue to be the most valuable tools available." The principle of prudence as it applies in the commons is, in fact, broader than Wooster's statement, since it applies not only to treasuries but also to collections and repertories. The key to the principle of prudence is avoidance of excessive risk. The trustees or agents who protect a priceless painting by placing it in a fireproof vault and those who protect the rigorous standards of a science or profession both may be said to act prudently.

Principles of Consensus

Together, these principles form the core of a normative model of common goods that can be found in operation in the everyday life of most American commons. In the most general sense, the principles of satisfaction, proportion, contextualism, conservation, and prudence as they operate in the commons are all *principles of consensus and community*. As such, they prove most workable in circumstances of cooperation. Their greatest collective weakness (and the greatest weakness of common action in general) is the inability to adequately resolve contested, controversial, or difficult issues. It is this inability, and not inefficiencies or mismanagement, that is the most frequent target of contemporary concern by the management scientists.

Examples of this basic inability abound among common institutions. The Protestant Reformation and the continuing tendencies toward schism evident in many contemporary religious bodies are evidences of the unsatisfactory nature of this process. When religious factions quarrel over doctrine, ritual, or belief, the issues often have major economic implications involving the proper use of collective treasuries and collections or the proper selection and enactment of presentations—rituals, music, and other ritual elements. Luther's concern over the sale of indulgences, Puritan opposition to displays of religious icons, and the schism of two branches of the American Church of Christ over the use of music in worship services are examples of such quarrels.

Similar phenomena can be found in many types of commons. Indeed, contemporary efforts to apply market economic principles to the commons must be seen as arising from one such situation. Suggestions that nonprofit efforts are not sufficiently efficient or as effective as they might be are themselves expressions of latent or real conflict between factions within many contemporary commons. In many cases, the issue is further exacerbated as partisans of one point of view or the other appeal to academic economists on the one hand and decision makers in government on the other to reinforce their particular views. Regrettably, the scientific issues of nonprofit economics cannot be entirely divorced from these conflicts at present.

What is at issue in the current situation in public funding of social services and the arts in particular is often as much who shall control the definition of appropriate action in the commons as it is who shall control the actual resources. In general, the absence of adequate consensus and community, however, does not constitute a sufficient rationale for ignoring or violating the principle of contextualism and the autonomy of groups in the commons. Discovery of possible general solutions to the problem of hermeneutics that could be applied in the same way as the other economic principles of the commons is perhaps the single greatest theoretical challenge facing the theory of the commons.

Conclusion

Any theory of the commons must include a theory of values to be complete. Yet attempts to spell out value theories for the commons confront a fundamental contradiction: specifying the substance of common values deprives participants of a fundamental constitutive power. If participation in the commons is to be fully free and un-coerced, and resources (including symbolic resources of information and meaning) are truly to be shared, members of commons must be free to determine their own values. Consequently, in discussing values in the commons, we are reduced to discussing either values in specific contexts or the metavalues that form the basis of specific value choices. The very idea of a full or complete value theory to which all "right thinking" participants in commons would sub-scribe is a fundamental contradiction. Given that, however, this chapter has identified a number of value clusters that occur regu-larly in the context of the American commons. In this context, Dewey was essentially correct when he said that values are derived from common experience and used to make value judgments and solve practical problems.

One of the important dynamics that arises out of this is a role theory of value in which members of commons come to value ob-jects because of the roles those things play in the group. In partic-ular, members of commons come to value other people, things, and ideas because those things are valued by others whom they respect and admire.

Participants in commons also frequently demonstrate in their practical actions a value principle of satisfaction. When issues are discussed or decisions considered, search for information and meaning is continued and alternatives are discussed and debated until agreement is reached (through previously agreed-upon rules for terminating discussion) that a satisfactory solution has been arrived at. At that point, the attention of the commons can be ex-pected to turn elsewhere.

Closely related to this is the principal of proportion, by which a satisfactory distribution of resources is seen not as one that makes everyone happy, but rather as one that everyone can live with. In a working commons, compromise will ordinarily be rec-ognized as a legitimate and acceptable alternative to the full and free expression of every participant's self-interest. Such compromise is not a matter of a priori formulas or equations but of expression of consensus, whereby any who are dissatisfied with the result will not be sufficiently dissatisfied to prolong consideration of the issue.

In all commons, the value of contextualism is of essential

importance. Commons are composed in part of complex networks of interconnected values, meanings, and information, and great violence is ordinarily done to common values by considering them out of context. The values of any given commons (whether scientific, religious, charitable, social, or other) can only be fully determined and applied from within that commons.

From ancient Athens to the present, wealthy and powerful members of community elites have felt the influence of certain value obligations, so they acted as patrons to the community as a whole. Even though Andrew Carnegie sought to update and generalize these obligations through his gospel of wealth, elite members of contemporary communities frequently appear to ignore or reject any such obligations. An important concern raised in this chapter, therefore, is how to revive morally resilient forms of patronage.

Finally, two important values associated specifically with the handling of financial and material resources can be identified. A principle of conservation is one by which members of a commons strive to use only the resources necessary for any particular purpose and to conserve remaining resources for future use. A principal of prudence is one by which common financial resources may be invested, but only with due concern for minimizing risk to principal.

In a most general sense, all of these principals are expressions of the community represented by a commons and of the group consensus that binds members together: a consensus grounded in voluntary participation, common purposes, shared resources, mutuality, and justice.

(11)

Summing Up

The core of nonprofit and voluntary action encompasses a single theoretical domain that is only partially examined by current research investigations on nonprofit organizations, voluntary action, and prosocial behavior. The theory of the commons opens up a potentially powerful English-language vocabulary for treating many interrelated aspects of such action by using terms that have evolved over the centuries to discuss various associative, philanthropic, charitable, and related ideas. Linking all of these terms and concepts is the concept of the commons as a social, economic, and political space for uncoerced participation, sharing of resources and purposes, mutuality, and peer relations.

Commons are social spaces outside the home and away from family and independent of political states and economic markets. They are found in many different cultures, locations, and historical periods. We refer generally to participation in commons as voluntary association. True voluntary association is possible only under conditions of leisure, or freedom from subsistence living and labor. Those people who are thus free constitute, to varying degrees, leisure classes. They are engaged in what may be seen from some perspectives as paradoxical behavior: unproductive labor or productive consumption. Ultimately, the volunteer labor of such leisure classes is justified by the observation that civilizations are built up of such common goods.

Purposes shared in association can be called common goods. The pursuit of common goods is rational behavior, albeit distin-

272

guishable from the self-interested pursuit of profit that characterizes markets. Such behavior often consists of prosocial mixtures of self-interested and altruistic behavior, whether the prosocial behavior involved is philanthropic (for the common good of all who would benefit), charitable (for the common good of others), or mutual (for the common good of the group).

The shared resources of commons constitute endowments—treasuries of money and marketable goods and services; collections of valued objects; and repertories of routines, rituals, and performances. Mutuality and fairness find expression in explicit preference for the values of satisfaction, proportion, contextualism, conservation, and prudence and the social responsibility of leisure classes.

The theory of the commons as offered here is a fit platform to issue a number of challenges to the multidisciplinary community of nonprofit and voluntary action scholars. Psychological researchers have built up a large body of findings in the area of altruistic, charitable, bystander, and donor behavior and in other forms of prosocial behavior. They have generally shown little inclination or interest in connecting this work with the main body of interdisciplinary commons studies. Researchers engaged in the study of common social organizations have, on the whole, shown relatively little imagination in looking beyond the traditional U.S. view of associations and nonprofit social agencies to the broader world of multicultural common activity. Political researchers have been generally reluctant to acknowledge the link between their studies of parties, interest groups, and factions and the broader research community of organizational studies, restricted though it is. Economic researchers have concentrated chiefly upon a rather narrow band of "profitable nonprofits"—particularly hospitals and nursing homes—as indicative of the entire domain. And social welfare researchers have until recently neglected the continuing importance of the process of organizing volunteer charity.

There are many examples of hybrid institutions that mix characteristics of commons with families, states, and markets. Recent preoccupation with revenue-generating nonprofit corporations, for example, is such a concern. Such organizations are neither truly market oriented nor truly in the commons.

Many other types of organized benefactories in addition to

social agencies and public bureaus can be identified. Recently, the trend has been away from group trusteeships of nonprofit organizations toward the effective control of a solo trustee. Campaigns, committees, conferences, producer and consumer cooperatives, disciplines (whether academic disciplines, religious orders, or professions), festivals, foundations, literary and scientific journals, political parties, pilgrimages, research institutes, secret societies, and sciences are among the many types of benefactories.

The democratic political state can be seen as a special type of commons that has been called a dominant protective association. Political states arise out of the common goods and mutual actions of interest groups, factions, and political parties and in turn exercise a measure of control over the activities of commons. The U.S. constitutional tradition, and in particular the First Amendment rights of assembly, freedom of speech, freedom of religion, and redress of grievances, establish strong normative barriers against excessive state interference in the pursuit of common goods. They are a major institutional expression of the value of institutional harmony.

The problem of charity organization is a continuing concern, even in a period characterized by extensive networks of nonprofit charitable corporations and helping professions. Although the general approach of social work and other charitable professions has been to ignore or downplay the importance of charity commons, the phenomenon itself remains alive and vital.

Economists have grafted a substantial theory of nonprofit economics onto existing economic theory by relaxing definitions of the terms *firms* and *public goods* and related concepts on the basis of general rational choice models of human behavior. Beyond the limits of this model, where the customary assumptions of scarcity, production, profit maximization, and unrestrained self-interest do not apply, very little work has been done. Although there are numerous bold proposals and sound theoretical reasons for transcending this particular limit, the paradigm of the scientific commons of the economic profession still seeks to encompass all common goods economics within conventional perspectives.

Many additional disciplinary contributions are yet to be made to our collective understandings of the commons. In particular, further examination of psychological, anthropological, legal, and historical studies are likely to bear much fruit.

The focus in this book has been upon rethinking traditional perspectives on nonprofit organizations and voluntary associations, with particular concern for extending the scientific research commons of nonprofit and voluntary action studies; that is, in the language of the model presented and on identification of a plausible common good. By the very nature of common goods, however, the broader adoption and utilization of this good is dependent not on myself but on its acceptance and transformation by the community of readers. Mutual concerns were the starting point of this exercise. I have made an effort to call upon the rich endowment of the English language as a shared resource for the writing and speaking that make up the dialogue of this particular commons.

References

Abbott, G. *The Child and the State*. Chicago: University of Chicago Press, 1938.

Acton, H. "Medicean Florence." In A. Toynbee (ed.), *Cities of Destiny*. New York: McGraw-Hill, 1967.

Adams, J. L. *Voluntary Associations: Sociocultural Analyses and Theological Interpretations*. Chicago: Exploration Press, 1986.

Addams, J. *My Twenty Years at Hull House*. New York: Macmillan, 1930.

Adorno, T. W., Frenkel-Brunswik, E., Levinson, D., and Sanford, R. *The Authoritarian Personality*. New York: HarperCollins, 1950.

al Din Khairi, M. "Types of Relationships Between Some Nuclear Families and Relatives in the City of Amman: An Explorative Study." *Dirasat*, 1984, *11*(6), 43–74.

Alhadeff, D. A. *Microeconomics and Human Behavior: Toward a New Synthesis of Economics and Psychology*. Berkeley: University of California Press, 1982.

Amato, P. R. "The Helpfulness of Urbanites and Small Town

Dwellers: A Test Between Two Broad Theoretical Positions." *Australian Journal of Psychology*, 1983, *35*(2), 233–243.

Anderson, B., and Schiller, B. "Interest Group Focus on Market Expansion Alternatives and Governmental Policies: The Nordic Industrial Federations, 1960–1972." *Journal of Voluntary Action Research*, 1976, *5*(3-4), 176–191.

Anheier, H. K. "Indigenous Voluntary Associations, Nonprofits and Development in Africa." In W. W. Powell (ed.), *The Nonprofit Sector: A Research Handbook*. New Haven, Conn.: Yale University Press, 1987.

Anheier, H. K. "Themes in International Research on the Nonprofit Sector." *Nonprofit and Voluntary Sector Quarterly*, 1990, *19*(4), 371–392.

Anheier, H. K., and Knapp, M. "Voluntas: An Editorial Statement." *Voluntas*, 1990, *1*(1), 1–12.

Anthony, R. N. *Financial Accounting in Nonbusiness Organizations: An Exploratory Study of Conceptual Issues*. New York: Financial Accounting Standards Board, 1978.

Anthony, R. N., and Young, D. W. *Management Control in Nonprofit Organizations*. (3rd ed.) Homewood, Ill.: Dow Jones-Irwin, 1984.

Arberry, A. "Muslim Cordoba." In A. Toynbee (ed.), *Cities of Destiny*. New York: McGraw-Hill, 1967.

Arendt, H. *The Human Condition*. Chicago: University of Chicago Press, 1958.

Argyle, M. *Cooperation: The Basis of Sociability*. New York: Routledge & Kegan Paul, 1991.

Arrington, B., and Haddock, C. C. "Who Really Profits from Not-for-Profits?" *Health Service Research*, 1990, *25*(2), 291–304.

Asprea, A., and Betocchi, G. V. "Comportamento Prosociale, Altruismo e Teoria dell'Equita" (Prosocial Behavior, Altruism, and the Theory of Equity). *Giornale Italiano di Psicologia*, 1981, *8*(3), 377–402.

Attwood, D. W., and Baviskar, B. S. *Who Shares? Cooperatives and Rural Development*. New York: Oxford University Press, 1989.

Austin, D. M. "The Political Economy of Social Benefit Organizations: Redistributive Services and Merit Goods." In H. D. Stein (ed.), *Organization and the Human Services*. Philadelphia: Temple University Press, 1981.

Austin, D. M. "The Political Economy of Human Services." *Policy and Politics,* 1983, *11*(3), 343–359.

Ayubi, N. *Political Islam*. New York: Routledge & Kegan Paul, 1991.

Babchuk, N., and Schmidt, A. J. "Voluntary Associations, Social Change and Racial Discrimination: An Analysis of Means and Ends." *Journal of Voluntary Action Research,* 1976, *5*(2), 65–74.

Badelt, C., and Weiss, P. "Non-Profit, For-Profit and Government Organizations in Social Service Provision: Comparison of Behavioural Patterns for Austria." *Voluntas,* 1990, *1*(1), 77–96.

Baer, M. A. "The Development of Political Interest Groups in a Local Environment: Evidence from British New Towns." *Journal of Voluntary Action Research,* 1979, *8*(3-4), 57–66.

Balsdon, J. *Life and Leisure in Ancient Rome*. New York: McGraw-Hill, 1969.

Bandelier, A. *The Delight Makers: A Novel of Prehistoric Pueblo Indians*. Orlando, Fla.: Harcourt Brace Jovanovich, 1971. (Originally published 1890.)

Banton, M. "Voluntary Associations: Anthropological Aspects." In D. Sills (ed.), *Encyclopedia of Social Sciences*. Vol. 16. New York: Macmillan, 1965.

Banu, S., and Puhan, B. N. "Social Responsibility and Dependence Proneness in Indian and Bangladeshi Men and Women." *Personality Study and Group Behaviour,* 1983, *3*(1), 1–5.

Barker, A. "Citizen Participation in Britain: A Widening Landscape." *Journal of Voluntary Action Research,* 1979, *8*(1-2), 76–83.

Barnes, J. "Hellenistic Art and Science." In J. Boardman, J. Griffin, and O. Murray (eds.), *The Oxford History of the Classical World*. New York: Oxford University Press, 1986.

Bar-Tal, D. "Sequential Development of Helping Behavior: A Cognitive-Learning Approach." *Developmental Review,* 1982, *2*(2), 101–124.

Batson, C. D. "Sociobiology and the Role of Religion in Promoting Prosocial Behavior: An Alternative View." *Journal of Personality and Social Psychology,* 1983, *45*(6), 1380–1385.

Batson, C. D. "How Social an Animal? The Human Capacity for Caring." *American Psychologist*, 1990, *45*(3), 336–346.

Batson, C. D., Bolen, M. H., Cross, J. A., and Neuringer-Benefiel, H. E. "Where Is the Altruism in the Altruistic Personality? *Journal of Personality and Social Psychology*, 1986, *50*(1), 212–220.

Bauer, R. "Voluntary Welfare Associations in Germany and the United States: Theses on the Historical Development of Intermediary Systems." *Voluntas*, 1990, *1*(1), 97–111.

Baumol, W., and Bowen, W. *Performing Arts: The Economic Dilemma*. Cambridge, Mass.: MIT Press, 1968.

Bays, C. "Why Most Private Hospitals Are Nonprofit." *Journal of Policy Analysis and Management*, 1983, *2*(3), 366–385.

Becker, G. S. *The Economic Approach to Human Behavior*. Chicago: University of Chicago Press, 1976.

Beers, C. W. *A Mind That Found Itself: An Autobiography*. Pittsburgh, Penn.: University of Pittsburgh Press, 1983. (Originally published 1921.)

Ben-Ner, A. "Producer Cooperatives: Why Do They Exist in Capitalist Economies?" In W. W. Powell (ed.), *The Nonprofit Sector: A Research Handbook*. New Haven, Conn.: Yale University Press, 1987.

Bennett-Sandler, G. "Citizen Participation in Policing: The Social Control of a Social Control Agency." *Journal of Voluntary Action Research*, 1978, *7*(1-2), 15–24.

Ben Zadok, E., and Kooperman, L. "Voluntary Associations in West Africa: A Political Perspective." *Community Development Journal*, 1988, *23*(2), 74–85.

Berelson, B., and Steiner, G. L. *Human Behavior: An Inventory of Scientific Findings*. Orlando, Fla.: Harcourt Brace Jovanovich, 1964.

Berger, P. L., and Luckmann, T. *The Social Construction of Reality: A Treatise in the Sociology of Knowledge*. Garden City, N.Y.: Anchor, 1966.

Berleant, A. "Subsidization of Art as Social Policy." *Journal of Behavioral Economics*, 1979, *8*(1), 23–37.

Bernstein, B. "Carnegie Hall Takes a Bow." *Town and Country*, July 1990, pp. 61–80.

Bernstein, R. *Praxis and Action*. Philadelphia: University of Pennsylvania Press, 1971.

Bernstein, R. *The Restructuring of Social and Political Theory*. Philadelphia: University of Pennsylvania Press, 1976.

Bernstein, R. *Beyond Objectivism and Relativism: Science, Hermeneutics and Praxis*. Philadelphia: University of Pennsylvania Press, 1983.

Bernstein, S. R. "Contracted Services: Issues for the Nonprofit Manager." *Nonprofit and Voluntary Sector Quarterly*, 1991a, *20*(4), 429–444.

Bernstein, S. R. *Managing Contracted Services in the Nonprofit Agency: Administrative, Ethical and Political Issues*. Philadelphia: Temple University Press, 1991b.

Bestor, A. *Backwoods Utopias: The Sectarian Origins and the Owenite Phase of Communitarian Socialism in America, 1663–1829*. Philadelphia: University of Pennsylvania Press, 1970.

Beyan, A. J. *The American Colonization Society and the Creation of the Liberian State: A Historical Perspective, 1822–1900*. Washington, D.C.: University Press of America, 1991.

Biemiller, L. "Tracing a Culture's Metamorphosis in Its Cemeteries." *Chronicle of Higher Education*, Dec. 4, 1991, p. A5.

Bilinkoff, J. *The Avila of Saint Teresa: Religious Reform in a Sixteenth-Century City*. Ithaca, N.Y.: Cornell University Press, 1989.

Billis, D. "The Roots of Voluntary Agencies: A Question of Choice." *Nonprofit and Voluntary Sector Quarterly*, 1991, *20*(1), 57–70.

Bishai, W. B. *Humanities in the Arab-Islamic World*. Dubuque, Iowa: Brown, 1973.

Blanchi, R. *Unruly Corporatism: Associational Life in Twentieth-Century Egypt*. New York: Oxford University Press, 1989.

Blau, P. M. *Exchange and Power in Social Life*. New York: Wiley, 1967.

Blau, P. M., and Scott, W. R. *Formal Organizations*. San Francisco: Chandler, 1962.

Blaug, M. *The Economics of the Arts*. Boulder, Colo.: Westview Press, 1976.

Blaug, M. "Justifications for Subsidies to the Arts: Reply to F. F. Ridley." *Journal of Cultural Economics*, 1983, 7(1), 19–22.

Blumer, H. *Symbolic Interactionism*. Englewood Cliffs, N.J.: Prentice Hall, 1969.

Boardman, J. "Greek Art and Architecture." In J. Boardman, J. Griffin, and O. Murray (eds.), *The Oxford History of the Classical World*. New York: Oxford University Press, 1986.

Bonnett, A. W. "Instrumental and Expressive Voluntary Organizations Among Black West Indian Immigrants in New York." *Journal of Voluntary Action Research*, 1977, 6(1-2), 89–97.

Bontempo, R., Lobel, S., and Triandis, H. "Compliance and Value Internalization in Brazil and the U.S.: Effects of Allocentrism and Anonymity." *Journal of Cross Cultural Psychology*, 1990, 21(2), 200–213.

Boorstin, D. *The Americans: The Colonial Experience*. New York: Vintage Books, 1958.

Borkman, T. Review of *Explorations in Self-Help and Mutual Aid*, by L. D. Borman. *Journal of Voluntary Action Research*, 1978a, 7(3-4), 138.

Borkman, T. Review of *Self-Help Groups in the Modern World*, by A. H. Katz and E. I. Bender. *Journal of Voluntary Action Research*, 1978b, 7(3-4), 138.

Borman, L. D. "Self-Help/Mutual Aid in Changing Communities." *Social Thought*, 1984, 10, 49–62.

Boulding, K. E. *The Economy of Love and Fear: A Preface to Grants Economics*. Belmont, Calif.: Wadsworth, 1973.

Boulding, K. E., Pfaff, M., and Horvath, J. "Grants Economics: A Simple Introduction." *The American Economist*, 1972, 16(1), 19–35.

Bouman, F.J.A. *Small, Short and Unsecured: Informal Rural Finance in India*. New York: Oxford University Press, 1990.

Bouressa, G., and O'Mara, R. J. "Ethical Dilemmas in Organ Procurement and Donation." *Critical Care Nursing Quarterly*, 1987, 10(2), 37–47.

Bowra, M. "Athens in the Age of Pericles." In A. Toynbee (ed.), *Cities of Destiny*. New York: McGraw-Hill, 1967.

Bradshaw, B. *The Dissolution of the Religious Orders in Ireland Under Henry VIII*. London: Cambridge University Press, 1974.

Brandon, W. *The American Heritage Book of Indians.* New York: Dell, 1961.

Braudel, F. *Civilization and Capitalism, 15th–18th Century.* Vol. 1: *The Structures of Everyday Life: The Limits of the Possible.* New York: HarperCollins, 1981.

Braudel, F. *Civilization and Capitalism, 15th–18th Century.* Vol. 3: *The Perspective of the World.* New York: HarperCollins, 1986a.

Braudel, F. *Civilization and Capitalism, 15th–18th Century.* Vol. 2: *The Wheels of Commerce.* New York: HarperCollins, 1986b.

Braybrooke, D., and Lindblom, C. A. *A Strategy for Decision.* New York: Free Press, 1963.

Bremner, R. H. *The Public Good: Philanthropy and Welfare in the Civil War Era.* New York: Knopf, 1980.

Bremner, R. H. *American Philanthropy.* (Rev. ed.) Chicago: University of Chicago Press, 1988.

Brief, A. P., and Motowidlo, S. J. "Prosocial Organizational Behaviors." *Academy of Management Review,* 1986, *11*(4), 710–725.

Brinkman, C. "Civilization." In E.R.A. Seligman (ed.), *Encyclopedia of the Social Sciences.* New York: Macmillan, 1937.

Brinton, C. "Making the Modern World II: Protestantism." *The Shaping of Modern Thought.* Englewood Cliffs, N.J.: Prentice Hall, 1963.

Brissett, D., and Edgley, C. (eds.). *Life as Theater: A Dramaturgical Sourcebook.* Hawthorne, N.Y.: Aldine, 1990.

Britton, N. "Permanent Disaster Volunteers: Where Do They Fit?" *Nonprofit and Voluntary Sector Quarterly,* 1991, *20*(4), 395–414.

Brown, D. *Human Universals.* Philadelphia: Temple University Press, 1991.

Brown, M. K. "The Impact of Alternative Forms of Citizen Control on Police Organization and Police Discretion." *Journal of Voluntary Action Research,* 1978, 7(1-2), 85–101.

Brown, R. D. "The Emergence of Voluntary Associations in Massachusetts, 1760–1830." *Journal of Voluntary Action Research,* 1973, *2*(2), 64–73.

Brown, S. G. *Revolution, Confederation and Constitution.* East Norwalk, Conn.: Appleton and Lange, 1971.

Brudney, J. L. "Coproduction and Privatization: Exploring the Relationship and Its Implications." *Journal of Voluntary Action Research,* 1987, *16*(3), 11–21.

Brudney, J. L. *Fostering Volunteer Programs in the Public Sector: Planning, Initiating, and Managing Voluntary Activities.* San Francisco: Jossey-Bass, 1989.

Brudney, J. L., and England, R. E. "Toward a Definition of the Coproduction Concept." *Public Administration Review,* 1983, *43,* 59–65.

Brunn, S. D., and others. *Cities of the World: World Regional Urban Development.* New York: HarperCollins, 1983.

Bruno, F. J. "New Light on Oriental and Classical Charity in the Pre-Christian Era." *The Family,* 1944, *2,* 260–265.

Buchanan, J. M. *Cost and Choice: An Inquiry in Economic Theory.* Chicago: Markham, 1969.

Bukkyo Dendo Kyokai (Buddhist Promotional Foundation). *The Teachings of Buddha.* (293d ed.) Tokyo: Kosaido Printing Co., 1983.

Bultena, G. L., and Rogers, D. L. "Voluntary Associations and Political Equality: An Extension of Mobilization Theory." *Journal of Voluntary Action Research,* 1975, *4,* 3–4.

Burns, J. M., Peltason, J. L., and Cronin, T. E. *Government by the People: The Dynamics of American National Government.* (12th ed.) Englewood Cliffs, N.J.: Prentice Hall, 1984.

Butora, M. "Self-Help: A New Concept in Health Care. II: Present Status in Czechoslovakia and Its Perspectives." *Cesk-Zdrav,* 1989a, *37,* 245–255.

Butora, M. "Self-Help: New Concepts in Health Care. I: The Situation Worldwide." *Cesk-Zdrav,* 1989b, *37*(3), 129–138.

Cabral, S. L. "Ritual Change Among Portuguese-Americans in New Bedford, Massachusetts." *Journal of Voluntary Action Research,* 1978, *7*(3-4), 75–85.

Campbell, B. *Before the Black Death: Studies in the 'Crisis' of the Early Fourteenth Century.* New York: Manchester University Press, 1991.

Cantor, N. F. *Inventing the Middle Ages: The Lives, Works, and Ideas of the Great Medievalists of the Twentieth Century.* New York: Morrow, 1991.

Caplan, G., and Killilea, M. (eds.). *Support Systems and Mutual*

Help: Multidisciplinary Explorations. New York: Grune and Stratton, 1976.

Carducci, B. J., and others. "An Application of the Foot in the Door Technique to Organ Donation." *Journal of Business and Psychology,* 1989, *4*(2), 245–249.

Carlson, M., and Miller, N. "Explanation of the Relation Between Negative Mood and Helping." *Psychological Bulletin,* 1987, *102*(1), 91–108.

Carnegie, A. "The Gospel of Wealth." In B. O'Connell (ed.), *America's Voluntary Spirit.* New York: Foundation Center, 1983. (Originally published 1889.)

Cass, R. H., and Manser, G. "Roots of Voluntarism." In B. O'Connell (ed.), *America's Voluntary Spirit.* New York: Foundation Center, 1983. (Originally published 1889.)

Caulkins, D. D. "A Note on the Prevalence of Voluntary Associations in Two Norwegian Provinces." *Journal of Voluntary Action Research,* 1976, *5*(3-4), 155–159.

Cavallaro, R. "Sociological Analysis and Theory of Social Groups: Some Proposals of Contemporary Sociology." *Sociologica,* 1983, *17*(1), 89–113.

Cavan, R. S. "From Social Movement to Organized Society: The Case of the Anabaptists." *Journal of Voluntary Action Research,* 1977, *6*(3-4), 105–111.

Chadwick, H. "The Early Christian Community." In J. McManners (ed.), *Encyclopedia of Christianity.* New York: Cambridge University Press, 1990.

Chadwick, N. *The Celts.* New York: Viking Penguin, 1971.

Chalmers, T. *On the Use and Abuse of Literary and Ecclesiastical Endowments.* London: 1827.

Chambers, C. A. *Paul Underwood Kellogg and the Survey: Voices of Social Welfare and Social Justice.* Minneapolis: University of Minnesota Press, 1971.

Chambers, M. M. "Articles on Charity and Almsgiving." In J. Hastings (ed.), *Encyclopaedia of Religion and Ethics.* Vol. 3. New York: Scribner's, 1917.

Chambré, S. M. "Kindling Points of Light: Volunteerism as Public Policy." *Nonprofit and Voluntary Sector Quarterly,* 1989, *18*(3), 237–248.

Cherniack, M. *The Hawk's Nest Incident: America's Worst Industrial Disaster.* New Haven, Conn.: Yale University Press, 1986.

Childe, V. G. "The Urban Revolution." *Town Planning Review,* 1950, *21,* 3–17.

Chrisman, N. J. "Middle Class Communitas: The Fraternal Order of Badgers." *Ethos,* 1974, *2*(4), 356–376.

Cialdini, R. B., Baumann, D. J., and Kenrick, D. T. "Insights from Sadness: A Three-Step Model of the Development of Altruism as Hedonism." *Developmental Review,* 1981, *1*(3), 207–223.

Clary, C. G. "Social Support as a Unifying Concept in Voluntary Action." *Journal of Voluntary Action Research,* 1987, *16*(4), 58–68.

Clayre, A. *Political Economy of Cooperation and Participation: Third Sector.* London: Oxford University Press, 1980.

Cleverley, W. "Return on Equity in the Hospital Industry: Requirement or Windfall?" *Inquiry,* 1982, *19*(2), 150–159.

Cohen, J. L., and Arato, A. *Civil Society and Political Theory.* Cambridge, Mass.: MIT Press, 1992.

Collins, A. H., and Pancoast, D. L. *Natural Helping Networks: A Strategy for Prevention.* Washington, D.C.: National Association of Social Workers, 1975.

Collins, C. D. *The Iconography and Ritual of Siva at Elephanta.* New York: State University of New York Press, 1988.

Commons, J. R. *Institutional Economics: Its Place in Political Economy.* Madison: University of Wisconsin Press, 1961. (Originally published 1934.)

Constantelos, D. J. *Byzantine Philanthropy and Social Welfare.* New Brunswick, N.J.: Rutgers University Press, 1968.

Cornes, R., and Sandler, T. *The Theory of Externalities, Public Goods, and Club Goods.* New York: Cambridge University Press, 1986.

Cornwall, S. "The Social and Working Condition of Artists." *International Labor Review,* 1979, *118*(5), 537–556.

Coulson, N. J. *A History of Islamic Law.* Edinburgh: Edinburgh University Press, 1978.

Crawford, M. "Early Rome and Italy." In J. Boardman, J. Griffin, and O. Murray (eds.), *The Oxford History of the Classical World.* New York: Oxford University Press, 1986.

Crew, M. *Theory of the Firm.* White Plains, N.Y.: Longman, 1975.

Crosby, C. "Social and Economic Benefits from Regional Investment in Arts Facilities: Theory and Application." *Journal of Cultural Economics,* 1982, *6*(1), 1–13.

Cummings, L. D. "Voluntary Strategies in the Environmental Movement: Recycling as Cooptation." *Journal of Voluntary Action Research,* 1977, *6*(3-4), 153–160.

Cwi, D. "Public Support of the Arts: Three Arguments Examined." *Journal of Behavioral Economics,* 1979, *8*(1), 39–68.

Daly, H. E., and Cobb, J. B. *For the Common Good: Redirecting the Economy Toward Community, the Environment and a Sustainable Future.* Boston: Beacon Press, 1989.

Daniel, R. L. *American Philanthropy in the Near East, 1820–1960.* Athens: Ohio University Press, 1970.

Daniels, A. K. "Good Times and Good Works: The Place of Sociability in the Work of Women Volunteers." *Social Problems,* 1985, *32*(4), 363–374.

Das, A. "Federal Support for Art: An Economic Analysis." *Journal of Cultural Economics,* 1979, *3*(2), 89–97.

Deegan, M. J. *American Ritual Dramas: Social Rules and Cultural Meanings.* Westport, Conn.: Greenwood Press, 1989.

de Guzman, J. "Helping a Lost Passenger: An Analysis of the Number of Bystanders and Dependency of the Victim in an Urban and a Rural Community." *Philippine Journal of Psychology,* 1979, *12*(2), 10–16.

DeLaat, J. "Volunteering as Linkage in the Three Sectors." *Journal of Voluntary Action Research,* 1987, *16*(1-2), 97–111.

Delgado, G. *Organizing the Movement: The Roots and Growth of ACORN.* Philadelphia: Temple University Press, 1986.

Demott, B. J. *Freemasonry in American Culture and Society: A History of the Masonic Fraternity.* Washington, D.C.: University Press of America, 1986.

DePaor, M. L. *Early Christian Ireland.* New York: Praeger, 1958.

Desruisseaux, P. "What Would Andrew Carnegie Think About How His Money Is Used Today?" *Chronicle of Higher Education,* Aug. 7, 1985, p. 11.

deSwaan, A. "Workers' and Clients' Mutualism Compared: Perspectives from the Past in the Development of the Welfare State." *Government and Opposition,* 1986, *21*(1), 36–55.

de Tocqueville, A. *Democracy in America.* 2 vols. New York: Vintage, 1945. (Originally published 1862.)

DeVall, W. B., and Harry, J. "Associational Politics and Internal Democracy." *Journal of Voluntary Action Research,* 1975, *4*, 1–2.

de Vaux, R. *Ancient Israel.* Vol. 2: *Religious Institutions.* New York: McGraw-Hill, 1965.

Dharmasiri, G. *Fundamentals of Buddhist Ethics.* Antioch, Calif.: Golden Leaves, 1989.

Diaz, L. R., Earle, W., and Archer, R. L. "Empatia y Valores Pro-Sociales como Precursores de Conductas de Ayuda" (Empathy and Prosocial Values as Antecedents of Helping Behavior). *Revista de Psicologia Social y Personalidad,* 1987, *3*(2), 1–9.

Diaz, L. R., and others. "Empatia: Antecedentes Historicos y Su Relacion con Conductas Prosociales y Antisociales" (Empathy: Historical Antecedents and Its Relationship to Prosocial and Antisocial Behaviors). *Revista de Psicologia Social y Personalidad,* 1985, *1*(2), 77–92.

DiMaggio, P. "Nonprofit Organizations in the Production of Culture." In W. W. Powell (ed.), *The Nonprofit Sector: A Research Handbook.* New Haven, Conn.: Yale University Press, 1987.

Douglas, D. "The Paris of Abelard and St. Louis." In A. Toynbee (ed.), *Cities of Destiny.* New York: McGraw-Hill, 1967.

Douglas, J. "Political Theories of Nonprofit Organization." In W. W. Powell (ed.), *The Nonprofit Sector: A Research Handbook.* New Haven, Conn.: Yale University Press, 1987.

Douglas, S. A. "Voluntary Associational Structure in Malaysia: Some Implications for Political Participation." *Journal of Voluntary Action Research,* 1972, *1*(1), 24–37.

Dozier, J. B., and Miceli, M. P. "Potential Predictors of Whistle-Blowing: A Prosocial Behavior Perspective." *Academy of Management Review,* 1985, *10*(4), 823–836.

Dumazedier, J. "Leisure." In D. Sills (ed.), *Encyclopedia of the Social Sciences.* Vol. 9. New York: Macmillan, 1968.

Dworkin, R. *Taking Rights Seriously.* Cambridge, Mass.: Harvard University Press, 1977.

Easton, D. *A Framework for Political Analysis.* Englewood Cliffs, N.J.: Prentice Hall, 1965.

Eber, M., and Kunz, L. B. "The Desire to Help Others." *Bulletin of the Menninger Clinic,* 1984, *48*(2), 125–140.

Edelman, M. *Political Language.* New York: Academic Press, 1977.

Edney, J. J., and Bell, P. A. "Sharing Scarce Resources: Group-Outcome Orientation, External Disaster, and Stealing in a Simulated Commons." *Small Group Behavior,* 1984, *15*(1), 87–108.

Edwards, A. "Decentralization of Arts Subsidy for Orchestra/Theater in the Netherlands." *Journal of Cultural Economics,* 1983, *7*(1), 83–94.

Edwards, P. W., and Zeichner, A. "Blood Donor Development: Effects of Personality, Motivational and Situational Variables." *Personality and Individual Differences,* 1985, *6*(6), 743–751.

Eichelman, B. "Aggressive Behavior: Animal Models." *International Journal of Family Psychiatry,* 1985, *6*(4), 375–387.

Eisenberg, N. "The Relation Between Empathy and Altruism: Conceptual and Methodological Issues." *Academic Psychology Bulletin,* 1983, *5*(2), 195–207.

Eisenberg, N., and Miller, P. A. "The Relation of Empathy to Prosocial and Related Behaviors." *Psychological Bulletin,* 1987, *101*(1), 91–119.

Eisenberg, N., and others. "Relation of Sympathy and Personal Distress to Prosocial Behavior: A Multimethod Study." *Journal of Personality and Social Psychology,* 1989, *57*(1), 55–66.

Eisenstadt, S. N. "The Social Conditions of the Development of Voluntary Association: A Case Study of Israel." *Journal of Voluntary Action Research,* 1972, *1*(3), 2–13.

Elizur, A. "An Integrated-Development Model of Empathy." *Israel Journal of Psychiatry and Related Sciences,* 1985, *22*(1-2), 29–39.

Elkin, F., and McLean, C. "Pressures Towards Cooperation in Voluntary Associations: The YMCA and YWCA in Canada." *Journal of Voluntary Action Research,* 1976, *5*(1), 16–26.

Elkin, R., and Molitor, M. *Management Indicators in Nonprofit Organizations: Guidelines to Selection and Implementation.* Baltimore: University of Maryland Press, 1984.

Ellsworth, E. W. *Science and Social Science Research in British*

India, 1780–1880: The Role of Anglo-Indian Associations and Government. Westport, Conn.: Greenwood Press, 1991.

Emerson, T. I. "Freedom of Association and Freedom of Expression." *Yale Law Journal*, 1964, *74*(1), 2.

Emerson, T. I. *The First Amendment and Freedom of Expression*. New York: Random House, 1970.

Erikson, J. M. "Vital Senses: Sources of Lifelong Learning." *Journal of Education*, 1985, *167*(3), 85–96.

Etzioni, A. *A Comparative Theory of Complex Organizations*. New York: Free Press, 1963.

Etzioni, A. *The Active Society: A Theory of Societal and Political Processes*. New York: Free Press, 1968.

Etzioni, A. (ed.). *The Semi-Professions and Their Organization: Teachers, Nurses, Social Workers*. New York: Free Press, 1969.

Evans, J. *Monastic Life at Cluny, 910–1157*. London: Archon Books, 1968. (Originally published 1931.)

Fairclough, A. *To Redeem the Soul of America: The Southern Christian Leadership Conference and Martin Luther King, Jr.* Athens: University of Georgia Press, 1987.

Fama, E., and Jensen, M. "Agency Problems and Residual Claims." *Journal of Law and Economics*, 1983, *26*(2), 327–349.

Faramelli, N. J. "From Protest to Planning: Some Reflections on Citizens' Participation." *Journal of Voluntary Action Research*, 1976, *5*(2), 106–115.

Fasting, K., and Sisjord, M. "Verbal Behavior and Power in Sports Organizations." *Scandinavian Journal of Sport Sciences*, 1986, *8*(2), 81–85.

Fedler, F., and Pryor, B. "An Equity Theory Explanation of Bystanders' Reactions to Shoplifting." *Psychological Reports*, 1984, *54*(3), 746.

Ferrari, J. R., Barone, R. C., Jason, L. A., and Rose, T. "The Use of Incentives to Increase Blood Donations." *Journal of Social Psychology*, 1985, *125*(6), 791–793.

Filer Commission. *Giving in America: Toward a Stronger Voluntary Sector*. Washington, D.C.: Commission on Private Philanthropy and Public Needs, 1975.

Finley, M. I. *The Ancient Economy*. Berkeley: University of California Press, 1974a.

Finley, M. I. "Aristotle and Economic Analysis." In M. I. Finley (ed.), *Studies in Ancient Society.* New York: Routledge & Kegan Paul, 1974b.

Finley, M. I., and Pleket, H. W. *The Olympic Games: The First Thousand Years.* New York: Viking Penguin, 1976.

Fisher, A. L. "Mormon Welfare Programs: Past and Present." *Social Science Journal,* 1978, *15*(2), 75–100.

Fisher, D. "American Philanthropy and the Social Sciences in Britain, 1919–1939: The Reproduction of a Conservative Ideology." *Sociological Review,* 1980, *28*(2), 277–315.

Fisher, J. L. "The Growth of Heartlessness: The Need for Studies on Philanthropy." *Educational Record,* 1986, *67*(1), 25–28.

Fiske, A. P. *Structures of Social Life: The Four Elementary Forms of Human Relations.* New York: Free Press, 1991.

Fitzgerald, M. W. *The Union League Movement in the Deep South: Politics and Agricultural Change During Reconstruction.* Baton Rouge: Louisiana University Press, 1989.

Fletcher, L. P. "Some Economic Aspects in the Decline of Friendly Societies in the Windward Islands." *Journal of Voluntary Action Research,* 1977, *6*(3-4), 191–203.

Flynn, M. *Sacred Charity: Confraternities and Social Welfare in Spain, 1400–1700.* Ithaca, N.Y.: Cornell University Press, 1989.

Flynn, J. P., and Webb, G. E. "Women's Incentives for Community Participation in Policy Issues." *Journal of Voluntary Action Research,* 1975, *4*(3-4), 137–147.

Ford Foundation. *The Common Good: Social Welfare and the American Future—Policy Recommendations of the Executive Panel.* New York: Ford Foundation, 1989.

Forster, E. *Alexandria: A History and Guide.* Garden City, N.Y.: Anchor Books, 1961.

Foundation Center. *The Literature of the Nonprofit Sector: A Bibliography with Abstracts.* New York: Foundation Center, 1989.

Frankel, M. "Tax Treatment of Artists' Charitable Contributions." *Yale Law Journal,* 1979, *89*(1), 144–167.

Franklin, J. H. *From Slavery to Freedom: A History of Negro Americans.* (5th ed.) New York: Knopf, 1980.

Fraser, C., and Hite, R. E. "The Effect of Matching Contribution Offers and Legitimization of Paltry Contributions on Compliance." *Journal of Applied Social Psychology*, 1989, *19*, 1010–1018.

French, R. S. *From Homer to Helen Keller: A Social and Educational Study of the Blind*. New York: World, 1932.

Frohlich, N., and Oppenheimer, J. "Beyond Economic Man: Altruism, Egalitarianism, and Difference Maximizing." *Journal of Conflict Resolution*, 1984, *28*(1), 3–24.

Fultz, J., and others. "Social Evaluation and the Empathy-Altruism Hypothesis." *Journal of Personality and Social Psychology*, 1986, *50*(4), 761–769.

Furlough, E. *Consumer Cooperation in France: The Politics of Consumption, 1834–1930*. Ithaca, N.Y.: Cornell University Press, 1991.

Gainotti, G., Nocentini, U., Sena, E., and Silveri, H. C. "Discovery of Simple Binary Sequences in Brain Damaged Patients." *International Journal of Clinical Neuropsychology*, 1986, *8*(3), 99–104.

Galaskiewiscz, J. *Social Organization of an Urban Grants Economy*. San Diego, Calif.: Academic Press, 1985.

Garcia, I. M. *United We Win: Rise and Fall of La Raza Unida Party*. Tucson: Mexican American Center, University of Arizona, 1991.

Gassler, R. S. "Nonprofit and Voluntary Sector Economics: A Critical Survey." *Nonprofit and Voluntary Sector Quarterly*, 1990, *19*(2), 137–150.

Geanakoplos, D. J. *Byzantium: Church, Society and Civilization in Contemporary Eyes*. Chicago: University of Chicago Press, 1985.

Gibb, H.A.R., and Kramers, J. H. "Zakat." In *Shorter Encyclopedia of Islam*. Leiden, Netherlands: E. J. Brill, 1953.

Gibbons, F. X., and Wicklund, R. A. "Self-Focused Attention and Helping Behavior." *Journal of Personality and Social Psychology*, 1982, *43*(3), 462–474.

Gifis, S. H. *Law Dictionary*. (3d ed.) New York: Barrons, 1991.

Ginsberg, E., and Vojta, G. J. "The Service Sector of the U.S. Economy." *Scientific American*, 1981, *244*(3), 48–55.

Girouard, M. *Cities and People: A Social and Architectural History*. New Haven, Conn.: Yale University Press, 1985.

Girouard, M. *The English Town*. New Haven, Conn.: Yale University Press, 1990.

Gluck, P. R. "An Exchange Theory of Incentives of Urban Political Party Organization." *Journal of Voluntary Action Research,* 1975, *4*(1-2), 104–115.

Gluck, P. R. "Citizen Participation in Urban Services: The Administration of a Community-Based Crime Prevention Program." *Journal of Voluntary Action Research,* 1978, 7(1-2), 33–44.

Goff, F. H. *Community Trusts.* Cleveland, Ohio: Cleveland Trust Company, 1919.

Gold, B. K. (ed.). *Literary and Artistic Patronage in Ancient Rome.* Austin: University of Texas Press, 1982.

Gold, B. K. *Literary Patronage in Greece and Rome.* Chapel Hill: University of North Carolina Press, 1987.

Goldberg, D. J., and Rayner, J. D. *The Jewish People: Their History and Religion.* New York: Viking Penguin, 1989.

Goldman, R. M. *The National Party Chairmen and Committees: Factionalism at the Top.* Armonk, N.Y.: Sharpe, 1990.

Goodman, C., and Pynoos, J. "A Model Telephone Information and Support Program for Caregivers of Alzheimer's Patients." *Gerontologist,* 1990, *30*(3), 399–404.

Goodman, P., and Goodman, P. *Communitas: Means of Livelihood and Ways of Life.* New York: Vintage, 1960.

Goodman, S. H., and Johnson, M. S. "Life Problems, Social Supports, and Psychological Functioning of Emotionally Disturbed and Well Low-Income Women." *Journal of Community Psychology,* 1986, *14*(2), 150–158.

Goodwin, J. R. "Alms for Kasagi Temple." *The Journal of Asian Studies,* 1987, *46*(4), 827–840.

Gordon, W. C., and Babchuk, N. "A Typology of Voluntary Associations." *American Sociological Review,* 1959, *24*(1), 22–29.

Gouldner, A. "The Norm of Reciprocity." *American Sociological Review,* 1960, *25,* 161–178.

Grady, B. "Indian Costume: A Ritual of Pride." *New Orleans Times-Picayune,* Mar. 16, 1991, p. 1.

Graham, A. "Informal Networks of Care: Issues Raised by Barclay." *British Journal of Social Work,* 1983, *13*(4), 417–433.

Gramajo, G.N.N. "La Familia Tapatia: 'Los Hijos Regalados'" (The Family in Guadalajara: "Donated Children"). *Revista de Psicoanalisis,* 1988, *45*(1), 187–204.

Gray, B. K. *A History of English Philanthropy: From the Dissolution of the Monasteries to the Taking of the First Census.* London: Cass, 1967. (Originally published 1905.)

Gray, P. S. "Voluntary Organizations in Ghana." *Journal of Voluntary Action Research,* 1976, *5*(3-4), 221–230.

Gutmann, D. "Age and Leadership: Cross-Cultural Observations." *Psychoanalytic Inquiry,* 1982, *2*(1), 109–120.

Hahm, S. "Meanings of Village Codes by Toegye and Yulgok on Social Culture." In Proceedings of the Third International Conference on Universal Values and Indigenous Cultures, Morgantown, W. Va., 1991.

Hale, J. "Quattrocento Venice." In A. Toynbee (ed.), *Cities of Destiny.* New York: McGraw-Hill, 1967.

Hall, J. N. "Towards a Psychology of Caring." *British Journal of Clinical Psychology,* 1990, *29*(2), 129–144.

Hall, P. D. "A Historical Overview of the Nonprofit Sector." In W. W. Powell (ed.), *The Nonprofit Sector: A Research Handbook.* New Haven, Conn.: Yale University Press, 1987.

Hallenstvedt, A., Kalela, A., Kalela, J., and Lintonen, R. "The Nordic Transnational Association Network: Structure and Correlates." *Journal of Voluntary Action Research,* 1976, *5*(3-4), 123–154.

Hands, A. R. *Charities and Social Aid in Greece and Rome.* Ithaca, N.Y.: Cornell University Press, 1968.

Hansmann, H. B. "The Role of Nonprofit Enterprise." *Yale Law Journal,* 1980, *89*(5), 835–901.

Hansmann, H. B. "Nonprofit Enterprise in the Performing Arts." *Bell Journal of Economics,* 1981a, *36*(3), 613–617.

Hansmann, H. B. "Reforming Nonprofit Corporation Law." *University of Pennsylvania Law Review,* 1981b, *129*(3), 500–563.

Hansmann, H. B. "Economic Theories of Nonprofit Organization." In W. W. Powell (ed.), *The Nonprofit Sector: A Research Handbook.* New Haven, Conn.: Yale University Press, 1987.

Hardin, G. "The Tragedy of the Commons." *Science,* 1968, *162*, 1243–1248.

Hardin, G. "Discriminating Altruisms." *Zygon Journal of Religion and Science,* 1982, *17*(2), 163–186.

Hardoy, J. *Urban Planning and Pre-Columbian America.* New York: Braziller, 1968.

Harris, M. "The Governing Body Role: Problems and Perceptions in Implementation." *Nonprofit and Voluntary Sector Quarterly,* 1989, *18*(4), 317–334.

Harvey, J. W., and McCrohan, K. F. "Voluntary Compliance and the Effectiveness of Public and Non-Profit Institutions: American Philanthropy and Taxation." *Journal of Economic Psychology,* 1988, *9*(3), 369–386.

Hastings, J. (ed.). *Encyclopaedia of Religion and Ethics.* New York: Scribner's, 1917.

Heal, F. *Hospitality in Early Modern England.* New York: Oxford University Press, 1990.

Heath, A. *Rational Choice and Social Exchange.* London: Cambridge University Press, 1976.

Hechter, M., Opp, K., and Wippler, R. (eds.). *Social Institutions: Emergence, Maintenance and Effects.* Hawthorne, N.Y.: Aldine, 1990.

Helton, A. "A Buddy System to Improve Prenatal Care." *MCN: The American Journal of Maternal Child Nursing,* 1990, *15*(4), 234–237.

Herm, G. *The Celts: The People Who Came Out of the Darkness.* New York: St. Martin's Press, 1975.

Herman, G. *Ritualized Friendship and the Greek City.* Cambridge, England: Cambridge University Press, 1987.

Herman, R. D., and Van Til, J. (eds.). *Nonprofit Boards of Directors.* New Brunswick, N.J.: Transaction Books, 1988.

Heshka, S., and Lang, D. "Predicting Student Participation in Voluntary Associations from Attitudes and Personality: A Preliminary Report." *Journal of Voluntary Action Research,* 1978, *7*(3–4), 28–35.

Hessing, D. J., and Elffers, H. "Attitude Toward Death, Fear of Being Declared Dead Too Soon, and Donation of Organs After Death." *Omega Journal of Death and Dying,* 1986–87, *17*(2), 115–126.

Hill, J. N. "Prehistoric Social Organization in the American Southwest: Theory and Method." In W. A. Longacre (ed.), *Re-*

constructing Prehistoric Pueblo Societies. Albuquerque: University of New Mexico Press, 1970.

Hill, L. E. "The Pragmatic Alternative to Positive Economics." *Review of Social Economics,* 1983, 1–11.

Hillary, G. *Communal Organizations: A Study of Local Societies.* Chicago: University of Chicago Press, 1963.

Hodgkinson, V. A., Lyman, R. W., and Associates. *The Future of the Nonprofit Sector: Challenges, Changes, and Policy Considerations.* San Francisco: Jossey-Bass, 1989.

Hodgkinson, V. A., and Weitzman, M. S. *Dimensions of the Independent Sector: A Statistical Profile.* Washington, D.C.: INDEPENDENT SECTOR, 1986.

Homans, G. C. *Social Behavior: Its Elementary Forms.* Orlando, Fla.: Harcourt Brace Jovanovich, 1961.

Homans, G. C. "Social Behavior as Exchange." *American Journal of Sociology,* 1968, *63,* 597–606.

Hook, J. G. "Development of Equity and Altruism in Judgment of Reward and Damage Allocation." *Developmental Psychology,* 1982, *18*(6), 825–834.

Hornblower, S. "Greece: The History of the Classical Period." In J. Boardman, J. Griffin, and O. Murray (eds.), *The Oxford History of the Classical World.* New York: Oxford University Press, 1986.

Horvath, J. "Grants Economics." In D. Greenwalt (ed.), *Encyclopedia of Economics.* New York: McGraw-Hill, 1982.

Hourani, A. *A History of the Arab Peoples.* Cambridge, Mass.: Harvard University Press, 1991.

Howe, J. *The Kuna Gathering: Contemporary Village Politics in Panama.* Austin: University of Texas Press, 1986.

Huang, N. "Study on the Problem of Personality." *Acta Psychologica Sinica,* 1984, *16*(1), 1–7.

Hull, D. L. *Science as a Process: An Evolutionary Account of the Social and Conceptual Development of Science.* Chicago: University of Chicago Press, 1988.

Hunter, L. "Comments on E. James and E. Neuberger, 'The University Department as a Nonprofit Labor Cooperative.'" *Public Choice,* 1981, 613–617.

Hurvitz, N. "'We'd Rather Do It Ourselves!' A People's Movement for Mental Health Rejects Professional Assistance." *Journal of Voluntary Action Research*, 1977, *6*(1-2), 69–72.

Idson, T. L., and Ullmann, S. G. "Participation in Policy Development by Registered Nurses in Not-for-Profit and Proprietary Facilities." *Nonprofit and Voluntary Sector Quarterly*, 1991, *20*(1), 25–37.

INDEPENDENT SECTOR. *National Taxonomy of Exempt Entities [NTEE]: A System for Classifying Nonbusiness, Tax-Exempt Organizations in the U.S. with a Focus on IRS Section 501(c)(3) Philanthropic Organizations.* Washington, D.C.: INDEPENDENT SECTOR, 1987.

Ireland, T. R., and Johnson, D. B. *The Economics of Charity.* Blackburg, Va.: Center for the Study of Public Choice, 1970.

Iwata, O. "Some Correlates of Differences Caused by Intimacy Level in Person Perception and Affiliative/Altruistic Behavior Intention." *Psychologia: An International Journal of Psychology in the Orient*, 1989, *32*(3), 185–193.

James, E. "How Nonprofits Grow: A Model." *Journal of Policy Analysis and Management*, 1983, *2*(3), 350–365.

James, E. "The Nonprofit Sector in Comparative Perspective." In W. W. Powell (ed.), *The Nonprofit Sector: A Research Handbook.* New Haven, Conn.: Yale University Press, 1987.

James, E., and Neuberger, E. "The University Department as a Nonprofit Labor Cooperative." *Public Choice*, 1981, *36*(3), 585–612.

James, F. G. "Charity Endowments as Sources of Local Credit in Seventeenth- and Eighteenth-Century England." *Journal of Economic History*, 1948, *8*, 153–170.

Jankovsky, K. P., and Steicher, U. H. "Altruism: Reflections on a Neglected Aspect in Death Studies." *Omega: Journal of Death and Dying*, 1983–84, *14*(4), 335–353.

Jarrige, A., and Moron, P. "Aspects Psychologiques de l'Insemination Artificielle par Donneur" (Psychological Aspects of the Donor by Artificial Insemination). *Psychologie Medicale*, 1982, *14*(8), 1209–1213.

Jason, L. A., Rose, T., Ferrari, J. R., and Barone, R. "Personal Versus Impersonal Methods for Recruiting Blood Donations." *Journal of Social Psychology*, 1984, *123*(1), 139–140.

Jeanneret, M. *God and Mammon: Universities as Publishers.* Champaign: University of Illinois Press, 1990.

Jenkins, S., and others. *Ethnic Associations and the Welfare State: Services to Immigrants in Five Countries.* New York: Columbia University Press, 1988.

Jeremy, M., and Robinson, M. *Ceremony and Symbolism in the Japanese Home.* Honolulu: University of Hawaii Press, 1989.

Johnson, D. *The Roman Law of Trusts.* New York: Oxford University Press, 1989.

Johnson, K. "Fair Housing Councils: An Exploration of the Law Enforcement Role of Voluntary Organizations." *Journal of Voluntary Action Research,* 1975, *4,* 3-4, 184-193.

Johnson, N. *The Welfare State in Transition: The Theory and Practice of Welfare Pluralism.* Boston: University of Massachusetts Press, 1988.

Jones, A., and Moskoff, W. *Ko-ops: The Rebirth of Entrepreneurship in the Soviet Union.* Bloomington: Indiana University Press, 1991.

Jordan, B. *The Common Good: Citizenship, Morality, and Self-Interest.* New York: Blackwell, 1989.

Kan, S. "The 19th Century Tlingit Potlatch: A New Perspective." *American Ethnologist,* 1986, *13*(2), 191-212.

Karst, K. L. "The Efficiency of the Charitable Dollar: An Unfulfilled State Responsibility." *Harvard Law Review,* 1960, *73*(3), 433-483.

Karuza, J., and others. "Responsibility and Helping." *Academic Psychology Bulletin,* 1983, *5*(2), 183-194.

Katz, A. H. "Self-Help and Mutual Aid: An Emerging Social Movement?" *Annual Review of Sociology,* 1981, *7,* 129-155.

Kauffmann, D. "Altruism as (Non)selfishness: A Christian View of Prosocial Behavior." *Journal of Psychology and Christianity,* 1984, *3*(3), 50-57.

Kayden, X., and Mahe, E. *The Party Goes on: The Persistence of the Two Party System in the U.S.* New York: Basic Books, 1986.

Kelly, R. M. "Sources of the Community Control over Police Movement." *Journal of Voluntary Action Research,* 1978, *7*(1-2), 25-32.

Kent, R. C. *The Anatomy of Disaster Relief: The International Network in Action.* New York: Pinter Publishers, 1987.

Kerber, K. W. "The Perception of Nonemergency Helping Situations: Costs, Rewards, and the Altruistic Personality." *Journal of Personality,* 1984, *52*(2), 177–187.

Kerri, J. N. "An Inductive Examination of Voluntary Association Functions in a Single-Enterprise Based Community." *Journal of Voluntary Action Research,* 1972, *1*(2), 43–51.

Kerri, J. N. "Studying Voluntary Associations as Adaptive Mechanisms: A Review of Anthropological Perspectives." *Current Anthropology,* 1976, *17*(1), 23–35.

Kessler, R. C. "A Descriptive Model of Emergency On-Call Blood Donation." *Journal of Voluntary Action Research,* 1975, *4,* 3–4.

Kestenbaum, C. J. "Pathological Attachments and Their Relationship to Affective Disorders in Adult Life." *American Journal of Psychoanalysis,* 1984, *44*(1), 33–49.

Kettner, P. M., and Martin, L. L. *Purchase of Service Contracting.* Newbury Park, Calif.: Sage, 1987.

Klobus-Edwards, P. A., and Edwards, J. M. "Women as Citizen Participants: The Case of Blacks and Whites." *Journal of Voluntary Action Research,* 1979, *8*(3-4), 43–50.

Knoke, D. *Organizing for Collective Action: The Political Economy of Associations.* Hawthorne, N.Y.: Aldine, 1990.

Kobasa, S., and others. "Social Environment and Social Support." *Cancer,* 1991, *67*(3), 788–793.

Kodym, M., and Kebza, V. "K Pojeti Nadani a Talentu v Hudebni Psychologii" (On the Conception of Endowment and Talent in Musical Psychology). *Ceskoslovenska Psychologie,* 1982, *6*(3), 222–232.

Kofta, M. "Freedom to Choose Among Modes of Helping, Value System, and Willingness to Help." *Polish Psychological Bulletin,* 1982, *13*(1), 13–21.

Kohler, E. L. *A Dictionary for Accountants.* (5th ed.) Englewood Cliffs, N.J.: Prentice Hall, 1975.

Kramer, R. M. "Voluntary Agencies and the Use of Public Funds: Some Policy Issues." *Social Service Review,* 1966, *40*(1), 15–26.

Kramer, R. M. "The Future of the Voluntary Service Organization." *Social Work,* 1973, *18*(6), 59–69.

Kramer, R. M. *Voluntary Agencies in the Welfare State.* Berkeley: University of California Press, 1981.

Kramer, R. "Voluntary Agencies and the Personal Social Services." In W. W. Powell (ed.), *The Nonprofit Sector: A Research Handbook.* New Haven, Conn.: Yale University Press, 1987.

Kratchadourian, H. "Proper Distribution of Public Subsidies Among Art Forms and Purposes." *Journal of Cultural Economics,* 1979, *8*(1), 77–91.

Krishnan, L. "Recipient Need and Anticipation of Reciprocity in Prosocial Exchange."*Journal of Social Psychology,* 1988, *128*(2), 223–231.

Krivich, M. "Effects of Type of Ownership of Skilled Nursing Facilities on Residents' Mobility Rates in Illinois." *Public Health Reports,* 1990, *105*(5), 515–518.

Kroll-Smith, J. S. *The Real Disaster Is Above Ground: A Mine Fire and Social Conflict.* Lexington, Ky.: University Press of Kentucky, 1990.

Kronick, J. C. "Public Interest Group Participation in Congressional Hearings on Nuclear Power." *Journal of Voluntary Action Research,* 1982, *11*(1), 46–59.

Kropotkin, P. *Mutual Aid: A Factor of Evolution.* Boston: Extended Horizon Books, n.d.

Kuhn, T. S. *The Structure of Scientific Revolutions.* Chicago: University of Chicago Press, 1962.

Kurtz, L. F., and Chambon, A. "Comparison of Self-Help Groups for Mental Health." *Health and Social Work,* 1987, *12*(4), 275–283.

Kvavik, R. B. "Interest Group Cooptation in a Comparative Perspective: Norway and the United States." *Journal of Voluntary Action Research,* 1976, *5*(3-4), 169–175.

Lanfant, M. F. "Voluntary Associations in France." (J. C. Ross and D. Ross, trans.) *Journal of Voluntary Action Research,* 1976, *5*(3-4), 192–207.

Langer, S. *Philosophy in a New Key: A Study in the Symbolism of Reason, Rite and Art.* (3d ed.) Cambridge, Mass.: Harvard University Press, 1967.

Langton, S. "Envoi: Developing Nonprofit Theory." *Journal of Voluntary Action Research,* 1987, *16*(1-2), 134–146.

Laskin, R. *Leadership of Voluntary Organizations in a Saskatchewan Town.* Saskatoon: Center for Community Studies, University of Saskatchewan, 1962.

Latour, B. *Science in Action.* Cambridge, Mass.: Harvard University Press, 1987.

LaTour, S. A., and Manrai, A. K. "Interactive Impact of Informational and Normative Influence on Donations." *Journal of Marketing Research,* 1989, *26*(3), 327-335.

Lawrence, C. H. *Medieval Monasticism: Forms of Religious Life in Western Europe in the Middle Ages.* (2nd ed.) New York: Longman, 1989.

Lederman, L. M. "The Value of Fundamental Science." *Scientific American,* 1984, *251*(5), 40-47.

Lee, P. *Social Work as Cause and Function and Other Papers.* New York: Columbia University Press, 1937.

Lenkersdorf, C. "Voluntary Associations and Social Change in a Mexican Context." *Journal of Voluntary Action Research,* 1976, *5*(3-4), 214-220.

Lenski, G., and Lenski, J. *Human Societies: An Introduction to Macrosociology.* (3d ed.) New York: McGraw-Hill, 1978.

Levi, P. "Greek Drama." In J. Boardman, J. Griffin, and O. Murray (eds.), *The Oxford History of the Classical World.* New York: Oxford University Press, 1986.

Levitt, M. J., and Feldbaum, E. G. "Councilmembers, Lobbyists and Interest Groups: Communication and Mutual Perceptions in Local Politics." *Journal of Voluntary Action Research,* 1975, *4*(1-2), 98-103.

Lewis, A. *Make No Law: The Sullivan Case and the First Amendment.* New York: Random House, 1991.

Lewis, A. R. *Nomads and Crusaders, A.D. 1000-1368.* Bloomington: Indiana University Press, 1988.

Lidz, T. *The Person: His and Her Development Throughout the Life Cycle.* (Rev. ed.) New York: Basic Books, 1976.

Lieberman, P. *Uniquely Human: The Evolution of Speech, Thought and Selfless Behavior.* Cambridge, Mass.: Harvard University Press, 1991.

Lightman, E. S. "Technique Bias in Measuring Acts of Altruism:

The Case of Voluntary Blood Donation." *Social Science and Medicine,* 1982, *16*(18), 1627–1633.

Lincoln, B. *Discourse and the Construction of Society: Comparative Studies of Myth, Ritual and Classification.* New York: Oxford University Press, 1989.

Lindeman, E. C. *Wealth and Culture: A Study of One Hundred Foundations and Community Trusts and Their Operations During the Decade 1921–1930.* Orlando, Fla.: Harcourt Brace Jovanovich, 1936.

Lipsitz, A., Kallmeyer, K., Ferguson, M., and Abas, A. "Counting on Blood Donors: Increasing the Impact of Reminder Calls." *Journal of Applied Social Psychology,* 1989, *19,* 1057–1067.

Loewenberg, F. "Voluntary Associations in Developing Countries and Colonial Societies: The Social Service Department of the Palestine Jewish Community in the 1930s." *Nonprofit and Voluntary Sector Quarterly,* 1991, *20*(4), 415–428.

Lohmann, R. A. "And Lettuce Is Non-Animal: Toward a Positive Economics of Nonprofit Action." *Nonprofit and Voluntary Sector Quarterly,* 1989, *18*(4), 367–383.

Lohmann, R. A. "The Administration of Hull House." Unpublished paper, 1990a.

Lohmann, R. A. "Automating the Social Work Office." *Computers in Human Services,* 1990b, 7(1–2), 19–30.

Lohmann, R. A., and Bracken, M. S. "The Buddhist Commons in Japan and Asia." In *Collaboration: The Vital Link Across Practice, Research and the Disciplines.* Proceedings of the Annual Conference, Association for Research on Nonprofit Organizations and Voluntary Associations, October 1991.

Lohmann, R. A., and Johnson, C. "The Monongah Mines Disaster Relief Committee." Unpublished paper, 1991.

Lorentzen, R. *Women in the Sanctuary Movement.* Philadelphia: Temple University Press, 1991.

Lorenzo, G. "Current Issues in the Assessment and Treatment of Ethnic Minority Populations." *Psychotherapy in Private Practice,* 1989, 7(3), 133–140.

Lowi, T. J. *The End of Liberalism: Ideology, Policy and the Crisis of Public Authority.* New York: Norton, 1969.

Lubove, R. *The Professional Altruist*. Cambridge, Mass.: Harvard University Press, 1965.

Lux, D. S. *Patronage and Royal Science in Seventeenth Century France: The Académie de Physique in Caen*. Ithaca, N.Y.: Cornell University Press, 1989.

Lyman, R. "Reagan Among the Corinthians." *Nonprofit and Voluntary Sector Quarterly*, 1989, *18*(3), 203–210.

Lystad, M. H. "Human Response to Mass Emergencies: A Review of Mental Health Research." *Emotional First Aid: A Journal of Crisis Intervention*, 1985, *2*(1), 5–18.

Ma, H. K. "A Cross Cultural Study of Altruism." *Psychological Reports*, 1985, *57*(1), 337–338.

MacAloon, J. J. *Drama, Festival, Spectacle: Rehearsals Toward a Theory of Cultural Performance*. Philadelphia: Institute for the Study of Human Issues, 1984.

McCarthy, P. R., and Rogers, T. "Effects of Gain Versus Loss of Reward on Actual and Perceived Altruism." *Psychological Reports*, 1982, *51*(1), 319–322.

McChesney, R. *Waqf in Central Asia: 400 Years in the History of a Muslim Shrine, 1480–1889*. Princeton, N.J.: Princeton University Press, 1991.

McDermott, J. J. (ed.). *The Philosophy of John Dewey*. (2 vols.) New York: Putnam, 1973.

McFate, P. "The Effects of Inflation on the Arts." *Annals of the American Academy of Political and Social Science*, 1981, *456*, 70–87.

McGee, S., and Brown, C. "A Split in the Verbal Comprehension Factor in WAIS and WISC-R Profiles." *Journal of Clinical Psychology*, 1984, *40*(2), 580–583.

McGlashan, T. H. "Schizotypal Personality Disorder: Chestnut Lodge Follow-Up Study: VI. Long-Term, Follow-Up Perspectives." *Archives of General Psychiatry*, 1986, *43*(4), 329–334.

MacIver, R. M. *The Modern State*. Oxford, England: Clarendon Press, 1926.

MacIver, R. M., and Page, C. H. *Society: An Introductory Analysis*. Troy, Mo.: Holt, Rinehart & Winston, 1949.

McManus, M., Brickman, A., Alessi, N. E., and Grapentine, W. L.

"Neurological Dysfunction in Serious Delinquents." *Journal of the American Academy of Child Psychiatry,* 1985, *24*(4), 481–486.

McMillen, D. B. "The UMW as a Social Movement." *Journal of Voluntary Action Research,* 1978, 7(3-4), 106–119.

McNeill, W. H. *Plagues and People.* New York: Anchor, 1977.

McWilliams, W. C. *The Idea of Fraternity in America.* Berkeley: University of California Press, 1973.

Maritain, J. *The Person and the Common Good.* (J. J. Fitzgerald, trans.) South Bend, Ind.: Notre Dame University Press, 1972.

Marlowe, H. A. "Social Intelligence: Evidence for Multidimensionality and Construct Independence." *Journal of Educational Psychology,* 1986, *78*(1), 52–58.

Marts, A. C. *Philanthropy's Role in Civilization: Its Contribution to Human Freedom.* New York: HarperCollins, 1953.

Marty, M. E. *A Short History of Christianity.* San Diego, Calif.: Harcourt Brace Jovanovich, 1959.

Masterson, M. P. "The Creation of Scotland's National System of Official Voluntarism." *Journal of Voluntary Action Research,* 1979, *8*(1-2), 102–110.

Mather, C. *Bonifacius: An Essay upon the Good.* Cambridge, Mass.: Harvard University Press, 1966.

Maton, K. "Meaningful Involvement in Instrumental Activity and Well-Being: Studies of Older Adolescents and At Risk Urban Teen-Agers." *American Journal of Community Psychology,* 1990, *18*(2), 297–320.

Matson, W. I. *A History of Philosophy.* New York: American Book Company, 1968.

Mauss, M. *The Gift.* New York: Norton, 1967.

Mead, G. H. *Mind, Self, and Society from the Standpoint of a Social Behaviorist.* (C. W. Morris, ed.) Chicago: University of Chicago Press, 1934.

Mead, M. "Conferences." In D. L. Sills (ed.), *Encyclopedia of the Social Sciences.* Vol. 3. New York: Macmillan, 1965.

Mehta, V. *Mahatma Gandhi and His Apostles.* New York: Viking Penguin, 1976.

Meier, K. G. "Some Problems of Defining Corporatism as State/Interest Groups Constellation." *Journal of Voluntary Action Research,* 1982, *11*(4), 53–62.

Meindl, J. R., and Lerner, M. J. "The Heroic Motive: Some Experimental Demonstrations." *Journal of Experimental Social Psychology*, 1983, *19*(1), 1–20.

Melville, H. *Mardi and a Voyage Thither*. New York: Library of America, 1982a. (Originally published 1849.)

Melville, H. *Omoo: A Narrative of Adventures in the South Seas*. New York: Library of America, 1982b. (Originally published 1847.)

Melville, H. *Typee: A Peep at Polynesian Life*. New York: Library of America, 1982c. (Originally published 1846.)

Meritt, B. D., Wade-Gery, H. T., and McGregor, M. F. *The Athenian Tribute Lists*. Cambridge, Mass.: Harvard University Press, 1939.

Miceli, M. P., and Near, J. P. "Individual and Situational Correlates of Whistle-Blowing." *Personnel Psychology*, 1988, *41*(2), 267–281.

Michels, R. *Political Parties: A Sociological Study of the Oligarchical Tendencies of Modern Democracy*. New York: Free Press, 1949.

Michels, R. *Political Parties: A Sociological Study of the Oligarchical Tendencies of Modern Democracy*. New York: Free Press, 1962. (Originally published 1915.)

Middleton, M. *The Place and Power of Nonprofit Boards of Directors*. Working paper no. 78. New Haven, Conn.: Institute for Social and Policy Studies, Yale University, 1983.

Middleton, M. "Nonprofit Boards of Directors: Beyond the Governance Function." In W. W. Powell (ed.), *The Nonprofit Sector: A Research Handbook*. New Haven, Conn.: Yale University Press, 1987.

Midlarsky, E., and Hannah, M. "The Generous Elderly: Naturalistic Studies of Donations Across the Life Span." *Psychology of Aging*, 1989, *4*(3), 346–351.

Miller, J. G. "Culture and the Development of Everyday Social Explanation." *Journal of Personality and Social Psychology*, 1984, *46*(5), 961–978.

Mills, C. W. *The Sociological Imagination*. New York: Oxford University Press, 1959.

Mills, R. S., Pedersen, J., and Grusec, J. E. "Sex Differences in

Reasoning and Emotion About Altruism." *Sex Roles,* 1989, *20*(11-12), 603–621.

Milofsky, C. *Community Organization.* New York: Oxford University Press, 1987.

Milofsky, C., and Blades, S. D. "Issues of Accountability in Health Charities: A Case Study of Accountability Problems Among Nonprofit Organizations." *Nonprofit and Voluntary Sector Quarterly,* 1991, *20*(4), 371–394.

Milofsky, C., and Hall, P. D. "Commentary on Van Til's 'Independence of Research': Another View." *Nonprofit and Voluntary Sector Quarterly,* 1989, *19*(1), 79–84.

Mingione, E. *Fragmented Societies: A Sociology of Economic Life Beyond the Market Paradigm.* Cambridge, Mass.: Basil Blackwell, 1991.

Mitchell, J. N. *Social Exchange, Dramaturgy and Ethnomethodology.* New York: Elsevier Science, 1978.

Molnar, J. J., and Purohit, S. R. "Citizen Participation in Rural Community Development: Community Group Perspectives." *Journal of Voluntary Action Research,* 1977, *6*(1-2), 48–58.

Moore, J. "The Evolution of Reciprocal Sharing." *Ethology and Sociobiology,* 1984, *5*(1), 5–14.

Moore, T. *The Economics of the American Theatre.* Durham, N.C.: Duke University Press, 1968.

Moren, J. "Ad Hoc Voluntary Organizations: Devices for Spontaneous Political Actions." *Journal of Voluntary Action Research,* 1976, *5*(3-4), 160–168.

Morgan, S. P. "A Research Note on Religion and Morality: Are Religious People Nice People?" *Social Forces,* 1983, *61*(3), 683–692.

Morgan, W., and Brask, P. "Towards a Conceptual Understanding of the Transformation from Ritual to Theatre." *Anthropologica,* 1988, *30*(2), 175–202.

Morris, R. *Rethinking Social Welfare: Why Care for the Stranger?* White Plains, N.Y.: Longman, 1986.

Mullen, B. "Operationalizing the Effect of the Group on the Individual: A Self-Attention Perspective." *Journal of Experimental Social Psychology,* 1983, *19*(4), 295–322.

Muncy, R. L. *Creating a Female Dominion in American Reform, 1890-1930.* New York: Oxford University Press, 1991.

Murray, O. "Greek Historians." In J. Boardman, J. Griffin, and O. Murray (eds.), *The Oxford History of the Classical World.* New York: Oxford University Press, 1986.

Neal, M. A. "Reaching Out and Letting Go: Societal Transformations." *Religious Education,* 1984, *79*(4), 495-509.

Nelson, A. L. "Patients' Perspectives of a Spinal Cord Injury Unit." *SCI Nursing,* 1990, *7*(3), 44-63.

Nelson, K. "The Evolution of Financing Ballet Companies in the United States." *Journal of Cultural Economics,* 1983, *7*(1), 43-62.

Netting, F. E., McMurtry, S. L., Kettner, P. M., and Jones-McClintic, S. "Privatization and Its Impact on Nonprofit Service Providers." *Nonprofit and Voluntary Sector Quarterly,* 1990, *19*(1), 33-46.

Netton, I. R. *Muslim Neoplatonism: An Introduction to the Thought of the Brethren of Purity.* Edinburgh: Edinburgh University Press, 1991.

Neville, G. K. *Kinship and Pilgrimage: Rituals of Reunion in American Protestant Culture.* New York: Oxford University Press, 1987.

Newsome, B. L., and Newsome, M. "Self Help in the United States: Social Policy Options." *Urban and Social Change Review,* 1983, *16*(2), 19-23.

Newton, K. "Voluntary Organizations in a British City: The Political and Organizational Characteristics of 4,264 Voluntary Associations in Birmingham." *Journal of Voluntary Action Research,* 1977, *4*(1-2), 43-62.

Nolan, M. L., and Nolan, S. *Christian Pilgrimage in Modern Western Europe.* Chapel Hill: University of North Carolina Press, 1989.

Norbeck, E. "Japanese Common-Interest Associations in Cross-Cultural Perspective." *Journal of Voluntary Action Research,* 1972, *1*(1), 38-45.

Norberg, K. *Rich and Poor in Grenoble, 1600-1814.* Berkeley: University of California Press, 1985.

Northrup, F.S.C. *The Logic of Science and the Humanities.* Orlando, Fla.: Harcourt Brace Jovanovich, 1965.

Nozick, R. *Anarchy, State and Utopia.* New York: Basic Books, 1974.

O'Connell, B. *America's Voluntary Spirit.* New York: Foundation Center, 1983.

Odendahl, T. "The Culture of Elite Philanthropy in the Reagan Years." *Nonprofit and Voluntary Sector Quarterly,* 1989, *18*(3), 237–248.

Oleck, H. L. *Non-Profit Corporations and Associations.* (4th ed.) Englewood Cliffs, N.J.: Prentice-Hall, 1980.

Olesko, K. M. *Physics as a Calling: Discipline and Practice in the Königsberg Seminar for Physics.* Ithaca, N.Y.: Cornell University Press, 1991.

Olson, M. *The Logic of Collective Action.* Cambridge, Mass.: Harvard University Press, 1956.

O'Malley, M. N., and Andrews, L. "The Effect of Mood and Incentives on Helping: Are There Some Things Money Can't Buy?" *Motivation and Emotion,* 1983, *7*(2), 179–189.

O'Neill, M. *The Third America: The Emergence of the Nonprofit Sector in the United States.* San Francisco: Jossey-Bass, 1989.

O'Reilly, C. A., and Chatman, J. "Organizational Commitment and Psychological Attachment: The Effects of Compliance, Identification, and Internalization on Prosocial Behavior." *Journal of Applied Psychology,* 1986, *71*(3), 492–499.

Organ, D. W. "A Restatement of the Satisfaction-Performance Hypothesis." *Journal of Management,* 1988, *14*(4), 547–557.

Orive, R. "Group Similarity, Public Self-Awareness, and Opinion Extremity: A Social Projection Explanation of Deindividuation Effects." *Journal of Personality and Social Psychology,* 1984, *47*(4), 727–737.

Orloff, A. *Carnival: Myth and Cult.* Petlinger, 1980.

Ostrander, S. A. "Toward Implications for Research, Theory and Policy on Nonprofits and Voluntarism." *Journal of Voluntary Action Research,* 1988, *16*(1-2), 126–133.

Ostrander, S., Langton, S., and Van Til, J. *Shifting the Debate: Public/Private Sector Relations in the Modern Welfare State.* New Brunswick, N.J.: Transaction, 1988.

Ostrom, E. "Citizen Participation in Policing: What Do We Know?" *Journal of Voluntary Action Research,* 1978, *7*(1-2), 102.

Palisca, C. V. *The Florentine Camerate: Documentary Studies and Translations.* New Haven, Conn.: Yale University Press, 1989.

Palisi, B. J., and Jacobson, P. E. "Dominant Statuses and Involvement in Types of Instrumental and Expressive Voluntary Associations." *Journal of Voluntary Action Research,* 1977, *6*(1-2), 80–88.

Paris, C., and Blackaby, B. "Public Participation and Urban Renewal: Theoretical Issues and a Local Study." *Journal of Voluntary Action Research,* 1979, *8*(1-2), 94–101.

Parisi, N., and Katz, I. "Attitudes Toward Posthumous Organ Donation and Commitment to Donate." *Health Psychology,* 1986, *5*(6), 565–580.

Parker, R. "Greek Religion." In J. Boardman, J. Griffin, and O. Murray (eds.), *The Oxford History of the Classical World.* New York: Oxford University Press, 1986.

Pauly, M., and Redisch, M. "The Not-for-Profit Hospital as a Physicians' Cooperative." *American Economic Review,* 1973, *63,* 87–95.

Pavitt, P. *Charity and Children in Renaissance Florence: The Ospedale degli Innocenti, 1410-1536.* Ann Arbor: University of Michigan Press, 1990.

Penner, L. A., Escarraz, J., and Ellis, B. B. "Sociopathy and Helping: Looking Out for Number One." *Academic Psychology Bulletin,* 1983, *5*(2), 209–220.

Perkins, K. B. "Volunteer Firefighters in the United States: A Descriptive Study." *Nonprofit and Voluntary Sector Quarterly,* 1989, *18*(3), 269–278.

Perlmutter, F., and Adams, C. "The Voluntary Sector and For-Profit Ventures." *Administration in Social Work,* 1990, *14,*1–13.

Perlstadt, H. "Voluntary Associations and the Community: The Case of Volunteer Ambulance Corps." *Journal of Voluntary Action Research,* 1975, *4*(1-2), 85–89.

Peschek, J. G. *Policy-Planning Organizations: Elite Agendas and America's Rightward Turn.* Philadelphia: Temple University Press, 1987.

Petersen, J. C. "Ideological Diffuseness and Internal Democracy in Voluntary Associations." *Journal of Voluntary Action Research,* 1976, *5*(1), 33–41.

Peterson, S., and Peterson, V. "Voluntary Associations in Ancient Greece." *Journal of Voluntary Action Research,* 1973, *2*(1), 2-15.

Picon-Salas, M. *A Cultural History of Spanish America: Conquest to Independence.* (E. A. Leonard, trans.) Berkeley: University of California Press, 1971.

Piechowski, M. M., and Cunningham, K. "Patterns of Overexcitability in a Group of Artists." *Journal of Creative Behavior,* 1985, *19*(3), 153-174.

Pierce, C. S. *Collected Papers of Charles Sanders Pierce.* Vols. 1-6. (C. Hartshorne and P. Weiss, eds.) Cambridge, Mass.: Harvard University Press, 1931-1935.

Pierce, C. S. *Collected Papers of Charles Sanders Pierce.* Vols. 7-8. (A. Burks, ed.) Cambridge, Mass.: Harvard University Press, 1958.

Pifer, A. "The Nongovernmental Organization at Bay." In B. O'Connell (ed.), *America's Voluntary Spirit.* New York: Foundation Center, 1983.

Pigou, A. C. *The Economics of Welfare.* (4th ed.) London: Macmillan, 1932.

Piliavin, J. A., Callero, P. L., and Evans, D. E. "Addiction to Altruism? Opponent-Process Theory and Habitual Blood Donation." *Journal of Personality and Social Psychology,* 1982, *3*(6), 1200-1213.

Poplawski, W. T. "On the Origin of Altruism and Charitable Behavior Conceptions: Chosen Ancient Sources as a Contribution to Prosocial Behavior Theory." *Psychologia,* 1985, *28*(1), 1-10.

Préaux, C. "Alexandria Under the Ptolemies." In A. Toynbee (ed.), *Cities of Destiny.* New York: McGraw-Hill, 1967.

Previté-Orton, C. W., and others (eds.). *The Cambridge Medieval History.* New York: Macmillan, 1924-1936.

Price, S. "The History of the Hellenistic Period." In J. Boardman, J. Griffin, and O. Murray (eds.), *The Oxford History of the Classical World.* New York: Oxford University Press, 1986.

Pulkkinen, L. "The Inhibition and Control of Aggression." *Aggressive Behavior,* 1984, *10*(3), 221-225.

Purcell, N. "The Arts of Government." In J. Boardman, J. Griffin, and O. Murray (eds.), *The Oxford History of the Classical World.* New York: Oxford University Press, 1986.

Quigley, B., Gaes, G. G., and Tedeschi, J. T. "Does Asking Make a Difference? Effects of Initiator, Possible Gain, and Risk on Attributed Altruism." *Journal of Social Psychology,* 1989, *129*(2), 259–267.

Ransel, D. L. *Mothers of Misery: Child Abandonment in Russia.* Princeton, N.J.: Princeton University Press, 1988.

Rapoport, A., Bornstein, G., and Erev, I. "Intergroup Competition for Public Goods: Effects of Unequal Resources and Relative Group Size." *Journal of Personality and Social Psychology,* 1989, *56*(5), 748–756.

Rapoport, A., and Eshed-Levy, D. "Provision of Step-Level Public Goods: Effects of Greed and Fear of Being Gypped." *Organizational Behavior and Human Decision Processes,* 1989, *44*(3), 325–344.

Raskin, M. *The Common Good: Its Politics, Policies and Philosophy.* New York: Routledge & Kegan Paul, 1986.

Rawls, J. *A Theory of Justice.* Cambridge, Mass.: Harvard University Press, 1971.

Redfield, R. *The Primitive World and Its Transformations.* Ithaca, N.Y.: Cornell University Press, 1953.

Reykowski, J., and Smolenska, Z. "Personality Mechanisms of Prosocial Behavior." *Polish Psychological Bulletin,* 1980, *11*(4), 219–230.

Rice, T. T. "Eighteenth Century St. Petersburg." In A. Toynbee (ed.), *Cities of Destiny.* New York: McGraw-Hill, 1967.

Rich, R. C. "A Cooperative Approach to the Logic of Collective Action: Voluntary Organizations and the Prisoners' Dilemma." *Journal of Voluntary Action Research,* 1988, *17*(3-4), 5–18.

Richardson, J. T., Simmonds, R. B., and Stewart, M. "The Evolution of a Jesus Movement Organization." *Journal of Voluntary Action Research,* 1979, *8*(3-4), 93–100.

Riecken, G., and Yavas, U. "Seeking Donors via Opinion Leadership." *Journal of Professional Services Marketing,* 1986, *2*(1-2), 109–116.

Riley, P. *The General Will Before Rousseau.* Princeton, N.J.: Princeton University Press, 1986.

Riley-Smith, J. *The Atlas of the Crusades.* New York: Facts on File, 1991.

Rimland, B. "The Altruism Paradox." *Psychological Reports,* 1982, *51*(2), 521-522.

Risse, G. B. *Hospital Life in Enlightenment Scotland: The Royal Infirmary.* New York: Cambridge University Press, 1985.

Robbins, L. R. *Politics and Economics.* New York: St. Martin's Press, 1963.

Rogers, D. L., and Bultena, G. L. "Voluntary Associations and Political Equality: An Extension of Mobilization Theory." *Journal of Voluntary Action Research,* 1975, *4*(3-4), 174-183.

Rose, A. M. *Theory and Method in the Social Sciences.* Minneapolis: University of Minnesota Press, 1954.

Rose, A. M. "Voluntary Associations Under Conditions of Competition and Conflict." *Social Forces,* 1955, *34,* 159-163.

Rose, A. M. *The Institutions of Advanced Societies.* Minneapolis: University of Minnesota Press, 1958.

Rose, A. M. "The Impact of Aging on Voluntary Associations." In C. W. Tibbitts (ed.), *Handbook of Social Gerontology.* Chicago: University of Chicago Press, 1960.

Rosenbaum, W. A. "Slaying Beautiful Hypotheses with Ugly Facts: EPA and the Limits of Public Participation." *Journal of Voluntary Action Research,* 1977, *6*(3-4), 161-173.

Rosenzweig, R. "Boston Masons, 1900-1935: The Lower Middle Class in a Divided Society." *Journal of Voluntary Action Research,* 1977, *6*(3-4), 119-126.

Ross, J. C. "Religious Fraternity to Club and Sect: A Study of Social Change in Voluntary Associations in England, 1000-1800 A.D." *Journal of Voluntary Action Research,* 1974a, *3*(1), 31-42.

Ross, J. C. "The Voluntary Associations of Ancient Jews: A Neglected Research Area." *Journal of Voluntary Action Research,* 1974b, *3*(3-4), 84-90.

Ross, J. C. "Anthropological Studies of Voluntary Associations: A Reassessment." *Journal of Voluntary Action Research,* 1976, *5*(1), 27-32.

Ross, J. C. "Arnold Rose on Voluntary Associations." *Journal of Voluntary Action Research,* 1977, *6*(1-2), 7-17.

Ross, J. C. "Differentiation of Gilds and Fraternities in Medieval Europe." *Journal of Voluntary Action Research,* 1983, *12*(1), 7-19.

Ross, R. J. "Primary Groups in Social Movements: A Memoir and Interpretation." *Journal of Voluntary Action Research,* 1977, *6*(3-4), 133-138.

Rourke, F. E. (ed.). *Bureaucratic Power and National Politics.* (Rev. ed.) Boston: Little, Brown, 1977.

Rowland, J. "Italy's Plundered Treasures: Thefts in the Thousands Threaten Cultural Heritage." *Washington Post,* Dec. 15, 1991, p. G-1.

Rubin, M. *Charity and Community in Medieval Cambridge, 1200-1500.* New York: Cambridge University Press, 1987.

Rudney, G. "The Scope and Dimensions of Nonprofit Activity." In W. W. Powell (ed.), *The Nonprofit Sector: A Research Handbook.* New Haven, Conn.: Yale University Press, 1987.

Runciman, S. "Christian Constantinople." In A. Toynbee (ed.), *Cities of Destiny.* New York: McGraw-Hill, 1967.

Rushton, J. P. "Altruism and Society: A Social Learning Perspective." *Ethics,* 1982, *92,* 425-446.

Russell, M. "Comments on Art Subsidy: Distributive Effects on the Public Purse." *Journal of Behavioral Economics,* 1979, *8*(1), 69-75.

Russell-Wood, A. *Fidalgos and Philanthropists: The Santa Casa de Misericórdia of Bahia, 1550-1755.* Berkeley: University of California Press, 1968.

Rutter, M. "Aggression and the Family." *Acta Paedopsychiatrica,* 1985, *6*(11), 25.

Ryan, E. B., and Heaven, R. K. "The Impact of Situational Context on Age-Based Attitudes: Aging, Technology and Society." *Social Behaviour,* 1988, *3*(2), 105-117.

Rybczynski, W. *Waiting for the Weekend.* New York: Viking Penguin, 1991.

Ryle, M., and Richards, P. G. *The Commons Under Scrutiny.* London: Routledge, 1988.

Saddhatissa, H. *Buddhist Ethics: Essence of Buddhism.* New York: Braziller, 1970.

Sahlins, M. *Stone Age Economics.* Chicago: Aldine, 1972.

Saidel, J. R. "Dimensions of Interdependence: The State and Voluntary-Sector Relationship." *Nonprofit and Voluntary Sector Quarterly,* 1989, *18*(4), 335-348.

Salamon, L. M. "Of Market Failure, Voluntary Failure and Third Party Government: Toward a Theory of Government-Nonprofit Relations in the Modern Welfare State." *Journal of Voluntary Action Research,* 1987a, *16*(1-2), 29–49.

Salamon, L. M. "Partners in Public Service: The Scope and Theory of Government-Nonprofit Relations." In W. W. Powell (ed.), *The Nonprofit Sector: A Research Handbook.* New Haven, Conn.: Yale University Press, 1987b.

Salem, G. W. "Maintaining Participation in Community Organizations." *Journal of Voluntary Action Research,* 1978, 7(3-4), 18–27.

Samter, W., and Burleson, B. R. "Cognitive and Motivational Influences on Spontaneous Comforting Behavior." *Human Communication Research,* 1984, *11*(2), 231–260.

Sassone, P. G. "Welfare Economics." In D. Greenwalt (ed.), *Encyclopedia of Economics.* New York: McGraw-Hill, 1982.

Schlenker, B. R., Hallam, J. R., and McCown, N. E. "Motives and Social Evaluation: Actor-Observer Differences in the Delineation of Motives for a Beneficial Act." *Journal of Experimental Social Psychology,* 1983, *19*(3), 254–273.

Schlesinger, S. C. *The New Reformers: Forces for Change in American Politics.* Boston: Houghton Mifflin, 1975.

Schmitt, M., Dalbert, C., and Montada, L. "Prosoziale Leistungen Erwachsener Tochter Gegenuber Ihren Muttern: Unterschiede in den Bedingungen von Absicht und Ausfuhrung" (Prosocial Behavior of Adult Daughters Towards Their Mothers: Differences in the Determinants of Intention and Realization). *Psychologische-Beitrage,* 1986, *28*(1-2), 139–163.

Schneider, M. "Primary Envy and the Creation of the Ego Ideal." *International Review of Psycho Analysis,* 1988, *15*(3), 319–329.

Schulman, D. C. "Voluntary Organization Involvement and Political Participation." *Journal of Voluntary Action Research,* 1978, 7(3-4), 86–105.

Schutz, A. *On Phenomenology and Social Relations: Selected Writings.* Chicago: University of Chicago Press, 1970.

Schwartz, M. R. *The Party Network: The Robust Organization of Illinois Republicans.* Madison: University of Wisconsin Press, 1990.

Schwartz, S. "The Facts First: A Reply to Baumol and Baumol" (On Finances of the Performing Arts During Stagflation: Some Recent Data). *Journal of Cultural Economy*, 1981, 85–87.

Schwartz, S. H., and Bilsky, W. "Toward a Theory of the Universal Content and Structure of Values." *Journal of Personality and Social Psychology*, 1990, *58*(5), 878–891.

Schwartzman, S. *A Space for Science: The Development of the Scientific Community of Brazil*. University Park: Pennsylvania State University Press, 1992.

Scully, S. *Homer and the Sacred City*. Ithaca, N.Y.: Cornell University Press, 1991.

Scully, V. *Pueblo: Mountain, Village, Dance*. New York: Viking Penguin, 1975.

Scully, V. "The Greek Temple." In *Architecture: The Natural and the Manmade*. New York: St. Martin's Press, 1991.

Segelman, L., and Bookheimer, S. "Is It Whether You Win or Lose? Monetary Approaches to Big-Time College Athletic Programs." *Social Science*, 1983, 347–359.

Seibel, W. "Government/Third Sector Relationship in a Comparative Perspective: the Cases of France and West Germany." *Voluntas*, 1990, *1*(1), 42–61.

Sen, A. K. *Collective Choice and Social Welfare*. San Francisco: Holden-Day, 1970.

Seppanen, P. "Sport Clubs and Parents as Socializing Agents in Sports." *International Review of Sport Sociology*, 1982, *17*(1), 79–90.

Seth, I. R., and Gupta, P. "Altruism in Hindus and Muslims." *Psychological Studies*, 1983, *28*(2), 69–73.

Seth, I. R., and Gupta, P. "Religion, Alter, Situation and Altruism." *Journal of Psychological Researches*, 1984, *28*(2), 107–113.

Seymour, H. J. *Designs for Fund-Raising*. New York: McGraw-Hill, 1966.

Shaffer, D. R., and Graziano, W. G. "Effects of Positive and Negative Moods on Helping Tasks Having Pleasant or Unpleasant Consequences." *Motivation and Emotion*, 1983, 7(3), 269–278.

Shaffer, D. R., and Smith, J. E. "Effects of Preexisting Moods on Observers' Reactions to Helpful and Nonhelpful Models." *Motivation and Emotion*, 1985, *9*(2), 101–122.

Shainess, N. "The Roots of Creativity." *American Journal of Psychoanalysis,* 1989, *49*(2), 127–138.

Shane, M., and Shane, E. "The Struggle for Otherhood: Implications for Development in Adulthood." *Psychoanalytic Inquiry,* 1989, *9*(3), 466–481.

Sharma, V. K., and Enoch, M. D. "Psychological Sequelae of Kidney Donation: A 5–10 Year Follow-Up Study." *Acta Psychiatrica Scandinavica,* 1987, *75*(3), 264–267.

Sharp, E. G. "Citizen Organization in Policing Issues and Crime Prevention: Incentives for Participation." *Journal of Voluntary Action Research,* 1978, *7*(1-2), 45–58.

Shaw, R. D. *Kandila: Samo Ceremonialism and Interpersonal Relationships.* Ann Arbor: University of Michigan Press, 1991.

Sherman, D. G., and Sherman, H. B. *Rice, Rupees and Ritual: Economy and Society Among the Samosir Batak of Sumatra.* Palo Alto, Calif.: Stanford University Press, 1990.

Sherover, C. M. *Time, Freedom, and the Common Good.* New York: State University of New York Press, 1989.

Sherwood, J. M. *Poverty in Eighteenth Century Spain: The Women and Children of the Inclusa.* Toronto, Canada: University of Toronto Press, 1989.

Shiffrin, S. H. *The First Amendment, Democracy and Romance.* Cambridge, Mass.: Harvard University Press, 1990.

Shotland, R. L., and Stebbins, C. A. "Emergency and Cost as Determinants of Helping Behavior and the Slow Accumulation of Social Psychological Knowledge." *Social Psychology Quarterly,* 1983, *46*(1), 36–46.

Shumaker, S. A., and Brownell, A. "Toward a Theory of Social Support: Closing Conceptual Gaps." *Journal of Social Issues,* 1984, *40*, 11–36.

Sieder, V. M. "The Historical Origins of the American Volunteer." In W. A. Glaser and D. L. Sills (eds.), *The Government of Associations.* New York: Bedminster Press, 1966.

Sills, D. L. "Voluntary Associations: Sociological Aspects." In D. L. Sills (ed.), *Encyclopedia of the Social Sciences.* Vol. 16. New York: Macmillan, 1965.

Silva, E. T., and Slaughter, S. A. *Serving Power: The Making of an*

Academic Social Science Expert. Westport, Conn.: Greenwood Press, 1984.

Simmel, G. "The Sociology of Secrecy and of Secret Societies." *American Journal of Sociology,* 1906, *11,* 441–498.

Simon, H. A. *Administrative Behavior: A Study of Decision-Making Processes in Administrative Organization.* (3d ed.) New York: Free Press, 1976.

Simon, H. "Economic Rationality: Adaptive Artifice." In *The Sciences of the Artificial.* Cambridge, Mass.: MIT Press, 1981.

Simon, J. G. "The Tax Treatment of Nonprofit Organizations: A Review of Federal and State Policies." In W. W. Powell (ed.), *The Nonprofit Sector: A Research Handbook.* New Haven, Conn.: Yale University Press, 1987.

Simon, Y. *A General Theory of Authority.* South Bend, Ind.: University of Notre Dame Press, 1962.

Simsar, M. A. *The Waqfizah of 'Ahmed Pasa.* Philadelphia: University of Pennsylvania Press, 1940.

Sloane, D. C. *The Last Great Necessity: Cemeteries in American History.* Baltimore, Md.: Johns Hopkins University Press, 1991.

Smith, A. *The Wealth of Nations.* New York: Viking Penguin, 1981. (Originally published 1776.)

Smith, C., and Freedman, A. *Voluntary Associations: Perspectives on the Literature.* Cambridge, Mass.: Harvard University Press, 1972.

Smith, C. A., Organ, D. W., and Near, J. P. "Organizational Citizenship Behavior: Its Nature and Antecedents." *Journal of Applied Psychology,* 1983, *68*(4), 653–663.

Smith, D. H. "The Importance of Formal Voluntary Organizations for Society." *Sociol. Soc. Res.,* 1966, *50*(4), 483–495.

Smith, D. H. "Ritual in Voluntary Association." *Journal of Voluntary Action Research,* 1972a, *1*(4), 39–53.

Smith, D. H. "Types of Volunteers and Voluntarism." *Volunteer Administration,* 1972b, *6,* 6–13.

Smith, D. H. "Research and Communication Needs in Voluntary Action." In J. Cull and R. Hardy (eds.), *Volunteerism: An Emerging Profession.* Springfield, Ill.: Thomas, 1974.

Smith, D. H. "Altruism, Volunteers, and Volunteerism." *Journal of Voluntary Action Research,* 1981, *11,* 2.

Smith, D. H. "Four Sectors or Five? Retaining the Member-Benefit Sector." *Nonprofit and Volunteer Sector Quarterly*, 1991, *20*(2), 137–151.

Smith, D. H., Seguin, M., and Collins, M. "Dimensions and Categories of Voluntary Associations/NGOs." *Journal of Voluntary Action Research*, 1973, *2*(2), 116–120.

Smith, D. H., and others. "Major Analytical Topics of Voluntary Action Theory and Research: Version 2." *Journal of Voluntary Action Research*, 1972, *1*(1), 6–19.

Smith, K. D., Keating, J. P., and Stotland, E. "Altruism Reconsidered: The Effect of Denying Feedback on a Victim's Status to Empathic Witnesses." *Journal of Personality and Social Psychology*, 1989, *57*(4), 641–650.

Smith, L. M. "Women as Volunteers: The Double Subsidy." *Journal of Voluntary Action Research*, 1975, *4*(3-4), 119–136.

Smith, R. W., and Preston, F. W. *Sociology: An Introduction*. New York: St. Martin's Press, 1977.

Smith, W. R. *The Fiesta System and Economic Change*. New York: Columbia University Press, 1977.

Snow, C. P. *The Two Cultures and the Scientific Revolution*. London: Macmillan, 1959.

Sober, E. "What Is Psychological Egoism?" *Behaviorism*, 1989, *17*(2), 89–102.

Sontz, A.H.L. *Philanthropy and Gerontology: The Role of the American Foundation*. Westport, Conn.: Greenwood Press, 1989.

Spates, J. L., and Macionis, J. J. *The Sociology of Cities*. Belmont, Calif.: Wadsworth, 1986–1987.

Spiegel, H.B.C. "Coproduction in the Context of Neighborhood Development." *Journal of Voluntary Action Research*, 1987, *16*(3), 54–61.

Spiro, M. *Buddhism and Society*. New York: HarperCollins, 1970.

Stanback, T. M. *Understanding the Service Economy: Employment, Productivity, Location*. Baltimore, Md.: Johns Hopkins University Press, 1979a.

Stanback, T. M. "The Urbanization of Services." In T. Stanback, *Understanding the Service Economy: Employment, Productivity, Location*. Baltimore, Md.: Johns Hopkins University Press, 1979b.

Stanfield, J. H. *Philanthropy and Jim Crow in American Social Science.* Westport, Conn.: Greenwood Press, 1985.

Staw, B. M. "Organizational Behavior: A Review and Reformulation of the Field's Outcome Variables." *Annual Review of Psychology,* 1984, *35,* 627–666.

Steele, C. M., Critchlow, B., and Liu, T. J. "Alcohol and Social Behavior. II: The Helpful Drunkard." *Journal of Personality and Social Psychology,* 1985, *48*(1), 35–46.

Steinberg, M. P. *The Meaning of the Salzburg Festival: Austria as Theater and Ideology, 1890–1938.* Ithaca, N.Y.: Cornell University Press, 1989.

Steinberg, R. "Nonprofit Organizations and the Market." In W. W. Powell (ed.), *The Nonprofit Sector: A Research Handbook.* New Haven, Conn.: Yale University Press, 1987.

Steinberg, R. "Labor Economics and the Nonprofit Sector: A Literature Review." *Nonprofit and Voluntary Sector Quarterly,* 1990, *19*(2), 151–170.

Stephenson, P. H. *The Hutterian People: Ritual and Rebirth in the Evolution of Communal Life.* Washington, D.C.: University Press of America, 1991.

Stewart, M. "From Provider to Partner: A Conceptual Framework for Nursing Education Based on Primary Health Care Premises." *ANS,* 1990, *12*(2), 9–27.

Stinson, T. F., and Stam, J. M. "Toward an Economic Model of Voluntarism: The Case of Participation in Local Government." *Journal of Voluntary Action Research,* 1976, *5*(1), 52–64.

Stockard, J., Van de Kragt, A. J., and Dodge, P. J. "Gender Roles and Behavior in Social Dilemmas: Are There Sex Differences in Cooperation and in Its Justification?" *Social Psychology Quarterly,* 1988, *51*(2), 154–163.

Strong, J. *The Legend of King Asoka: A Study and Translation of the Asplavadana.* Princeton, N.J.: Princeton University Press, 1983.

Sugden, R. "Reciprocity: The Supply of Public Goods Through Voluntary Contributions." *The Economic Journal,* 1984, *94,* 772–787.

Sumariwalla, R. D. *UWASIS II: A Taxonomy of Social Goals and*

Human Service Programs. Alexandria, Va.: United Way of America, 1976.

Sundeen, R. A. "A Comparison of Factors Related to Volunteering to the Local Government Sector in the U. S.: 1985 and 1988." In *Proceedings of the 1990 Conference of the Association of Voluntary Action Scholars.* London: Center for Voluntary Organization, 1990.

Suntharalingam, R. "The Madras Native Association: A Study of an Early Indian Political Organization." *Indian Economic and Social History Review,* 1967, *4*(3), 233–254.

Taylor, C. J. "The Kingston, Ontario, Penitentiary and Moral Architecture." *Social History,* 1979, *12*(24), 251–260.

Thielen, G. L., and Poole, D. L. "Educating Leadership for Effecting Community Change Through Voluntary Associations." *Journal of Social Work Education,* 1986, *22*(2), 19–29.

Thrupp, S. "Gilds." In D. L. Sills (ed.), *Encyclopedia of the Social Sciences.* Vol. 6. New York: Macmillan, 1965.

Tietjen, A. M. "Prosocial Reasoning Among Children and Adults in a Papua New Guinea Society." *Developmental Psychology,* 1986, *22*(6), 861–868.

Titmuss, R. *The Gift Relationship.* London: Allen and Unwin, 1970.

Toseland, R., and Hacker, L. "Social Workers' Use of Self-Help Groups as a Resource for Clients." *Social Work,* 1985, *30*(3), 232–237.

Toseland, R., Rossiter, C., Peak, T., and Smith, G. "Comparative Effectiveness of Individual and Group Interventions to Support Family Caregivers." *Social Work,* 1990, *35*(3), 209–217.

Toynbee, A. *Cities of Destiny.* New York: McGraw-Hill, 1967.

Trattner, W. I. *From Poor Law to Welfare State: A History of Social Welfare in America.* (4th ed.) New York: Free Press, 1989.

Traunstein, D. M., and Steinman, R. "Voluntary Self-Help Organizations: An Exploratory Study." *Journal of Voluntary Action Research,* 1973, *2*(4), 230–239.

Tucker, L. R. "Profiling the Heavy Blood Donor: An Exploratory Study." *Health Marketing Quarterly,* 1987, *4*(3-4), 61–74.

Turnbull, C. M. *The Mountain People.* New York: Simon & Schuster, 1972.

Tyler, T. R., Orwin, R., and Schurer, L. "Defensive Denial and High Cost Prosocial Behavior." *Basic and Applied Social Psychology,* 1982, *3*(4), 267–281.

Udoidem, S. *Authority and the Common Good in Social and Political Philosophy.* Washington, D.C.: University Press of America, 1988.

Underwood, B., and Moore, B. "Perspective-Taking and Altruism." *Psychological Bulletin,* 1982, *91*(1), 143–173.

Urban, G. A. *Discourse Centered Approach to Culture: Native South American Myths and Rituals.* Austin: University of Texas Press, 1991.

U.S. Bureau of the Census. *Statistical Abstract of the United States: 1985.* (105th ed.) Washington, D.C.: U.S. Government Printing Office, 1984.

U.S. Bureau of the Census. *Statistical Abstract of the United States: 1986.* (106th ed.) Washington, D.C.: U.S. Government Printing Office, 1987.

U.S. Bureau of the Census. *Statistical Abstract of the United States: 1990.* (110th ed.) Washington, D.C.: U.S. Government Printing Office, 1989.

U.S. Internal Revenue Service. *Annual Report.* Washington, D.C.: IRS, 1985.

Valelly, R. M. *Radicalism in the States: The Minnesota Farmer-Labor Party and the American Political Economy.* Chicago: University of Chicago Press, 1989.

Van Bavel, T. J. *The Rule of St. Augustine.* New York: Doubleday, 1984.

Van den Haag, E. "Should the Government Subsidize the Arts?" *Policy Review,* 1979, *10*, 62–73.

Van der Veer, P. "The Power of Detachment: Disciplines of Body and Mind in the Ramanandi Order." *American Ethnologist,* 1989, *16*(3), 458–470.

Vander Zander, J. W. *Social Psychology.* New York: Random House, 1977.

Van Doren, J. *Big Money in Small Sums: A Study of Small Contributions in Political Party Fund-Raising.* Chapel Hill: Institute for Research in Social Science, University of North Carolina, 1956.

Van Gennep, A. *The Rites of Passage*. Chicago: University of Chicago Press, 1960.

Van Lange, P. A., and Liebrand, W. B. "On Perceiving Morality and Potency: Social Values and the Effects of Person Perception in a Give-Some Dilemma." *European Journal of Personality*, 1989, *3*(3), 209–225.

Van Til, J. "Citizen Participation in Criminal Justice: Opportunity, Constraint, and the Arrogance of the Law." *Journal of Voluntary Action Research*, 1975, *4*(1-2), 69–74.

Van Til, J. *Mapping the Third Sector: Voluntarism in a Changing Social Economy*. New York: Foundation Center, 1988.

Van Vugt, J. P. *Democratic Organization for Social Change: Latin American Christian Base Communities and Literacy Campaigns*. Westport, Conn.: Bergin & Garvey, 1991.

Wagner, A. "On Sharing: A Preface to an Economic Theory of Voluntary Action." *Nonprofit and Voluntary Sector Quarterly*, 1991, *20*(4), 359–370.

Walker, M. J. "Organizational Change, Citizen Participation, and Voluntary Action." *Journal of Voluntary Action Research*, 1975, *4*(1-2).

Walkey, F. H., Siegert, R. J., McCormick, I. A., and Taylor, A. J. "Multiple Replication of the Factor Structure of the Inventory of Socially Supportive Behaviors." *Journal of Community Psychology*, 1987, *15*(4), 513–519.

Walter, V. "Volunteers and Bureaucrats: Clarifying Roles and Creating Meaning." *Journal of Voluntary Action Research*, 1987, *16*(3), 22–32.

Waltzing, J. P. *Etude Historique, sur les Corporatios Professionelles chez les Romaines*. Brussels: F. Hayerz, L'Academie Royale, 1895–1900.

Ward, L. *Lester Ward and the Welfare State*. (H. S. Commager, ed.) Indianapolis, Ind.: Bobbs-Merrill, 1967.

Warner, A. G. *American Charities: A Study in Philanthropy and Economics*. New Brunswick, N.J.: Transaction, 1988. (Originally published 1908.)

Warren, A. K. *Anchorites and Their Patrons in Medieval England*. Berkeley: University of California Press, 1985.

Warren, R. *The Community in America*. Skokie, Ill.: Rand McNally, 1963.

Weathers, J. E., Messe, L. A., and Aronoff, J. "The Effects of Task-Group Experiences on Subsequent Prosocial Behavior." *Social Psychology Quarterly*, 1984, *47*(3), 287-292.

Weber, M. "Economy and Society: An Outline of Interpretive Sociology." (G. Roth and C. Wittich, eds.) New York: Bedminster Press, 1968.

Weber, M. "Geschäftsbericht, Verhandlungen des Ersten Deutschen Soziologentages vom 19-22 Oktober, 1910 in Frankfurt A.M. Tubingen, 1911." *Journal of Voluntary Action Research*, 1972, *1*(1), 20-23.

Wedgewood, C. H. "The Nature and Functions of Secret Societies." *Oceania*, 1930, *1*, 129-145.

Weiner, B., and Graham, S. "Understanding the Motivational Role of Affect: Lifespan Research from an Attributional Perspective: Development of Emotion-Cognition Relations." *Cognition and Emotion*, 1989, *3*(4), 401-419.

Weinstein, E. "Forging Nonprofit Accounting Principles—An Update." *Accounting Review*, 1980, *55*(4), 685-691.

Weisbrod, B. *The Voluntary Nonprofit Sector*. Lexington, Mass.: Heath, 1977.

Weisbrod, B. *The Nonprofit Economy*. Cambridge, Mass.: Harvard University Press, 1988.

Wenocur, S., and Reisch, M. *From Charity to Enterprise: The Development of American Social Work in a Market Economy*. Urbana: University of Illinois Press, 1989.

Wertheim, E. G. "Evolution of Structure and Process in Voluntary Organizations: A Study of Thirty-Five Consumer Food Cooperatives." *Journal of Voluntary Action Research*, 1976, *5*(1), 4-16.

Weyant, J. M. "Applying Social Psychology to Induce Charitable Donations." *Journal of Applied Social Psychology*, 1984, *14*(5), 441-447.

White, J. M. *Everyday Life in Ancient Egypt*. New York: Putnam, 1963.

Wiarda, H. J., and Kline, H. F. *Latin American Politics and Development*. (2nd ed.) Boulder, Colo.: Westview Press, 1979.

Wiesenthal, D. L., Austrom, D., and Silverman, I. "Diffusion of

Responsibility in Charitable Donations." *Basic and Applied Social Psychology*, 1983, *4*(1), 17–27.

Wiesenthal, D. L., and Spindel, L. "The Effect of Telephone Messages/Prompts on Return Rates of First-Time Blood Donors." *Journal of Community Psychology*, 1989, *17*(2), 194–197.

Williams, J. A., Jr., and Ortega, S. T. "The Multidimensionality of Joining." *Journal of Voluntary Action Research*, 1986, *15*(4), 35–44.

Williams, K. D., and Williams, K. B. "Impact of Source Strength on Two Compliance Techniques." *Basic and Applied Social Psychology*, 1989, *10*(2), 149–159.

Wilson, D. J. *Science, Community and the Transformation of American Philosophy, 1860–1930*. Chicago: University of Chicago Press, 1990.

Wilson, J. P., and Petruska, R. "Motivation, Model Attributes, and Prosocial Behavior." *Journal of Personality and Social Psychology*, 1984, *46*(2), 458–468.

Wilson, P. J. *The Domestication of the Human Species*. New Haven, Conn.: Yale University Press, 1989.

Winkle, C. R. "Supply-Side Theory of the Role of the Nonprofit Sector: An Analysis of Two Case Studies." In *Proceedings of the 1990 Conference of the Association of Voluntary Action Scholars*. London: Center for Voluntary Organization, 1990.

Wiseman, T. "Pete Nobiles Amicos: Poets and Patrons in Late Republican Rome." In B. K. Gold (ed.), *Literary and Artistic Patronage in Ancient Rome*. Austin: University of Texas Press, 1982.

Wolch, J. R. *The Shadow State: Government and Voluntary Sector in Transition*. New York: Foundation Center, 1990.

Wolensky, R. P. "Toward a Broader Conceptualization of Volunteerism in Disaster." *Journal of Voluntary Action Research*, 1979, *8*(3-4), 33–42.

Wolff, R. P. *In Defense of Anarchism*. New York: HarperCollins, 1970.

Wolozin, H. "The Economic Role and Value of Volunteer Work in the United States: An Exploratory Study." *Journal of Voluntary Action Research*, 1975, *4*(1-2), 23–42.

Wood, S. *English Monasteries and Their Patrons in the Thirteenth Century.* London: Oxford University Press, 1955.

Woodward, G.W.O. *The Dissolution of the Monasteries.* London: Blandford Press, 1966.

Woo-Kuen, H. *The History of Korea.* Seoul: Eul-Yoo Publishing, 1970.

Wooster, J. W. "Current Trends and Developments in the Investment Practices of Endowments and Pension Funds." *Law and Contemporary Problems,* 1952, *17*(1), 162–171.

Worach, K. H. "Dwie Koncepcje Sposobu Zycia—Aktywnosc Instrumentalna i Aktywnosc Ekspresywna" (Two Concepts of the Way of Life—Instrumental Activeness and Expressive Activeness). *Studia Socjologiczne,* 1980, *79*(4), 259–273.

Wright, A. F. "Changan." In A Toynbee (ed.), *Cities of Destiny.* New York: McGraw-Hill, 1967.

Yalom, I. D. "The 'Terrestrial' Meanings of Life." *International Forum for Logotherapy,* 1982, *5*(2), 92–102.

Yamagishi, T. "The Provision of a Sanctioning System as a Public Good." *Journal of Personality and Social Psychology,* 1986, *51*(1), 110–116.

Yeo, S., and Yeo, E. (eds.). *Popular Culture and Class Conflict, 1590–1914.* New York: Harvester/Humanities, 1981.

York, A., and Lazerwitz, B. "Religious Involvement as the Main Gateway to Voluntary Association Activity." *Contemporary Jewry,* 1987, *8,* 7–26.

Young, D. R. "Executive Leadership in Nonprofit Organizations." In W. W. Powell (ed.), *The Nonprofit Sector: A Research Handbook.* New Haven, Conn.: Yale University Press, 1987.

Zurcher, L. A. "Ephemeral Roles, Voluntary Action, and Voluntary Associations." *Journal of Voluntary Action Research,* 1978, 7(3–4), 65–74.

Name Index

A

Abas, A., 248
Abbott, G., 185
Acton, H., 61, 117
Adams, J. L., 41, 134
Adorno, T. W., 80
al Din Khairi, M., 103
Alessi, N. E., 68
Alhadeff, D. A., 25, 162
Amato, P. R., 241
Anderson, B., 52, 187
Andrews, L., 248
Anheier, H. K., 8, 40, 47, 101, 181
Anthony, R. N., 24, 25, 26, 28, 29,
    30, 34, 37, 166
Arato, A., 80
Arberry, A., 102
Archer, R. L., 241
Arendt, H., 86, 161
Argyle, M., 143
Aronoff, J., 242, 244
Arrington, B., 159

Asprea, A., 240
Attwood, D. W., 143
Austrom, D., 204
Ayubi, N., 146

B

Babchuk, N., 39, 42, 57
Badelt, C., 175
Baldson, J., 99
Bandelier, A., 87
Banton, M., 40
Banu, S., 242
Barker, A., 42
Barnes, J., 97, 155
Barone, R. C., 247, 248
Bar-Tal, D., 241, 244
Batson, C. D., 239, 240, 241, 243,
    244
Baumann, D. J., 237
Baumol, W., 159
Baviskar, B. S., 143
Bays, C., 159

Becker, G. S., 25, 162
Beers, C. W., 228
Bell, P. A., 17, 251
Ben-Ner, A., 143
Bennett-Sandler, G., 179
Ben Zadok, E., 177
Berelson, B., 40
Berger, P. L., 63, 260
Bernstein, B., 138, 139, 140
Bernstein, R., 6, 63, 211, 254, 255, 256, 260, 262
Bernstein, S. R., 134, 135, 182, 227
Bestor, A., 181
Betocchi, G. V., 240
Beyan, A. J., 184
Biemiller, L., 3, 124
Bilinkoff, J., 111
Billis, D., 4, 48
Bilsky, W., 254
Bishai, W. B., 102
Blackaby, B., 42
Blades, S. D., 6
Blanchi, R., 102, 143
Blau, P. M., 25, 56, 57, 196
Boardman, J., 94
Bolen, M. H., 240
Bonnett, A. W., 42
Bontempo, R., 240
Bookheimer, S., 164
Boorstin, D., 228
Borkman, R., 222
Borman, L. D., 228, 229
Boulding, K. E., 99, 170, 198
Bouman, F.J.A., 230
Bouressa, G., 250
Bowen, W., 159
Bowra, M., 94
Bracken, M. S., 106, 110, 199, 219
Bradshaw, B., 110
Brandon, W., 121
Brask, P., 207
Braudel, F., 113, 175
Braybrooke, D., 260
Bremner, R. H., 84, 121, 136, 221, 228
Brickman, A., 68
Brief, A. P., 241, 242, 243
Brinton, C., 118
Brissett, D., 208

Britton, N., 251
Brown, C., 67
Brown, D., 52, 254
Brown, M. K., 123, 179
Brown, R. D., 122
Brown, S. G., 122
Brudney, J. L., 162, 177, 224, 226
Brunn, S. D., 116
Buchanan, J. M., 175
Bukkyo Dendo Kyokai (Buddhist Promotional Foundation), 218
Burleson, B. R., 241
Burns, J. M., 193, 194
Butora, M., 232, 233

C

Cabral, S. L., 228
Callero, P. L., 248
Caplan, G., 233
Carducci, B. J., 249
Carlson, M., 241
Carnegie, A., 139, 149, 263, 264
Cass, R. H., 122, 199, 216, 220
Caulkins, D. D., 39, 52
Cavallaro, R., 40
Cavan, R. S., 52
Chadwick, H., 103
Chadwick, N., 137
Chalmers, T., 16
Chambers, C. A., 150
Chambers, M. M., 84
Chambon, A., 232
Chambré, S. M., 263
Chatman, J., 241
Cherniack, M., 250
Childe, V. G., 90
Chrisman, N. J., 154
Cialdini, R. B., 237
Clary, C. G., 232, 233
Clayre, A., 143, 160
Cleverly, W., 159
Cobb, J. B., 172
Cohen, J. L., 80
Collins, A. H., 232
Collins, C. D., 90
Commons, J. R., 37, 38, 39
Constantelos, D. J., 116
Cornes, R., 175

Coulson, N. J., 102
Crawford, M., 100
Crew, M., 16, 160
Critchlow, B., 241
Cronin, T. E., 193
Cross, J. A., 240
Cummings, L. D., 52
Cunningham, K., 67

D

Daly, H. E., 172
Daniel, R. L., 103
Daniels, A., 241
Deegan, M. J., 89
de Guzman, J., 246
DeLaat, J., 224
Delgado, G., 178
Demott, B. J., 154
DePaor, M. L., 93
deSwaan, A., 115
de Tocqueville, A., 19, 36, 41, 44, 121, 178
DeVall, W. B., 172
de Vaux, R., 73, 92, 137
Dharmasiri, G., 203, 213
Diaz, L. R., 241
DiMaggio, P., 27
Dodge, P, J., 241
Douglas, D., 107
Douglas, J., 177, 178
Dozier, J. B., 241, 245
Dumazedier, J., 39
Dworkin, R., 191

E

Earle, W., 241
Easton, D., 60
Eber, M., 246
Edgley, C., 208
Edney, J. J., 17, 251
Edwards, A., 159
Edwards, J. M., 42
Edwards, P. W., 247
Eichelman, B., 68
Eisenberg, N., 240, 241, 243
Eisenstadt, S. N., 184
Elffers, H., 247

Elizur, A., 241
Elkin, F., 24, 143, 166
Ellis, B. B., 241
Ellsworth, E. W., 120
Emerson, T. I., 189, 191
England, R. E., 162
Enoch, M. D., 247
Erikson, J. M., 67
Escarraz, J., 241
Etzioni, A., 49, 55, 136, 146, 181
Evans, D. E., 248
Evans, J., 219

F

Fairclough, A., 136
Fama, E., 133
Faramelli, N. J., 42
Fedler, F., 240
Feldbaum, E. G., 187
Ferari, J. R., 248
Ferguson, M., 248
Ferrari, J. R., 247
Filer Commission, 181
Finley, M. I., 58, 93, 94, 95, 132
Fisher, A. L., 213
Fisher, D., 155
Fisher, J. L., 10
Fitzgerald, M. W., 154
Flynn, J. P., 42
Ford Foundation, 171
Forster, E., 75, 97
Foundation Center, 1
Franklin, J. H., 184
Fraser, C., 248
Freedman, A., 40, 127, 184, 225
French, R. S., 116
Frohlich, N., 160, 238
Fultz, J., 242
Furlough, E., 143

G

Gaes, G. G., 250
Gainotti, G., 68
Galaskiewiscz, J., 171
Garcia, I. M., 151
Gassler, R. S., 160
Geanakoplos, D. J., 116

Gibb, H.A.R., 218
Gifis, S. H., 11, 26, 27, 28, 55, 65,
    66, 67, 199
Ginsberg, E., 35
Girouard, M., 99, 100, 108, 109, 110,
    111, 113, 114, 118, 119, 120, 121,
    175–176
Gitlow v. New York, 193
Gluck, P. R., 42, 151
Goff, F. H., 223
Gold, B. K., 93, 100
Goldberg, D. J., 112, 217
Goldman, R. M., 152
Goodman, C., 231
Goodman, P., 61–62
Goodwin, J. R., 203
Gordon, W. C., 42, 57
Gouldner, A., 200
Grady, B., 132
Graham, S., 239
Grapentine, W. L., 68
Gray, B. K., 51, 106
Gray, P. S., 52
Graziano, W. G., 242
Grusec, J. E., 239
Gupta, P., 239
Gutmann, D., 67

H

Hacker, L., 232
Haddock, C. C., 159
Hague v. C.I.O., 192
Hahm. S., 110, 218
Hale, J., 117
Hall, J. N., 26, 41, 84, 181, 241
Hall, P. D., 5
Hallam, J. R., 242
Hallenstvedt, A., 52
Hands, A. R., 89, 93
Hannah, M., 250
Hansmann, H. B., 28, 158, 159
Hardin, G., 8, 204, 237
Hardoy, J., 90
Harry, J., 172
Harvey, J. W., 226, 249
Hastings, J., 84
Heal, F., 54, 109
Heath, A., 168, 196

Hechter, M., 167
Heffron v. International Society for
    Krishna Consciousness, 192
Helton, A., 232
Herm, G., 137
Herman, G., 89
Herman, R. D., 134
Heshka, S., 42
Hessing, D. J., 247
Hill, J. N., 40
Hill, L. E., 68, 254–255
Hillary, G., 62
Hite, R. E., 248
Hodgkinson, V. A., 33
Homans, G. C., 25, 196
Hornblower, S., 94, 95, 99
Horvath, J., 99, 170, 198
Hourani, A., 102, 107, 218
Huang, N., 67
Hull, D. L., 155
Hunter, L., 143

I

Idson, T. L., 159
INDEPENDENT SECTOR, 29, 30
Ireland, T. R., 167
Iwata, O., 239

J

Jacobson, P. E., 42
James, E., 143
James, F. G., 40
Jarrige, A., 241
Jason, L. A., 247, 248
Jenkins, S., 228, 229
Jensen, M., 133
Jeremy, M., 89
Johnson, C., 250
Johnson, D., 100, 149
Johnson, D. B., 167
Johnson, K., 179
Johnson, N., 178
Jones, A., 143
Jones-McClintic, S., 177
Jordan, B., 171

K

Kalela, A., 52
Kalela, J., 52
Kallmeyer, K., 248
Kan, S., 202
Karst, K. L., 267
Karuza, J., 238
Katz, A. H., 229
Katz, I., 247
Kauffmann, D., 237
Kayden, X., 151
Keating, J. P., 245
Kebza, V., 68
Kenrick, D. T., 237
Kent, R. C., 251
Kerber, K. W., 246
Kerri, J. N., 8, 40, 177
Kessler, R. C., 246
Kestenbaum, C. J., 67
Kettner, P. M., 177
Killilea, M., 233
Klobus-Edwards, P. A., 42
Knapp, M., 47, 181
Knoke, D., 167, 168, 227
Kobasa, S., 232
Kodym, M., 68
Kofta, M., 241
Kooperman, L., 177
Kramer, R. M., 39, 43, 133, 178, 227
Kramers, J. H., 218
Kravik, R. B., 52, 187
Krishnan, L., 160, 241, 242
Krivich, M., 159
Kroll-Smith, J. S., 250
Kronick, J. C., 250
Kropotkin, P., 115, 222, 223, 228
Kuhn, T. S., 63, 260
Kunz, L. B., 246
Kurtz, L. F., 232

L

Lanfant, M. F., 39, 52
Lang, D., 42
Langer, S., 52, 207
Langton, S., 4, 78, 178
Latour, B., 155
LaTour, S. A., 248

Lawrence, C. H., 105, 107, 219
Lazerwitz, B., 40
Lederman, L. M., 156
Lee, P., 26
Lenkersdorf, C., 39, 52
Lenski, G., 88
Lerner, M. J., 245
Levi, P., 95
Levitt, M. J., 187
Lewis, A., 191
Lewis, A. R., 116
Lidz, T., 68
Lieberman, P., 86
Liebrand, W. B., 241, 242
Lightman, E. S., 249
Lincoln, B., 89
Lindblom, C. A., 260
Lindeman, E. C., 150
Lintonen, R., 52
Lipsitz, A., 248
Liu, T. J., 241
Lobel, S., 240
Loewenberg, F., 184
Lohmann, R. A., 24, 106, 110, 133,
    134, 160, 199, 219, 250
Lorenzo, G., 67
Lowi, T. J., 80, 180, 200
Lubove, R., 26, 223–224
Luckmann, T., 63, 260
Lux, D. S., 120, 155
Lystad, M. M., 241, 250

M

Ma, H. K., 239
MacAloon, J. J., 148
McCarthy, P. R., 226
McChesney, R., 102
McCormick, I. A., 244
McCown, N. E., 242
McCrohan, K. F., 226, 249
MacGee, S., 67
McGlashan, T. H., 67
McGregor, M. F., 97
Macionis, J. J., 92
MacIver, R. M., 40, 166, 181
McLean, C., 143
McManus, M., 68
McMurtry, S. L., 177

McWilliams, W. C., 122
Mahe, E., 151
Manrai, A. K., 248
Manser, G., 112, 199, 216, 220
Maritain, J., 173
Marlowe, H. A., 241, 244
Marts, A. C., 217
Marty, M. E., 103
Masterson, M. P., 177
Mather, C., 263
Maton, K., 232, 233
Matson, W. I., 61
Mauss, M., 11, 200, 203, 204
Mead, M., 141, 211
Mehta, V., 137
Meier, K. G., 185
Meindl, J. R., 245
Melville, H., 87
Meritt, B. D., 97
Messe, L. A., 242, 244
Miceli, M. P., 240, 241, 245
Michels, R., 131, 134, 185
Middleton, M., 133, 134
Midlarsky, E., 250
Miller, N., 241
Miller, P. A., 241, 243
Mills, C. W., 212
Mills, R. S., 239
Milofsky, C., 5, 6
Mitchell, J. N., 54, 196
Molitor, M., 24, 166
Molnar, J. J., 42
Moore, B., 242–243
Moore, J., 246
Moore, T., 159
Moren, J., 52
Morgan, W., 207, 241
Moron, P., 241
Morris, R., 89, 108, 116, 199, 216,
    218, 221, 263
Moskoff, W., 143
Motowidlo, S. J., 241, 242, 243
Muncy, R. L., 222
Murray, O., 95, 105

N

NAACP v. Alabama, 192
Near, J. P., 241, 243

Nelson, A. L., 231
Nelson, K., 159
Netting, F. E., 177
Netton, I. R., 102
Neuberger, E., 143
Neuringer-Benefiel, H. E., 240
Neville, G. K., 152
Newsome, B. L., 230
Newsome, M., 230
Newton, K., 178
Nocentini, U., 68
Nolan, M. L., 152
Nolan, S., 152
Norbeck, E., 40, 60
Norberg, K., 108
Northrup, F.S.C., 144
Nozick, R., 64, 181, 183

O

O'Connell, B., 216
Odendahl, T., 125, 263
Oleck, H. L., 25, 65, 143, 191
Olesko, K. M., 155
Olson, M., 168, 169
O'Malley, M. N., 248
O'Mara, R. J., 250
O'Neill, M., 28, 29, 43
Opp, K., 167
Oppenheimer, J., 160, 238
O'Reilly, C. A., 241
Organ, D. W., 242, 243
Orive, R., 242
Orloff, A., 113, 148
Ortega, S. T., 58
Orwin, R., 241
Ostrander, S. A., 4, 78, 178
Ostrum, E., 42

P

Page, C. H., 40
Palisca, C. V., 117
Palisi, B. J., 42
Pancoast, D. L., 232
Paris, C., 42
Parisi, N., 247
Parker, R., 93–94
Pauly, M., 159

Pavitt, P., 117
Peak, T., 232
Pedersen, J., 239
Peltason, J. L., 193, 194
Penner, L. A., 241
Perkins, K. B., 250
Perlstadt, H., 39
Peschek, J. G., 153
Petersen, J. C., 172
Pfaff, M., 99, 170, 198
Picon-Salas, M., 122
Pierce, C. S., 255
Pierchowski, M. M., 67
Pifer, A., 43
Pigou, A. C., 165
Piliavin, J. A., 248
Pleket, H. W., 95
Poole, D. L., 184
Poplawski, W. T., 252
Préaux, C ., 75
Preston, F. W., 59
Previté-Orton, C. W., 106
Price, S., 97, 98
Pryor, B., 240
Puhan, B. N., 242
Pulkkinen, L., 243
Purcell, N., 101
Purohit, S. R., 42
Pynoos, J., 231

Q

Quigley, B., 250

R

Raskin, M., 172
Rawls, J., 52, 59
Rayner, J. D., 112, 217
Redfield, R., 141
Redisch, M., 143, 159
Reisch, M., 224
Reykowski, J., 241
Rich, R. C., 205
Richards, P. G., 17
Riley, P., 171
Riley-Smith, J., 135
Robbins, L. R., 158
Robinson, M., 89

Rockefeller, J. D., 150
Rogers, T., 226
Rose, A. M., 20, 39, 40, 41, 208
Rose, T., 247, 248
Rosenbaum, W. A., 42
Rosenzweig, R., 154
Ross, J. C., 8, 20, 106, 114
Ross, R. J., 39, 52
Rossiter, C., 232
Rourke, F. E., 180
Rowland, J., 75
Rubin, M., 109
Rudney, G., 35, 162
Runciman, S., 116
Rushton, J. P., 237
Russell-Wood, A., 111, 112, 117,
    121, 220
Rutter, M., 241, 243
Rybczynski, W., 39
Ryle, M., 17

S

Saddhatissa, H., 213
Sahlins, M., 87
Salamon, L. M., 4, 28, 33, 159
Salem, G. W., 42
Samter, W., 241
Sandler, T., 175
Sassone, P. G., 165
Schiller, B., 52, 187
Schlenker, B. R., 242
Schlesinger, S. C., 152
Schmidt, A. J., 39
Schulman, D. C., 42
Schurer, L., 241
Schutz, A., 48, 50
Schwartz, M. R., 152
Schwartz, S. H., 254
Schwartzman, S., 63
Scott, W. R., 56, 57, 196
Scully, S., 73
Scully, V., 91
Segelman, L., 164
Seibel, W., 84
Sen, A. K., 166–167
Sena, E., 68
Seth, I. R., 239
Seymour, H. J., 125

Shaffer, D. R., 241, 242
Shainess, N., 67
Shane, E., 239
Shane, M., 239
Sharma, V. K., 247
Sharp, E. G., 42
Shaw, R. D., 88
Sherman, D. G., 149
Sherman, H. B., 149
Sherover, C. M., 171
Shiffrin, S. H., 189, 190
Shotland, R. L., 245
Siegert, R. J., 244
Sills, D. L., 40
Silva, E. T., 145
Silveri, H. C., 68
Silverman, I., 204
Simmel, G., 153
Simon, H. A., 209, 260
Simon, H., 206
Simon, J. G., 28, 46, 177
Simon, Y., 173
Simsar, M. A., 102, 103, 116, 264
Slaughter, S. A., 145
Sloane, D. C., 3, 124
Smith, A., 36, 37, 39, 43, 161
Smith, C., 40, 127, 184, 225
Smith, C. A., 243
Smith, D. H., 19, 29, 40, 43, 44, 46,
   56, 57, 84, 208, 253
Smith, G., 232
Smith, J. E., 241
Smith, K. D., 245
Smith, R. W., 59
Smith, W. R., 148, 202
Smolenska, Z., 241
Snow, C. P., 144
Sober, E., 238
Sontz, A.H.L., 144
Spates, J. L., 92
Spiegel, H.B.C., 162
Spindel, L., 249
Spiro, M., 213
Stam, J. M., 38, 42
Stanback, T. M., 38
Stanfield, J. H., 144, 178
Staw, B. M., 166, 241, 243
Stebbins, C. A., 245
Steele, C. M., 241

Steinberg, M. P., 148
Steinberg, R., 160
Steiner, G. L., 40
Steinman, R., 230
Stephenson, P. H., 178
Stewart, M., 233
Stinson, T. F., 38, 42
Stockard, J., 241
Stotland, E., 245
Strong, J., 203
Sugden, R., 160
Sumariwalla, R. D., 31
Sundeen, R. A., 226
Suntharalingam, R., 151

T

Taylor, A. J., 244
Taylor, C. J., 20
Tedeschi, J. T., 250
Thielen, G. L., 184
Thrupp, S., 114
Tietjen, A. M., 241
Titmuss, R., 246
Toseland, R., 232
Toynbee, A., 91
Trattner, W. I., 121, 229
Traunstein, D. M., 230
Triandis, H., 240
Tucker, L. R., 249
Turnbull, C. M., 87
Tyler, T. R., 241

U

Udoidem, S., 168, 172, 173, 174
Ullmann, S. G., 159
Underwood, B., 242–243
United States v. *Mary T. Grace*, 192
Urban, G. A., 63
U.S. Bureau of the Census, 32, 35

V

Valelly, R. M., 151
Van Bavel, T. J., 219
Van de Kragt, A. J., 241
Van der Veer, P., 71, 144
Vander Zander, J. W., 59

Van Doren, J., 136, 151
Van Lange, P. A., 241, 242
Van Til, J., 4, 21, 42, 78, 134, 178, 179
Van Vugt, J. P., 135
Vojta, G. J., 35

W

Wade-Gery, H. T., 97
Wagner, A., 158, 160
Walker, M. J., 42
Walker v. *Birmingham*, 192
Walkey, F. H., 244
Walter, V., 12
Waltzing, J. P., 100
Ward, L., 12
Warner, A. G., 10, 223
Warren, A. K., 107
Warren, R., 62
Weathers, J. E., 242, 244
Webb, G. E., 42
Weber, M., 48, 60, 118, 180, 181
Wedgewood, C. H., 153
Weiner, B., 239
Weinstein, E., 158
Weisbrod, B., 32, 34, 38, 158, 159, 160, 164, 168, 178
Weitzman, M. S., 33
Wenocur, S., 224
Wertheim, E. G., 143
Weyant, J. M., 248
White, J. M., 90

Wiesenthal, D. L., 204, 249
Williams, J. A., Jr., 58
Williams, K. B., 249
Williams, K. D., 249
Wilson, D. J., 145, 155
Winkle, C. R., 159
Wippler, R., 167
Wiseman, T., 93
Wiss, P., 175
Wolch, J. R., 181
Wolensky, R. P., 250
Wolozin, H., 38
Wood, S., 107
Woodward, G.W.O., 106, 220
Wooster, J. W., 268
Worach, K. H., 238
Wright, A. F., 93

Y

Yalom, I. D., 237
Yamagishi, T., 204, 241
Yeo, E., 86
Yeo, S., 86
York, A., 40
Young, D. R., 16, 135
Young, D. W., 24, 25, 26, 28, 29, 30, 37

Z

Zeichner, A., 247
Zurcher, L. A., 58

Subject Index

A

Academic discipline, 144–145. *See also* Universities

Accounting fund, 66

Acts of common good: Buddhist perspective, 213–214; and common goods exchange, 205–213; defined, 206; and discourse/presentation, 206–208; and information/meaning, 208–211; and problem solving, 211–213; social, 20, 62; and tangible gifts, 205–206. *See also* Commons action; Social action

Affluence: and leisure, 162; prehistorical, 87–88, 91; and scarcity, 161; and theory of the commons, 48–49

Age of Reason: art/science/literature academies, 119–121; charity, 221–222; and commons, 119–121

Agencies: defined, 132–133; group

trusteeship, 133; solo trusteeship, 134–135

Altruism: acquisition, 237–238; comparative studies, 238–239; defined, 237; and egoism/hedonism, 238–239; hierarchy, 239; and personality, 240; and prosocial behavior, 242

Altruism theory, 9–10

American commons, 121–124

American Communist Party, 154, 191

Arabia: and Islam, 102–103; and urban development, 102. *See also* Islamic

Art: academies, 119–121; collections, 75–76; repertory, 77; and ritual, 90. *See also* Monuments

Association for Research on Nonprofit Organizations and Voluntary Action (ARNOVA), 7, 18, 19, 39–40, 44

Associations: and benefactories,

132; defined, 27, 132; mutual
aid, 227–229; protective, 183,
187–188; and state, 178, 180–183;
study, 181. *See also* Mutual aid
societies; Protective associations;
Voluntary associations
Authenticity, 49–50
Autonomy, 53

B

Beau monde society. *See* Polite
society
Behavior: altruistic, 237; bystander,
245–246; donor, 246–250; ethical,
216–222; helping, 244–251; organizational, 243; prosocial,
240–244; rational, 273
Benefactories: and agencies, 132–
135; and associations, 132; and
campaigns, 135–136; and collections, 74; and common places,
136–140; and commons, 131–156;
and committees, 140–141; and
conferences, 141–142; and cooperatives, 143; defined, 55–56; and
disciplines, 144–148; and fiestas,
148–149; and foundations, 149–
150; and incorporation, 131; in-
trinsic/extrinsic/mixed, 57; and
journals, 150–152; organization,
128–131; and political parties,
151–152; professional, 77; pur-
posive/expressive, 57–58; and re-
ligious/sacred pilgrimages, 152–
153; and research institutes, 153;
and science, 155–156; and secret
societies, 153–155; and theory of
the commons, 55–58; type A/B,
57; typology, 131–156
Boards of directors, 65, 133–134
Buddhism, 213–214, 218–219
Bylaws, 65
Bystander behavior, 245–246
Byzantium, 115–116

C

Campaigns, 135–136
Carnegie Hall, 138–140

Carnegie principle, 262–267
Cathedrals/churches, 104–105, 137
Ceremonies, 208. *See also* Dramas;
Presentation; Ritual
Chantries, 107–108
Charity: Buddhist tradition, 218–
219; early Christian tradition,
217–218; early modern, 221–222;
and ethical behavior, 216–222;
ethical precepts, 215–216; and
Hull House, 134–135; Islamic
tradition, 218; Jewish tradition,
217; medieval European, 108–
109; and monastic tradition,
219–220; and mutual aid societies, 227–229; and offerings, 203;
organization, 227–233, 274; origins, 222–224; and potlatch, 202;
and recipients, 203; and self-help
groups, 229–233; and volunteers,
224–227. *See also* Gift giving
Charity theory: defined, 12; and efficiency, 26; transformation,
215–216
Chronicle of Philanthropy, 7
Civil liberties: and freedom of religion, 194; and freedom of
speech, 193; and redress of grievances, 194; and right of assembly, 191–192; and theory of the
commons, 188–194
Civilization: and Age of Reason,
119–121; and agricultural/urban
revolutions, 91–93; Arabic, 101–
103; Byzantine, 115–116; classical Greek, 93–97; and collection,
75; and common goods, 69; and
commons, 70, 85; early American, 121–124; and endowment,
68–71; Hellenistic Greek, 97–99;
medieval European, 103–115;
prehistoric, 86–91; and Reformation, 117–119; and Renaissance,
117; Roman, 99–101; and social
surpluses, 85–86
Club sector, 44
Club theory, 175
Collection: art, 75–76; and civiliza-

tion, 75; defined, 73–74; types, 74–75

Collective choice theory, 167–169

Committees, 65, 140–141

Common goods: as acts, 205–206; and commons, 60; conceptual origins, 172; defined, 17–18, 69, 173–175; and democracy, 172; economics, 163–164; exchanges, 197–204; and metric measurement, 69; and political theory, 171–172; and public goods, 19, 69, 158, 168, 172–175; and rational behavior, 51–52, 273; and state, 187; and symbols, 207; and values, 256–257

Common goods exchange: and acts of common good, 205–206; and free-riding, 204–205; and gift giving, 200–202; and offerings, 203–204; and patronage/tributes, 198–200; and potlatch, 202–203

Common theory of value, 257

Commons: and Age of Reason, 119–121; and ancient urban communities, 91–93; and Arabic civilization, 101–103; and art/science/literature academies, 119–121; and Byzantine civilization, 115–116; and Carnegie Hall, 138–140; and classical Greek civilization, 93–97; and common goods, 60; and coproduction, 162; defined, 17–18, 58–59; and democratic governance, 65; and discourse, 63, 206–207; and early American civilization, 121–124; and emerging state, 183–185; and endowment, 18–19; and Greek philosophical schools, 96–97; and Hellenistic Greek civilization, 97–99; institutions, 64; language, 63–64; and markets/states, 59–60, 62–63, 177–179; and medieval European civilization, 103–115; and monuments, 90–91; and mutual reciprocity, 60; organization, 63; places, 136–140, 272; and polite

society, 124–125; prehistoric, 86–91; and public goods, 171; and Reformation, 117–119; and Renaissance, 117; and research, 19–20; and rituals, 88–89, 149; and Roman civilization, 99–101; and satisfaction, 258; as social acts, 20, 62; as social worlds, 64; symbolic role, 61–62; and theoretical basis, 58–65; and third sector, 20; and value theory, 254–257; and values, 166–167; and village communities, 91. *See also* Common goods; Commons action; Theory of the commons

Commons action: and benefactories, 128–131; and discourse/presentation/offering, 210–211; and microeconomic model, 211; and Pareto optimality, 167; and problem solving, 211; types, 209. *See also* Acts of common good; Learning; Nonprofit/voluntary action; Search; Social action; Technique

Community, 255, 268

Company, 27

Conferences, 103–104, 141

Consensus, 268–269

Conservation, 267–268

Contextualism: and amateurism, 261; and common values, 261–262; and objectivity, 260; principle, 260–262

Continuity, 50–51

Cooperatives, 28, 143

Coproduction, 162–163. *See also* Production

Core/periphery distinction, 78–79

Corporation, 27

D

Democracy, 65, 172, 179–180. *See also* State

Disaster response, 250–251

Discipline, 144–148

Discourse, 63, 206–207, 210

Donations, 246–249

Donor behavior: and donations,
246–247; and emotions, 248; factors, 249–250; and motivation,
247; and solicitation skills, 248–
249
Dramas, 208. *See also* Ceremonies

E

Economics: and club theory, 175;
defined, 158; of fairs/festivals,
175–176; and maximization paradigm, 163, 176; and surplus
theory, 163. *See also* Economics
of common goods; Grant economics; Nonprofit economics;
Microeconomics; Welfare
economics
Economics of common goods, 163–
164, 170–171. *See also* Nonprofit
economics
Efficiency, 26
Empathy, 242–243
Endowment: and civilization, 68–
71; and collection, 73–76; defined, 18–19, 65–67; genetic, 68;
and gifts, 67; and patronage, 80–
82; personal, 67–68; and regime,
78–80; and repertory, 76–78; and
shared resources, 273; and social-
ization/technique/search, 71–72;
and treasury, 73
Endowment theory: defined, 12–13;
and problem solving, 213; and
rational choice, 19
Ethics, 213–222
Ethnic mutual aid associations. *See*
Mutual aid societies
Europe. *See* Age of Reason; Middle
Ages; Reformation; Renaissance
Exchange. *See* Common goods
exchange
Existential scarcity, 161

F

Festivals/holidays: anthropological
studies, 149; economics, 175–176;
medieval European, 113–114

Fiestas, 148–149. *See also* Festivals/
holidays
Foundation, 149–150
Freedoms. *See* Civil liberties
Free-riding: and collective choice
theory, 168–169; and common
goods exchange, 204–205; defined, 169, 204; likelihood conditions, 205
Fund accounting, 66
Fund raising, 125, 136

G

Gift giving: and commons, 11–12;
and common goods exchange,
200–202; and discourse/presenta-
tion, 210; and endowment, 67;
and gifts, 200–201; Greek village, 93–94. *See also* Charity
Gift theory, 11–12, 201–202
Gifts, 200–201, 205–206
Gilds, 114–115, 147
Goods. *See* Common goods; Private
goods; Public goods
Grant economics, 170–171
Greece: and associations, 98–99;
classical, 93–97; and gift giving,
93–94; Hellenistic, 97–99; and
patronage, 95, 98; and religious/
philosophical schools, 95–97
Group trusteeships, 133

H

Helping behavior, 245–251
Holidays. *See* Festivals/holidays;
Fiestas
Hull House, 134–135

I

Incentives, 169
Incorporation, 65, 131
Independent sector, 43–44
INDEPENDENT SECTOR, 7, 35
Information, 208–209
Intangible commodities. *See*
Services

Internal Revenue Service, 30–31
Islamic: charity, 218; commons, 102–103. *See also* Arabia

J

Jewish: charity, 217; medieval European, communities, 112; secret societies, 154–155
Journal of Voluntary Action Research, 46
Journals, 150–151

K

Ku Klux Klan, 154, 191

L

Labor: defined, 86; organizations, 230; productive/unproductive, 36–37; 160; volunteer, 39, 164–165, 225–227. *See also* Unproductive labor
Law: and agencies, 133; and endowment, 66–67; nonprofit, 27; organization, 27–28; and self-help groups, 230
Learning, 209
Leisure, 39, 162

M

Maximization, 163, 176
Measurement, 165–166, 209
Medieval Europe. *See* Middle Ages
Meetings, 65
Microeconomics, 165, 211
Middle Ages: cathedrals, 104–105; chantries, 107–108; charity, 108–109, 219–220; defense/sport organizations, 109–112; fairs/holidays, 113–114; gilds, 114–115; monasteries, 105–106; synagogues/Jewish communities, 112; synods/conferences, 103–104; universities, 106–107
Monasteries, 105–106
Monuments, 90–91. *See also* Art
Mutual aid societies, 228–229

N

National Taxonomy of Exempt Entities (NTEE), 30, 31
Nazi party, 154, 191
Nondistribution constraint, 28
Nongovernmental organizations, 27
Nongovernmental sector, 44
Nonprofit and Voluntary Sector Quarterly, 7
Nonprofit business perspective, 13
Nonprofit economics: and collective choice theory, 167–168; market-government failure theory, 159; and measurement, 165–166; and scarcity theory, 160–162; and unproductive labor, 38–39, 160; voluntary failure theory, 159; and volunteer labor, 164–165. *See also* Economics of common goods
Nonprofit Management and Leadership, 7
Nonprofit organizations: criteria, 25; definitions, 25–27; economic theory, 38–39; for-profit assumption, 26; IRS approach, 30; and nondistribution constraint, 28; and not-for-profit organizations, 24–25; NTEE approach, 31–32; and productive/unproductive labor, 36–37; and profit, 24–26, 28; and terminology, 23–25; type A/B subclasses, 33–36; typologies, 30–32. *See also* Nonprofit sector; Nonprofit/voluntary action; Voluntary associations
Nonprofit sector: definition/organization, 28–29; and fund accounting, 66; popular view, 23–24; size, 32–33; and tax exemption, 29–30; and voluntary sector, 42–44. *See also* Club sector; Independent sector; Nongovernmental sector; Nonprofit organizations; Nonprofit/voluntary action; Third sector; Voluntary sector

NonProfit Times, 7
Nonprofit/voluntary action:
  American-style, 1–2; bibliography, 2; and Eastern European
  changes, 2; four-part dialogue,
  5–6; history, 84; new terminology, 4–5; political view, 177–178;
  rethinking, 3–5; and ritual, 89–
  90; scholarly community, 6–8;
  and self-help groups, 230–231;
  and social exchange theory, 196–
  197; social theories, 127–128;
  theoretical origins, 36–39, 44;
  and theory of the commons, 272.
  See also Nonprofit organizations; Nonprofit sector; Research; Voluntary associations;
  Voluntary sector
Not-for-profit organizations, 24–25.
  See also Common action; Nonprofit organizations

O

Offerings, 203–204, 210–211
Order, 145–147
Organizations, 27–28, 58. *See also*
  Nongovernmental organiza-
  tions; Nonprofit organizations;
  Not-for-profit organizations

P

Pareto optimality, 167
Parsimony, 9
Patronage: and ancient civilization,
  92–93; classical Greek, 95; as
  common goods exchange, 198–
  200; defined, 11, 80–81, 199; and
  endowment, 80–82; and interest
  group liberalism, 200; merit,
  199; Ptolomeic, 98; Roman, 100
Patronage theory, 10–11, 81
Philanthropy, 10. *See also* Charity;
  Gift giving
Pilgrimages, 152–153
Plenary session, 65
Polite society, 124–125
Political parties, 151–152

Potlatch: as common goods exchange, 202–203; defined, 11,
  202; examples, 202; and tax-
  exempt organizations, 202–203,
  210
Presentation, 207–208, 210. *See also*
  Ceremonies
Principle: Carnegie, 262–267; of
  consensus, 268–269; of conservation, 267–268; of contextualism,
  260–262; of proportion, 259–260;
  of prudence, 268; of satisfaction,
  257–259
Private goods, 69, 168
Problem solving, 259
Production, 162–163. *See also*
  Coproduction
Program on Nonprofit Organizations, Yale University, 7
Proportion, 259–260
Prosocial behavior: and aggression,
  243–244; and altruism, 242; basis, 241–242; and empathy, 242–
  243; factors, 244; and organizational behavior, 243; range, 240–
  241
Protective associations: nonstate,
  187–188; state, 178, 180–183. *See
  also* Associations
Protestant Reformation. *See*
  Reformation
Prudence, 268
Public choice theory, 168
Public goods: and collective choice
  theory, 168; and common goods,
  19, 69, 158, 168, 172–175; and
  commons, 171; and free-rider
  problem, 169; and rational
  choice model, 274; and state,
  185–187; theory, 167. *See also*
  Common goods

R

Rational choice theory, 19, 21, 274
Rationality, 51–52
Reformation, 117–119, 221
Regime, 78–80
Renaissance, 117

Repertory, 76–77

Research: areas of interest, 6–7; and commons, 19–20; conference, 142; and nontraditional disciplines, 8; scientific, 156; voluntary action, 46–47. *See also* Nonprofit/voluntary action: scholarly community; Theory of the commons

Research institute, 153

Rites, 208. *See also* Ritual

Ritual: and art/sculpture, 90; and commons, 88–89; feasting, 88–89; initiation, 88; and nonprofit/voluntary action, 89–90; and offerings, 204; and secret societies, 154. *See also* Festivals/holidays; Rites; Symbols

Role taking, 256–257

Rome, 100–101

Russell Sage Foundation, 150

S

Satisfaction, 257–259

Scarcity, 161–162

Science: benefits, 155–156; and community, 255; defined, 155; fundamental, 156; and peer review, 257; research, 156

Search, 72, 209

Secret societies, 153–154

Sector theory, 78–79

Selective incentives, 169

Self-help groups: benefits, 231–232; and charity, 229–233; and cults, 231; defined, 229; health-oriented, 232–233; legal status, 230; and nonprofit/voluntary action, 230–231; theoretical basis, 233; types, 230

Self-interest, 162

Service production. *See* Production

Services, 162–163

Social action, 47–48. *See also* Acts of common good; Commons action

Social exchange theory, 196–198

Social surpluses, 85–86

Socialization, 71

Sociology, 20

Solo trusteeships, 134

State: and common/public goods, 185–187; and commons, 177–179, 183–185, 274; defined, 180; democratic, 179–180; as protective association, 178, 180–183; welfare, 178. *See also* Democracy

Surplus, 163–164

Symbols, 207. *See also* Ritual

Syndicate, 28

Synods. *See* Conferences

T

Tax-exempt status, 28–30

Technique, 72, 209

Theory. *See* Altruism theory; Charity theory; Collective choice theory; Endowment theory; Gift theory; Nonprofit economic theory; Patronage theory; Philanthropic theory; Public choice theory; Rational choice theory; Sector theory; Social exchange theory; Theory of the commons; Value theory

Theory of the commons: and affluence, 48–49; and altruism theory, 9–10, 236; and authenticity, 49–50; and autonomy, 53; and benefit/benefactory, 55–58; and charity theory, 12; and civil liberties, 188–194; and commons, 17–18, 58–65; and continuity, 50–51; and endowment, 12–13, 65–82; and gift theory, 11–12; goal, 20–21; intrinsic valuation, 53–54; language resources, 13–16; near universality, 52–53; and nonprofit business perspective, 13; and nonprofit/voluntary action, 272; and ordinary language, 54; overview, 17–21; and parsimony, 9; and patronage theory, 10–11; and philanthropic theory, 10; premises/assumptions, 47–54; and rational choice

theory, 21; and rationality, 51–
52; and social action, 47–48; and
sociological theory, 20; terms/
concepts, 54–65; theoretical chal-
lenge, 273; and values, 254–256.
See also Commons
Third sector, 20–21, 44. *See also*
Club sector; Independent sector;
Nongovernmental sector; Non-
profit sector; Voluntary sector
Treasury, 73
Triage, 161
Tributes, 198–200
Trusteeships, 133–134

U

Underground Railroad, 154, 191
Unions/professional organizations,
147–148
Universities, 106–107. *See also* Academic discipline
Unproductive labor, 36–39, 160. *See
also* Labor

V

Value judgments, 167
Value theory, 254–256

Values, 166–167
Voluntary action theory, 46–47
Voluntary associations: defined,
39–40; expressive vs. social influence, 41–42; legal/environmen-
tal distinctions, 40–41; and
nonprofit sector, 42–44; and sodality, 40; theoretical origins, 41,
44. *See also* Nonprofit organizations; Voluntary sector
Voluntary sector, 42–43. *See also*
Club sector; Independent sector;
Nongovernmental sector; Nonprofit sector; Independent sector;
Third sector
Voluntas, 7, 47
Volunteer labor, 39, 164–165, 225–
227. *See also* Disaster response;
Donor behavior; Helping
behavior
Volunteerism, 224–227

W

Welfare economics, 165–166. *See
also* Microeconomics: normative
Welfare state, 178